D0758418

THE POWER OF RESILIENCE

THE POWER OF RESILIENCE

How the Best Companies Manage the Unexpected

Yossi Sheffi

The MIT Press
Cambridge, Massachusetts
London, England

© 2015 Massachusetts Institute of Technology

All rights reserved. No part of this book may be reproduced in any form by any electronic or mechanical means (including photocopying, recording, or information storage and retrieval) without permission in writing from the publisher.

MIT Press books may be purchased at special quantity discounts for business or sales promotional use. For information, please email special_sales@mitpress.mit.edu.

This book was set in Sabon and Helvetica Condensed by the MIT Press. Printed and bound in the United States of America.

Library of Congress Cataloging-in-Publication Data

Sheffi, Yosef, 1948-
The power of resilience : how the best companies manage the unexpected / Yossi Sheffi.
pages cm
Includes bibliographical references and index.
ISBN 978-0-262-02979-7 (hardcover : alk. paper)
1. Risk management. 2. Strategic planning. 3. Crisis management. 4. Business logistics—Management. I. Title.

HD61.S443 2015
658.4'056—dc23

2015011432

10 9 8 7 6 5 4 3 2 1

CONTENTS

PREFACE

When the Pacific tectonic plate slipped under the Okhotsk plate off the northeast coast of Japan, it unleashed a massive 8.6-magnitude earthquake. Yet nobody outside the affected area knew about it. Buildings, warehouses, and walls collapsed under the shaking. But the rest of the world was oblivious. Then came the terrible tsunami spawned by the quake; it surged 4 kilometers inland, obliterating towns and farms across the Sendai plain and throughout the Fukushima prefecture. And still people in Europe, the Americas, the Middle East, China, and even the Japanese outside of the directly affected were utterly unaware that this tragic disaster even occurred.

That massive earthquake took place in 869 AD. In those early days, industrial power came from local sources such as horses, oxen, water wheels, and windmills; production was local. Consequently, supply chain disruptions were local, too. Earthquakes, tsunamis, famines, plagues, and floods struck around the world, but the effects did not travel far because most goods did not travel far. Since 869, the world has become much more reliant on long-distance supply chains—and "Made in Japan" products—to provide the necessities of life. Modern technology has added new capabilities, but it has also added new vulnerabilities.

When those same tectonic plates off the northeast coast of Japan ruptured again in 2011, producing a similar quake and tsunami, the results were felt worldwide. The world of 869 had no nuclear reactors, electrical power grids, or digital communications—those infrastructure elements that underpin the modern world—but that could be broken, disrupting enterprises and lives on a large scale. Those new vulnerabilities, however, are offset by new tools for supply chain resilience. This book explores the encroaching threats that face today's corporate supply chains and the new processes and tools used to prepare for, manage, and learn from disruptions.

My 2005 book, *The Resilient Enterprise* (MIT Press, 2005), was motivated by the 9/11 attacks. While on sabbatical at Cambridge University in 2002, I participated in a meeting at the UK Home Office during which the issue of vulnerability of critical infrastructure and systems came up. The group realized that the private sector—at least in the Western world—owns and operates most of these systems. A high-level civil servant asked if anybody knew of companies' readiness to prevent and overcome disruptions. Neither the academics, nor the security services, nor the companies around the table had an answer. As a result, I embarked on a three-year research project, involving more than 30 students and researchers at the MIT Center for Transportation and Logistics (CTL), which culminated in the publication of *The Resilient Enterprise.*

In 2011, several of the executives I had interviewed for that book suggested that it was time for a new one. New threats had emerged and, at the same time, companies had increased their investments in business continuity, risk management, and resilience. Again, I brought together a group of students and researchers at the MIT CTL and embarked on the efforts that produced this book.

In the decade since the publication of *The Resilient Enterprise*, the landscape of supply chain risks and companies' implementations of resilience has changed. The world's GDP grew 30 percent from 2003 to 2013, and global trade outpaced economic growth—growing 55 percent during that time.[1] The number of middle-class consumers almost doubled to two billion, and companies' supply chains expanded upstream and downstream to serve them. Disasters such as Hurricane Katrina, a tsunami in Japan, floods in Thailand, and a worldwide financial crisis, as well as rising concerns about global warming, social exploitation, aging populations, cyber vulnerabilities, and many other events and trends tested the resourcefulness and resilience of companies. Many companies have learned from these and have created much more effective resources for prevention, detection, and response. The risks have ramified, but resilience management has matured.

The Power of Resilience: How the Best Companies Manage the Unexpected is neither a sequel to nor a second edition of *The Resilient Enterprise*. Each book stands on its own. Although the two books do overlap on some central messages about redundancy and flexibility, each book has a different focus and uses different examples. The two books differ in the types of risks and in the mitigation tactics discussed. *The Power of Resilience* focuses on deep-tier risks, corporate social responsibility (CSR) risks, cybersecurity risks, global raw material risks, long-term disruptions, business continuity planning, emergency operations centers, risk and disruption detection, and the potential for systemic disruptions. Readers of this book may find *The Resilient Enterprise* useful for its deeper treatment of freight security, flexibility, culture, and postponement.

The Power of Resilience benefits from interviews with dozens of companies and draws on research at the MIT Center for Transportation and Logistics to document the wide range of strategies that organizations can use to detect, prevent, and mitigate a wide range of risks. In some cases, the book explains how different companies handled the same disruption; in other instances, the book describes how one company handled different disruptions over time. The aim is to offer cross-sectional and longitudinal insights, respectively, on risk management and resilience; to show how firms can build assets and processes to manage events that have not yet happened, at once adding optionality and flexibility, often at low relative cost.

ANATOMIES OF CATASTROPHES

From a pure supply chain perspective, the 2011 earthquake, tsunami, and nuclear disaster in Japan was the single largest and broadest natural disaster in recent times. The event affected companies around the world that depend on semiconductors, electronics, specialty chemicals, and other manufactured goods coming from Japan's prodigious industrial network. Chapter 1 describes the event and Intel's response to it in depth, to illustrate many of the issues faced and tactics used by companies in big disruptions. The chapter ends with a short primer on supply chains to help frame the *what*, *who*, and *where* of supply chain risks and risk management.

Chapter 2 offers a quick tour of the many kinds of disruptions confronting today's companies. The chapter introduces the two-dimensional *impact-and-likelihood* framework that is often used to categorize and prioritize risks. The chapter introduces a third dimension—*detection*—to frame the differences between disruptions that can be forecast to happen in the future (e.g., a hurricane) and disruptions that may not be detected until long after the fact (e.g., a serious product defect). The chapter offers ways to think about what is known and what is not known about disruptions, and what kinds of knowledge might be important.

The 2011 Japanese quake affected many companies and illustrates the growing problem with deep-tier supply chain disruptions in which the suppliers of suppliers are affected. Chapter 3 examines GM's handling of the Japan crisis and the management of what GM calls "white-space"—the gap in parts' supply left between predisruption inventories in the supply chain and the postrecovery refilling of the chain. The white-space conceptual framework allows companies to estimate a value-at-risk from various types of disruptions and to prioritize prevention and preparation initiatives.

Whereas chapter 3 focuses on GM's response to a single disruption, chapter 4 uses a different lens. It looks at a wide range of short examples of different disruptions and different companies to illustrate many other elements of disaster response. These examples highlight the differences between normal operations and operations during a crisis. Crises often disrupt or degrade the basic human, physical, and informational infrastructure on which companies operate.

In 2008, the global financial system came to the brink of collapse. Chapter 5 shows how a disruption in the money supply chain became a disruption in physical supply chains on both the supply and demand sides. The crisis created a global bullwhip that amplified the drop in consumer spending further up the supply chain. Yet as brutal as the near-depression might have been, it spurred many companies toward more systematic programs for assessing supplier risk. The financial crisis also illustrated the difference between managing a localized, short-term, event-focused disruption (e.g., a storm or quake) and a global step-change that lasts for months or years.

FOREARMED AND FOREWARNED

Whereas the first five chapters talk primarily of companies' reactions to disruptions, chapter 6 begins the discussions of more proactive preparations. These preparations include the fundamental steps of creating redundancy and building flexibility. Yet the maturation of risk management has also led companies to prepare other kinds of specialized risk-management assets in the form of business continuity plans, emergency operations centers, and formalized processes for managing disruptions.

Globalization implies that suppliers play a growing role in the companies' risks, disruptions, and response options. Chapter 7 delves into companies' proactive approaches toward supplier risk management, using a segmentation of the procurement conditions. It is based, on the one hand, on the complexity and risk associated with the input purchased from the supplier and, on the other hand, on the company's annual expenditure with that supplier. The chapter also discusses the growing problem of counterfeit materials that arise as supply chains grow longer and more opaque.

Companies' increasing awareness of supply chain risks, coupled with the growing use of technology, has led to a greater emphasis on detection, which is the subject of chapter 8. The sooner a company knows about a general risk or a specific event, the sooner it can address it; the first company to lock in alternative supplies has an advantage. New technologies and new services help companies detect risks and events sooner than ever before.

EMERGING THREATS

Internet technologies are now indispensable communications tools within and between companies. Yet the openness of these networks and the high potential value of corporate and personal information make these systems a tempting target for criminals, terrorists, and state-sponsored espionage. Furthermore, the rise of the Internet-of-Things, with digital "smarts" being added to ever more consumer products and industrial systems, creates physical vulnerabilities rooted in digital vulnerabilities. Chapter 9 describes these threats and offers potential solutions.

The rising economies of China, India, Brazil, and others have contributed to the globalization of supply chains in terms of new markets and new sources of supply. Yet the growing global economy in the last decade has also created a new class of supply chain risks tied to price shocks and commodity shortages. Oil, grains, metals, rare earths and other materials have all seen extreme volatility in which prices for key commodities might double, triple, or plunge over a short time and disrupt the companies dependent on them. Chapter 10 discusses several strategies used by companies to handle input price volatility and material shortages.

With the rise of social media and 24 × 7 news cycles comes a growing brand risk based on public opinions of suppliers' actions, especially for consumer-facing companies. Chapter 11 covers corporate social responsibility risks in which the perceived misdeeds of a company or any of its remotest suppliers can turn into a public relations challenge, disrupt demand, and can lead to impactful regulatory changes. These intentional disruptions, wrought in many cases by social activists, lead companies to tighten control over supply chain partners, including deep-tier suppliers, using several strategies.

Long-term changes in the world such as demographic trends, climate change, and disruptive innovation create permanent shifts in patterns of supply or demand. Chapter 12 explores the nature and effects of these kinds of disruptions, which create a "new normal" rather than a short-term shock that quickly reverts to the old normal. The chapter suggests methods for attending to and even benefiting from these long-term changes.

FRAGILITY, RESILIENCE, AND COMPETITIVE ADVANTAGE

One of the major themes of the book, explored in chapter 13, is the growing dependency of companies on deep-tier suppliers as well as on concentrations of supply sources that create fragile chokepoints in the global economy. Although the world has yet to see a true systemic collapse of any supply chain for a major product category, these chokepoints and other trends signal potential near-misses that presage a more serious event. Supply chain risk management is in a race between the fragility of complex global supply chains and the resilience created by better risk management.

The final chapter of the book takes a step back from specific risk management and response tactics to the problem bedeviling every risk, resilience, and business continuity manager. How can one justify investments in these initiatives when they seem like a waste of resources when nothing happens? The chapter argues that unlike insurance, which pays off only in a crisis, resilience drives everyday improvements in costs, operations, revenues, reputation, and agility. A company's ability to confidently manage its risks implies that it can take strategic risks to create growth. That, in turn, implies that a resilient company can avoid the most insidious risk of all: the risk of stagnation and irrelevance in the dynamic global economy of the future.

THANKS

This book was based, in large part, on primary research, including interviews all over the world with many business executives. As a result I owe deep thanks to the people who gave their time generously, provided data, and pointed me in new directions. Without them this book would not have been possible.

The full list of individuals who helped with this research effort is given at the end of this book (my apologies if I omitted someone). In particular, however, I would like to mention Bill Hurles of GM, Jackie Sturm and Jim Holko of Intel, Tom Linton of Flextronics, and Chris Sultemeier of Walmart, who not only contributed their own time generously but also helped arrange interviews and meetings with many others.

Many people also helped directly with the research and the writing. First and foremost these include the talented and friendly Andrea and Dana Meyer of Working Knowledge, who were instrumental in helping develop the concepts, as well contributing to the research and ensuring that the results were presented in readable English; Jennifer Yip, my student at MIT who helped me think through some concepts; and Dan Dolgin, who edited and made numerous suggestions, enhancing the manuscript.

Finally, I would like to thank my wife of over 46 years, Anat. I cannot imagine a better mate to go through life with. This book is dedicated to her.

1

A QUAKE BREAKS A SUPPLY CHAIN

AFTERNOON, MARCH 11, 2011, JAPAN

Jackie Sturm and Jeff Selvala sat with a dozen other Intel colleagues in the Narita Airport outside Tokyo, Japan. They were waiting for the long flight home after a conference with their Japanese suppliers. At the conference, they had discussed routine operations, quality improvements, forthcoming production plans, and technology roadmaps to ensure a continuing smooth supply of the hundreds of arcane materials that feed Intel's $36.5 billion in fabrication facilities (fabs). Staying ahead of the world's ravenous demand for chips required choreographing a global supply chain, which meant traveling to Japan to visit the many silicon wafer and specialty chemical suppliers who produce the ultrapure materials needed for Intel's chips.

Change of Plans

Unbeknownst to the Intel employees—and the world—a horrendous accumulation of geophysical energy had reached a breaking point. At 2:46 pm local time, some 72 kilometers off the coast of Japan, the Pacific plate broke its locked fault line and began to shear downward and westward while the Okhotsk plate beneath northern Japan thrust upward and eastward. More than 1,000 years of accumulated strain broke free, sending a seismic shockwave racing at over 7,000 kilometers per hour through the solid rock of the floor of the Pacific. The shock caused more of the surrounding fault lines to rip like a broken zipper. A 500-kilometer-wide sheet of the earth's plate east of Japan slid under the islands, the coastline sank about one-half meter, the adjacent seabed rose up to three meters, and that part of Japan lurched over two meters toward North America.[1] As the sheet shifted, a prolonged and growing shockwave radiated in all directions. In less than a minute, the first earthly shudders reached Japan.

A few minutes later, the shockwave reached the Narita airport. Those who live in Japan or spend any amount of time there know about the ordinary tremors that remind the Japanese of where they live. But this was no ordinary tremor. In Narita, the quake began with a long low rumble that turned into a rolling motion that steadily gathered strength. This was a big one and everyone knew it. As the quake built, people who were standing sat down. As the strength increased, many sat on the floor. And there they remained for four to five minutes as the quake rumbled on.

The Japanese know they live on a treacherous island prone to quakes, tsunamis, and even the occasional volcano. Born of bitter experience and untold hundreds of thousands of deaths throughout their history, today's Japanese erect heavily reinforced structures and heady seawalls to survive most of the worst that the earth can throw at them. But history does not always repeat itself, and the disaster that followed was worse than anything the Japanese planners had anticipated.

The Living Assess the Situation

When the shaking stopped at Narita, everyone looked around and breathed a sigh of relief. They were alive and unhurt. The airport's well-designed buildings had withstood the shaking. Then came the fears: worries about the safety of family, friends, and coworkers in Japan. Intel has some 600 employees in Japan at two facilities, plus innumerable friends and acquaintances at the company's long-term suppliers. The travelers also worried about what their families would think when they heard of the devastating quake. Immediately, people started calling, texting, and emailing to determine if everyone was safe and to tell everyone that they were safe.

The Intel employees and others found communications to be difficult in the immediate aftermath. The barrage of anxious callers overwhelmed local cell towers. Internet access was sporadic. Long lines of people clustered around working landline phones. Moreover, no calls were reaching the most damaged areas. The disaster had knocked out power plants, downed power lines, and severed telecommunications cables. Three prefectures had no power, and two additional ones had partial blackouts.

The Quake Was the Least of the Worries

Although the worst of the shaking had stopped and inspectors were rushing around Narita to confirm the lack of damage, the disaster was only just beginning. Earthquakes on the Pacific's ring of fire have the ironic tendency to produce walls of water. When that Pacific plate of rock dropped, the Japanese land mass lifted, as did the thousands of meters of water above the seabed. Drop a stone in a bathtub and the ripples expand to slosh against the sides. Move thousands of square kilometers of rock in an underwater quake, and the sloshing is immense. The Japanese know this, too, and they have elaborate processes for detecting quakes, estimating the potential magnitude of any tsunami spawned by a quake, and alerting seaside authorities of potential wave heights.

As Japan's network of 3,700 seismic sensors[2] relayed data on the quake, the seismologists of the Japan Meteorological Agency (JMA) quickly estimated the size of the quake and tsunami and sounded the alarm in the first three minutes of the event. Unfortunately, the system was actually too quick—it used only the first minute of quake data, not the full duration of the shaking, in initially estimating a 7.9 magnitude value to the quake. In reality, the quake was a magnitude 9, making it the largest earthquake ever to hit Japan in the country's 1,500 years of recorded history. Solid engineering, reinforced concrete, and lofty seawalls can handle a lot, but a magnitude 9 quake is more than a lot. An earthquake of magnitude 9 on the moment magnitude scale releases over 31.6 times more destructive energy than a magnitude 8 and 44.7 times more energy than the initially estimated 7.9.[3]

About half an hour after the shaking ended, a tsunami two to three times higher than projected overwhelmed coastal defenses and inundated the shores nearest to the quake's epicenter. In some areas, a fateful conspiracy of the direction of the tsunami and the shapes of land, harbors, and sea bottom acted to concentrate the tsunami into a 20-meter-high wall of water. Large container ships were lifted over piers and wharves and were shoved inland as the water invaded the land. Along the Sendai coast, seawater flowed more than four kilometers inland across the broad coastal plain. As the waters retreated, houses, buildings, cars, and thousands of people were dragged out to sea. In some areas, rubble created by the quake was simply wiped from the land.

The violent ground motion, waves, and fires started by the quake damaged or destroyed some 1.2 million buildings across a large swath of northern Japan. Far worse was the human toll. Over 19,000 people lost their lives, some 50,000 were injured, and 400,000 became homeless. Of those who died, nearly 3,000 were never found—sucked into briny depths. The tsunami was responsible for 80 percent of the destroyed buildings and over 94 percent of the deaths.[4,5]

Too Hot to Handle

Even as the Japanese quickly started their rescue and inspection efforts, more phases of the disaster began unfolding. Some 180 kilometers away from the quake's epicenter lay the nuclear power complex of Fukushima Daiichi, with six nuclear reactors. The reactor complex was part of Japan's strategy of avoiding the risks of reliance on foreign supplies of fossil fuels. On March 11, three reactors were live and three were shut down for routine maintenance. When the quake struck, the three operating reactors immediately performed an emergency shutdown, dropping control rods into the reactor to suspend power production.

The Japanese thought they understood the seismic risks of Fukushima. A long historical record of earthquakes and careful modeling of the faults near Fukushima suggested that the region had manageable seismic and tsunami risks. "With firm geological foundations and major earthquakes rare, Fukushima is a safe and secure place to do business," said the government website for Fukushima prefecture.[6]

But the seismic modeling failed to include the potential for coseismic coupling—a knock-on effect in which the rupture in one fault induces larger ruptures in the many other faults around the Japanese islands.[7] The violence of the quake exceeded the design specifications of three of the reactors; eyewitness accounts and postquake activities suggest significant quake-related damage to the reactor cooling systems.[8]

The cold seawater that was the reason for the plant's seaside location became the facility's ultimate nemesis. About 50 minutes after the quake, the tsunami arrived. The sea rose to the 10-meter-high level of the plant, began flooding it, and kept rising. High waters soaked various parts of the plant for between 30 minutes to one hour.[9] Seawater flooded the backup diesel generators, thoroughly soaked critical controls with corrosive seawater, and shorted key electrical systems.

Even when powered down, the nuclear byproducts inside the reactor core's fuel rods generated tremendous heat. Without a continuous supply of cooling water, the remaining water sitting in the reactor chamber began to boil and raise the pressure of the chamber. To prevent catastrophic failure, emergency valves vented radioactive steam. Worse, as the water boiled and exposed the core, high-temperature chemical reactions produced explosive hydrogen gas.

If too much of the core is exposed, temperatures can rise to 2,800°C, melt the core assembly, and potentially allow uncontrolled fission to create vastly larger amounts of heat and radioactive debris. The ultrahot molten mass of reacting fuel could literally melt down through the bottom of the reactor, through any other containment walls, and begin melting into the concrete foundation of the reactor.

Nor were the reactors the only concern. The Fukushima operators faced a similar threat with the spent fuel rods sitting in the adjacent cooling pools. Without recirculating water, these pools began to heat toward the boiling point. If the pools boiled and evaporated, the rods would be exposed, become extremely hot, and release radioactive materials directly into the air.

The quake and tsunami led to a desperate battle to cool the reactors and fuel pools. At every turn, the workers faced horrible choices with significant risks of radiation leakage, explosions, and irreversible damage to the reactors' systems. The plant's lack of power and damaged sensor infrastructure meant the operators had limited visibility into conditions inside the reactor building and had limited control. The workers at the Fukushima tried valiantly to cool the reactor cores and the fuel pools. They brought in fire trucks and helicopters to dump water into the stricken reactor buildings. They sent rotating crews of workers and firemen to limit each worker's exposure to radiation. Rather than risk an immediate explosion because of lack of water, they used seawater in an attempt to cool the reactor, knowing that the salt could utterly ruin the reactor and potentially clog the pipes.

Yet without power, without large supplies of fresh water, without full sensor data on what was happening, and without the ability to enter the extremely radioactive reactor buildings, the workers had little hope of preventing a catastrophe. Only 24 hours after the tsunami, a hydrogen explosion shattered the reactor unit #1 building, followed by similar explosions in unit #3 (March 14), unit #2 (March 15), and unit #4 (March 15). Each explosion brought renewed fears of major radiation releases and created unknown amounts of damage to internal systems. Postanalysis of the disaster showed that unit #1 suffered a complete meltdown, and units #2 and #3 suffered partial meltdowns.[10,11,12]

From Reactors to Reactions

The third phase of the disaster arose from the horrible realities and uncertainties about radiation spewing from the stricken reactors. On many days, the radiation drifted out to sea to rain down into the Pacific. But on other days, radiation moved inland, motivating evacuations of the area around the reactors and causing concerns for the water supplies of Japanese cities. (Detectable amounts of radioactive materials even crossed the Pacific to appear in US air and rain samples.[13]) The invisible nature of radiation and the potential that it might coat objects or be absorbed into plants and animals created frightening uncertainties about the short-term and long-term safety of residents, businesses, farmers, and fishermen in the affected area. It also created worries for Japanese companies with parts and goods in the area. No one knew how far the radiation might spread and whether it could contaminate shipments sent to customers around the world.

TV images showed the grim aftermath of the explosions and fires—shattered buildings and a miasma of radioactive smoke rising unabated from the remains. News stories buzzed with data on rising heat levels, falling coolant levels, new attempts to stabilize the situation, and new fears of worsening conditions. As the threat of radiation grew, Japanese authorities created progressively larger and larger evacuation zones at 2, 10, 20, and 30 kilometers and asked citizens over a larger area to remain indoors. But were the evacuation zones large enough? Revelations showed that the plant's operator (TEPCO) and the Japanese government had repeatedly downplayed the extent of the crisis.

Uncertainties about the amount of radiation spewing from the smoldering plant and the potential shifting direction of the winds added to the anxiety. Intel considered evacuating all of its Japanese personnel, but the personnel themselves vetoed the idea.

Companies with business in Japan, who bought Japanese products, or who simply moved goods through Japanese waters began to wonder: were their goods radioactive? Fear of radioactive foods, materials, and dust created questions about the safety of Japanese exports. Intel and others worried about freight transiting Japanese ports—radioactive dust might settle on or get into shipping containers passing through the area. This potentially affected 7,000 of Intel's shipping lanes, because it affected lanes with Japanese origins or destinations as well as all Asia-Pacific lanes that might sail near Japanese waters. Another company, chemical giant BASF, worried about radioactive ingredients getting into consumer products. For example, BASF supplies the ingredients that go into lipstick manufactured and sold by Procter & Gamble. To assure itself and its customers of the safety of the ingredients originating from Japan, BASF installed Geiger counters on both the Japanese and German sides of its supply chain.

Intel had an added worry. Even if the chips themselves were clean of any radioactive contamination, exposure to radiation during manufacturing or transportation could affect their functioning. Irradiating the chips wouldn't make them radioactive but could reduce their long-term reliability. The company had specs for the issue but had heretofore not needed to enforce these specs. In this case, however, Intel had to work with key suppliers to ensure that silicon and chips weren't exposed to radiation at any stage. In addition to attempting to cope with the existing crisis, Intel planned for an expansion of its crisis response if the evacuation zone grew and encompassed more suppliers.

A Nuclear Powerless Country

At the time of the quake, Fukushima Daiichi was supplying less than 1 percent of Japan's electricity needs. Other reactors in the quake zone—totaling 4 percent of Japan's power needs—were shut down for inspection. Yet quake- and tsunami-related damage to nonnuclear power plants and to Japan's electric grid, coming on top of Japan's unique split grid system, created power shortages in the eastern half of the country. Power outages and rolling blackouts became a problem for almost a month.[14]

The government began an intensive media campaign called *setsuden* (Japanese for "power saving"). It encouraged citizens and companies to conserve as much power as possible by turning off lights, adjusting thermostats, and wearing clothing appropriate for the temperature. Retailers turned off neon lights, office buildings went dark, escalators stopped, trains slowed, and some manufacturers adopted staggered weekly schedules to reduce the weekday peak in demand. Rather than promoting consumption, the glowing giant neon signs of the retailers in Tokyo's Ginza district went dark to promote conservation.[15,16]

As the Fukushima crisis worsened, public opinion turned against Japan's energy strategy,[17] and the risks from dependence on foreign fossil fuels seemed the lesser of two evils.[18,19] The extreme loss of confidence in nuclear power caused the government to progressively shut down all the country's reactors.[20] By August 2011, three-quarters of Japan's nuclear reactors were shut down. By August 2012, only two of Japan's 54 reactors remained online.[21] This created a more sizable disruption to the country's power supplies, reducing capacity by over 30 percent. More than three years after the disaster, power shortages still threatened Japan, especially during the hot summer months when electrical demand spikes.[22]

WHEN THE CHIPS ARE DOWN

When the quake occurred, Intel's well-honed and extensively practiced crisis management processes sprang into action. Business unit crisis management teams had kickoff meetings on the day of the quake. On Saturday, March 12, Intel activated its Corporate Emergency Operation Center (CEOC) to help coordinate the response at the highest level. Intel split its response to the Japan disaster into two parallel streams of activities, which is Intel's standard approach for such incidents.

Emergency Management: Stabilizing the Local Situation

First, Intel's Emergency Management team ensured the safety of Intel's people and facilities in the disaster zone. Intel deployed predesignated local Emergency Response Teams, who are the first responders in a disaster, and local Emergency Operations Center (EOC) personnel to stabilize the situation and prevent further casualties. At the time of the quake, 300 Intel employees worked in downtown Tokyo and a similar number in Tsukuba, about 100 kilometers northeast of Tokyo.

Intel's office in downtown Tokyo survived intact, but the Tsukuba facility was another matter. Intel had no fabs in Japan, but its Tsukuba facility housed 300 personnel who worked on materials operations, quality assurance, information technology, e-business, and related functions.[23] Although the building wasn't structurally damaged, the quake broke fire sprinkler pipes in the ceiling. Ten inches of water flooded the offices and shorted the building's electrical systems. The Tsukuba office was uninhabitable.

Finding a temporary location for the 300 Tsukuba workers would not be easy given the 1.2 million buildings that had been damaged in the quake. Many companies had been forced out of their offices by the quake, tsunami, and Fukushima evacuations. "We have an organization at Intel called CRESD (Corporate Real Estate and Site Development), and so they worked night and day to try to find alternative work space," said Jim Holko, program manager of Intel's corporate emergency management.[24] Even with its corporate resources, Intel couldn't find a site large enough for all 300 people, so CRESD had to split the workforce across two locations. As a result, Intel also had to set up Internet and collaboration tools across the two sites.

Meanwhile, the company used its large global construction arm—which builds Intel's fabs—to accelerate the repair of the Tsukuba facility. Intel flew structural engineers, electricians, plumbers, and other technicians to Japan to inspect the building, define the requirements for the repair job, and find local contractors to do the repairs.

Business Continuity: Ensuring Global Operations

The second stream of Intel's crisis response, Business Continuity (BC), focused on Intel's products and processes. BC had to make sure that all the raw materials flows, chip making, and customer-related activities didn't stop—or that they restarted as soon as possible. Whereas the Intel's Emergency Management team took care of the safety issues within a couple of weeks of the quake, the BC side took six months.

Intel's first step in BC was to determine the impact of the disaster on the business operations of the company and its suppliers. Because Intel had no factories in Japan, supplier issues were its main BC focus. Intel assessed the status of 365 materials. By March 15, four days after the disaster, Intel knew it had no major problems with its direct (or "Tier 1") suppliers. At worst, a few Tier 1 suppliers had a few days of downtime, but nothing that was a threat to Intel's production schedules.

Tracing the status of deeper tier suppliers—suppliers to Intel's Tier 1 suppliers—took longer. By March 20, Intel knew that Tier 2 also had only minor problems, but Tier 3, Tier 4, and deeper tiers had more substantive problems. Intel identified 60 suppliers who had issues. Many of them were single-source specialty chemical manufacturers with unique capabilities. Making chips with layers only a few atoms thick depends on highly-specialized, exotic chemicals. In many cases, only one supplier (and sometimes even only one plant) in the world knew how to make the molecules "dance in just the right way," as Intel's Jackie Sturm, vice president, technology and manufacturing and general manager of global sourcing and procurement, put it.[25]

Even as Intel resolved many uncertainties about the quake's impact on suppliers, the company could not be certain that it had identified all the impacts. "Everything that was a risk for us in that earthquake, [it turned out] we knew about in the first 10 days, but we didn't know that fact on the 11th day," said Jeff Selvala, Intel's director, assembly test global materials.[26] Intel continued to probe suppliers, looking for any additional problems. News of issues at other chip makers would make Intel ask more questions, continuously digging for additional hidden disruptions and risks. Although no new problems appeared after day 10, Selvala said that Intel continued to search for more problems for at least a month.

More than 50 percent of Intel's assembly and test materials suppliers had manufacturing locations in Japan. The number was even higher for the deeper tiers, due to the high concentration of specialty chemicals makers in Japan. In all, Intel realized that 75 percent of assembly/test materials were at risk. One of the more significant challenges was getting enough silicon, which was the base material used for almost all of Intel's chips at every plant around the world. Five minutes after the shaking had stopped, Sturm was on the phone from the Narita tarmac, calling Intel's fab materials people to check the status of the company's silicon suppliers.

Quakes and Crystals

In 2011, the Shin-Etsu Handotai (SEH) plant in Shirakawa Japan was producing 20 percent of the world's supply of 300-millimeter silicon—the large platter-like wafers used to make chips.[27] The factory's delicate crystal pullers slowly grew boules of silicon—heavy crystal ingots 300 millimeters in diameter—that were sliced into 600,000 to 700,000 wafers per month.[28]

To give the 250 kilograms of molten silicon time to coalesce into a perfect crystal, the equipment slowly lifts the nascent boules out of the yellow-hot pool of molten silicon over a period of more than a day. The quake's shaking jostled these quiet pools, disordered the crystal growth, and ruined the crystals. When the power died, the gestating boules, representing tens of millions of dollars of chips, froze into stillborn cold gray lumps.

SEH's first order of business was to ensure the safety of its employees, three of whom had been injured in the quake. Next, SEH needed to inspect its facilities for damage to ensure it could restart production as quickly as possible. But even as the company worked to inspect and begin repairs at the affected site, the area came under threat from the nuclear reactor crisis and radiation leakage from Fukushima Daiichi, only 80 kilometers away. Moreover, the Shirakawa plants got their power from the Fukushima nuclear plant. Although the area around the Shirakawa was never under government evacuation orders, some concerned area residents did leave on their own. Local fears were so strong that TEPCO was forced to agree to pay all children and pregnant women living in the area at the time of the crisis 200,000 yen (about $2,600 at the time) each, as compensation for their fears and added costs.

SEH also initiated a series of communications to the business world about the status of damage to the company's facilities and its efforts to recover.[29] The day after the quake, SEH reported three facilities damaged by the quake, including the Shirakawa semiconductor plant. By March 15, SEH announced it had found damage to the production equipment at Shirakawa but did not know how long it might take to repair the facility. By March 17, SEH decided to shift as much wafer production as possible to other SEH facilities. Inspections and assessment took almost a month. By April 11, SEH was in the process of recovering inventory from Shirakawa to increase wafer shipments. Not until April 28 could SEH restart partial production. The Shirakawa plant was the last SEH facility to return to full production on July 1, more than three and half months after the quake.[30]

The larger obstacles to SEH's recovery came from the aftereffects of the quake. Between the quake damage and Japan's decision to take its nuclear plants off line, the country faced severe power shortages and rolling blackouts. Whereas individuals and many businesses experienced power outages as an inconvenience and a loss of productivity, other businesses—especially those like SEH who were running delicate industrial processes—faced potential safety concerns and equipment damage if the power went out. "We are requesting the electric power companies to provide a stable supply of electric power because we have facilities and equipment that need to be operated continuously due to the safety reasons," pleaded SEH in its March 22 report on the company's postquake efforts.[31]

Acquire, Search, and Prolong Existing Supplies

Where possible, Intel sought to maintain business continuity using existing suppliers and prequalified materials. Its efforts were focused on three work streams. The first was to quickly acquire materials from its normal portfolio of prequalified suppliers. For example, Intel knew it had to acquire more silicon to fill the gap created by the downed factories. The company's first step was to approach its major suppliers, asking them to increase Intel's allocation.[32] Despite suppliers' best efforts, the global wafer industry did not have the spare production capacity to replace what was lost in the quake.

Intel's second tactic was to search and secure the supply chain's inventories of critical materials. All supply chains have inventories at every level, some of it by design and some resulting from inefficiencies. Companies maintain inventories as a hedge against demand fluctuations and to take advantage of economies of scale in manufacturing and shipping. Inventory levels depend on lead times, manufacturing technologies, demand, and process uncertainty (see the section titled "Views on the Risks" in this chapter). At the same time, lack of intracompany communications, incorrect incentive systems and other factors can mean that companies often have more inventories than optimal.[33] "You do have some amount of time, because you have inventory, your supplier has inventory, their supplier has inventory, and so on. And so there's a natural buffer there that you have a period of time to resolve issues," Selvala said.[34] Chapter 6 explores how some companies use inventory to help them recover from disruptive events.

Third, Intel also worked to prolong the life of constrained supplies by minimizing the quantity consumed by each step of the chip-making process. For example, in one case, Intel diluted a key chemical, qualified it for use, and used the alternative formulation for eight weeks. Another engineering group found a way to clean off and reuse test wafers that would have gone to the scrap pile. Moreover, the company pushed the tactic up the supply chain—working with Tier 3 suppliers to minimize consumption of critical Tier 4 supplies. By boosting supplies from second-source suppliers, finding as much material as possible and prolonging its use, Intel hoped to fill the gap until the affected suppliers could resume normal production.

The Backup Response: Replace Disrupted Supplies

In some cases, Intel couldn't find enough prequalified suppliers with inventory or capacity to meet Intel's demands while its Japanese suppliers recovered. This unfortunate fact was especially true for sole-source suppliers. The lack of prequalified suppliers had the potential to create a lag during which time Intel could face production interruptions. Needless to say, the entire reason for the business continuity effort was to avoid such disruptions.

The threat of a production disruption led Intel to look for alternative suppliers and alternative products. Under normal circumstances, Intel's fab managers would resist quick qualification of alternative chemicals and materials. But these were not ordinary times. Intel would need to buy previously unqualified materials and quickly qualify them to ensure they met Intel's high quality standards.

Engineers sought alternatives to constrained materials and used fast-track qualification processes—jumping the normal queue of engineering work—to get the replacement materials into use. Intel also gave purchasing managers wide freedom to buy large quantities of materials "just in case" and accelerate the usual materials and spending approvals processes. "We were out there using letters of intent, if that was sufficient, or placing purchase orders if that was necessary, or non-cancelable purchase orders. Whatever was necessary to secure supplies. And we were doing that in real time," Selvala said.[35]

In seeking alternatives to disrupted supplies, Intel made sure that the lead-time of the alternative was less than the recovery time of the original supplier. Intel's supplier contracts often include "have made" rights, whereby Intel can have a proprietary material made by another supplier if the original supplier cannot meet the contract terms. Often, however, the lead-time on getting a material made elsewhere was longer than the anticipated recovery time of the original qualified sole-source supplier.

Collaboration for Better Crisis Response

Intel wasn't the only chip maker affected by the quake. The loss of the SEH plant created a global shortage of silicon. Other chip makers started calling Intel for help in locating silicon. Because the silicon shortage created imbalances in the PC supply chain, Intel assisted some of them in locating additional supplies. "If we were aware of capacity, we certainly tried to assist because the whole industry was down," Intel's Jackie Sturm said.[36] Even if Intel could make its chips, PC makers would not buy them unless they could get all the other chips and components from other suppliers so that they have everything needed to build complete PCs.

Intel also tried to help in other ways. It joined a group of Japanese companies in asking METI—Japan's Ministry of Economy, Trade, and Industry—to expedite the repair of the electrical grid around key suppliers and to exempt certain key facilities from the mandatory daily blackouts. Although it took some convincing, METI did help. Key suppliers were able to get continuous supplies of power even as blackouts affected other parts of Japan.[37]

"We'll work with governments. We will work with competitors if that's what it takes. We'll work with our local authorities and try to engage wherever we think there's opportunity to help fix the situation," Sturm said.[38] Nor was Intel unique in this respect. In the other disruptions described later in this book, companies often collaborated with government, suppliers, and competitors.

Returning to Normal Operations: Winding Down Response

Some aspects of Intel's response were settled relatively soon after the quake. As the BC effort progressed, the frequency of meetings declined. During the first two weeks of the crisis, the crisis management teams of the Worldwide Materials Group had daily meetings over the status of issues such as silicon, chemicals, and back-end supplies. Then, they reduced the frequency to three times a week during April and May. In June, they further reduced the frequency to just once a week. At no time were factories down for lack of silicon, noted Sturm

Once the recovery effort was under control, the CEOC closed on April 6. Similarly, the logistics crisis management team wound down on April 7, after figuring out the shipping lane issues and how to divert products to avoid radiation. Other business unit crisis management teams kept working until June 30. Overall, the business continuity effort took six months. Some follow-on actions continued thereafter, but operations were mostly back to normal. Complete rehabilitation of the Tsukuba office took 10 months. Throughout the entire crisis, Intel never had to halt production at any of its fabs.

THE GLOBALIZATION OF SUPPLY CHAINS

To understand why the Japanese quake and tsunami had global effects and how other kinds of distant disruptions can affect companies and economies, it helps to understand something about supply chains. From the point of view of a single company, a supply chain—which is actually a network of suppliers, subsuppliers, and service providers[39]—can be thought of as having five different aspects:

- The parts that go into the company's products,
- The identities of the network of suppliers who make those parts,
- The locations where parts and products are made, assembled, and distributed,
- The flows of parts and products (including the transportation links that move materials along the chain), as well as the flow of information and cash, and
- The inventories of materials, parts, and finished goods stored or being handled in various stages of the chain.

Each of these five aspects provides different insights into the risks to which supply chain operations are exposed.

Exploding the BOM: The "What" of Supply Chains

The first aspect of a supply chain for a given product, such as an automobile, encompasses all the materials and parts that go into that product—the "what." To manage the myriad subassemblies, parts, and raw materials required to build a particular unit (a car, for instance, may have 50,000 parts), companies create a bill of materials (BOM) that lists the quantities of subassemblies, parts, and raw materials required to make one unit of a product. For example, the BOM for an automobile would include: one body, one engine, one transmission, four door assemblies, two axles, four brake assemblies, five wheel assemblies, one navigation system, and so forth. Each of these parts, in turn, includes other parts and subassemblies, and so on. The assembled engine might include one engine block, six pistons, six fuel injectors, six spark plugs, twelve valves, etc. Each piston might include: one connecting rod, three piston rings, and so on. The BOM is a hierarchy that, if drawn, looks like a tree in which a set of leaves makes a twig, a set of twigs makes a branch, and the entire collection of branches makes the finished product.

Companies with multiple products will have a different BOM for each product, and each product will differ in the types and quantities of parts that go into that product. To make some planned number of products on an assembly line, companies use material requirements planning (MRP) software to ensure that they make or purchase the right quantities of every part on the BOM with sufficient lead time. Given a production schedule, the planned number of units of each product during each time period multiplied by the number of parts per product to be manufactured during this time tells the company the number of parts to make or buy (e.g., one car with six pistons and three piston rings per piston needs 18 piston rings) for the manufacturing plan during that time unit. MRP takes a production schedule and generates a purchasing schedule, given the lead time for each part. Each supplier, in turn, uses its own MRP process to ensure that it, too, buys or makes the required raw materials and parts in time to deliver the requested parts to the product manufacturer by the scheduled delivery date.

Organizations in the Supply Chain: The "Who" of Supply Chains

The second aspect of the supply chain is of a network of facilities and companies that manufacture the parts of the BOM, assemble parts into finished goods, and then distribute and sell the products—the "who." This aspect encompasses a spectrum of manufacturing strategies. At one extreme, a supply chain might be vertically integrated. In this case, a single company owns almost all the stages of production, in one or more facilities. For example, Ford's famous River Rouge plant was renowned for taking raw iron ore, glass, and rubber in on one side and rolling vehicles out of the other side of the massive, sprawling facility. A more modern example is Samsung, which makes many of the parts—such as processors, memory chips, and displays—for its own televisions, smartphones, and computer products.

At the other extreme is an outsourced supply chain in which a company buys complex, preassembled parts from a wide, tiered network of independent suppliers, with each supplier responsible for one or more steps in the production process, which might encompass a single simple part or a complete subassembly. In fact, some companies outsource their entire manufacturing operations, buying finished goods in retail packaging from contract manufacturers. For example, Cisco, Microsoft, and Apple do not have any manufacturing facilities of their own—they only handle the design, marketing, sales, and supply chain of their products.

Regardless of a company's level of vertical integration, the direct suppliers of the company are known as Tier 1 suppliers. Tier 1 suppliers would include the providers of steel or aluminum sheets and coil to Ford's stamping plants or contract manufacturers such as Flextronics International Ltd., Hon Hai/Foxconn, or Pegatron Corp, that manufacture computers, phones and tablets for Apple.[40] A company's Tier 2 suppliers are the suppliers to the company's Tier 1 suppliers. Tier 3 supplies Tier 2, and so on. These echelons of tiers often correspond to the echelons of branches in the BOM tree.

Today's supply chains can be quite deep. For example, Intel traced tantalum, a metal essential its microprocessors, through as many as a dozen supply chain tiers back through the makers of tantalum-containing electronic components to the metal processors, smelters, ore exporters, ore transporters, ore consolidators, and then to the artisanal miners (see chapter 11). In some cases, the structure of the BOM is more complicated as companies both buy from and sell to the same company, or where one part may "visit" the same supplier more than once for different manufacturing processes, a situation that is common in the information technology industry.

Manufacturing and Services Locations: The "Where" of Supply Chains

Whether vertically integrated or outsourced, supply chains can also vary by their geographic deployment—the "where." Manufacturers may choose to locate production facilities close to raw materials supplies (e.g., a chemical plant near an oil field), close to sources of labor (e.g., low-cost or high-skill regions), close to centers of demand (e.g., major customers or major population centers), in some industrial cluster location (close to other, similar manufacturers) or in a location influenced by government (e.g., via incentives and regulations).

The structure of the supply chain for acquiring and moving raw material and parts to final assembly (the so called "upstream supply chain") is determined by the choice of suppliers. At most manufacturing companies, the choice of suppliers is managed by the procurement organization. Naturally, engineering, finance, and logistics also contribute to the decisions in order to ensure quality, capacity, financial viability, and timely deliveries of parts and raw materials. Lastly, departments such as risk management, compliance, and corporate social responsibility also influence supplier choice and factory location decisions.

To get the product to market (the "downstream" part of the process), the supply chain encompasses the distribution function. Distribution determines the location and operations of the company's warehouses and distribution centers. Distribution also usually manages the movement of the finished products to customers—be they retail distribution centers, retail outlets, e-commerce fulfillment centers, or directly to consumers. Many companies outsource distribution, too, either by selling their finished goods to wholesalers who distribute the product, or by using logistics service providers to handle warehousing and distribution to their downstream echelons of retailers and consumers.

Going with the Flows: "How Things Move" in Supply Chains

All of these locations of supply, production, distribution, and demand are connected by flows—the fourth aspect of the supply chain. Supply chains encompass three essential types of flows: material, information, and money. The most salient and costly flows of a supply chain are the material flows. In general, materials flow downstream from mines and farms to factories that process raw materials, to the factories that make parts and subassemblies, to original equipment manufacturers (OEMs) that make finished goods products, to distributors and to retailers, and, finally, to end consumers. At each stage, companies add value to the materials, often differentiating them into many types of parts or products. Materials, parts, and products can travel on a variety of conveyances such as trucks, railroads, ocean freighters, canal barges, aircraft, and pipelines—the "how and where things move" in the supply chain. Intel, for example, manages 14,000 origin-destination "lanes" around the world, connecting the chipmaker to its suppliers, its network of internal facilities, and its customers.

At the same time that materials flow down the chain, money flows up the chain when consumers pay the retailer, the retailer pays the distributor, and so on. Information—in the form of, for example, forecasts, purchase orders, shipping notices, and invoices—flows in both directions to coordinate activities throughout the supply chain. In fact, both materials and money also go in both directions to some extent, as returns and defective goods travel back to the manufacturer, and as rebates and discounts flow from suppliers to customers. An increasingly important part of supply chain management involves the returns part of the supply chain, be it for responsible disposal, recycling, remanufacturing, or the return of packaging material.

Transportation carriers have their own operating strategies for how they handle and route freight. The two basic strategies are known as "direct operations" (DO) and "consolidated operations" (CO). In direct operations, a dedicated conveyance carries the cargo directly from origin to destination (like a taxicab). This is the case with full truckload movements, unit trains, and leased conveyances in all modes of transportation. Direct operations are not cost efficient for small shipments, however, so smaller shipments are usually consolidated geographically through transshipment hubs such as UPS's Louisville, FedEx's Memphis, or DHL's Leipzig terminal. Examples of CO modes (think public transit or passenger airline hubs) include less-than-truckload (LTL or "groupage"), boxcar trains, ocean container ships, and many others. CO also include in-vehicle consolidation, such as pickup and delivery operations in which shipments destined for a variety of places are loaded on a single vehicle for distribution (like postal service mail delivery). Numerous factors—the economies of scale in conveyance size, the economies of scope underlying carriers' networks, the efficiency of handling modal transshipments, delivery time requirements, and the need to mediate between concentrated sources of supply (e.g., a large factory) and diffuse regional demand (e.g., a network of retail outlets)—all affect the choice of transportation mode in each specific situation.[41]

The Story of Inventory: "Where Things Sit" in Supply Chains

Both the economics of production and the economics of transportation mean that products are typically shipped in batches of some minimum quantity. The *economic order quantity* is the production batch size (or shipment size) that has been optimized vis-à-vis inventory carrying costs and ordering costs. The batching of production and transportation implies that both manufacturer and customer must hold inventory—the manufacturer will hold finished goods inventory because of the efficiency of batch manufacturing and/or until it has produced enough for a cost-effective shipment; the customer company will hold this *cycle inventory* until it is sold off. In addition, each echelon in the supply chain may hold additional inventory—*safety stock*—to cover random fluctuations in customer demand or in parts' supply. Finally, because processes along the supply chain—especially transportation—take time, inventory also sits in trucks, on the high seas, or while undergoing some manufacturing process and is called the *work-in-process* (WIP) inventory.

Inventory is costly. It consumes capital on a company's balance sheet, consumes space for storage, and requires labor to put away, maintain, service, manage, and pick-and-pack. Inventory can degrade over time (e.g., perishable food, medicines, and chemicals) or go obsolete (e.g., last-year's skirts or silicon chips). Consequently, companies try to minimize the amount of inventory they hold. In the 1950s and 1960s, Toyota pioneered the just-in-time (JIT) manufacturing and supply chain inventory management method as part of the Toyota Production System. The system was designed to reduce inventory along the supply chain while increasing product quality and service levels. This practice spread within Japan and then throughout the world. JIT and the related strategy of lean manufacturing/lean supply chain enable companies to operate with less inventory and be more responsive to changing market conditions.

Views on the Risks

Each of these five aspects of the supply chain offers respective insights into the many different risks in supply chains. The "parts" aspect of the supply chain is associated with materials availability, defective parts, and pricing risks associated with the various inputs to the final product or assembly.

The "who" and the "where" of the supply chain affect many geographic and operational risks such as natural disasters, supplier bankruptcies, and regulatory risks. Outsourcing—especially offshore—reduces a company's level of control over the outsourced steps of the manufacturing process and can expose the company to geographic, legal/regulatory, and political upheaval risks. The "who" and "where" aspects also determine the natural resources footprints (e.g., energy, water, and carbon) and potential social responsibility risks in the supply chain (see chapter 11).

The "flow" aspect of the supply chain depicts the range of connective risks in the logistics, financial, or information infrastructure that underlies the fabric of the chain. The material flow aspect includes risks in the timeliness of shipments and potential disruptions in key transportation terminals, lanes, and hubs. The information flow aspect highlights the vulnerability of global supply chains to information technology disruptions (e.g., computer failures, software glitches, or cyber-attacks). The money flow aspect depicts the vulnerability of commerce to financial crises, bankruptcies, and exchange rate risks.

Finally, the "inventory" aspect of the supply chain includes geographic risks, product quality risks, and parts obsolescence. Yet, inventory also represents an opportunity to buffer many supply risks by allowing companies to maintain the flow of parts and products during a disruption.

RISING VULNERABILITY ON ALL SIDES OF THE SUPPLY CHAIN

Intel's vulnerability to the Japanese earthquake, and the many examples in the rest of this book, arise from a series of trends that have pushed companies toward more complex, broader, longer, and more fragile supply chains.

More Trade, More Distance, Longer Lead Times, More Players

The leading driver of this growing vulnerability is the explosion of global trade. Global merchandise exports surged from $7.38 trillion in 2003 to $17.93 trillion in 2012.[42] Rapidly declining costs of communications and growing efficiency of logistics are enabling all this trade, with the resulting lengthening of supply chains. Digital communications mean companies can more readily work with facilities, suppliers, and distribution centers on the other side of the world.

Containerization and larger conveyance sizes aid global trade by reducing transportation costs. In 1999, the largest container ships carried 8,700 TEU (twenty-foot equivalent unit) although 90 percent of container ships were 4,500 TEU or smaller (in order to fit through the Panama Canal, known as "Panamax" vessels). With the growth of trade came demand for bigger ships and the efficiencies they bring. By 2013, the largest ships carried 18,270 TEU[43] and nearly 50 percent of the total fleet capacity was in post-Panamax ships.[44] Larger ships, larger airplanes, longer trains, and larger trucks are all more efficient per ton-mile than smaller vehicles. Indeed, the trend in the industry has been to increase conveyance size in every mode of transportation, reducing the cost of long-distance trade in products. With the increase in size, however, comes a greater concentration of risk.

Global competition motivated companies to hunt for the best price and performance in global markets. As companies outsourced their manufacturing operations to distant lands and distant suppliers, lead time from order to delivery lengthened, meaning that there was more opportunity for things to go wrong. More actors were involved—from suppliers to service providers to multiple governments and regulatory regimes—thereby further increasing complexity and the probability of failure.

More Variety

Global trade, global competition, and the need for differentiation in the marketplace mean that companies now sell more varieties of each product—what companies refer to as SKUs (stock keeping units). For example, Colgate—one of the more than 16 competitors selling toothpaste in the United States—advertises 14 types of toothpaste. Higher SKU counts mean that each variant sells in relatively small quantity, making the problem of predicting demand difficult. The reason is that product demand is often subject to random variations. The relevant measure of the variability of demand is the coefficient of variation: the ratio of the standard deviation to the mean. As the average sales of each SKU grow smaller, this ratio increases (owing to a linear decrease in the mean but only a square-root decrease in the standard deviation), resulting in more difficulties in forecasting demand, and leading to overstock/understock and higher costs. The first rule of forecasting—that forecasts are always wrong—is truer today than ever before.

More Technology, More Complexity

Many products have become more complex through the addition of embedded information and communications technology. Automobiles now contain between 30 and 100 microprocessors, with each subsystem of the car having its own controller and software.[45] Every headlight, airbag, rearview mirror, seat, and door has its own dedicated microprocessor.[46] Even simple products such as coffee makers and other home appliances use microprocessors and associated electronic systems. And new technology includes more than just electronics; products now rely on a growing variety of engineered materials, additives, pigments, and treatments that enable high efficiencies, performance, and market acceptance.

With product complexity comes the need to use more suppliers, who, in turn, may use more suppliers, leading to more complex supply chains. A car seat used to be like a piece of furniture and depended only on suppliers of cloth, leather, stuffing, and some metal or plastic framing. But modern car seats are technological gizmos that also include switches, motors, heating elements, sensors, and the ubiquitous microprocessor to control them. Even the seat materials themselves are more advanced, with high-tech foams and more durable, fashionable, and sustainable textiles.[46]

Complex, Broad, Long, and ... Vulnerable

Computers may make complex global supply chains more efficient and they work constantly to make them easier to manage, but they don't make them less risky. Companies can more readily manufacture complex products using complex supply chains, but the systems are inherently more fragile precisely because modern computers and communications enable tighter coordination and lean, inventory-less operations. While such controls and processes make a company more competitive in normal times, they also make it more fragile to any event that disrupts the finely tuned global network of business machinery. In addition, complex supply chains mean "deep" bills-of-materials and thus many tiers in the supply chain. While companies may be able to pressure their direct suppliers to help manage risks, companies have little knowledge of these deep-tier suppliers and, in most cases, almost no influence over them to demand more resilience or adherence to a code-of-conduct.

In the end, the rise of global trade means that companies have more moving pieces stretched over greater distances and with less slack in the system. And with a growing global population and a growing global economy, significant supply chain disruptions are inevitable. Thus, when a quake hits Japan or anywhere else unexpectedly, the companies of the global economy find themselves shaking, too.

2

A CLASSIFICATION OF CATASTROPHES

Russian novelist Leo Tolstoy wrote, "Happy families are all alike; every unhappy family is unhappy in its own way."[1] This so-called Anna Karenina Principle applies to supply chain disruptions in that every disruption comes with its own litany of misery, its own roster of causes, and its own cascade of effects. No two disruptions follow identical scripts, but the management of risk and disruption does encompass three general activities: prevention, detection, and response. Those three activities can frame companies' resilience efforts.

A MENAGERIE OF MISADVENTURES

Before organizations can categorize various disruptions for purposes of resilience management, they need to examine the gallery of possibilities. Supply chains, with their complex global connections and diverse stakeholders, can have many failure modes. Disruptions might be tied to natural, negligent, or intentional causes. Disruptions might involve any of a combination of suppliers, workers, customers, competitors, the built environment, the natural world, governments, and nongovernmental organizations. The root-cause events may strike a company directly, or they may strike a deep-tier supplier or a customer's customer.

Natural Disasters

Ash from a volcano in Iceland in 2010 grounded air traffic across the European Union and, consequently, decimated fresh food and flower exporters in Africa. A 2011 flood in Thailand inundated 877 factories,[2] halted 30 percent of the global hard disk manufacturing industry,[3] and caused billions of dollars in losses for the PC industry. A drought in the US Midwest in 2012 damaged crop yields and sent corn and soybean prices soaring. The price spike hit food producers, especially meat and dairy producers.[4] Each year, nature supplies fresh insults to companies dependent on the smooth operations of their global supply chains. Supply chains and logistics are outdoor sports, and customers don't want to hear that the game was canceled because of rain.

In total, natural disasters created $360 billion in losses in 2011.[5] The year 2011 saw an especially severe litany of floods, hurricanes, earthquakes, and tsunamis. These events killed people, damaged property, disabled logistics infrastructure, and upended the lives of citizens and employees. Many natural disasters—such as the Thai floods and the Japanese quake and tsunami—affected large areas and entire industries. Annual surveys of businesses in 2009,[6] 2010,[7] 2011,[8] 2012,[9] and 2013[10] found that 50 percent of companies suffer supply chain disruption from adverse weather in any given year. Weather is the first or second most common cause of disruption. In addition to disruptions from adverse weather, about 20 percent of companies experience a supply chain disruption from an earthquake or tsunami in any given year.

Although many natural disasters involve too much water, some involve not enough. The 2012 drought in the US Midwest affected transportation by reducing the level of the Mississippi River to the point of impairing the navigability of the river.[11] River barges carry 60 percent of US grain exports and 20 percent of US coal[12] as well as other bulk commodities such as steel, petroleum, fertilizers, and construction materials. The resulting two-month disruption in the winter of 2012–2013 resulted in an estimated $6 billion in losses.[13] The Rhine River—a major route for bulk commodities in Europe—suffers from similar water-level problems in dry years.

Accidents, Safety Violations, and Noncompliance

Disruptive accidents, often caused by lax safety measures, run the gamut from massive conflagrations to simple failures in critical pieces of equipment: A German factory making cyclododecatriene exploded and car makers around the world suddenly realized they might face potential disruptions of thousands of different parts used on every vehicle they make.[14] A barge on the Rhine River capsized, closing the river for twenty days, causing a stack-up of 450 barges and hindering the 170 million tonnes of goods shipped on the river annually.[15] A paint supplier to a contract manufacturer of a toy maker had to find a second source for pigments but didn't have time for testing. Later, the pigments were found to contain lead, causing a highly publicized recall of 1.5 million toys.[16] After lithium-ion batteries in the aft compartment of a newly-introduced passenger jet caught fire at the end of a long flight, the Federal Aviation Administration grounded the entire worldwide fleet, the first such action by the FAA in 34 years; the grounding cost the manufacturer and airlines hundreds of millions of dollars.[17,18] A garment factory in Bangladesh collapsed, 1,100 workers died, and many blamed prominent Western clothing companies for the deaths and deplorable conditions in factories in Bangladesh. Accidents and safety violations can disrupt logistics infrastructure, manufacturing equipment, and the flow of goods or parts, and they can undo many years of reputation-building and brand loyalty.

Whereas natural disasters occur regardless of the preparations and vigilance of companies, other types of disruptions become less likely for the well-prepared and the attentive. Safety programs, intensive quality control, and prudence can reduce the likelihood of accidents and violations. And yet, the connectivity of supply chains and companies' dependence on shared resources such as key raw materials or key transportation lanes imply that even the most careful company can be disrupted by the imprudence and bad luck of others.

Intentional Disruptions

Intentional disruptions come in many forms. In November 2012, 400 office clerks walked off their jobs at the ports of Los Angeles and Long Beach, thereby halting the movement of $760 million a day worth of goods.[19,20] In 2005, terrorists attacked the lightly guarded London subway and bus system rather than the more heavily secured Heathrow Airport. To protest the destruction of tropical forests for the farming of palm oil, Greenpeace raided

Nestle's annual shareholders meeting in 2010. Activists dressed as orangutans stood outside Nestle's headquarters in Frankfurt, Germany, while other activists unfurled a banner inside the meeting itself.[21]

Intentional disruptions include attacks on a company's assets or processes, with the goal of disrupting its operations or robbing it. Such disruptions include criminal acts like cyber-disruptions (e.g., denial-of-service attacks and theft of customer data), cargo theft, extortion, kidnapping, embezzlement, sabotage, and corporate espionage, as well as legal actions such as labor strikes, management lockouts, and activist boycotts and protests.

Intentional disruptions are fundamentally different from natural disruptions or accidents in two major aspects. First, the attacker will usually choose the most impactful place and time for the event—thus, for example, the port workers chose to strike the month before Christmas when the volumes are at their highest and capacity strained.[22] Second, the disruption will be aimed at the least hardened target. Furthermore, whereas the likelihood of a hurricane or an earthquake is not influenced by protective measures (only the impacts are affected), hardening a target against an intentional disruption can lower the likelihood of such an attack. Furthermore, unlike, say, accident avoidance measures that primarily benefit the preparer, preparations against intentional disruption can increase the chance that the attacker will target a related, less protected target such as a different business unit or a competitor.

Creative (and Other) Destruction

Beginning with Apple's iPhone in 2007, the rise of touchscreen smartphones coupled with app stores decimated the sales of previous mobile phone industry leaders such as Nokia, Blackberry, and Motorola. The Toyota Production System, developed in the 1970s, resulted in American manufacturers not being able to compete on cost and quality, causing the US government to impose "voluntary" quotas on Japanese car imports from 1981 through 1994.[23] In his groundbreaking book *The Innovator's Dilemma*,[24] Clayton Christensen gives many other examples of new products and business processes that disrupted existing ones, from the transistor radio to

LCD TVs to steel mini-mills. Such innovations cause existing firms to cede their market leadership, lose profits, and even disappear. (See more on disruptive innovation in chapter 12).

Creative destruction may be disruptive, yet as the theory of evolution suggests, "survival of the fittest" is what keeps companies, industries, and economies competitive. Competition motivates innovations in products, services, costs, and consumer choices. As with the evolution of species, the more competitive and prone to failure individual players in an industry are, the more robust the industry as a whole is (see chapter 13).[25]

In addition, businesses also face illegal competition from counterfeiters. Copies of popular brands of clothes and shoes dominate the worldwide counterfeit trade, which had an estimated value of $600 billion in 2010, according to the US Immigration and Customs Enforcement Agency.[26] Counterfeit competitors sell $75 billion in fake pharmaceuticals, which bring the added threat of harming those who take them.[27] And, according to the BSA | The Software Alliance global piracy study, "42% of all PC software packages installed in the world in 2011 were pirated."[28] Although injured companies, governments, and international bodies have been working to fight this illegal trade, it has been growing with increasing globalization and e-commerce.[29]

Some threats, such as a competitor's predatory pricing, are difficult to prove and involve prolonged legal proceedings or unpredictable political forces. In 1996, Microsoft started to give away its Internet Explorer browser, driving Netscape out of the market and sparking a multiyear antitrust lawsuit against Microsoft.[30] Google faced complaints by European regulators that the free distribution of the Android operating system was predatory.[31] Believing that Chinese tire manufacturers enjoyed subsidies as well as an artificially low currency value, the United States slapped a tariff of 35 percent on imported Chinese tires in 2009.[32]

Global Crises: An Age of Contagion

In 1997, a crash in the value of the Thai currency created a financial contagion that swept through Asian economies[33] and even caused crises in financial markets in the United States, Europe, Russia, and

Latin America.[34] Then, in 2008, a housing bubble led to a foreclosure crisis that threatened to collapse the world financial system like a house of cards. Marked contractions in credit supply and consumer demand triggered a global bullwhip as imports plummeted, causing contraction and bankruptcies throughout global supply chains.

Nor are financial contagions the only potential causes for a global crisis. In 2003, severe acute respiratory syndrome (SARS) appeared in Asia and then rapidly spread to more than two dozen countries.[35] The unknown nature of the new disease and its accompanying high fatality rate led to quarantines and warnings about travel.[36] Ten years after the SARS outbreak, health officials were carefully monitoring a related disease, Middle East Respiratory Syndrome (MERS).[37] And in 2014, governments around the world were taking steps to stop the spread of the Ebola virus.[38] Health officials also worry that each new strain of flu could threaten to reenact the 1918 Spanish Flu pandemic that killed 50 to 100 million people worldwide.[39] In addition to the potential human toll, epidemic diseases threaten to curtail the free movement of people and goods that underpin global supply chains.

Last, there are internal and external political upheavals. A dispute between the governments of China and Japan over the ownership of a group of uninhabited islands led to a Chinese boycott of Japanese goods, resulting in a 17 percent drop in volume of Japanese exports to China between June and November 2012.[40] Following a 2014 decision by China to move an oil rig to disputed waters with Vietnam, Vietnamese mobs ransacked foreign factories, causing manufacturers around the world to halt production.[41] In 2011, Spanish fruit and vegetable exporters lost €200 million a week after a food poisoning scare caused Germany to ban Spanish cucumbers.[42]

The growing interconnectedness of the global economy makes it increasingly prone to contagion. Contagious events, including medical and financial problems, can spread via human networks that often correlate strongly with supply chain networks. Unlike the more localized disruptions of natural disasters, industrial accidents, or terrorist strikes, global crises deliver a near-simultaneous blow to multiple countries and multiple industries. Furthermore, the mere fear of contagion, especially with health and financial issues, can cause a reduction in demand because of caution as well as supply and price spike issues resulting from hoarding. Although everyone can get hit, the weaker and less-prepared companies suffer the most.

THE QUADRANTS OF CATASTROPHES: IMPACT AND LIKELIHOOD

The preceding anecdotes and surveys of business disruptions illustrate two key points about such events, which affect how companies prioritize risk management efforts. First, different disruptions have different degrees of impact. For example, a tsunami that drags an entire factory into the sea is more serious than a shortage of some part. Second, different disruptions occur with different frequencies or likelihoods. Adverse weather occurs more frequently than do major fires, epidemics, or disruptive innovations.

Thus, many risk experts categorize potential disruptions by their impacts and their likelihoods, creating a 2 × 2 matrix as shown in figure 2.1. This stylized plot also shows where various hypothetical types of disruptions might lie on the four quadrants of impact and likelihood. The figure depicts events defined by causes (e.g., flood, wind damage, recession) as well as events defined by their effects on the supply chain (e.g., loss of key supplier, IT failure, and downed transportation link).

Estimating Impact and Likelihood

Companies can estimate the impacts and likelihoods of disruptions using a range of historical, analytic, or subjective measures. The potential impact can be estimated in terms of revenue loss, operating income reduction, brand diminution, stock price reduction, and/or loss of market share. The likelihood of many disruptive events can be estimated based on their past frequency and various probability models; that is how insurance companies assess risk and calculate premiums. Although the impact of a downed plant or a supplier's inability to ship parts may be the same regardless of the cause, estimating likelihood entails examining the possible causes of the disruption and the chances of them being triggered.

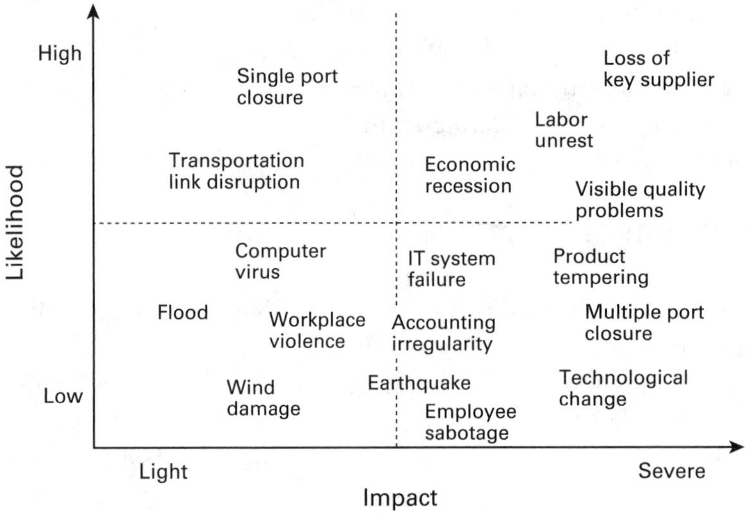

Figure 2.1

Prioritizing possible events

In the absence of good data and rigorous estimates of impact and likelihood, however, companies use more subjective scoring methods. For example, a large beverage company uses a scheme that divides each axis into five levels, creating a 5 × 5 matrix (rather than the 2 × 2 shown in figure 2.1). Furthermore, the numerical values associated with the levels are not linear. The company assigns the five levels of impact (the horizontal axis) a numerical score of 1, 3, 7, 15, and 31, respectively, and the five levels of likelihood (the vertical axis) a numerical score of 1, 2, 4, 7, and 11, respectively. The rationale for this pattern of levels is that impacts (e.g., "What happens if Supplier X can't ship for two months?") are often easier to assess than likelihoods ("What is the probability that something will disrupt Supplier X?") and therefore are given a higher weight. It also means that high-impact/low-probability events will have a higher risk score than high-probability/low impact events.

The company multiplies the impact and likelihood numerical scores to compute a total risk score, which can range from 1 (for insignificant risks with both low likelihood and low impact) to 341 (for perceived "worst-case" risks with both high likelihood and high impact). This number is, in fact, a mathematical expectation of the damage from a disruption, and the assumption is that the higher the expectation, the more resources should be directed toward mitigation and resilience. As mentioned later in this chapter (in the section titled "The Irony of Anxiety about Expected Losses"), however, the worst-case disruptions may not be the highest-expected-value disruptions.

The Power Law of Impacts versus Likelihoods

In the average year, seismologists tally about 1,300 earthquakes of magnitude 5 to 5.9, which are strong earthquakes capable of causing damage. They also detect an average of 134 earthquakes of magnitude 6 to 6.9, which are quakes that have 32 times the destructive energy but are about 1/10th as likely to occur as the magnitude 5 to 5.9 quakes. Finally, seismologists record about 15 quakes of magnitude 7 to 7.9, which are another 32 times more energetic and approximately another 1/10th as likely.[43] This pattern of increasing destructive magnitude and decreasing likelihood—in which each factor of multiplication of the seriousness of the event comes with a significant decrease in the likelihood of events (about 1/10th as many quakes for each 32 times increase in destruction)—is known as a power law distribution. The power law distribution is also known popularly as the 80/20 law or Pareto Rule, which, in the context of disruptions, posits that 80 percent of events will be frequent, minor events; and only a rare, small percentage will generate the major impact.

As it turns out, many types of disruptive events—including earthquakes, volcanoes, hurricanes, tornados, floods, landslides, forest fires, power outages, and even man-made events such as terrorist activities, cybercrimes, wars, and commodity price volatility—generally follow a power law. That is, they show a multiplicative inverse relationship between the likelihood and the impacts of events. Figure 2.2[44] presents, for example, the cumulative number of events for earthquakes, hurricanes and floods in the United States over a 90-year period versus the loss per event on a log-log scale. Figure 2.2 is similar to figure 2.1 in that it shows "likelihood" and impacts of disruptive events.

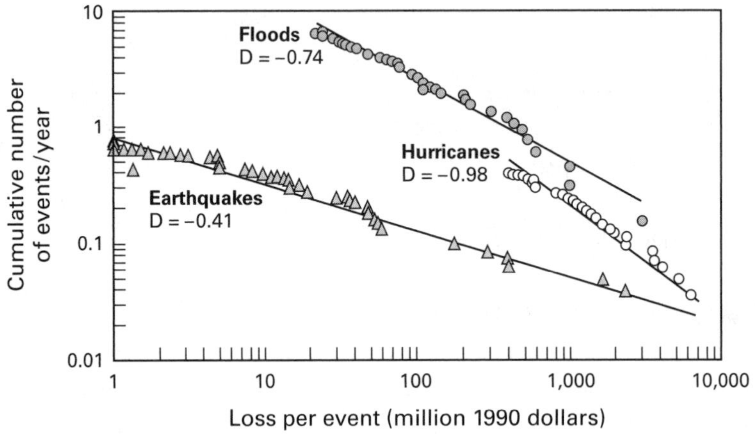

Figure 2.2

Hurricane and earthquake losses 1900–1989; flood losses 1986–1992

Yet figure 2.2 is different in four key ways. First, figure 2.2 shows a spectrum of events of a given type of disruption, such as a range of earthquakes of different impacts and different likelihoods. In contrast, figure 2.1 simply aggregates all quakes together as one average impact of average likelihood.

Second, the points on figure 2.2 are events that actually took place. Thus the plot shows the historical record, rather than an estimate of future likelihood and impact as in figure 2.1. Naturally, the historical records can be an input to the estimates of likelihood and impact. The plotted line can be used as an estimate for the future pattern of likelihoods and impacts, assuming that the future follows the same pattern as the past.

Third, figure 2.2 uses a log-log scale, which is a highly nonlinear, on both axes. Events in the highly likely upper half of the chart might be 10, 100, even 1,000 times more likely than those in the lower, unlikely half. And events in the high-impact right half might be 10, 100, even 1,000 times more destructive than those in the low-impact left half.

Fourth, figure 2.2 also reflects the total exposure of the entire United States rather than of a specific company. A given company with facilities and suppliers in only a few areas of the world would have lower likelihood of being hit by the natural disasters depicted in figure 2.2, but the impact on the company, if hit, may be significant. Thus, the slope of the log-log line may be shallower for a given company or facility.

Power law statistics also affect the expected losses for different levels of impacts. If 10 times bigger events are 1/10th as likely as the smaller events (a slope of –1.0 on the log-log plot), then the cumulative losses over a long time period from frequent, small disruptions will be as high as the total losses from rare, massive disruptions during the same time period. Yet, from a risk management standpoint, the high-likelihood/low-impact events do not require any significant response and, by and large, do not represent an existential threat. In contrast, high-impact disruptions—whether relatively likely or highly unlikely—are what risk management is all about.

A Daily Dribble of Microdisruptions: Low-Impact Events

Every single day, small events disrupt the smooth running of a business: late deliveries, digital communications disruptions, low yields, isolated workplace accidents, and similar small-scale events. Such small-scale disruptions may delay a shipment, alter customer commitment, or reduce productivity, but they don't threaten the company. Even significant demand spikes, critical machine breakdowns, or input price fluctuations do not generally pose an existential threat to most well-run companies. Being both modest in effect and likely to occur, such disruptions are handled tactically through companies' day-to-day operations that manage minor burbles in supply, demand, scheduling, and prices. Routine business processes are designed to smooth low-impact disruptions that barely merit any notice at all.

The Unexpected and Unimagined: High-Impact, Low-Likelihood Disruptions

On February 15, 2013, a modest space rock about 65 feet wide hurtled at 43,000 miles per hour into the dawn skies of central Russia. Although the meteor did not directly hit anything, it did explode high in the atmosphere with a detonation equivalent to a 500-kiloton nuclear weapon. Even at a distance of 20 miles, the blast damaged 7,200 buildings and seriously injured 1,500 people around Chelyabinsk, Russia.[45]

Scientists who study meteors and the outer space environment near the earth worry about the very rare but inevitable likelihood of much larger rocks hitting the earth.[46] A direct strike by a large "city killer" meteor could demolish a city or create a massive tsunami. Although strikes by larger meteors or asteroids might be extremely unlikely, the potential death toll and the resulting economic impact could be devastating.

Risk managers can fail to anticipate many other types of events besides meteor strikes. The 1996 Chernobyl nuclear accident caused a release of 400 times more radioactive materials than the Hiroshima atomic bomb, contaminating over 100,000 square kilometers with significant fallout.[47] The 1984 Bhopal industrial disaster in a Union Carbide plant exposed 500,000 people to methyl isocyanate gas, causing thousands of deaths and severe injuries.[48] The 2010 explosion of the BP Horizon oil rig in the Gulf of Mexico caused 11 deaths and the biggest oil spill in the history of the petroleum industry.[49] These and other events—such as the 2010 Eyjafjallajökull volcanic eruption, the 2005 Hurricane Katrina, and the 2011–2013 Arab Spring, to name an additional few—were neither envisioned nor planned for, causing significant disruptions as a result.

This category also includes so-called black swans, which are events that were thought to be impossible or that have never been imagined until they occur. The term derives from the historical experience that every swan seen by Europeans was a white swan and, therefore, black swans were assumed to be nonexistent. But then black swans were found in Australia in 1697. The term was popularized by Nassim Taleb in 2007 to indicate a category of flawed reasoning about unprecedented events:[50] the *lack of evidence* of a possible disruption does not constitute *evidence of lack* of possible disruption. As mentioned in chapter 1, Japanese planners underestimated the potential heights of tsunamis, such as the one that hit the Fukushima prefecture. The planners had centuries of earthquake and tsunami data but falsely concluded that a tsunami as high as the 2011 one was impossible and that therefore the nuclear reactors were safe from that threat. Black swans reflect a deeper kind of uncertainty than standard likelihood because experts misjudge the likelihood of a black swan risk to be zero when, in fact, it is not.

Here Comes Another "Big One": High-Impact, High-Likelihood Disruptions

Each year, the Atlantic Basin brews up an average of 12 named storms, of which six become hurricanes.[51] Thus, the 600 manned oil platforms in the Gulf of Mexico face a high chance of disruption every year. When a hurricane such as Isaac (2012) threatens the area, more than 90 percent of platforms prepare by shutting down production and evacuating personnel.[52] Similarly, every year, officials in extreme northern latitudes prepare for severe winter storms by restocking road salt, maintaining plowing equipment, replenishing airport de-icing mixtures, and so forth. For some types of disruptions, the question is not "if" but "when" and "how severe."

Anyone using statistical reasoning based on the expectation of losses would assess high-impact/high-likelihood events as the worst. They happen relatively often and hit hard. These are the types of events for which companies prepare, such as the oil platform operators preparing for seasonal hurricanes. These are the type of events that the methodology of taking the product of likelihood and impacts is designed to highlight. High expected losses occurring at relatively high likelihood justify proactive steps to reduce the likelihood of impacts. These events have enough salience that companies plan for them, prepare specific mitigation tools and processes to lessen their impact, and coordinate a planned response to these potential disruptions with their suppliers.

Of course, the term "high likelihood" is relative. As the power law indicates, the likelihood of specific high-impact events may still be very small. Yet chapter 1 noted that globalization has increased the length, breadth, and complexity of supply chains. Although small-likelihood events are individually unlikely, global enterprises are now exposed to large numbers of unlikely events through all their complex and lean networks of suppliers. In other words, the probability that a specific disruption will take place in a specific supplier's facility on a specific day may be very small. However, the probability that something significant will happen somewhere in a global supply chain sometime during a given year is not negligible.

THE IRONY OF ANXIETY ABOUT EXPECTED LOSSES

Impact and likelihood combine to affect the overall priority of each risk. As mentioned above, the standard logic of risk management prioritizes risk based on the expected value of the loss—which is impact multiplied by likelihood. In quadrant terms, high-impact/high-likelihood risks have the highest priorities, low-impact/low-likelihood risks have the lowest priorities, and both high-impact/low-likelihood and low-impact/high-likelihood risks have intermediate values. Expected value, however, is only partially effective in classifying risks. In particular, high-impact/low-likelihood risks may be more dangerous than their expected value implies because their rarity means that no one in the company will have had experience with the event, and the unlikelihood of the disruption makes it easy to ignore.

The contrast between more-likely versus less-likely disruptions illustrates a common pattern in how organizations think about and prioritize risk and uncertainty. Organizations plan for the expected (e.g., hurricane seasons) because its likelihood is historically high, and they pay less attention to the highly unlikely or the impossible ("black swans") because even the nature of the disruption may not be foreseen. Yet if an organization has thorough and inclusive preparation and a ready mitigation plan for an event, that event should be reclassified as lower-impact because the company has likely tempered those impacts. That is, risk management itself modulates the risks to the company.

Taking the logic of the effects of risk mitigation efforts to the next level suggests a different view of the actual dangers of different types of disruptions. The most dangerous events are not the well-known *high-impact/high-likelihood* ones for which the organization has experience and well thought-out "playbooks." Rather, the most dangerous events are the *high-impact/low-likelihood* ones. The reason is because such events are either unimaginable or are so rare that they have not taken place in recent memory, if ever, and as such are "not on the radar screen" of risk managers. And even if such events are imagined, they may be assessed as unlikely and therefore they don't justify proactive steps like mitigation procedures or playbooks.

Higher-Order Risks of Unknown-Unknowns

In a press briefing on February 12, 2002, US Secretary of Defense Donald Rumsfeld said, "There are known knowns; there are things we know that we know. There are known unknowns; that is to say, there are things that we now know we don't know. But there are also unknown unknowns—there are things we do not know we don't know."[53]

Risk managers can think about the analogs of these three categories of foreknowledge in a supply chain risk management context. The "known knowns" of disruptions are the everyday problems, referred to as the "daily dribble" earlier in this chapter. They also include seasonal variations and long-term trends, such as population aging, urbanization, and declining automobile ownership in the developed world.

The "known unknowns" are the foreseeable but random disruptive events whose probability can be estimated from historical evidence, power-law extrapolation, and logic. "Known unknown" events include tornados in Oklahoma and hurricanes in the Gulf of Mexico. Such disruptions may be significant, but they are not considered "outside the realm of possibility." These are the high-likelihood/high-impact events that can be prepared for through playbooks, drills, and experience. They can also be insured against because their probability density is known and thus a quantitative risk measure can be calculated.

Finally, there are the "unknown unknowns"—those events for which not only can the likelihoods not be calculated, but the events themselves have not been imagined. Such events should be discussed in terms of *uncertainty* rather than *risk*. The scenario of a record-breaking tsunami wave hitting Japan—triggered by a 9.0 earthquake that causes a nuclear disaster and subsequent power shortages—was not imagined by any planner; nor was there any historical precedence for such an event. Similarly, the 9/11 terrorist attack caught the United States by surprise. Furthermore, few foresaw the growing real estate bubble in the United States prior to 2008 and fewer still took actions to mitigate the financial meltdown that followed. The near-collapse of the international financial system did not enter into the risk management calculus of most executives. In comparing these three categories, Rumsfeld concluded, "And if one looks throughout the history of our country and other free countries, it is the latter category that tends to be the difficult one."[54]

The statistics of big, rare events hide a curse. No matter how bad the last "big one" was, a bigger one is inevitable. As history rolls onward, the list of major disruptions grows skyward. The next "bigger one" may take a long time to materialize, or it could happen tomorrow; but, unfortunately, the unlikely is not the impossible. With a growing global population and a growing global economy, the biggest disaster will always lie somewhere in the future.

Yet, companies don't prepare specifically for meteor strikes, calamitous accidents, or cataclysmic storms and other natural events. Such occurrences are too infrequent, especially within the scope of a single company and its supply chain. Preparation for unexpected events requires the development of general resilience—the ability and processes required to "bounce back" from whatever happens (see chapter 4 and chapter 6).

Resilience to Effects versus Resilience to Causes

The menagerie of disruptions illustrates the boundless causes of disasters. From toxic labor relations to toxic lead contamination, from viruses to volcanoes, and from regulation to innovation, companies face innumerable threats to their ongoing operations. Every day, media outlets report on catastrophes near and far, making the world seem a dangerous place. And yet, Cisco found that fixating on each and every cause wasn't the best way to think about business risks. Although the focus on causes did "scare the business" into funding risk management at Cisco, the cause-focused view didn't lead to effective risk management.[55] The overall rarity of each cause implies that next year's causes are almost inevitably different from last year's causes.

After the 2006 Taiwan earthquake, Cisco changed how it looks at risks.[56] In contrast to worrying about the never-ending litany of new causes of disruption in a diverse and complex world, Cisco started looking at the effects side of the risk picture, especially the question of "what if we can't make and deliver a given product," regardless of cause. Unlike the causes, the effects are tractable and known because they are linked directly to the companies' product portfolio and its global network of suppliers and contract manufacturers. Whereas Cisco can predict neither the cause of the next disaster nor its likelihood, it can consider the potential impacts of a disruption to each product in terms of interruption of product revenues. And the products' risks do follow a power law—a relative few of Cisco's products account for more than half its potential risk, simplifying risk prioritization efforts.[57] The impact estimation method and the crisis management dashboard described in chapter 3 use this focus on products.

The effects-focused view reflects the fact that *what* is disrupted matters more than *why* it is disrupted. Frank Schaapveld, senior director supply chain EMEA (Europe, the Middle East and Africa) at Medtronic, the medical equipment and technology company, said, "We do take into account natural disasters or internal root causes like power outages, but I'm not really interested in the nature of the disaster, only its impact. Will a location be out of action for one hour, one day, or one week? How long will it be without critical personnel? What caused the impact is less relevant."[58]

The Link between Causes and Likelihood

Despite the usefulness of the effects-focused view at stripping away the "noise" of the 24-hour news cycle, thinking about causes has its uses. The effects-focused approach is not associated with any disruption likelihood—it is just a "what if?" analysis. Yet some products rely on riskier technologies from riskier facilities and riskier suppliers in riskier geographies. The likelihood of a disruption is an important element in prioritizing the preparations for it. A second use of the cause-focused approach is in understanding correlated risks—the chance that two different effects (e.g., disruption of two suppliers or two products) might occur simultaneously and create greater damage or disrupt a back-up supplier. The cause-focused approach lets risk managers think about the scopes of different types of disruptions. For example, an industrial accident or fire may disrupt a single site of a given supplier; flooding or a regional political upheaval may disrupt multiple colocated sites; and bankruptcy or industrial action may disrupt all of the supplier's sites.

A CUBE OF CALAMITY: THE QUADRANTS AND DETECTABILITY

In addition to the two dimensions of likelihood and impacts, disruptions vary on a third crucial dimension: detectability. Some types of disruptions can be forecasted or detected well before they have an impact on the enterprise, while others hit without warning. Detectability adds a time dimension to the classification of disruptions and is defined as the time between knowing that a disruptive event will take place and the first impact. Note that the detectability of an event can be positive (detection *before* the impact), zero (realization at the instant of occurrence), or even negative (detection *after* the disruption has taken place).

Figure 2.3 shows the addition of the detectability dimension to the two dimensions depicted in the quadrant diagram in figure 2.1. The detectability axis can be divided into four main segments: very long-term trends that are well discussed in the media, for which companies have time to prepare strategically; disruptions that arise and hit after some short warning (e.g., hurricanes); disruptions that strike with no warning but can be instantly recognized if they happen (e.g., a fire); and disruptions that are hidden and are only discovered some time after the fact (e.g., a product contamination or design defect) or not at all (e.g., industrial espionage).

Forewarned Is Forearmed: Positive Detection Lead-Time

Trends such as the aging of the world's population in the Western world, China, and Japan, come as no surprise and can be detected years—even decades—in advance. Growing demand for energy and natural resources in China, India, and other emerging markets is also all but inevitable, with its concomitant implications

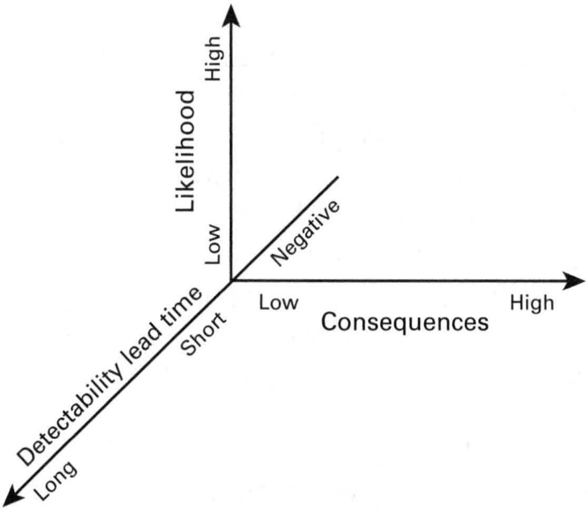

Figure 2.3
Likelihood-consequences-detectability axes

for supplies and prices. Long-term trends in urbanization, mobile phone usage, economic growth in sub-Saharan Africa, robotics (including drones), rising food prices, and water scarcity will affect investments and supply chain patterns. The difference between long-term trends and any other risk is that these trends offer an opportunity to incorporate them into a company's strategy, thereby profiting from them. Nonetheless, like the proverbial frog in gradually heating water, some companies may not detect, prepare for, or take advantage of slowly shifting trends.

The end dates of labor contracts are known on the signing date of the contract, yet some companies miss that signal of higher risk of labor strikes at that time. The phase-in dates of major regulatory changes (e.g., regarding toxic chemicals) can likewise have months or years of lead time. Most supplier bankruptcies should be of little surprise (see chapter 5). Companies can detect which suppliers have precarious balance sheets, unfavorable patterns of profits, or negative cash flows months before the supplier reaches a point of insolvency or bankruptcy. Furthermore, shipment errors, quality problems, and slow refunds can presage a troubled supplier even before this shows in the financial data.

Other threats have shorter detection horizons but still offer some chance of a warning. As capricious as the weather seems, the physics of moist air flowing at various altitudes and at various temperatures isn't impenetrably mysterious. Hurricanes, many floods, and winter storms now arrive with hours or days of warning. When a hurricane steams into the Gulf of Mexico, the oil rig workers know what to do. They are trained to carry out a series of "shut-in" procedures for closing key valves and securing equipment, thereby reducing the chances of an oil spill when the storm hits and enabling a rapid restart after the storm passes. Forewarning lets a company kick-off impact-avoidance and recovery efforts.

Even earthquakes can be detected as they start, enabling early warnings to those more distant from the epicenter. Businesses and residents of Tokyo knew the 2011 quake was coming about 80 seconds before it struck and had up to 40 minutes warning on the tsunami's arrival in Tokyo Bay. Data can flow faster than disaster (see chapter 8).

BANG! Hit in an Instant: Zero Detection Lead-Time

On the morning of December 8, 2010, the electricity supply dropped for just 0.07 of a second at Toshiba's Yokkaichi memory-chip plant in Mie prefecture. The power glitch caused the factory's equipment to reboot, which ruined all the wafers in production. That was all it took to create a two-month disruption in production of NAND[59] flash memory.[60] At the time, Toshiba provided 35.4 percent of the world's supply of NAND flash,[61] and the failure affected about 20 percent of Toshiba's production. "I don't think it could come at a worse time," said Krishna Shankar, an analyst at ThinkEquity, because of the surging demand for NAND flash in fast-growing product categories such as smartphones, tablets, digital cameras, and music players.[62] No one could have forecast the event. Toshiba had no warning of the disruption, but it did know in an instant that disruption had struck.

Some events strike with little or no warning, like a technology outage, an explosion in a factory, or a terrorist attack. One minute, everything is running smoothly and, the next second, chaos erupts. What happens afterward depends on the likelihood of the event.

High-impact/high-likelihood disruptions that strike suddenly trigger a playbook response based on experience and drills. High-impact/low-likelihood events are more of a surprise and require significant information gathering, assessment, and creative problem solving.

In both cases, the detection time includes the time required for the company to sufficiently understand what happened and to mount an appropriate response. During 9/11, for example, the first plane to hit the World Trade Center was presumed to be an accident. Only after the second plane hit and after enough of the US government's agencies realized what was happening, was the military able to launch jets to intercept United Flight 93, which crashed in western Pennsylvania before the military could intercept it.[63] A large disruption can affect an entire industry, in which case the company that identifies the nature and magnitude of the problem early on can minimize the impact by securing supply, transportation, and access before its competitors do.

Lurking Dangers in Hidden Events: Negative Detection Lead-Time

In early 2007, a long-time paint supplier to Mattel ran short of colorants for the paint and could not get more from its primary supplier. The supplier quickly found a backup supplier via the Internet, who assured that it could supply safe colorants that were certified as lead-free. The paint supplier didn't test the new colorant because testing would delay production, although paint workers noted that the new paint did not smell the same as the usual formulation.[64]

For two and half months, Mattel's contract manufacturer made and shipped some one million toys painted with the substitute colorants. The toys flowed from China across the seas to distributors and retailers. In early July 2007, testing by a European retailer revealed prohibited levels of lead in the paint and coatings on some Mattel toys. Mattel immediately halted production of the toys, investigated the cause, and confirmed the presence of lead in the paint. In early August of 2007, Mattel recalled nearly one million toys of 83 different types.

Fortunately, the impact was not as bad as it could have been because two-thirds of the contaminated toys were still in the distribution chain. Yet Mattel still needed to alert consumers to return some 300,000 sold toys made during the two-and-a-half month period before it realized the problem.[65] Subsequent testing found other lead-contaminated toys, which forced Mattel to recall another million toys that autumn.[66] Mattel also paid a $2.3 million fine for violating federal bans on lead paint.[67] The recall meant that Mattel had to incur significant costs, including the logistics of identifying, collecting, and destroying the toxic products. More important, the incident tainted the brand in the eyes of consumers and the media. As a result, Mattel's stock fell 25 percent off its 2007 high during the worst of the recall incident.[68]

Whereas everyone knows when an earthquake hits, some disasters have a hidden start. Food contamination incidents can take weeks to surface as a result of delays in the food reaching consumers, the incubation time of the food-borne pathogens, and the time required to trace the illness back to particular types and brands of food. Usually, the greater the delay in detecting a hidden problem, the greater the impact and the resulting damage. Product defects—caused by design errors or material quality issues—may not surface until long after the goods are in customers' hands and in use.

Some disruptions have a more insidious and less detectable character—they are unknown unknowns. For example, toys have contained magnets for decades without safety concerns, but a new breed of high-strength magnets created an unforeseen and serious safety problem. Unlike prior generations of magnets, if these types of high-strength magnets broke loose from the toy and if a child swallowed more than one magnet over time, then the magnets could potentially pinch together two parts of the child's intestines, cause a perforation, and lead to a serious infection. Toy makers sold tens of millions of toys with these types of magnets over a nine-year period before health and safety officials detected the problem and mandated an extensive recall.[69]

MANAGING THE MENAGERIE OF RISKS

Companies have many strategic options for managing the diverse risks that they face. Risk management may include prevention of avoidable risks, playbooks to respond to common types of disruptions, general resilience for unexpected or very rare disruptions, and improving awareness of both incipient risks and ongoing disruptions.

Reduce the Likelihood or the Impact?

The quadrant framework of likelihood and impact suggests two complementary approaches for reducing risks. First, a company can reduce the likelihood of disruptions by being compliant with regulations, adhering to social concerns, maintaining good labor relations, and avoiding situations that are prone to disruption (e.g., suppliers in floodplain locations or unstable countries). A company may also implement safety, quality, and security measures,[70] including cybersecurity, to prevent possible intentional attacks. Yet, prevention and likelihood-reducing measures cannot entirely eliminate risks. Furthermore, prevention generally targets the foreseeable causes of disruptions, which implies that it may not reduce the likelihood of unknown-unknown risks.

Second, companies can reduce the impact by preparing a timely and effective response to disruptions. Optional assets such as spare inventory, spare capacity, and alternative suppliers provide materials and resources that can be utilized to minimize impacts and accelerate recovery times. Flexible processes can help a company respond quickly and efficiently. To this end, companies can create emergency operations centers, business continuity plans, and predefined escalation procedures that help coordinate a response (see chapter 6). Increasing flexibility and adding "just-in-case" assets can provide general resilience that helps address unknown-unknown threats.

From Unknown to Known: Accelerating Detection

An important part of reducing the impacts of a disruption is quick detection (see chapter 8). The earlier the warning, the more a company can do in preparation, such as moving inventory and assets away from the affected area, preparing recovery materials, or securing second-source supplies. Detection also means perceiving the scope and magnitude of the disruption. Accelerating a company's information flow and its decision-making processes is an important factor in detection and fast response.

Temperature and smoke sensors can warn of a fire, and many industrial sites connect these sensors to automatic fire suppression, fire evacuation alarms, and emergency responders. Similarly, tsunami sensors around the Pacific Ocean not only detect incoming tsunamis but also automatically activate sirens and evacuation alerts.

In a similar fashion, consumer-facing companies use social media to detect problems with their products and even to mitigate developing problems. For example, Dell and Best Buy use social media to both monitor problems and communicate with affected customers, thus responding quickly in order to avoid a growing wave of bad publicity. Some companies go beyond "listening" to social media discussions by inserting "solutions" (e.g., "I heard that the company knows about the problem and a new keyboard will be shipping in two months…").

On June 7, 2013, Delta Airlines was jolted to discover an unfavorable YouTube video of soldiers returning from Afghanistan who were complaining about being charged extra for a fourth checked bag. The video went viral.[71] Delta immediately understood the looming public relations disaster. Later the same day, it issued a corporate apology and by the next morning it changed its policy to allow soldiers traveling on orders to check four bags for free. The policy change meant that software systems had to be updated, airport kiosks modified, and employees around the world notified. By noon of that next day, Delta updated its blog posts and Facebook page alerting the public to the changed policy.[72] The fast action prevented the video from gaining the notoriety of the video "United Breaks Guitars."[73,74]

Detecting trends and longer-term disruptions means monitoring the environment for changes. Detecting instant-impact events means monitoring operations, suppliers, and the regions in which they operate. Detecting hidden-impact events means intensive monitoring of less visible elements of the supply chain, such as deeper-tier suppliers, fringe groups that influence an industry, and unusual adverse events among customers that might signal a heretofore unknown problem in the company's products or processes.

Detection is a broader and deeper strategy than just installing smoke alarms or social media monitoring; rather, detection means vigilance toward both specific near-term events and potential future events that might disrupt the company. Detection depends on creating *visibility* into the supply chain; at its heart, detection is the conversion of the unknown into the known in a timely fashion. Via detection, a company might go from: 1) not even knowing it is exposed to disruption from Gulf Coast hurricanes because of a deep-tier supplier of critical raw material being in that region to 2) knowing it's exposed but only having an estimated likelihood and impact based on actuarial data to 3) knowing that the supplier will be hit by a hurricane in three days' time but that this supplier has four weeks of inventory at an inland distribution center and a business continuity plan for a five-week recovery time creating a potential one-week gap in supplies a month after the hurricane's landfall. Thus, detection converts unknown-unknowns into known-unknowns and converts known-unknowns into known-knowns.

3

REDUCING THE WHITE-SPACE

General Motors's Detroit headquarters lies a comfortable 6,400 miles from Japan. Whereas Intel had 600 people working in Japan and depended heavily on Japan's extensive network of semiconductor suppliers, GM's ties to the area were much less intensive. A scant 2 percent of its vehicle parts came from Japan, and only 25 of GM's 18,500 Tier 1 suppliers were in Japan. Yet GM's experience with the 2011 quake shows just how deeply interconnected companies have become, and how unknown risks can outweigh known ones.

RESPONDING TO DISRUPTIONS FROM AFAR

The quake and tsunami struck around 1 o'clock in the morning Detroit time on Friday, March 11. When GM's executives learned of the disaster in the morning, they were somewhat worried about those 25 Japanese Tier 1 suppliers but did not think that they faced a corporate-wide crisis. GM's purchasing department worked through the weekend, trying to get information from Japanese suppliers. However, like many other companies, GM had a difficult time reaching these suppliers. Power and telecommunications were down in the affected area. Japanese roads and railroads were closed pending inspection for damage, so workers could not get to suppliers' factories. By Monday, GM received some initial reports of the severity of the damage and which suppliers were impacted.

Convening the War-Room

By Tuesday, March 15, GM estimated that 30 suppliers and 390 parts were affected by the quake and tsunami. Although 390 parts out of a total of about 30,000 parts for an average car seems minor, a single missing part can prevent completion and shipment of a car. Initial estimates based on available inventories showed that outages of these parts would halt production at many GM assembly plants in only eight days. More ominously, the initial estimate was that by the end of March, all of GM's factories worldwide would be down. Worse, initial estimates suggested that production might be disrupted for at least seven months. That's when alarm bells rang throughout GM.

Past crises can help a company develop new skills, and GM was no exception. In 2005, Delphi Corporation, which was a spin-off from GM, declared bankruptcy. To work through the staggering implications of losing its biggest supplier, GM created "Project D." That effort provided a backbone of people and methods for what became "Project J"—the response to the Japanese quake, tsunami, and nuclear disaster six years later. Bankruptcies and earthquakes may be vastly different causes, but they have similar effects in terms of disrupting critical supplies.

Step one of GM's method was to create a crisis room. The room was actually three rooms: one for the central coordination of Project J, one for working on supply chain solutions for specific elements of the crisis, and one for working on engineering solutions for affected parts. All three rooms sat in the GM's futuristic VEC (Vehicle Engineering Center) in Warren, Michigan, 15 miles from GM headquarters at Detroit's Renaissance Center. The VEC houses GM's engineering and design functions as well as its supply chain management organization. Other smaller crisis rooms in other GM's global locations also joined the effort.

Tapping the Team

With 390 affected parts and all 16 assembly plants at risk of a shutdown within a couple of weeks, GM needed a team of people who were adept at solving tough problems quickly under pressure. That's where the experience of Project D provided its first benefits. "I knew exactly—I mean literally day one—I knew the people we wanted, because I pulled in people who had worked on Project D," said Rob Thom, manager, Global Vehicle Engineering Operations.[1]

Because the crisis was a supply chain disruption, supply chain people took the lead for managing the entire effort. Bill Hurles, executive director of Global Supply Chain, led the effort with a strong collaboration between the supply chain organization and the engineering organization.

Creating a Daily Cycle: Communicate, Act, Report

The team quickly established a daily routine heavily focused on communication and coordinated action on the highest priority issues. Candid communications helped focus the efforts on the toughest problems. "This is where it's hard because you don't want to convey bad information but sometimes you have to. I shared everything, I mean everything," said Ron Mills, director, GM Components Holding, who served as the key spokesman for the engineering side of GM.[2]

Each day began with a 6 am call to senior leaders, including Vice Chairman Steve Girsky. "I had every region on the phone; all North America was impacted by this crisis and we'd go through 'here's where we are, here's what we learned, here's our downtime, here's our challenge for the day,'" Mills said.

Next, the team defined the day's activities to reach that day's goals. Sub-teams had their own meetings, such as a 7:30 am supply chain meeting. By 8 am, the crisis team leaders were rolling out information to all the teams working on the crisis. The crisis team also held a 10:30 am update to the sales, service, and marketing teams.

"Then, at 4:00 pm, we did a follow-up on what we learned for the day and what progress we had made," said Mills. This call closed the loop on the team's daily recovery activities. Regular and consistent communications of status, goals, actions, and results kept the group steadily working toward their goal. Given the global nature of the event and the magnitude of the problems, many team members worked around the clock. "It was seven days a week, 24 hours a day that we ran," Mills said.

GM'S RESPONSE TASKS

Minimizing the impact of the crisis on GM's production and subsequent sales called for a multifaceted plan of attack. The crisis room teams worked on five basic tasks: identify disrupted parts, assess the risk involved, delay the shortage of parts, reduce any shortages, and optimize production during the disruption. These tasks mainly involved the supply chain, purchasing, engineering, and marketing sides of the organization. And all the tasks had to take place concurrently.

Task 1: Detect the Potential Disruptions

GM's first task, starting on the day of the quake, was to identify all the affected parts and their impact on GM operations. Although the team immediately knew of some two dozen affected suppliers and 390 affected parts, those were only the direct impacts based on very preliminary estimates.

Thom described the commencement of the recovery effort. "When we had the first meeting, it was like, 'OK, who are the players and who knows what?' Well, we didn't have any information yet. So, they handed us the 390 part numbers, and then an hour later said, 'Oh, by the way, we've got a hundred more.'"[3] Disruptions deeper in the supply chain would surface over time, but the sooner GM could detect those hidden problems, the sooner it could solve them.

Modern-day cars are electronic miracles with all manner of sensors, computers, and actuators for managing the engine to produce efficient and reliable power with the lowest possible tailpipe emissions. The cars' dashboards use computerized displays and touchscreens to provide more control and convenience for drivers and passengers. Although a dashboard assembly or antilock brake module might be made in America by an American Tier 1 supplier, some of the components on the circuit board may have come from Japan. Given the Japanese prowess for electronics manufacturing, it's no surprise that a big part of the disruption lay in the electronics. All of GM's cars had computer chips, sensors, displays, radios, and navigation systems made with parts from Japan.

Electronics weren't the only concern, however. GM soon discovered that almost every type of part on many different vehicles required something from Japan. Xirallic, a sparkly additive in the paint used on the Corvette, came from Japan. Special plastics for the body trim came from Japan. Rubber seals and gaskets came from Japan. High-tech chrome plating on turbochargers came from Japan.

Cooling fans, radiator caps, air conditioner compressors, starter motors, and many more parts had some tie to Japanese suppliers.

Like most companies, GM did not have direct business relationships with those deeper-tier suppliers. Each Tier 1 supplier was typically responsible for its own engineering and sourcing decisions from deeper tiers. Furthermore, suppliers consider these relationships to be proprietary and confidential—part of the supplier's intellectual property—thereby limiting GM's awareness of how the quake might affect various suppliers' production and recovery alternatives. Fortunately, GM's team benefited from some ongoing efforts to map the deeper tiers of the company's supply chain. Even before the quake, the company knew it was exposed to risks in semiconductors. "We already had a pretty good roadmap, and it helped us navigate our way through," said Bill Hurles.[4] Collaboration with the engineering side of GM helped, too. In many cases, GM's engineers knew some of the Tier 2 and Tier 3 suppliers because they knew which sensor or chip was used inside a particular subsystem.

The deeper the team dug, however, the more problems they found. Some of GM's non-Japanese suppliers had Japanese suppliers. And some of GM's non-Japanese suppliers had other non-Japanese suppliers who had Japanese suppliers. And so on. "The list kept growing. And every day, it went up. It was a moving target for us," Thom said.[5]

From the known 390 affected parts on March 14, the number grew to 1,551 parts on March 24, 1,889 on March 29, and to a staggering 5,329 on April 13. During the month after the quake, GM discovered an average of 160 disrupted parts each day. Nor was the problem helped by the ongoing crisis with the Fukushima nuclear plant and the persistent power shortages in Japan.

As the number of affected parts grew into the thousands, tracking each individual part became difficult. The volume of inscrutable part numbers impeded communications and obfuscated the effort. To cope with this, the team switched from tracking individual parts to tracking what GM called "commodities," which were common categories of parts or subassemblies used on most vehicles, such as a seat, door pad, or radio. The long list of 5,329 affected parts became a more manageable list of 116 affected commodities. And because GM's purchasing, engineering, and supply base functions are largely organized around commodities, this view made sense in terms of finding the right internal and external people to address each affected commodity.

In the end, it took more than two months to even know how many parts were affected. The final figure of 5,830 affected parts was nearly 15 times higher than the initial estimate of 390 parts associated with the Tier 1 suppliers in Japan. And each missing part raised the specter of halting production somewhere in GM's system.

Task 2: Chart the White-Space

From the beginning and as the number of affected parts grew, GM needed a way to track the impact of the developing crisis. It needed a visual "dashboard" to show at a glance which vehicle platforms were affected, which parts were affected, when critical parts would run out, when fresh parts or alternatives might appear, and when each one of its 16 assembly plants might be shut down for lack of parts. Again, the company's experience with Project D provided the solution.

"We call these white-space charts," said Mills.[6] The solution was a very long, room-spanning whiteboard chart showing the timelines on each of GM's 16 global assembly plants along a horizontal axis. "This is something that we've come up with to show impact. It helps us communicate to our leadership where we are with the problem," Mills said.

On the left edge of the time axis was the current day and near-term weeks. These near-term weeks were shaded, marked, and annotated to show when shortages of any parts might affect that assembly plant. A circle on the timeline showed when a part would run out for some vehicle options but that GM could "build through" by continuing to produce the other variants of that vehicle. A triangle indicated a potential problem affecting production. And an "X" marked a definite disruption to production. As GM gathered data from suppliers, marks began to pepper the various timelines for each plant on the giant chart.

The timeline for each plant covered further months—out to almost a year on the right-hand-side of the chart. This side of the chart showed when GM expected to restart production through one of three methods: the recovery of the original supplier, bringing alternative suppliers on line, or finding an engineering work-around. It also showed previously scheduled halts in production, such as the traditional midsummer shutdown—the annual suspension of production while the company did maintenance and retooling, switched over to the new model year, and gave workers a vacation.

In the middle of the chart was the namesake white-space—the ominous time gap during which GM would run out of supplies and before it expected to have a solution to the disruption. Very early in the crisis, every one of the 16 rows of the chart had sickening "X's," sometimes many, somewhere on the timeline. Those marks showed the date when GM would be forced to shut down production at that plant as a result of parts shortages.

The crisis team shaded in and color-coded the two sides of the chart to reflect progress on managing the gap. Red meant they did not yet have a plan; yellow meant they had a plan but had not implemented it yet; and green meant they were executing the plan. Because different groups were working on the two sides of the chart by extending existing suppliers on the left side and resuming supplies on the right side, the two sides might have different colors. The primary goal of GM's response to the crisis was to eliminate all white-space. Moreover, as the recovery teams worked, they also aimed to make both sides of the white-space chart turn green to demonstrate confidence about parts supplies and recovery plans.

GM staffers also used this same color notation to talk about the status of different commodities: "We're red on paint. We're yellow on heated seat modules." By April 13, of the 116 commodities known to be affected, GM was executing recovery plans for 44 (status: green), had plans for another 61 (status: yellow) and only had 11 "red" commodities. By May 27, the scope of the problems had grown from 116 to 118 commodities, but the engineers and Japan's suppliers had made significant progress in finding alternatives or in restoring production. The number of commodity groups marked as "red"—a serious problem—dropped from 11 groups to only 2. And the number of commodities deemed to be "green" grew from 44 to 82.

Task 3: Delay the Shutdown

"The first couple of weeks were kind of white knuckle time," said General Motors Chairman & CEO Daniel Akerson.[7] With each bit of news of another part disruption, the team quickly re-estimated when GM would run out and which vehicles would be affected by that new shortage. Those estimates added more "X" marks on the left side of the white-space chart and defined that boundary of the white-space.

The supply chain team worked hard to find any extra inventory of the affected parts that might be available—in an undamaged warehouse in Japan, in transit to GM, in a contract subassembly maker's site, and so forth. The team searched up and down the supply chain. They even tapped into the replacement parts inventories in the field and at dealers' locations. Each time they found more parts, they were able to push critical "X" marks a little further into the future and shrink the white-space on that side.

These delaying tactics worked, and the left edge of the white-space moved further and further into the future. The first assessment of the crisis on March 14 estimated that all plants would shut down by the end of March—only two weeks away. By March 24, the team had found enough supplies to keep all the plants running until April 11. By the end of March, the shutdown had been pushed to May 16—providing more than six weeks for finding other solutions to the toughest problems.

Task 4: Reduce Time-to-Recovery

At the same time that the supply chain professionals of GM worked to extend supplies to delay the shutdown, the engineering side of GM looked for ways to recover parts' supplies and production as quickly as possible. To reduce the time-to-recovery, both procurement and engineering helped with the recovery of the affected suppliers and, at the same time, looked for substitute parts. Part substitutions involved a double search both for new suppliers and for ways to adapt well-stocked parts to cover the shortages in parts affected by the Japanese quake.

For example, Renesas Electronics, maker of 40 percent of the world's automotive microcontrollers, was severely hit by the disaster. Fortunately, General Motors CEO Dan Akerson had been on the board of directors of Freescale, another supplier of these kinds of chips. "So I picked up the phone, I called the CEO of Freescale and I said, 'I know you make chips of this type.' We came up with a solution," Akerson said. At the same time that GM was seeking second sources, the company also had supplier quality engineers in Japan helping suppliers recover and restart production. "So we have a two-track solution if this becomes a problem for us," Akerson concluded.[8]

Yet finding an alternative part meant more than just slapping a different part into the vehicle. Under normal circumstances, engineers take six to twelve months to qualify and validate a new part or new supplier. In building cars designed to last for years and run hundreds of thousands of miles, every part must be carefully checked to ensure it will perform its job effectively, safely, and reliably. Validating a new part requires checking that part's ability to withstand the rigors of years of expected life on the road in terms of heat, cold, mechanical stress, and exposure to gasoline, motor oil, antifreeze, and so forth. The size, weight, and materials of the proposed substitute must be compatible with the other parts and materials already on the vehicle. Finally, engineers need to make sure each part is compatible with manufacturing (e.g., if assembly workers must bend a substitute hose to maneuver it into place, the chosen hose won't be damaged).

Engineers also had to make sure that any change they made didn't adversely affect the rest of the vehicle. For instance, the weight of the latch in the hood affects the required strength of the spring needed to hold the hood open. Substitute a heavier latch, and the hood needs a heavier spring. But then the weight of the hood assembly affects the front suspension, and so on. An important part of the qualification process was the effort to minimize the threat of cascading changes. This effort was complicated by the fact that alternatives for several parts were considered simultaneously.

Recovery also meant that suppliers had to work to create capacity for new or changed parts. Vehicles depend on a great many custom-made parts that fit a very limited set of vehicles. Suppliers often use specialized tooling to make complexly-shaped parts such as seals, gaskets, floor mats, rubber boots, and plastic trim, as well as stamped, forged, or cast metal parts. And any visible parts on the exterior or interior need to match in color. For these reasons, qualifying a part from a new supplier, or even just a new plant of an existing supplier, takes time.

Task 5: Allocate Scarce Supplies If Needed

"We still have issues, and the issues we have now are getting tougher to solve," said Robert E. Socia, GM's vice president for global purchasing and supply chain in mid-May.[9] Despite the heroic efforts to find inventories, alternate suppliers, and alternative engineering solutions, GM could not totally close the gap. "Now the long tent pole appears to be semiconductors," said Akerson.[10] The specialized nature of chips, the extent of the damage, and the long recovery times meant that some white-space remained. Because an unsolvable white-space gap had been a looming threat from the beginning, GM had thought carefully about what to do if it could not eliminate all of the white-space.

In many cases, parts such as engine controllers, mass airflow sensors, and brake control modules were shared across multiple vehicles. As Bill Hurles noted, "a lot of the stuff we were working with, you could allocate. We could make a decision to build and use that same engine controller in multiple products in Europe, multiple products in China, and multiple products in North America."[11]

"Our goal was to keep them all," Hurles continued, "but we set up a protocol if we got into a situation and needed to make a prioritization." First, and from the beginning, GM prioritized all the assembly plants on the white-space chart using a proprietary measure of each vehicle's financial contribution to the company. The rows of the chart listed the plants in financial priority order. This ensured that the crisis team focused its efforts on the vehicles that could help GM sustain itself if the disruption proved to be worse than expected.

Second, GM also factored in the operating stock levels in the field. How many cars, in terms of days of sales, did it have on dealers' lots, and was that number lower or higher than planned? Stopping production on a vehicle that had a low number of days in inventory raised the risk of lost sales. "So the stock level would kind of determine the relative importance of vehicles," explained Bob Glubzinski, manager of North American scheduling and order fulfillment at GM.[12]

On March 21, concern about a very near-term shortage of airflow sensors led GM to idle production of Chevrolet Colorado small trucks in Shreveport, Louisiana, for one week. Although this step made headlines, it did not influence sales because GM and its dealers had sufficient stocks of finished vehicles. GM took this step because managers knew that the sooner they idled a low-priority plant, the longer they'd be able to guarantee the supply of airflow sensors to plants making full-size trucks that had both a larger profit margin and lower field inventory of finished vehicles. As it turned out, the closing was not even needed; GM subsequently found it had enough sensors to supply all its truck plants, and Shreveport restarted the following week.

KEY LESSONS

In the end, GM weathered the crisis well. From the perspective of the average car buyer, almost nothing happened. Dealer lots still offered plenty of cars, although a few colors of some models weren't available for a time. Inside GM, it was a major event and hundreds of people put in very long hours to insulate dealers and customers from the disaster half a world away. As one GM staffer joked, "My neighbor thought I was divorced because I wasn't home for nine weeks."

The success of GM's efforts illustrates an important lesson in coping with large supply chain disruptions. When dealing with complex manufacturing operations, team members should stick to their roles and expertise in order to avoid impeding progress and minimize extra needless work. It also highlighted the role of senior management.

"Stay in Your Swim Lane"

"Because this was such a visible crisis, everyone was trying to be a hero in their own function," said GM's Dr. Marc Robinson, assistant director & economist, enterprise risk management.[13] One of the toughest challenges for GM was in reining in the good intentions of everyone's attempts to find solutions to the many different part shortages. GM employs a broad staff of veterans with decades of experience and extreme loyalty to the company. They knew their cars and factories inside and out. That meant that everyone had lots of ideas on how to tackle the various shortages.

Yet people's well-intentioned interventions could easily create other problems. In the same way that changing a part has cascading engineering implications on the engineering of other parts, changing a manufacturing plan has cascading implications on other plans and on the supply chain. As an example, consider heated seats, which faced a disruption in their electronic control modules. "We received a lot of pressure from engineering to stop ordering these seats for vehicles yet-to-be-manufactured," Glubzinski said.[14] But GM wanted to avoid three types of impacts that this intuitive and well-meaning change to the company's mix of products could create.

The first cascading impact of changing the mix was a potential capacity issue. Hurles explained the chain of logic: "I can build vehicles without heated seats. But now that starts shifting the mix because almost all heated seats go with leather. If I go out of heated seats, I now go into cloth. Now I can create an issue with cloth."[15] Moreover, the cloth vs. leather mix affects other vehicle features linked to selling basic vs. sport vs. luxury variants of a given model. So one small change could have significant impacts on the volumes of other parts and create shortages in other parts that were not disrupted. "We could move ourselves right into a hurricane," Hurles concluded.

The second cascading impact was caused by the sheer complexity of GM's supply chain and manufacturing systems. Building cars involves a carefully choreographed, weeks-long pipeline of coordinated production activities around the globe. Canceling heated seats means that all subassemblies and components that were destined to go into vehicles with heated leather seats become stranded somewhere in the supply chain. "And the supply chain, which was already in a very delicate state, could not survive more change," Glubzinski said.

Finally, the third impact came on the sales side. Dealers and consumers may not want more cloth seat vehicles. And the lack of heated seats might put GM at a competitive disadvantage in the marketplace relative to other car makers who could offer heated seats. "We want to provide the dealers the product that's going to turn. They know what they want. They know what they can sell. We want to supply it to the best ability that we can," Glubzinski said. "All of our efforts were to keep building every product every day to the plan, trying to minimize changes to the mix," Hurles added.

Hurles continued, "I still remember the night I called John Calabrese [vice president, Global Vehicle Engineering] and Ron Mills and just said, 'guys, I need your help. I'm seeing people starting to make decisions to shift mix. I can't have them do that. We don't need to do that. It's a good intention, but if they start removing part A, I'm going to have a problem with part B. So I need you to make it very clear, they're not to make a change without our authorization.'"

This battle to limit unintended consequences from well-intentioned interventions led to a mantra: "Stay in your swim lane." Although the crisis team wanted creative solutions from everyone, they didn't want everyone implementing independent decisions that affected other parts of the organization and created more problems elsewhere. GM had to balance between people having the flexibility to solve the problem any way they could and the discipline not to disrupt the functioning of the rest of the company.

Strong Support from Top Management

From the beginning, the team had strong support from GM's executives. And, possibly, the biggest contribution of senior management was not to get involved in the details. Steve Girsky, vice chairman of General Motors told the war room team, "You are the brain trust. Just tell me what you need; otherwise I'm staying out of the way." And the executives meant it. One team member was very pleasantly surprised to notice that the "execs were going to Jimmy Johns [a local sandwich shop] to pick up food so that we [the crisis team] could keep working."[16]

That support from top management grew stronger during the crisis as the team steadily found solutions to almost every element of the disruption. "Here was this life-threatening crisis that the team showed they could manage, and it gave the leadership confidence. The leadership didn't need to tour the crisis room again in later crises," Hurles said.

Finding Cross-Functional Firefighter/Engineer/Supply-base Experts

GM found that this crisis, like others, helped build bench strength by revealing people who had the required combination of the right psychological profile and the right skills. In the wake the 2011 Japan earthquake, GM's Mills said, "I know who to call in the organization, who works well in crisis, who has the right skill set, who has the stamina to survive in the environment, and who also has know-how to work within their function and across the functions." And he added, "You can't just have an engineer who knows a steering system. You've got to have an engineer who knows the steering system and knows the supply base and knows the competitive alternatives to your solutions. You've got to have some breadth and depth. I know who those guys are in the organization, which helps."

OTHER COMPANIES' RESPONSE TACTICS

Many companies used similar strategies and had similar experiences during the Japan quake and during other disruptions. Delphi noted that it faced a five-day information blackout during the Japanese quake and tsunami that made assessing the situation difficult. Intel also had to contend with the time required for engineering validation of alternatives involving complex products with intricate interactions. Yet other companies used somewhat different response tactics to handle the multiple tasks demanded in a disaster response.

Risk Identification: Triage under Uncertainty

In October 2011, a massive wave of flooding reached Bangkok, Thailand, inundating the country's industrial parks. Over 1,000 factories were flooded, including many suppliers to the computer and electronics industries (see chapter 7). Among the affected companies was Flextronics, the large global contract manufacturer headquartered in Singapore. Flextronics knew that it bought some 2,000 different electronic components from dozens of suppliers that might be in the affected area. But with little information coming from the flooded area, Flextronics couldn't know exactly which parts were actually affected or how best to respond.

To focus its efforts in the midst of unresolvable high uncertainty, Flextronics defined four mutually exclusive, collectively exhaustive categories of parts. The "green" category included well-stocked parts with more than three months of inventory. These were parts that were not likely to cause production and customer shortages problems because they were not likely to run out. This large supply of inventory likely exceeded the time-to-recovery, or, in GM's vernacular, these parts had no white-space. The "yellow" category comprised dual-sourced parts, which were less likely to be disrupted because Flextronics had access to supplies from its (already qualified) second supplier. Contacting the second source would presumably ensure a fast recovery.

The last two categories covered single-sourced and low-inventory parts—ones that had a high likelihood of causing supply disruptions. These parts were prioritized by revenue impact. The "orange" category parts were those feeding into lower-revenue business activities. And the "red" category parts were the high-revenue-impact parts.

Overall, this categorization let Flextronics winnow down the daunting list of 2,000 potentially disrupted parts to a short list of about 100 high-priority parts. The team then identified recovery strategies, such as placing risk buys, qualifying alternate sources, or adjusting build schedules and allocating available inventory to the higher priority products. Using this information, the team was in a position to have targeted conversations with suppliers and customers about the 100 parts that were on the "high risk" list. Categorization by sourcing, inventory, and revenue impact was critical to ensure that the parts with the highest risk were addressed first.

IMPACT: WHITE-SPACE = VALUE-AT-RISK

GM's approach to assessing the white-space provides a general framework for companies to roughly estimate the impact of future disruptions. The white-space duration of a potential disruption in days or weeks can be converted into a financial number—the value-at-risk (VaR)—by multiplying the white-space duration of disrupted production (or sales) in days times the daily impact (e.g., revenues or profits) of a day's worth of production (or sales). Although the actual VaR may vary as a result of the many nuances of disruptions and the company's response, this VaR estimate can provide a starting point for quantifying impact. Estimating VaR requires the terms described in the four sections below.

The VaR calculated below is an effects-focused view on risk in that it is an estimate of the financial effects of a disruption—regardless of the cause—on the company. It is a conditional estimate of loss, rather than an expected value of loss: if disruption occurs, then VaR may be the impact. Calculating the VaR for multiple types of disruptions helps companies to prioritize proactive risk mitigation efforts or reactive recovery efforts during crisis response.

White-Space Left Edge = Time-to-Impact

The first factor for estimating value-at-risk is defined by the left edge of the white-space, which is the lag between the disruptive event at its point of occurrence (e.g., the earthquake) and the disruption of production, sales, or deliveries[17] for the company. Inventories—often measured as days of supply (DOS)—between the source of the disrupted part and the customer enable the company to maintain operations for some period of time after the disruptive event occurs. This number represents the inventory anywhere in the supply chain where inventories might lurk, such as suppliers' warehouses, safety stocks of inbound parts, work-in-process, and finished goods. These inventories delay the time when a product's disrupted part becomes unavailable and consequently that product cannot be made and shipped to customers. Each added day of inventory means one fewer day of lost production, sales (and profits). The duration of normal operations that these inventories offer before customers are affected is the time-to-impact (*TTI*).

White-Space Right Edge = Time-to-Recovery

The second factor is the anticipated time-to-recovery (*TTR*), which is the lag between when the disruptive event occurs and when the company can restart normal production. *TTR* is the point marked by the right-hand edge of the white-space in GM's chart. As mentioned in the "Task 4: Reduce Time-to-Recovery" section, the *TTR* is the earliest of several durations. These include the duration of the recovery efforts to restart production and resume deliveries at the disrupted supplier; the duration of procurement and engineering processes to find, qualify, buy, and use parts from a second source; and the duration of product and manufacturing reengineering processes to use other types of available parts or capacities. *TTR* also includes any transportation lead-time, which may be expedited.

The concept of *TTR* raises an issue: what counts as recovery? Often, production from a restored supplier or new second source will take time to ramp from zero volume to full production. For example, automotive chip maker Renesas announced a series of expected recovery levels with different recovery times as it rebuilt after the 2011 quake: a 10 percent capacity resumption at 12 weeks, 35 percent at 16 weeks, 55 percent at 20 weeks, 75 percent at 24 weeks, and 100 percent at 28 weeks.[18] Later, the company announced an accelerated recovery schedule that reduced the 100 percent recovery point from 28 weeks to 24 weeks.[19] Using new or existing second-source suppliers has similar issues with the lead-time for ramping to volume production or bringing more capacity online to deliver replacement supplies for the disrupted part.

Different companies might use different *TTR* thresholds to manage risks. For example, Cisco uses the 100 percent *TTR* definition, which is conservative and may over-estimate the impact because it's highly likely that a disrupted supplier would resume partial production before it recovers 100 percent. In contrast, Medtronic assesses the 50 percent, 90 percent, and 100 percent *TTR* points to model the ramp of the recovery. Moreover, to the extent that the affected company can prioritize the use of partial supplies, it can further reduce the impact by allocating the limited supplies to its most profitable or important product lines and customers—a 50 percent recovery in supplies is then likely to produce more than a 50 percent recovery in sales or profits (see the section titled "Mitigating the VaR").

The gap between the estimated time-to-impact (when inventories run out) and the estimated time-to-recovery (when production can resume) is the estimated customer impact time (*CIT*). In other words, $CIT = TTR - TTI$. For GM, this was the white-space or production down time, when GM would not be able to fulfill dealers' orders. For other companies, CIT is the time during which they will not be able to fulfill customers' orders.

The Daily Financial Impact

The third factor for estimating the value-at-risk for a given disrupted part or facility is the financial impact of the disrupted element to the company. To estimate the daily financial impact, one uses Bill of Materials (BOM) data to identify all the products that use the disrupted part and then uses Enterprise Resource Planning (ERP) order data to estimate the daily financial impact on different channels, products or customers.

The financial contribution per day of each disrupted product can be calculated from the financial contribution per unit of the product sold and the number of units sold per day. The daily financial contribution is then the sum of the financial contributions per day of all the products that use the disrupted part (accounting also for the number of such parts used in each product). It can be based on revenue (e.g., sales/day), gross profit, net profit, or some other measure of the financial outcome per day. Naturally, the contribution per unit of product may be different across customers as well.

As mentioned above with respect to the VaR, the financial impact is just a rough initial estimate that assumes demand does not change, that the disruption has no other side effects on customer relations, and that the company serves customers fairly.[20] A company's response actions (see the section titled "Mitigating the

VaR"), customer demand patterns, customer importance, parts' interactions, competitors' capacities and behaviors, and many other factors mean that during a disruption the actual impact may be different.

Partial Supply

In many disruptions, parts production does not cease entirely. Second sources, undamaged capacity at the disrupted supplier, and alternative parts can be used to provide partial parts supply for the duration of the *TTR* and allow some partial rate of production during the *CIT*. In some cases, predisruption inventory plus partial supply may suffice to satisfy demand during the entire time-to-recovery.[21] However, once existing inventories run out (assuming that both finished product inventories and part inventories will be used to satisfy the full demand as long as possible), then the partial supply of parts implies that the company can only satisfy a portion of the demand until the *TTR* is reached.[22]

The impact of the lost sales during the *CIT* depends on the unsatisfied sales volume, which in turn depends on the level of missing parts (calculated as one minus the partial supply). Thus, if the partial supply can cover 25 percent of the normal volume, the fraction of missing parts would be 75 percent and, as a rough approximation, the company would be losing 75 percent of its usual revenue or profits during the *CIT*. To a first approximation, the VaR of a disrupted part or ingredient under conditions of partial supply is the total daily impact multiplied by the CIT and by the fraction of missing parts.

MITIGATING THE VAR

A simplistic estimate of the value-at-risk can overestimate the potential impact of a disruption because companies have many tactics for minimizing the financial impact of a disruption, such as: preferential allocation, auctions, dilution, and substitution. Each tactic can mitigate the VaR by increasing the amount of demand satisfied using the available disrupted supplies or by increasing the financial returns from those disrupted supplies.

Algorithms of Allocation

Both GM during the 2011 Japan earthquake and Flextronics during the 2011 Thai floods allocated scarce parts to those products or customer segments with the highest financial performance. GM used a confidential profit margin metric for its allocations during Project J as well as finished product inventory levels in the field. Flextronics based its allocation decisions on value-at-risk calculations but adjusted the decisions because the different product lines represented different contract manufacturing clients. Issues such as profitability, the overall value of the client to Flextronics, and the impact on the client were taken into account.

Customer size matters. During the Thai floods and the disruption of the hard disk industry, large PC makers such as HP, Dell, and Apple were "highest on the priority list to get the products," said Bob O'Donnell, program vice president at IDC, the market intelligence company.[23] The top makers were followed by PC original design manufacturers (ODMs), while channel retailers were last.[24] Yet it is not always just the large customers who get parts in short supply. Verifone's senior vice president of global supply chain, Patrick McGivern, commented that tiny customers might get good allocations because their volumes are very small and suppliers may be sympathetic to the plight of the smallest customers who may have fewer options and may face an existential threat from a significant disruption.

Of course, suppliers are likely to use allocation, too. Flextronics's head of procurement and chief supply chain officer, Tom Linton, said that during the first two days after the 2011 Japan quake, everyone was frantic to find out what happened; then it was a mad rush to lock in suppliers. Some suppliers allocated "fairly" (that is, they did not commit their limited supplies to those who called them first or to the best customers only) and others didn't. When floods in Thailand devastated some hard disk drive makers, Stephen J. Luczo, CEO of Seagate, said, "It's going to be very interesting to see who gets drives and who doesn't."[25] Financial and marketing considerations, as well as company culture and regulations, can affect how companies decide which customers to serve and how.

The Effect of Preferential Allocation on VaR

Preferentially allocating scarce supplies can mitigate the financial impact of a disruption by making only those products that get the highest financial return from the fewest number of parts. That allocation depends on both the financial return on each unit of product and the number (or amount) of the scarce part used to make that product. For example, a product with a financial contribution of $1 that requires only one part of the disrupted type to build, should be preferred to a product with a higher financial contribution—say $2, but which requires five units of parts to build. Thus, for the simple case of a single disrupted part, products could be ranked by their financial contribution *per part* and orders for higher-ranked products could be fulfilled ahead of orders of lower-ranked products.

The feasibility of preferential allocation depends on three primary prerequisites. The first is the availability of some parts via inventories or partial supply to support some rate of production and sales. The second is that the products' financial contribution per unit of the scarce part must vary across products or customers. If all products and customers have the same financial returns per unit of scarce part, then preferential allocation offers no benefits. The third prerequisite is that the company must have the regulatory freedom, contractual flexibility, and cultural willingness to sacrifice low-performing products (and customers).

If the company can use preferential allocation, then the allocation-mitigated VaR can, in theory, be estimated via a formal optimization process that allocates units of each partially available part to the various products so as to minimize the VaR. The result is a *mitigated VaR*, which is smaller than the VaR under *fair allocation*, in which each product or customer is given the same partial fraction of demand.[26]

The optimization needed to calculate the mitigated VaR can grow quite complex if the disruption affects multiple parts and multiple products. During an actual supply disruption, such an optimization is not practical because of the time constraints, changing dynamics, and ongoing uncertainty. As demonstrated by GM's Project J and Flextronics's actions during the Thailand floods, companies rely in such cases on their knowledge of engineering, supply chain, and customers, using heuristics and inventiveness to mitigate the VaR.

Even in a planning mode, when the objective is to prioritize risky parts (and suppliers), formal optimization for risk prioritization may not be useful given the large number of parts and products at even medium-sized manufacturers. More important, formal optimization may not be useful given the uncertainties and unpredictable dynamics in the levels of demand, pricing, inventory, time-to-recovery, and partial supply levels. For purposes of risk prioritization, the mitigated VaR can be estimated numerically by simulating a wide range of scenarios and modeling the mitigated VaR as a function of key parameters.

The most important parameter is the variability of the financial contribution per unit part across all the products using the disrupted part. A set of one-time simulations (with an embedded optimization to calculate the mitigated VaR for each realization) can give a company the data to estimate an approximate mitigated VaR resulting from a disrupted part or a combination of parts. The mitigated VaR estimate for various potential disruptions can then be expressed as a function of the variability of financial contributions, as well as the number of disrupted parts per each product, expected sales volumes, inventory levels, partial supplies, and *CIT*.[27]

Preferential allocation will have no effect if all the products using a disrupted part have the same financial contribution, but will have a large effect if the variation is high. The greater the differences in financial outcomes between high-value and low-value products, the more the company can mitigate VaR by preferentially making only high-value products or serving only high-value customers. The impact of preferential allocation will be especially high (per available part) in the case of low partial supplies because if the company has only a scant supply and allocates it to the highest of the high-value products, then that will have a higher mitigation effect than if the company has greater partial supply and is producing more of the average-valued products.

Highest Bidder

In the wake of the Thai floods and the decimation of Western Digital's disk drive production capacity, Seagate temporarily took the #1 disk drive maker's crown from its disrupted rival. Seagate also took a rather unusual approach to allocation—auctioning some disk drives to the highest bidder.[28] "In addition to making drives available for those qualified customers not covered by an LTA (long-term agreement) or where LTA volumes are not sufficient to cover their needs, this will allow us to fully understand and gauge marginal pricing," said William David Mosley, Seagate's chief operating officer.[29] Seagate's move also prompted more customers to sign LTAs to avoid potential price spikes that might result from an auction.[30]

But the auction approach may have affected customer relations. "Seagate, where they are playing the auction approach—whoever is going to pay the most money is going to get the product—has left a real bad taste in many OEM's mouths," explained a source within the industry.[31] "OEMs are doing business with (Seagate) because they have to right now. Once everything is back to normal, I feel that they are going to lose a lot of market share for that."[32] Tellingly, when Western Digital recovered its capacity, it also retook the lead.[33]

Auctioning a scarce commodity after a disruption might seem extortionate, but a well-designed auction actually improves economic efficiency by allocating the resource to those who can create the greatest value with that resource. Moreover, a high post-disruption price encourages those companies who have ways of foregoing the scarce commodity to deploy their flexibility or substitute options, thereby leaving more of the scarce commodity for those who have no such options. In fact, government auctions are justified in many cases on this characteristic of auction mechanisms. For example, in the opening letter of the information package for the US broadband personal communications service auctions, Reed Hundt, chairman of the US Federal Communications Commission wrote: "I am confident that the auction method we have chosen will put the spectrum in the hands of those who most highly value it and who have the best ideas for its use."[34]

The response of some of Seagate's corporate customers to the auction demonstrates that this approach should be used with care and probably never in consumer markets, where social networks and "equality activists" can hurt a company's reputation. Using an auction during a disruption—despite its theoretical appeal—reeks of profiteering.

Let's Be Fair

Other companies insist on fair allocations for commercial, cultural, or legal reasons. The most common fair allocation gives every customer the same fraction of their orders. Joe McBeth, vice president of global supply chain management at Jabil, noted that many Japanese companies employed strict fair allocation schemes after the 2011 earthquake. Intel said that as a large supplier in the PC industry, it generally uses a fair allocation approach to avoid the appearance of favoritism.

Yet being fair isn't easy, especially if customers try to game the system by asking for large orders knowing that they may get only a fraction of what they ordered. Customers could also over-order in an attempt to hoard supplies if they anticipate future shortages. Naturally, over-ordering makes it difficult for a company to serve all its customers. To avoid these difficulties, many suppliers used an allocation formula based on historical sales level.

Continental Teves Inc., a supplier of automotive, industrial, and agricultural products, had to make tough decisions when 9/11 shut down all US airfreight traffic and disrupted cross-border freight flows between the United States and both Canada and Mexico. On the afternoon of 9/11, the company assembled a list of all outstanding orders from customers and to suppliers. Most important, it collected data on its North American customers' inventory levels. Knowing these customers' production rates from past order patterns, Continental Teves calculated the number of days of parts supplies each customer had before its operations would run out of parts. This statistic—days of supply—was the one on which Continental Teves based its fair allocation, trying to ensure that all its customers had the same days of supply.

Dilution Is a Solution

Another approach is dilution—using less of a key raw material when formulating a product in order to extend partial supplies. Dilution reduces VaR by extending both the DOS of existing inventory as well as partial supplies. Chapter 1 described how Intel successfully used this strategy for stretching disrupted supplies of some specialized chemicals after the Japan earthquake. But whereas a properly reengineered and qualified manufacturing process might tolerate dilution, customers might not be as accepting.

In February 2013, premium bourbon distiller Maker's Mark faced a shortage of bourbon. "Fact is, demand for our bourbon is exceeding our ability to make it, which means we're running very low on supply," wrote Rob Samuels, the company COO and grandson of the founder.[35] Choosing not to raise prices, the distiller found a way to add a "touch more water" without affecting the taste—diluting the alcohol content of its product from its historic level of 45 percent, or 90 proof, to 42 percent, or 84 proof. "This will enable us to maintain the same taste profile and increase our limited supply so there is enough Maker's Mark to go around, while we continue to expand the distillery and increase our production capacity," wrote Rob Samuels in a letter to customers.[36] The action, however, did not sit well with customers, as described in chapter 4.

Substitution

Another mitigating factor is substitution by customers of an alternate product sold by the same firm. When General Mills estimates the impact of ingredient shortages, it knows that a shortage of one type of General Mills breakfast cereal does not imply that the consumer stops buying cereal for breakfast. Instead, consumers may buy a different flavor, which is often another General Mills product. To the extent that consumers substitute a different flavor of General Mills cereal, General Mills does not lose any sales, which reduces the potential impact. The potential amount of mitigation provided by substitution depends on the percentage of customers who will substitute another product offered by the affected firm, the efforts of the company to promote substitute products, the difference in the financial contribution of the original versus the substituted product (after accounting for special promotional costs), and the availability of spare capacity to satisfy the incremental demand for the substitute product. Substitution reduces VaR. The availability of substitutes and an estimate of the extent of substitutability should be taken into account when calculating the impact of other mitigation methods such as auctions, dilution, and preferential allocation.

4

CRISIS RESPONSE

When disaster strikes, companies' first order of business is to help first responders. These responders could be firefighters and medical personnel, or they could be plant employees responsible for performing emergency procedures to prevent further damage, such as the release of harmful material into the environment or the loss of property. Simultaneously, or shortly thereafter, companies start the effort to minimize the business impact of the disruption and to recover as quickly as possible. Doing so requires nonroutine activities: putting special teams to work, creating *ad hoc* supply chains, communicating the unusual situation to stakeholders, and collaborating with others (even competitors). In terms of the "quadrant of events" discussed in chapter 2, these response activities are all aimed at reducing the impact of an event. (At this point, the probability of the event is 1; it already happened.)

WAKE UP AND SMELL THE HURRICANE

Every year, an average of six hurricanes form in the Atlantic Ocean, although 2005 saw a record 15 hurricanes.[1] Almost half of these, on average, are classified as major storms (category 3 or higher), which are deadly and can create substantial damage. Even though each storm follows its own track, long-term statistics, short-term forecasting, and substantial experience allow companies to know how to respond to these events, even if the details may vary from storm to storm.

A Storm Is Brewing

Hurricane Katrina began as a tropical depression near the Bahamas. As the storm strengthened, The Procter & Gamble Company (P&G) started tracking the potential threat. With several facilities in the coastal southern United States, and millions of customers in the region, P&G watched carefully. When Katrina turned north toward Louisiana, the storm became a serious threat to P&G. Half of P&G's coffee production and 20 percent of all coffee drunk in American homes was roasted, ground, and canned in Folgers's plant in Gentilly, Louisiana, just east of New Orleans. P&G also operates several other facilities in the same geographic area: the smaller Millstone coffee plant adjacent to Gentilly, a coffee storage operation, and the Lacombe coffee distribution center.

On August 25, 2005, four days before Katrina's landfall, P&G activated its emergency preparations, even though at that point the storm was not predicted to hit New Orleans. This activation included moving product out of the region, getting backup data tapes, and preparing for a possible shutdown. Inventory from New Orleans was shipped out to Cincinnati. On August 27, two days before landfall, the hurricane turned north and veered toward New Orleans. In response, P&G shut down its New Orleans sites at 10 pm on Saturday night (August 27) and told employees to evacuate the city.[2]

On August 29, at 5:10 am, Hurricane Katrina made landfall in Louisiana. At 8:14 am, the US National Weather Service issued a flash flood warning for several parishes in New Orleans, citing a levee breech in the Industrial Canal. By the afternoon, three more levees ruptured. Within hours, the city of New Orleans flooded as the levee system failed catastrophically. Rising water surged 6–12 miles inland from the waterfront,[3] flooding many low-lying districts, including Gentilly.[4] The death toll reached 1,836, and property damage was estimated at $81 billion.[5]

Response Team on the Move[6]

Even as Katrina lashed the coast, P&G convened its crisis management team at the company's Cincinnati headquarters. As the team members met at headquarters, while Katrina blasted Louisiana, they had two priorities: to support P&G's employees, and to save the business. P&G needed to restore its supply chain before October because the months of October to December are peak times for consumer coffee buying.

When the storm moved out of the area, P&G's team moved in. They set up a command center in Baton Rouge, 80 miles from New Orleans, which was as close as they could get to the affected area. The crisis team oversaw recovery efforts, with team members working on a two-weeks-on, two-weeks-off cycle. Baton Rouge also became P&G's logistical staging area for construction materials, recovery supplies, and generators.

Access Denied: Assessment from the Air

P&G's first task was to assess the damage. But this was impossible, because all roads into the area were impassible and authorities were prohibiting entry to the disaster area. P&G didn't even know when the roads would open or when the company would be allowed access to its property. Rather than wait for a government-provided assessment of the damage, P&G hired a helicopter just after the storm to take hundreds of aerial photographs of its facilities, the surrounding area, and New Orleans's damaged roads, railroads, and port infrastructure.

The photos revealed a mixed picture. The first bit of good news was that P&G's plant was located on high ground and was protected by a long railroad embankment that saved it from the storm surge and flooding from the breeched levees. The plant itself had suffered only minor wind damage.

The bad news was the dire state of the infrastructure. All the surrounding roads were flooded and covered with debris from the high winds and flood waters; P&G's team would have no access by road to the plant for 12 days. Railways suffered damage to tracks as well as to rolling stock. Almost every rail line was out of service for months. One third of the port of New Orleans where P&G imported its coffee beans was destroyed. Beyond the damage to logistical infrastructure, P&G faced the absence of utilities: supplies of power and natural gas were out for two weeks, and phones were out for several weeks.

Helping Employees

One of the biggest uncertainties and biggest challenges faced by P&G was tracing the fates of its employees. After the storm, P&G tried to locate its employees and ensure their safety. The task was difficult given the complete failure of the phone system in New Orleans. P&G used local broadcast systems and its own phone networks, asking people to call into its toll-free consumer relations hotline in Cincinnati. Fortunately, no P&G employees lost their lives in the storm. Yet it took P&G three nerve-wracking weeks to learn that everyone was alive, because so many employees had evacuated out of the state.

In addition to resurrecting the Gentilly coffee plant, P&G helped employees solve three major issues that workers faced in their own lives. First, the company promised continuity of pay for its employees, regardless of the reopening date of the plant, so workers would know that their livelihoods were protected. In addition, the company offered interest-free loans, with approval in less than 24 hours, to employees who needed emergency funds. Second, it soon became clear that the storm had traumatized on-the-ground leaders as well as employees, so P&G brought in leaders from unaffected areas to help, and provided counseling to employees. Third, most employees lost their homes in the flood. In fact, most houses in the New Orleans area were unsuitable for habitation because of the flooding. As a result, there was a lack of housing and hotel accommodations. The company needed shelter for its employees and for the construction workers at the plant who were repairing the facility. The company looked at three options: chartering an anchored cruise ship, partnering with a hotel, or building a trailer village.

P&G's solution was to build a trailer village, which offered the most flexibility for expansion during construction phases and post-construction when housing would be needed for employees only. Named Gentilly Village, it had 125 trailers that slept more than 500 people—employees and their families as well as contractors. The village included laundry and recreation facilities. To accommodate workers whose families had evacuated to other states, P&G provided money for them to visit their families twice a month and created a seven-days-on, seven-days-off work schedule that let plant employees have time to rebuild their lives after the disaster. To deal with the lack of access to groceries or restaurants, the company brought in its own kitchen and cafeteria, serving three meals a day and providing snacks around the clock—all free to employees and contractors working at the site.

Recovery Challenges

One of the immediate challenges was getting potable water to the plant. Initially, the company arranged for 20 trucks to run in a continuous supply loop bringing water in from Baton Rouge. Then, because the plant uses 18,000 gallons of potable water per hour when operating at full capacity, P&G decided to dig a well—drilling 700 feet deep—to get the needed water. The decision to drill the well proved prescient because city water was not restored to the plant until mid-December. P&G kept using the well even after the municipal water system was restored because it was a less-costly source of fresh water.

During the crisis, the recovery coordination plan was organized around three daily meetings (at 9:00 am, noon and 6:00 pm) to review various facets of the recovery. The morning meeting covered business continuity issues, the midday meeting handled resource issues, and the end-of-day meeting tackled engineering work to ensure that all tasks were proceeding as planned.

Finding Alternate Production Capacity

Part of P&G's response effort was focused on finding alternate sources of supply to make up for lost production during the time-to-recovery of the Gentilly plant. The challenges were to gain access to additional coffee production capacity, and to do it quickly. P&G wanted to avoid the literal white-space of empty store shelves and the potential that competitors could block P&G's replacement of lost capacity by filling retailers' shelves with their own brands, securing retail shelf space for the long term.

In its effort to secure emergency second sources, P&G temporarily changed its procedures for negotiating large supply deals and let procurement teams make decisions on the spot using existing competitive analysis to ensure that P&G was getting acceptable contract terms. The two guidelines for the new contracts were that the supply be a quality product and that P&G could still make a profit. P&G used a "should-cost" methodology to estimate a reasonable cost for a second-source supply. Having a precalculated cost estimate accelerated negotiations with suppliers and avoided bureaucratic delays, while not damaging profit margins with excessive payments for that needed capacity. If those guidelines were met, employees were empowered to commit to the contract to ensure that P&G product got to retailers' shelves. The company was successful in locking up needed capacity in all but one case and was able to lock out competitors from taking P&G's retail space.

The Government Grind

In addition to the damage caused by the storm, local regulators caused further slowdowns. The area was put under martial law with dusk-to-dawn curfews, hampering P&G's efforts to travel to the facility and to move needed supplies. Fortunately, P&G was able to sort through the bureaucratic issues because many of its local managers had prior established relationships with local government officials. This helped speed the process of working with the four different agencies involved in infrastructure issues. As a result of these relationships, P&G was even able to get a police escort through the road checkpoints that would otherwise have added hours of delay trying to confirm the legitimacy of their permits.

Production Perks Up

P&G's New Orleans plant started production on September 17, three weeks after the hurricane. Each operation at the plant that was brought back online went through quality assurance, and each operation was audited by the FDA in two days. By October, the plant was operating at full capacity. The recovery teams and top management celebrated each successful step along the way. This recognition contributed to keeping the teams motivated to continue working seven days a week for six weeks.

In all, P&G was the first company back in operation after the hurricane. The governor of the state called the company a role model, and President George W. Bush visited the facility on September 20.[7] From a business standpoint, P&G in 2005 shipped 96 percent of the previous year's volume despite the disruption, and its first-quarter 2006 brought record volumes, with business back stronger than ever.

CREATING AD HOC SUPPLY CHAINS

As was the case with P&G during hurricane Katrina, disruptions force companies to create ad hoc supply chains—temporary flows of products, recovery materials, and personnel that are unlike the company's workaday supply chain. These ad hoc supply chains might reroute product around damaged nodes of the supply network, use different modes of transportation instead of disrupted ones, use emergency procurement procedures, or connect secondary suppliers into the network.

A Phoenix Arises from the Ashes

Just seven weeks before Christmas, on Tuesday, November 1, 2005, UK-based clothing retailer Primark Stores Limited suffered a devastating warehouse fire. Some £50 million in apparel—half of its stock—went up in flames as TNT Fashion Group's 440,000 square feet warehouse at Magna Park near Lutterwirth and adjacent offices burned.[8] Fire is often a significant disruption, and it's not a rare or beyond-the-pale hazard, which places it in the high-impact/high-likelihood category of risks (see figure 2.1). "This is as bad as it gets, but the disaster recovery plan is designed to cope with this. The loss of a key distribution center is a top-10 risk on our list," said a Primark spokesperson.[9]

"Our first priority was to get the warehouse management system back up. The second priority was to provide the necessary equipment for the new warehouse location," said Jim Flood, IT director at TNT Fashion Group, which ran the warehouse for Primark.[10] "We had the alternative site operational by [Wednesday at] 8:30 am on the same business park," the Primark spokesperson said.[11] TNT Fashion Group invoked its recovery contracts with its IT suppliers to deliver equipment to the new location. By

Wednesday afternoon, TNT was uploading Primark's data onto the datacenter-based warehouse management system from daily backup tapes. By Thursday, TNT had installed the hardware to run the warehouse management system locally.[12]

The company took three steps that weren't part of its usual supply chain strategy. First, the company rushed extra orders to suppliers to replace the lost inventory.[13] Second, the company chartered a giant Russian six-engine Antonov-225 aircraft to bring in replacement stock by air from Shanghai, Hong Kong, and Dhaka.[14] Third, the company rerouted shipments directly to stores to reduce distribution delays.[15] Accelerating the supply chain helped ensure that Primark had good 2005 holiday-season sales.

Can You Fuel Me Now?

When Hurricane Sandy roared through New York City, the storm surge pushed the Atlantic Ocean into lower Manhattan and flooded underground utility tunnels with corrosive seawater. Water six feet deep surrounded Verizon's main switching office in lower Manhattan and flooded the ground floor and four subbasements full of equipment. It took Verizon a week to pump out almost one billion gallons of water. In the areas surrounding the city, high winds downed trees, power lines, and telecommunications towers.

Verizon faced a significant challenge repairing flooded equipment boxes, repairing downed lines, and repairing damaged cell towers. The company brought in hundreds of trucks, hundreds of linemen, and tons of repair and replacement equipment that it had prestaged in the area. But that wasn't all Verizon needed to supply its repair efforts. The disruption to New York City also curtailed fuel supplies through a confluence of three storm-related disruptions: filling stations had no power, the local gasoline refineries were down, and the port was closed. Verizon needed 50,000 gallons per day to run trucks and emergency backup generators around the area.

So in addition to bringing in all the needed telecommunications supplies for repairs, Verizon had to create a fuel supply chain. The company built 18 temporary fueling depots in the region using 1,000-gallon gasoline tanks and 500-gallon diesel tanks with pumps and safety features (such as spilled fuel retention berms and firefighting equipment). The company obtained special approvals from local officials to store and handle large amounts of fuel. Then it transported fuel up from Louisiana and Texas, with drivers carrying wads of cash to pay the $200 tolls on the bridges into New York City. Finally, Verizon managed the distribution of fuel to trucks and to 220 thirsty backup generators.

As with P&G during Katrina, Verizon also had to provide transportation, housing, food, water, and essentials to a recovery workforce of 900 technicians, engineers, and managers in the New York/New Jersey area. To house many of them, Verizon found a 250-room hotel that was without power. The company brought in a big generator and spliced it into the hotel's electrical system to make that hotel a home away from home for its troops.

The Logistics of Recovery

Even before waters of the 2011 Thai flood retreated, companies moved in to extract equipment, raw materials, inventory, and office records to begin recovery efforts by shifting production to other sites. For example, Japan's Nidec Corp., a leading manufacturer of small motors, cut a hole in the roof of its Rajana factory, sent divers in to disconnect the equipment, and hoisted to equipment out onto boats.[16] At other factories, teams of dozens of workers waded through knee-deep noisome water and hand-carried materials to small skiffs that could navigate in the shallow flood waters.

Workers operating in the flood zone never knew what they would encounter: sand, mud, sewage, spilled fuel, industrial waste, and the occasional crocodile. When workers at Hana Microelectronics encountered a cobra lurking in a dark, damp, flooded factory, they quickly evacuated and then fumigated the building. "The concern now is employees' health because this water is pretty dirty. A lot of what we were bringing in was bathing water, as well as drinking water and food, because when they get out of the water, the first thing everybody wants to do is wash," said Bruce Stromstad, general manager of Hana Microelectronics.[17]

After retrieving the equipment and materials, companies needed to clean things carefully, calibrate machinery, and requalify the systems. "Equipment that passes our initial assessment of its working condition is shipped to our Pinehurst campus," said Fabrinet, a precision optical, electromechanical, and electronic manufacturing services supplier in Thailand, in its update messages, "where further tests validate whether the equipment is functioning and in good working order. Equipment passing these stages is calibrated and stored in a controlled environment. The remaining equipment continues to be cleaned and debugged, an exercise that can be laborious and time consuming."[18]

CRISIS COMMUNICATIONS: FROM CONFUSION TO CONFIDENCE

Supply chains comprise three flows—the flow of goods, the flow of money, and the flow of information. Disruptions certainly hit the flow of goods, but they also impede the flow of information. In fact, the disconcerting unknowns inherent in disruptions stem entirely from the disruption of information flows about the extent of damages, mitigation efforts, and anticipated time-to-recovery. Customers in disrupted supply chains are looking for as much information as possible so they can plan and execute a proper response. But disrupted suppliers often don't know the extent of the damage or know how quickly they can recover.

From Blackouts to Transparency

Serious disasters often create a literal communications blackout resulting from physical damage to power and telecommunications infrastructure. After the Japan quake, some suppliers were entirely unreachable for as long as five days. Similarly, hurricane Sandy took out power to more than 7.9 million people[19] and damaged one quarter of the cell towers in the storm-affected areas of 10 states.[20] The storm also damaged critical back-haul links that connect cell towers to the rest of the world.

During the unrest in Egypt in 2011, the government shut down telecommunications systems to prevent antigovernment forces from coordinating their riots or attacks.[21] Anticipating that these kinds of situations can happen, Intel equips each of its facilities with a satellite phone. Unfortunately, according to Jim Holko, Intel's program manager of corporate emergency management,

Intel's Egyptian sales office managers could not get to the phone during the 2011 unrest because the phone was in an office near Tahrir Square, the epicenter of heavy clashes between police and demonstrators.[22]

Even if the infrastructure is not damaged physically, disasters create disrupted communications caused by congestion at two levels of the system. First, the high volume of attempted communications clogs the telecommunications infrastructure. This creates busy signals, dropped calls, and a degraded ability to reach people in the affected area. Here, technology can help with communications channels such as SMS (short message service, aka "texting") and email, both of which use much less of the scarce bandwidth than voice communications. A single SMS text message uses less network capacity than a fraction of a second of voice. In disasters like the 2011 Japan quake or hurricane Sandy, the voice telecommunications network typically collapses when many people try to reach loved ones, but text messages can still go through. A similar reduction in network availability took place in Madrid in 2004 after the March 11 terrorist bombing in the Atocha train station and following the July 7, 2005, London bombing.

Second, the volume of demands for information overwhelms the people and companies in the affected area with every customer calling, calling, calling to get updates. For example, during the aftermath of the 2012 Evonik Industries's fire (see the section titled "Massively Horizontal Collaboration" below for more on the event), Delphi faced the challenge of communicating very complex information sets concerning the effects of the PA-12 resin shortage. The company needed to communicate to its customers the status of each part or assembly from each supplier and to each customer that might be affected by the shortage of PA-12. Delphi used spreadsheets, distributed via SharePoint, for two-way communications internally and with customers and suppliers. The only problem was that others had the same idea, and Delphi was frustrated by each OEM customer using his or her own clever format for crisis-related data. "We spent more time trying to provide them data in their format than in chasing parts," said Rick Birch, global director, Operational Excellence at Delphi.[23] Delphi hoped that the

AIAG (Automotive industry Action Group)-moderated collaborative response to the Evonik crisis would help coordinate a shared approach and common formats.

During interviews for this book, Intel, GM, Delphi, Flextronics and others all mentioned the problem of disruption-affected suppliers being inundated by customer calls and demands. Some companies try to reduce this. For example, contract manufacturer Jabil centralized supplier contacts in the aftermath of the Japan earthquake so that its 59 sites weren't all calling the same suppliers and creating chaos. "We centralized that through our global commodity management team and put a point person for each supplier," said Joe McBeth, vice president of global supply chain at Jabil.[24]

Cacophony and Distrust

At 1:19 am on March 8, 2014, Malaysia Airlines flight 370 (MH370) stopped communicating with air traffic controllers while flying over the Gulf of Thailand. Eventually, the plane's disappearance triggered a massive search for the jet airliner and its 239 passengers and crew members. But the search did not go smoothly. Some of the problems with the search were unavoidable because of issues such as mistaken witnesses who thought they saw a plane crash,[25] satellite images that found garbage instead of wreckage,[26] an oil slick that turned out to be bunker fuel from a ship,[27] and the overall mystery of how a large aircraft could disappear and yet fly on for seven hours after its last seemingly routine communication. The deeper problems stemmed from how the disaster was managed and communicated to the world. "At best, Malaysian officials have thus far been poor communicators; at worst, they are incompetent," said Peter Goelz, former managing director of the United States government's National Transportation Safety Board.[28]

Delays in releasing information began with Malaysia Airlines, who did not announce that the plane was missing until six hours after contact was lost and one hour after the slated landing time.[29] Then came the revelation that Malaysian military radar had detected an unidentified aircraft at the time of the disappearance of flight 370 but did not alert anyone. When reporters asked for more information about where the aircraft was spotted, Malaysian authorities said that the answers were "too sensitive." Chinese authorities—representing 154 Chinese passengers—repeatedly urged Malaysia "to report what they have … in an accurate and timely fashion."[30]

With so little known about the fate of the flight, each meager bit of information was scrutinized by the families, the media, and governments. On March 15, for example, Malaysia's prime minister reported that the last words from the cockpit were "All right, good night."[31] Pundits and passengers' families tried to divine the mental state of the cockpit and assess the potential for terrorism, hijacking, or suicide that might be hidden in those terse words. But then the transcript for the air traffic control released two weeks later showed the final words as "Good night Malaysian three seven zero" with no explanation for the discrepancy with the earlier report.[32] Similar inconsistencies occurred in various reports by Malaysian authorities about the timing of events,[33] whether and where the plane had flown over Malaysia,[34] and whether the plane had communicated at all after someone in the cockpit deliberately turned off the transponder.[35] "There have been misinformation and corrections from Malaysian authorities on the whereabouts of MH370," said Goelz, who told CNN that it was the worst disaster management he had ever seen.[36]

A major cause of the problem was the lack of a coordinated approach to communications. At various times, statements came from the prime minister of Malaysia, the minister of transport, the inspector general of Malaysian police, the Malaysian Maritime Enforcement Agency, the Department of Civil Aviation, and the director-general of Civil Aviation, as well as various representatives of the airline. "It seems the Malaysians internally are not talking very well to each other," said Taylor Fravel of the security studies program at the Massachusetts Institute of Technology.[37] The delayed and inconsistent information provoked mistrust of Malaysian authorities and sparked theories that the Malaysian Air Force shot down the plane or that Malaysia was conspiring to cover up the true location of the plane and the fate of the missing people.[38] "We will never forgive for covering the truth from us and the criminal who delayed the rescue mission," said Jiang Hui, the families' designated representative.[39]

Of course, the Malaysian government does not have a monopoly on unhelpful communications in the face of a disaster. The US government public communications during the 2014 Ebola epidemic, Hurricane Katrina, or the obfuscating and contradictory statements following the Benghazi attack in Libya, are examples of similar shortcomings. For example, during the Ebola crisis, the US Centers for Disease Control and Prevention changed its recommendations several times.[40] To add to the chaotic communications, the White House made conflicting statements, and several states took matters into their own hands and issued their own quarantine and isolation rules, only to change them later, adding to the confusion and fear.[41] Similarly, the statements by various Japanese government and TEPCO officials following the 2011 Tohoku earthquake and tsunami shook confidence and contributed to public fears.

These examples of governments' failures to communicate clearly in crises provide a warning to corporations. Mixed messages coming from different parts of a disrupted organization can add to the confusion rather than calm the fears of customers and investors. One of the most important preparatory initiatives is a crisis communications protocol. GM's mantra of "stay in your swim lane" is just as important in terms of communications as it is in terms of operational decisions. The ubiquity of social media, round-the-clock news channels, and everybody being always "in touch" amplifies the impact of rumors and misinformation, accentuating the importance of unified crisis communications.

After AirAsia lost an aircraft flying from Indonesia to Singapore on December 28, 2014, the airline's CEO was lauded for his consistency, openness of communications, and willingness to take responsibility from the beginning. "I am the leader of this company; I take responsibility" said AirAsia founder and CEO, Tony Fernandes.[42]

On Valentine's Day, February 14, 2007, an ice storm hit the New York City region and JetBlue's hub in New York's JFK airport. A JetBlue spokesman said, "We had planes on the runways, planes arriving, and planes at all our gates. We ended up with gridlock."[43] Hundreds of passengers were stranded in planes on the tarmac because the planes could not take off but had no open gates to which to return. The JFK disruption plunged the airline into chaos, forcing it to cancel over a thousand flights during a six-day period, ruining the travel plans of more than 131,000 passengers.[44]

David Neelman, the company CEO at the time, cited multiple operational failures that compounded the crisis. Among the primary culprits: inadequate communication protocols (caused by, in his words, a "shoestring communications system") to direct the company's 11,000 pilots and flight attendants on when and where to go; an overwhelmed reservation system; and the lack of cross-trained employees who could work outside their primary area of expertise during an emergency.[45] The CEO added, "We had so many people in the company who wanted to help who weren't trained to help. We had an emergency control center full of people who didn't know what to do. I had flight attendants sitting in hotel rooms for three days who couldn't get a hold of us. I had pilots e-mailing me saying, 'I'm available, what do I do?' "[46] The airline lost its stellar reputation with customers, and three months later the CEO was replaced.

Of course, consistency of communications requires consistency of the policies and information that feed communications. For corporations, this means that business continuity plans and crisis management playbooks should include a plan for communicating effectively with all stakeholders during a crisis. Such a plan may include a special media center, identification and empowerment of a spokesperson, and identification of a variety of technical experts who can support the media center. In the case of major disruptions, the top executive often takes a leading role as the face of the company. For example, after the Japanese quake, GM's CEO, Dan Akerson, spoke to reporters at various times about the company's efforts and progress on mitigating the disruption.[47,48,49,50]

Marketing/Customer Relations[51]

In handling the aftermath of hurricane Katrina, P&G's communications delivered messages tailored to three audiences: consumers, retailers, and the general public. First, P&G needed to handle the consumer reaction to its emergency second-sourcing of coffee canning. The company ran consumer television ads to reassure the public that its high-quality coffee would be on shelves but that it may come in unfamiliar containers because P&G needed to second-source coffee canning to other companies.

Second, P&G also knew that competitors were visiting retail chain customers to try and wrest valuable shelf-space from P&G. Some competitors tried to spread fear, uncertainty and doubt ("FUD," as P&G referred to it) about P&G's promises to restore coffee production in light of the serious damages. For P&G, this meant reassuring its retailers, showing them P&G's recovery plans, allocating available capacity, and staying on schedule for the recovery.

Third, P&G took an unusual step (contradictory to its typical policy) and announced all the philanthropic activities it was undertaking as part of the Katrina recovery effort. P&G is usually reticent about broadcasting its charitable efforts, but the company realized that it would need to do this, in the case of Katrina, as part of the company's accelerated efforts to restart the New Orleans plant. The company didn't want to be portrayed as cruel in "forcing" hurricane victims back on the job, so P&G got in front of the media with what management considered to be a balanced, forthright portrayal of its total set of efforts.

We All Make Mistakes: From Perdition to Redemption

The decision by bourbon producer Maker's Mark to handle an unsustainable surge in demand by diluting its bottled beverage (see chapter 3) sparked outrage from consumers.[52,53] Jim Martel, a longtime Maker's Mark purist and a brand ambassador since 2001, said, "My favorite bourbon is being watered down so they can 'meet market demand.' In other words, so Beam, Inc. [the parent company] can fatten their wallets a little more. I'll help lower their demand by not buying any more."[54]

The company was forced to address the criticism. "We've been tremendously humbled over the last week or so," Maker's Mark president Bill Samuels said about customers' negative reactions.[55] "Our focus was on the supply problem. That led to us focusing on a solution," Samuels said. "We got it totally wrong."[56] The company reversed its decision to dilute the product. "You spoke. We listened. And we're sincerely sorry we let you down," the distiller wrote on its Facebook page on February 17, eight days after announcing the dilution.

The public apology and reversal of the policy helped. Nearly 28,000 people clicked "like" on the Facebook announcement of the reversal. A *Forbes* magazine article headline proclaimed: "Maker's Mark's Plain Dumb Move Proved to Be Pure Marketing Genius."[57] In fact, sales of Maker's Mark surged 44 percent. "There's no doubt that with the change of the proof and then the reversal of that decision, we did see sort of a buying forward from consumers," said Matthew Shattock, chief executive of the parent company, Beam.[58] Ironically, the surge in popularity exacerbated the original problem, which was a shortage of aged spirits for bottling. A bottle of Maker's Mark takes more than five years to make, so the time-to-recovery is very long.

Similarly, JetBlue's response to what it still calls its Valentine's Day Massacre earned it many kudos and helped the airline recover its reputation relatively quickly. The CEO immediately apologized publicly; the airline provided refunds to any passengers stuck on the tarmac for more than three hours; and it issued a "passenger bill of rights," providing compensation for various customer service failures, including $1,000 for any passenger bumped from an oversold flight. While the apologies helped the firm, they were not enough to save the CEO's job.

Online Technology = New Opportunities for Communications

The Maker's Mark and JetBlue sagas played out on a modern medium. Social media such as Facebook and Twitter offer new communication channels to reach customers, mixing the properties of one-way broadcast media and two-way interactive discussion channels. This is in addition to their role in sensing and detecting brewing problems, mentioned in 2. Social media channels are likely to rise in importance in crisis communications because of several factors including: the rising penetration of smartphones; the large portion of the population on social media; the bandwidth leanness of Internet communications relative to voice or video communications; and the finer-grain mechanisms that enable both senders and receivers to control which messages they see or to whom they send them.

ALL FOR ONE AND ONE FOR ALL

In many large disruptions, companies tend to help each other. Clearly, it makes business sense to help a customer in trouble. During the interviews conducted as part of the research for this book, most companies credited their suppliers for working tirelessly to help them. It also makes sense for companies to help suppliers in trouble when the company depends on the supplier's material or parts. Such collaboration between suppliers and customers is typically referred to as "vertical collaboration"—collaborations along the supply chain.

Large disruptions, however, also bring companies in the same echelon of a supply chain—and even competitors—to work together when their resource pooling and joint actions can accelerate recovery. This is referred to as "horizontal collaboration."

Customers Helping Suppliers Helping Customers

When tropical storm Lee trundled up the East Coast in September 2011, companies in Louisiana, Mississippi, Alabama, Texas, Pennsylvania, and New York prepared for torrential rains and local flooding. Automotive carpet maker Autoneum in Bloomsburg, Pennsylvania, had 72 hours to prepare its factory and inventory for the sure-to-come flood.[59] Unfortunately, the rains caused a local dam to burst, and seven to eight feet of muddy water flooded the carpet factory, wrecked the equipment, and ruined the carpeting being made by the plant.

Autoneum made carpet for six different car makers, including GM, and the manufacturers flew teams of specialists to the stricken supplier. Yet different manufacturers behaved differently. GM people joined in to help on Autoneum's muddy factory floor, while representatives from several other manufacturers stayed in their conference rooms and demanded the product. GM brought in 200 electricians and used GM's supply chain people and suppliers to procure needed parts.

For GM's team at Autoneum, the most gut-wrenching part of their stay was getting a tour of the town and seeing all the damaged houses. Workers were putting in 12-hour shifts to get the factory running and then going to their flooded homes to deal with that. Thus, GM also helped to build morale—buying pizza for everyone and handing out GM jackets. Autoneum repaid GM's help with better service during the recovery. GM never missed a beat, whereas other OEMs were forced to park thousands of carpet-less vehicles and add carpet later.

Massively Horizontal Collaboration

On March 31, 2012, a tank filled with highly flammable butadiene exploded in a chemical factory in Marl, Germany. Intense flames and thick black smoke billowed from Evonik Industries's cyclododecatriene (CDT) plant at the 7,000-worker chemical complex in the heavily industrialized Ruhr river valley. Roughly 130 firefighters fought the blaze for 15 hours to prevent its spread to the rest of the facility and ultimately to extinguish it. The explosion and fire killed two workers and severely damaged the plant.[60]

Cyclododecatriene sounds like an obscure chemical, and the fact that it's used to synthesize cyclododecane, dodecanoic acid, and laurolactam may mean nothing to most readers. But CDT is a key ingredient in making certain polyamides, which are high-strength plastics more commonly known as nylon. In particular, CDT goes into a high-tech type of nylon—PA-12 or nylon-12—that is especially prized for its chemical resistance, abrasion resistance, and fatigue resistance. That makes PA-12 a favorite of the auto industry, which uses this tough plastic for fuel lines, brake lines, and plastic housings. And if that wasn't enough, using nylon makes cars quieter and more fuel-efficient. The average light vehicle in 2011 used over 46 pounds of nylon, up from just 7 pounds in 1990.[61,62]

Nor were carmakers the only industry using these materials. PA-12 also goes into solar panels, athletic shoes, ski boots, optical fibers, cable conduits, and flame-retardant insulation for copper wire. CDT is a key precursor for making many other chemicals, such as brominated flame retardants, fragrances, hot-melt adhesives, and corrosion inhibitors.[63] The March 2012 explosion and fire in Marl destroyed almost half the world's production capacity for CDT. Worse, at the time of the explosion, CDT supplies were already tight as a result of its use in the booming solar panel industry. For automotive companies, the potential value-at-risk resulting from the Evonik fire was arguably similar to the value-at-risk during 2011 Japanese quake. Every vehicle they made depended on PA-12, and the fire threatened a significant and prolonged disruption of car production.

When a maker of fuel lines and brake lines—TI Automotive—raised the alarm about the dire implications of the Evonik fire, the entire automotive industry sprang into action. The industry convened an emergency summit on April 17 in Troy, Michigan. The summit was moderated by a neutral third party, the Automotive Industry Action Group (AIAG).[64] The AIAG is a volunteer-run, nonprofit organization that provides shared expertise, knowledge, and standards on quality, corporate responsibility, and supply chain management to a thousand member firms in the automotive industry.[65] Two hundred people attended the summit, representing eight automakers and 50 suppliers.[66] All tiers of the affected sectors of the automotive supply chain came, including the big OEMs, their Tier 1 suppliers, component makers, polymer resin makers, and on down to chemical makers such as Evonik and BASF.[67]

The participants had three objectives that required the collective expertise of the entire industry. First, they wanted to understand and quantify the current state of global PA-12 inventories and production capacities throughout the automotive supply chain. Second, they wanted to brainstorm options to strategically extend current PA-12 capacities and/or identify alternative materials or designs to offset projected capacity shortfalls. Third, they wanted to identify and recruit the necessary industry resources required to technically vet, test, and approve the alternatives.

The group formed six committees to help quickly create action plans to lessen any impact of shortages on component and vehicle production.[68] Each committee tackled an assigned task such as managing remaining inventories, boosting production at existing suppliers, identifying new firms to produce resins, and finding replacement materials.[69,70] The group hosted multiple technical follow-up meetings during the subsequent weeks on these issues.[71]

This multifaceted collaboration was key to overcoming the challenge. Within a week of the meeting, the top OEMs had jointly drafted a plan to expedite their parts validation processes.[72] Harmonized validation processes ensured that a supplier didn't need a different process for each OEM customer. Suppliers from other industries lent their capacity to automotive applications. For example, Kansas-based Invista Inc., the maker of Stainmaster carpets, released capacity for production of CDT.[73] In the end, cars continued to roll off the line even though the Evonik factory was offline until December 2012, nine months after the explosion and fire.[74]

Industry-Level Flexibility: Neighbors Helping Neighbors

During the evening of June 29, 2012, a destructive roiling line of thunderstorms—called a derecho—knocked out power to more than 4.2 million customers in Midwest and Mid-Atlantic states.[75] One of the hard-hit utilities was Baltimore Gas and Electric Company (BGE), which saw 760,000 customers lose power. To augment its own workforce during the recovery, BGE called MAMA (Mid-Atlantic Mutual Assistance), a mutual aid network of nine utilities[76] as well as the Southeastern Electric Exchange,[77] another mutual aid network.

Utilities have prepared for large disruptions by creating semiformal mutual aid agreements that are made individually, through state agencies, or through the American Public Power Association (APPA). Mutual aid agreements were strengthened over the first decade of the 21st century when APPA worked with the Federal Emergency Management Agency and the National Rural Electric Cooperative Association (NRECA) to create the APPA-NRECA Mutual Aid Agreement. "Almost every co-op has signed it, about 880, and almost 1,000 public power utilities have signed it," said Mike Hyland, senior vice president for engineering services at APPA.[78] The aid networks use each other's repair crews to move across the country to provide capacity to member utilities.

The aid networks generally activate on a concentric ring basis—a stricken utility first asks for help from its nearest aid network neighbors and then calls progressively more distant rings of utilities. For larger storms in which neighboring utilities also need aid, the ring of calls can stretch across the United States and into

Canada.[79] In the case of the 2012 derecho, a total of nearly 25,000 utility workers from all parts of both countries worked on restoring power.[80] These networks also helped during Hurricane Irene and Hurricane Sandy.[81] Other public utilities, such as water and wastewater, have analogous mutual aid networks.[82]

Utilities are not the only industry to cooperate to create flexibility. Railroads that share territories also have mutual aid agreements. For example, BNSF and Union Pacific are the two largest railroads serving the western United States—from the Pacific Coast to the Mississippi River extending to points further east—and they are fierce competitors in the transportation marketplace. However, when a significant service interruption occurs on either railroad, they will sometimes help each other maintain a steady flow of freight by negotiating temporary alternate routing options where they have parallel routes that can operationally support the modified movements. Such service interruptions can be the result of derailments, flooding, or other issues that affect track or train operations as well as scheduled interruptions (track maintenance and construction). In addition, as a result of regulatory conditions imposed as part of a merger or other related agreements, some railroads have obtained shared rights on limited segments of track and coordinate operations over those segments. In fact, a small permanent group of Union Pacific personnel actually sits in BNSF's massive network operations center to provide operational coordination over the areas of the national networks where the two railroads operate jointly. So, while BNSF and Union Pacific compete for customers, they cooperate on capacity in certain situations.

Co-opetition

During the recovery effort from hurricane Sandy, cell phone carriers were working to fix their networks and provide service to customers as quickly as possible. In an effort to accelerate the resumption of customer service, AT&T and T-Mobile agreed to let each other's customers share both networks, because both carriers use the same GSM technology. Tim Harden, president of Supply Chain and Fleet Operations at AT&T, said, "It's the good of the community and the good of the nation at that point, as opposed to who the competitor might be."[83] Pooling the capacities of the two networks helped cover "holes" in coverage in each network resulting from local damage. The strategy for eliminating holes in the coverage was "divide and conquer," said Neville Ray, chief technology officer for T-Mobile, and they have "two companies working to bring up one network, rather than two companies working to bring up two networks."[84]

LEARNING FROM DISASTER

Friedrich Nietzsche, the German philosopher, quipped, "what does not kill me makes me stronger" in his book *Twilight of the Idols* published in 1888. For companies experiencing operational disruptions, in particular, this is true only if they learn from their experiences, draw the relevant lessons, and improve their risk management and disaster recovery processes.

Hardened by Experience

After recovering from Katrina, P&G reviewed its response to find potential improvements on two performance dimensions: the cost of recovery and the time to resuming production. P&G then evaluated hardening the facility against future hurricanes in order to reduce the cost and recovery time. One major lesson stemmed from the hot and humid climate of New Orleans. With no power and no air conditioning in the factory, mold grew very quickly, and the company spent millions of dollars to eradicate it. If they had had on-site emergency generators, they could have turned the air conditioning on immediately and prevented the mold damage.[85] The same problem plagued companies hurt by the Thai floods.

Similarly, better seals on food containers were more important than reinforcing the roof. P&G also decided it needed some emergency accommodations on site so that a team could fly in and have everything it needed to get started. The company is also looking at its supply sources, increasing its network of suppliers outside of New Orleans, and is helping its suppliers have the same robustness of response as P&G's in preparation for the next disruption.

People vs. Product: Managing Emergencies vs. Ensuring Continuity

The 2008 Sichuan earthquake near Chengdu was one of the worst earthquakes in China's history. The 7.9-magnitude earthquake was the deadliest and strongest to hit China since the one in 1976 in Tangshan. The 2008 quake killed nearly 70,000, injured 374,000, and destroyed the homes of 4.8 million people.[86] Intel's factory and assembly and testing facility in Chengdu were largely undamaged as a result of Intel's insistence on seismic building design principles. The company was able to quickly restore operations.

Although Intel's preparation and response worked—Intel's factories were at 95 percent production within seven days of the earthquake—the postevent review revealed an internal tension of priorities and scope of activities between caring for the local workers in Chengdu and managing Intel's broader global business continuity. Jackie Sturm, Intel's vice president and general manager of Global Sourcing and Procurement, explained that following the Chengdu quake, Intel decided to split its incident response activities into two independent streams. Emergency Management (EM) would care for people and the safety of local facilities without worrying about the broader business issues. While EM cared for the affected people, Business Continuity (BC) would focus on business issues such as the affected work-in-process inventory, alternative fabs, logistics, products, and customers. Under the new structure, EM starts immediately during the disaster (i.e., is a first responder) and BC follows quickly. EM ends as soon as Intel has ensured the safety of everyone; BC continues until the recovery of production and return to normal operations. EM operates locally, while BC may involve global activities such as shifting production to a different facility. Intel used this spilt response structure to handle the 2011 Japanese quake and tsunami, as described in chapter 1.

Learning the Alphabet: Projects D, J, T, and E

At GM, each major disruption of the last decade was a special project designated by a letter. "Project D" was the 2005 Delphi bankruptcy, "Project J" was the 2011 Japan earthquake, "Project T" was the late 2011 Thailand flood, "Project E" was the 2012 Evonik fire, and "Project S" was superstorm Sandy in 2012. Each created a learning opportunity. "Quite honestly, I think if we had not had Project D, we would have stumbled more," said Rob Thom, GM's global vehicle engineering operations manager, about Project J.[87] "Once you get into a crisis, I've found you learn so fast [that] it makes you creative," added Ron Mills, GM's general manager of Components Holdings Program Management and Product Engineering.[88] Thus, each crisis accumulates skills and better methods for response. After a crisis, many companies review and analyze the organization's response to the event. This may consist of two stages; a preliminary "hotwash" performed immediately after the event, and a more careful analysis later.[89] According to Thom, by the time Project E occurred, the company was much more aware of potential deep-tier issues, more realistic in its white-space analysis, better coordinated in sharing information internally, and faster in validating alternatives.

"There's going to be another crisis," said Carlos Ghosn, the CEO of Nissan, a few weeks after the November flooding in Thailand. "We don't know what kind of crisis, where it is going to hit us, and when it is going to hit us, but every time there is a crisis we are going to learn from it.[90]"

Whereas many crises involve natural disasters or accidents that strike a particular location, some events have worldwide scope.

5

THE FINANCIAL CRISIS AND THE MONEY SUPPLY CHAIN

Recall the discussion of supply chains in chapter 1 and, specifically, the three types of flows underlying supply chain management: material, information, and money. Most disruptions (e.g., a tsunami, a labor strike, or theft) affect material flows from suppliers to their customers. Material flow disruptions are often coupled with disruptions in the information flow (see chapter 4). In contrast, a financial crisis disrupts the flow of money and credit, which affects the ability of consumers to purchase goods from retailers and of manufacturers to purchase parts and products from suppliers. Thus, whereas many disruptions affect supply, a financial crisis affects demand as well.

A DISRUPTION OF THE MONEY SUPPLY CHAIN

If a tsunami of water takes minutes or hours to wreak its devastation, then a tsunami of debt takes months or years to inflict its ravages. And just as a massive earthquake arises from centuries of accumulated seismic strain, the 2008 financial crisis began much earlier, in the 1990s. Low interest rates after the 2001 recession made housing much more affordable to borrowers and created rising demand for housing at ever higher prices. And those same low rates pushed lenders and investors to seek innovative new investments with higher rates of return, as well as creating new financial instruments that transferred and hid the risks of default.

The Buildup to a Breakdown

Between 2002 and 2006, housing prices doubled in the United States[1] and also surged in other countries, including Spain, Ireland, and the United Kingdom.[2] The more housing prices appreciated, the more attractive housing became to housing buyers, real estate speculators, and the investors funding the mortgages. Financial innovations such as securitization—the bundling and redividing of collections of debts—enabled global investors to share in the profits of the housing boom. If housing prices could only go up, then even people with bad credit and no down-payment looked like safe investments. The percentage of subprime mortgage originations almost tripled to 20 percent of all mortgages.[3]

Between 2002 and 2006, some $14 trillion (!) in mortgage-backed securities (MBS) were issued in the United States alone.[4] Not only did these trillions finance a surge in construction and related durable goods purchases (e.g., home appliances), but cash-out financing and home-equity loans let home owners convert their home's rapidly rising equity into cash for other purchases (cars, recreational vehicles, flat-panel TVs, etc.). Between 2002 and 2008, US homeowners converted roughly $4.5 trillion of home equity into cash and took on increasing personal debts.[5] Flows in global supply chains grew significantly on the abundant money supply. Between 2002 and 2008, US exports[6] and US imports[7] doubled.

In June 2004, the US Federal Reserve began raising short-term interest rates to reduce monetary stimulus, but the initial hikes had no effect. In fact, long-term rates, such as mortgage rates, paradoxically dropped. This prompted then-chairman of the Federal Reserve, Alan Greenspan, to remark, "For the moment, the broadly unanticipated behavior of world bond markets remains a conundrum."[8] Housing, GDP, exports, imports, and the stock market marched exuberantly upward even as the Fed continued to raise rates.

The Crest of the Breaking Wave

But the debt-fueled housing-bubble economy could not grow forever, and a succession of peaks portended the coming declines. First, sales of new houses peaked (July 2005). Next, housing starts peaked (January 2006). Then housing prices reached their zenith in April 2006.[9] As real estate activity slumped, banks tightened lending standards on commercial real estate (Q4 2006), and residential mortgages (Q1 2007).[10]

The rising interest rates hit many mortgage borrowers with higher monthly payments. Tighter lending standards and declining housing prices locked them out of further refinancing. Real estate speculators—who relied on flipping real estate quickly—got stuck with houses they could not sell. Delinquencies and foreclosures began to rise in 2006, which began to erode banks' finances. At the end of 2007, banks further tightened lending terms for commercial and industrial loans and hiked interest rates on those loans.[11,12]

When it became clear that securitized subprime mortgages would not deliver their promised profits, the edifice of debt began crumbling. Both banks and borrowers found themselves overextended, which pushed the US economy into recession in January 2008.[13] By August 2008, unemployment had risen, durable goods sales had dropped 5 percent, and car sales had dropped 20 percent. The retreating economy revealed the rocks of risk lurking below the financial froth. Or, as Warren Buffett is credited with saying, "You only find out who is swimming naked when the tide goes out."[14]

The downturn entered a more dangerous phase shortly after midnight on Monday, September 15, 2008, when Lehman Brothers, the fourth largest investment bank in the United States, declared bankruptcy, citing debts totaling $768 billion and assets worth only $639 billion as a result of large losses on subprime mortgages.[15] The stock market lost 4 percent of its value that day. American International Group (AIG), an insurance company with $1 trillion in debts, including credit default swaps that backed $60 billion in subprime mortgages held by other financial institutions,[16] appeared to be the next company on the brink of collapse. The global financial system was unraveling quickly with a very real risk that the liquidation of one firm's holdings could drive down asset prices to the point that it forced the liquidation of other firms. To halt the domino effect, the Federal Reserve Board arranged an $85 billion bailout on September 16.[17] As part of the bailout, the United States became the owner of 79.9 percent of AIG's equity.[18]

From Breakdown to Bullwhip

The Lehman bankruptcy sent a shock throughout the financial system and the broader economy, affecting the *demand* for almost every good; US consumer spending fell 8 percent.[19] Hardest hit were capital goods industries, as a result of constriction in the supply of capital. New home sales fell by 80 percent.[20] New car sales dropped 30 percent,[21] and new orders for durable goods sales slumped 40 percent.[22] Chrysler filed for bankruptcy in April 2009, General Motors in June 2009. Demand for services fell, too, with declines in restaurant sales and airline passenger volumes. Europe also suffered as a result of a combination of the global recession, European bank exposure to US mortgages, Eastern European debt, unfunded state largess, and housing bubbles in Ireland and Spain. Exports from Europe fell and the economies of the peripheral countries of the EU nosedived.

The swift contraction in demand sparked an amplified reaction in upstream supply chain activities that grew more and more extreme as the disruption in demand propagated up the chain of suppliers—a phenomenon known as "the bullwhip effect."[23] In a hypothetical illustration of the bullwhip effect, if a retailer sees an X percent drop in sales, it might reason that future sales will be low, too, because most forecasts are based on past experience. In addition, it might realize that its current inventories are too high if future sales continue to be low. Consequently, the retailer might cut orders to the wholesaler by, say, 2X percent (reflecting both lower future sales and desire to decrease the high current inventory). The wholesaler, seeing the 2X percent drop in orders from the retailer, might prepare for future lower sales and too much inventory by cutting orders to the wholesaler by 4X percent. At each tier of the supply chain, the decline in demand sparks a bigger decline in orders from suppliers—each company reasoning that it needs to quickly cut production (to adjust to declining sales) and work off its bloated inventory.

The exaggerated decline in orders can be especially damaging to upstream suppliers who have high fixed costs tied to production assets. Ford CEO Alan Mulally tried to mitigate the impending bullwhip during the financial crisis by imploring the US Senate banking committee to save his competitors. He argued that otherwise the automotive Tier 1 suppliers would fail and then their suppliers would fail, and so on, affecting the entire US automobile industry.

When demand revives, the bullwhip pattern reverses as each echelon boosts ordering both to cover expected higher sales and to quickly replenish depleted inventories. Again, the effect amplifies up the chain with larger and larger order size increases upstream in the supply chain. However, because of cuts in capacity during a downturn, upstream companies take time to respond to orders. As orders flood in, lead times grow, suppliers start allocating partial shipments to customers, and customers respond by boosting orders even more in an effort to garner a greater percentage of the allocation. All of this causes significant swings in inventory and orders, such that the amplitude of the swings is larger the further upstream (and further from the consumer orders) a company is in its supply chain.

In the context of a normal economy with modest demand volatility, the bullwhip effect causes volatility to vary across the tiers of a supply chain—wholesale volumes will be more volatile than retail volumes, manufacturing volumes will be more volatile than wholesale volumes, and supplier volumes will be more volatile still. This phenomenon has been documented in consumer-packaged goods industries,[24] food,[25,26] semiconductor manufacturing,[27] and others.

Macroeconomic data during the 2008 financial crisis show the bullwhip effect operating on a much broader scale. For example, US retail sales (representing consumer demand) declined by 12 percent; yet US manufacturers pulled down inventories by 15 percent and manufacturing sales declined almost 30 percent, while imports plunged over 30 percent.[28] The financial crisis created a broad bullwhip across the globe. More than 90 percent of OECD countries exhibited simultaneous declines in exports and imports of more than 10 percent.[29] A survey of 125 Dutch companies found that those in Tier 1 and Tier 2 relative to end-consumers saw a 25 percent drop in revenues, while those in Tiers 3 and 4 saw a 39 to 43 percent drop.[30] The bullwhip showed in the financial data of individual companies, such as the life sciences and materials company Koninklijke DSM N.V.; Dutch multinational Akzo Nobel N.V.; German conglomerate ThyssenKrupp AG; and in Koninklijke Philips N.V., the Dutch diversified technology company commonly known as Philips.[31] Evidence of the bullwhip effect during the financial crisis was also found in studies of French import/export transaction data.[32] The bullwhip effect explains, in part, how a global financial earthquake can shift the tectonic plates underpinning the economy and create a global tsunami of economic disruption.

Disrupting the Supply of Trade Finance

The disruption of the banking system also had a direct impact on global trade.[33,34] Banks and other financial institutions act as financial intermediaries in foreign trade by issuing letters of credit that guarantee payments across international borders. These financial instruments require trust between banks, and trust was in short supply after Lehman failed. The TED-spread,[35] which represents the willingness of the largest banks in the world to lend to each other in short-term routine transactions, spiked from pre-crisis levels of 0.3 percent in April 2007 to over 4.5 percent by mid-October 2008.[36] Banks simply didn't know who was exposed to toxic debt—in some cases, the banks themselves weren't aware of risks lurking within their own portfolios. Analogous credit spreads in exporting countries were even higher than the TED-spread.[37]

Between 2008 and 2009, letter-of-credit messages in the SWIFT[38] network declined at a rate faster than the decline in merchandise trade.[39] Most banks tightened trade-related lending guidelines and increased the costs of lending to exporters.[40] The problem affected seaborne international trade more so than air or land-based international trade as a result of the much longer durations needed to cover slower modes.[41] In short, the supply of money for international trade dried up.

A DISRUPTION IN DEMAND

Whereas physical disasters usually have an obvious geographic epicenter, the financial crisis created more widespread uncertainty. At first, companies didn't know the impact on demand and supply. Would there be bank runs? How far would real estate prices fall? How far would the stock market drop? How high would unemployment climb? How would consumers, customers, retailers, suppliers, and governments react to the crisis? Which suppliers, logistics companies, and retailers would fail? No one knew. With the tightening of credit and so much financial uncertainty for consumers and businesses, consumer demand fell.

Given the disruption in the money supply and the fact that money to purchase goods and services enters the supply chain on the retail end, retailers had front row seats for the disruption. Many US retailers failed, including Circuit City, Linens 'n' Things, Filene's Basement, Eddie Bauer, Ritz Camera Centers, and many others. US retailers were responsible for 19 percent of the mass layoffs in 2009,[42] although the retail industry represented only 6 percent of US gross domestic product.[43]

Consumers Shift to Frugality

The uncertainty created angst everywhere, manifesting itself in consumers' anxieties over spending. Consumers embraced frugality and sought to stretch their constrained budgets.[44] Although Shaw's supermarket chain believed it was relatively recession-proof because people must eat, it noticed a strong shift in consumer buying habits away from higher-priced (and higher-margin) items toward less expensive store brands. While unit sales in food remained the same, both revenues and margins dropped as sales of low-cost staples such as pasta and Campbell's Soup grew. For Chiquita, banana sales increased while premium salad sales decreased. Other retailers, such as Staples, similarly noted the trend toward frugality among consumers.

Although most companies were negatively affected, those serving the lower end of the price spectrum garnered increased demand. "Walmart sells what you need to have as opposed to what you want to have," said Howard Davidowitz, chairman of a national retail investment-banking and consulting firm.[45] Similarly, when people ate out, they went to low-priced venues such as McDonald's.[46] To address the shift, some companies responded by creating "value-for-money" products to attract the growing numbers of price-conscious consumers. For example, the downturn forced

Starbucks to offer $1 cups of coffee and new instant coffee to offset declining sales of its premium coffee drinks.[47]

Paradoxically, the downturn actually created supply shortages in some industries, for two reasons. First, the increase in order cancellation rates caused suppliers to delay production. Suppliers didn't want to purchase raw materials for orders that might be canceled. They cut inventories and waited for firm orders, building a sales backlog as a "cushion." This reluctance of suppliers to commence production without firm orders (and upfront payments) caused supply shortages.[48] Second, changing demand patterns brought shortages of (now higher-volume) lower-priced goods and private-label brands.[49] Both Shaw's and Staples found that the shift from brand-name to private-label products strained the contract manufacturers making these generic products.[50]

Frugality Disrupts Forecasting

The changes in consumer's purchasing behavior upended years of historical data used by companies for forecasting. Before the crisis, grocery chain Shaw's "knew what you would have for dinner next week."[51] The retailer, with 169 stores, used 10 years' worth of data to forecast exactly what consumers would buy and even how they would react to promotions. During the crisis, however, demand shifted so much that a survey of 342 global companies between late 2009 and early 2010 found that the top two challenges for supply chain performance were "demand volatility and/or poor forecast accuracy" (74 percent of respondents) and "lack of visibility to current market demand" (33 percent).[52]

Along those lines, office supplies retailer Staples said that its forecasts were no longer as accurate as they once were. Other companies experienced abrupt customer events that changed demand patterns. For makers of computers and other electronic products, such as HP (the biggest creditor of Circuit City[53]), that meant a sudden shift of the business to other retail channels with different patterns of demand.[54] History stopped being a good a predictor for demand patterns.

Reacting to Forecast Inaccuracy

The downturn and disruption of forecast reliability forced companies to resort to reactive tactics rather than to planned strategy. Shaw's Supermarkets had neither sufficient historical data nor applicable forecasting models to estimate the new pattern of demand for the private-label products that consumers were suddenly seeking. As a result, the company had to become more nimble and short-term focused, using ad hoc communications as well as manual ordering from its suppliers. Rather than Shaw's promotions driving sales and marketing activities, consumer behavior was driving marketing—a complete reversal from the past; consequently, the company became focused on the next week, not on the next quarter.

Companies Shift to Survival Mode

"Hunkering down" for survival was the prevailing behavior of customers, suppliers, and companies in many industries. Responding to falling orders from their customers, companies cut orders to their suppliers even further, thus contributing to the bullwhip. Interviews with 20 companies, conducted at the MIT Center for Transportation and Logistics, documented that cost-cutting was the prevailing response to the crisis.[55] Many companies slashed budgets, cut staff, and eliminated non-essential expenses. In 2009, another survey found that companies reduced supply chain costs by negotiating supplier cost reductions (75% of respondents), reducing inventory levels (60%), moving to lower-cost suppliers (44%) and reducing the number of suppliers (40%).[56]

Even recession-proof industries such as healthcare and education were affected. Medical device makers saw customers such as hospitals having financial problems. Well-funded universities such as MIT and Harvard University saw their endowments decline in value by 25 to 30 percent. This caused the universities to curtail operating budgets and halt many capital projects.

Smaller Shipments, Slower Modes

Cost cutting affected demand patterns for logistics in two ways. First, C.H. Robinson, a third-party logistics provider, noticed that customers wanted smaller shipments. Companies switched from using full truckload (TL) to less-than-truckload (LTL) carriers and from LTL to parcel carriers. Even though the smaller shipments cost more per unit shipped, shippers chose smaller order sizes because they were more concerned about high inventory levels and customer nonpayment risks.[57]

Second, the financial crisis also coincided with high oil prices and growing concerns of greenhouse gas emissions, which reduced demand for faster modes. UPS and FedEx saw their customers shift from premium air service to less expensive ground delivery modes. Between 2008 and 2009, FedEx Express (air) shipments dropped nearly 5 percent but FedEx Ground shipments rose 1 percent.[58] The total volume of international airfreight fell 25 percent.[59] Mission-critical parts service providers noticed a decline in requested service levels: two-hour service became four-hour, and four-hour service requests became eight-hour, for example.[60] High oil prices also motivated ocean carriers to adopt "slow steaming" (see also chapter 10) to save fuel.[61,62] Slow steaming delayed delivery of goods, increasing inventories in transit. The longer transit times also increased exposure to a multitude of transoceanic trade risks such as customer bankruptcies, port disruptions, and tariff increases.

The interplay of shipment size, speed, cost, and inventory create complex tradeoffs, which many companies addressed through a segmentation of their supply chains. For example, Shaw's considered lower-cost transportation modes, such as rail instead of truck. Rail was cheaper, but it took 21 days to move rail containers across the country, which increased the inventory costs. Not all products were shifted to rail; strawberries were too perishable, but hardier fruits such as Washington apples could make the rail journey. Astute companies performed frequent reassessments of transportation costs because fuel prices fell during the latter part of the recession, making trucking, at times, attractive again for more products.

Looking at the Bigger Picture before Making Bigger Cuts

With the downturn in demand, BASF (the largest chemical company in the world) faced tough choices in operating its expensive, massive chemical plants. As a result of diminished demand, some plants were operating below economically productive volumes, and their managers wanted to shut them down in order to limit the losses. Yet BASF has many vertically integrated parts in its internal network, a strategy it calls *verbund* (which is German for "linked" or "integrated").[63] This integrated structure means that some of the most important suppliers and customers of BASF plants are other BASF plants.

Rather than analyze each plant in isolation (i.e., whether a given plant has enough direct customer demand to justify its continued operation), BASF looked at the bigger picture of its internal supply chain. Although a certain facility might have been economically unproductive on an individual basis, BASF kept the plant running if the plant made intermediate products that were used by other still-profitable parts of BASF. This was analogous to the value-at-risk calculations described in the last part of chapter 3, in the sense that BASF was calculating the total impact of disrupting production of an intermediate chemical on all the downstream products that use that chemical, and thus on the entire company's financial performance. The company could rely on this holistic strategy because it had control over all the company's divisions for purposes of cost sharing. This is not the case for most other companies, who rely on external suppliers, some of whom may go out of business, creating shortages.

The Upside of a Downturn

"A crisis is a terrible thing to waste," said economist Paul Romer, noting the opportunity for making changes that would be difficult at other times.[64] During downtimes, there is significantly less resistance to change, and companies also may have underutilized workers who can take on the restructuring tasks. With this in mind, some companies used the financial crisis to their advantage. Office supply giant, Staples, made major changes to its IT systems by merging two IT networks to improve its operations. Home Depot implemented a new distribution strategy, consolidating cross-docking flow centers to improve delivery efficiency.

While some companies reacted to the downturn by squeezing their suppliers for price reductions, others did the opposite by seeking reliable and stable suppliers. Thus, Trevor Schick, vice president of global supply chain management and chief procurement officer at EMC Corporation (an IT storage hardware solutions manufacturer) saw a "flight to quality" phenomenon among some customers. Schick also noticed that the biggest companies gained market share in a recession while the weaker ones lost. In an industry like storage devices, which had five large companies and 80 startups, fears about the survival of the startups pushed customers toward sourcing from the larger suppliers.

Other companies took advantage of the downturn by beginning expansion initiatives. Barrett Distribution Centers exploited distressed real estate prices to buy warehousing in new markets for geographic expansion. Other companies used the downturn to lure key people away from competitors. Robert W. Baird & Co., a 2,400-employee Milwaukee-based investment bank, hired 70 executives during 2009, many from rivals, and "significantly more" than in 2008, said Managing Director Robert Venable.[65] Nearly half (49 percent) of companies surveyed said that poaching was a concern, even in a down economy.[66] And 62 percent of companies were concerned about losing key talent as a result of the cutbacks made during the recession.[67]

Training employees was another low-cost, high-impact strategy for using the downtime labor surplus to create more opportunities during the recovery. For example, Toyota launched training and quality-enhancement projects rather than laying people off. "We used the downtime for environmental, OSHA, and diversity training as well as improving problem-solving skills and standardized work," said Wil James, senior vice president for manufacturing and quality.[68] Some countries, such as Germany and Singapore, provided government support for employers to retain and retrain employees—covering some of their salaries—rather than be passive as companies lay them off.[69,70] The programs benefited companies, workers, and the government: the company retained the worker at a reduced pay-rate, the workers kept their jobs and gained training, and the cost to the government was less than the cost of full unemployment benefits and social discord.

The start of the downturn didn't imply an end to innovation or new product introductions. Patent applications increased during the downturn, a pattern seen in other downturns including the Great Depression.[71] Apple released its 3G iPhone during the recession and saw a 240 percent increase in sales.[72] The first iPhone competitor based on Google's Android system, the HTC Dream, launched about a month after the Lehman failure, and yet it sold a million units during the worst two quarters of the recession.[73] A. G. Lafley, then chief executive of Procter & Gamble, said, "I think it's more essential to innovate through a recession ... to continue to bring disruptive new brands and products for our consumers."[74]

BANKRUPTCIES IN THE SUPPLY CHAIN

The disruption in the money supply, and the fall-off in demand, reverberated across global supply chains to create risks of bankruptcies everywhere. Flextronics summarized these risks in its 2009 annual report. The report stated that the company faced risks from "the effects that current credit and market conditions could have on the liquidity and financial condition of our customers and suppliers, including any impact on their ability to meet their contractual obligations."[75] During a 2009 MIT Center for Transportation Logistics conference, corporate participants agreed that they were all struggling with both suppliers' and customers' problems.

Demand Disruption Becomes Supply Disruption

In February 2009, Edscha, a maker of automobile roof modules for convertibles, declared bankruptcy. When car sales plummeted 30 percent, supplier revenues dropped further, straining them financially.[76] Not only did automotive suppliers suffer greater sales declines owing to the bullwhip effect, but many suppliers are capital-intensive businesses because of large investments in tooling and equipment. Thus, many suppliers carried high debt loads and were especially impacted by the disruption in the credit markets. Edscha had suffered a loss of almost 50 percent of sales, which pushed the €1.1 billion company over the edge.[77] In North America, nearly 60 suppliers' plants closed in the three years after 2008, with the loss of about 100,000 jobs.[78] Bankruptcies in the automotive industry more than tripled between 2007 and 2009.[79]

A Business Continuity Institute survey in the summer of 2009 found that 28 percent of companies had suffered a disruption caused by a financial failure of a supplier in the preceding 12 months, and 52 percent said such failures would be a major threat in the following 12 months.[80] Manufacturing companies were especially hard hit by this type of disruption, with 58 percent of them reporting supplier financial failures.[81] In another survey, 40 percent of respondents ranked "suppliers going out of business" among the risks are most likely to affect their own supply chains.[82]

Managing the Risks of Supplier Bankruptcy

During the depths of the downturn, one company said, "Supplier disruptions are now corporate risk number one. Risk management in the financial crisis is all about being very fast in reacting, since we lose millions of euros if a strategic supplier goes out of business. The faster we know that the supplier defaults, the less money we will lose."[83] Such efforts are discussed in greater depth in chapter 8.

Spending on supplier risk assessment and the frequency of reassessment increased dramatically during the crisis. For example, one automotive company went from a six-month assessment cycle to a weekly assessment for all first-tier and also some second-tier suppliers.[84] Companies such as EMC, Boston Scientific Corporation, and Shaw's Supermarkets had mounting concerns about supplier quality during the downturn. They saw suppliers' capacity and staff cutbacks as a potential threat to quality; fewer people meant more knowledge gaps, more sporadic production runs, and fewer people to do quality-critical tasks like maintenance and inspections.

Financial Support of Suppliers

The precarious state of supplier finances forced some companies to offer direct support to their ailing suppliers. Edscha's bankruptcy was a shock for BMW, which needed the supplier's roof modules for its new Z4 convertible and other models. BMW said, "We had to help Edscha and try and stabilize it. We had no choice to go to another supplier, as that would have taken six months and we don't have that."[85] Surveys found that between 9 and 12 percent of companies were providing financial assistance to suppliers.[86,87]

Most companies explicitly eschewed direct investment in suppliers because of the risks and the company's own needs to conserve capital. Instead, companies helped financially struggling suppliers in a number of other ways. For example, BASF, HP, and others helped some suppliers by accelerating payments or by buying raw materials on their behalf. Other companies prepaid for tooling or other capital-intensive supplier needs if suppliers couldn't get their own credit.[88] According to Dr. Hermann Krog, then executive director of logistics at Audi, the automotive OEM helped suppliers by agreeing to be the guarantor on some bank loans.

Jackie Sturm, vice president and general manager of Global Sourcing and Procurement at Intel, said that the company assisted suppliers in creating financial plans as well as in finding other customers or investors.[89] In some cases, however, Intel went a step further. It provided liquidity, by lending working capital against future production. Intel Capital even took equity stakes in a few suppliers and—as it turned out—profited from those investments when the economy recovered.

Solutions for Customer Insolvency

Supplier bankruptcies weren't the only risks faced by companies; customers failed, too. For example, in 2009 alone, Flextronics "incurred $262.7 million of charges relating to Nortel and other customers that filed for bankruptcy or restructuring protection or otherwise experienced significant financial and liquidity difficulties," according to Flextronics's 2011 annual report.[90] A customer bankruptcy might mean an indefinite delay in getting paid, if one got paid at all. A spring 2009 survey found that 7 percent of companies were providing financial assistance to customers.[91]

Nypro, a $1.2 billion global plastic parts manufacturer, reviewed all of its "customers-at-risk," sometimes on a daily basis during the crisis. For some customer accounts, the company was able to insure the receivables. On accounts for which it couldn't get insurance, such as on automotive customers, the company offered early payment discounts to customers to mitigate financial default risks, thus reducing Nypro's exposure to those risky customers. Some customers paid in as few as 15 days under this program. A survey by *World Trade* magazine found that 43 percent of companies offered pricing concessions to customers for early payment in an effort to conserve working capital.[92]

Compared to prior recessions, the rise of outsourcing and contract manufacturing created new customer-side risks during the 2008 financial crisis. For example, Nypro might make parts on behalf of a large low-risk firm, such as bottle caps for P&G or cell phone bodies for Nokia. But as a result of outsourcing by the OEM, Nypro's parts might actually be sent to a small regional copacker or a Chinese contract manufacturer before being shipped to the OEM. This intermediary contract manufacturer was then responsible for paying Nypro. This arrangement exposed Nypro to the credit risk of the contract manufacturer, rather than the OEM. Worse, when Nypro negotiated an agreement with a big OEM like P&G or Nokia, Nypro might not even know who these contract manufacturers would be. Consequently, Nypro sought guarantees from the OEM, or enlisted its help in performing due diligence on copackers and contract manufacturers.

RECOVERY: PHASE 2 OF THE BULLWHIP

During the downturn, US unemployment had more than doubled—reaching 10 percent in December 2009.[93] The rate of business failures increased 30 percent from the prerecession value to 235,000 failures per quarter in March 2009.[94] Although the world may have been staring into a financial abyss after Lehman's failure in the fall of 2008, global resilience absorbed the shock. Trillions of dollars in monetary stimulus stabilized the financial markets, and fiscal stimulus helped limit the depths of the downturn. Governments took over ailing financial institutions or agreed to take toxic assets off of banks' balance sheets. These concerted efforts by central bankers and governments prevented a deeper deflationary cycle, runs on banks, and other types of value-destruction processes that contributed to the 1930s Great Depression. Retail sales began to recover after March 2009, and by June 2009, the recession was officially over in the United States.

Risks in the Rebound

Managing during the downturn had been difficult, yet managing during the rebound wasn't easy, either. In the following 12 months, retail sales rebounded by a modest 7 percent, but imports surged 27 percent as distributors and retailers started to build inventory in anticipation of increased sales. The bullwhip was now again in effect.

"Sometimes it's easier to manage on the way down in a recession than on the way up," said Brian Hancock, vice president of supply chain at Whirlpool Corp. "It takes quite a bit of effort to bring capacity back on line, and everybody is hesitant to increase capacity in case they don't see the economy returning to 2006 and 2007 levels."[95] In Q3 2009, a survey by technology research firm AMR found that nearly one-quarter of respondents worried that the downturn would continue.[96]

To manage the recovery, USG Corp., a US-based maker of construction materials with 2009 sales of $3.2 billion, used advanced planning software. When the housing bubble burst, the company cut production capacity strategically and reduced costs. As construction slowly rebounded, the company planned for careful growth and determined the optimal use of manufacturing plants for specific products and markets.[97]

"Now, we are looking at long-term forecasts and running models five to 10 years into the future to help us determine when and what [capacity] we will need to bring back online first," said Timothy McVittie, senior director of logistics for USG Building Systems. "Finding the right balance is a big hairy beast," McVittie explained, "due the challenge of staying lean but still meeting customer expectations." He then added, "Considering that industry demand is as low as it is, the marketplace has little patience for manufacturers who cut too deep and can no longer effectively service their customers."[98] Corroborating this view, a supply chain risk survey by AMR Research in the third quarter of 2009 found that 44 percent of respondents believed the recovery cycle would pose the greatest risk in 2010.

Overextended Suppliers in a Fragile Economy

Companies worried about suppliers' abilities to handle a rebound; a company couldn't be poised for growth if its suppliers weren't poised for growth. EMC noted that the 2000–2001 tech industry recession had been a painful one because suppliers cut capacity too slowly. In contrast, during 2008–2009, EMC was surprised by how quickly technology suppliers reacted. DRAM memory chip capacity, for example, fell rapidly. But overly aggressive cutbacks could be just as damaging as overly cautious ones, so EMC prepared for the recovery by using contracts that required suppliers to maintain 20 percent upside capacity available. When EMC visited a supplier, it made sure that the supplier was devoting resources to EMC and that if the supplier cut capacity, it did not cut capacity devoted to EMC.

The automotive industry experienced similar effects. As automakers and other vehicle manufacturers increased their production volumes beginning in 2010, the growth strained their suppliers. Some of these suppliers grew too fast and without adequate capital. Small suppliers, especially, still didn't have access to capital, and other suppliers were too uncertain about the economy to make needed capital investments. Part of companies' concerns about these supply risks were driven by ongoing economic uncertainties such as the United States's "fiscal cliff," debt ceiling, budget sequestration battles, European sovereign debt crisis, government austerity moves, and mixed data about the robustness of the recovery.

In particular, Toyota watched for suppliers who respond to production launches with plans to work seven days a week. Although the financial results of these suppliers were impressive when judged according to traditional metrics, many were actually becoming more fragile and more risky as a result of deferred maintenance, lack of equipment renewal, and overworked employees. Around-the-clock production "immediately throws up a flag," said Toyota's North American purchasing chief Bob Young. "It means we have to visit them to understand their true condition."[99] As the recovery progressed and Toyota North America planned to boost production, the company doubled its supplier watch-list to 40 in April 2013 from 20 suppliers in 2012.

In thinking about long-term relationships and the stability of the entire supply base, companies were looking to aid selected suppliers as needed. They were again considering tooling buys, accelerated payables, buying materials for suppliers, loans, and so forth. In one case, a large company simply bought the small supplier when the supplier ran into trouble. Honda Motor Co.'s North American purchasing chief, Tom Lake, acknowledged that Honda can't just say "more" and expect suppliers to jump. "Because so many automakers are increasing production, suppliers have to pick and choose where to make an investment."[100]

CASH BECOMES KING: REDUCING WORKING CAPITAL

The financial crisis revealed the sharp distinction between profit and cash flow, making cash a much more important financial measure of company health.[101] The disruption of the money supply and the resulting recession-induced bullwhip meant companies had to rely, at first, on retained earnings or preexisting cash reserves. A Grant Thornton/World Trade magazine survey found that 90 percent of respondents worked to reduce their working capital in 2009 (up from 78 percent in 2008).[102] The financial crisis created urgency and an opportunity to both reduce operating costs and free up scarce capital locked in the supply chain. One of the results was increased collaboration between companies' finance departments and supply chain organizations.

Even strong companies faced liquidity issues. Nypro, for example, had two cash-related challenges. First, it had high capital costs associated with the injection molding machines and molds it needed to make plastic products. Nypro needed about $300,000 to $600,000 in capital assets to support each additional $1 million in revenues. Second, employees owned the privately held Nypro. When employees retire, the company had to have the cash to buy the retirees' shares in the company. Between 2010 and 2014, Nypro needed $200 million in cash to handle an upcoming rash of retirements. As described in the section titled "Terms of Endearment: Reducing Working Capital" below, Nypro was able to extract cash from its supply chain.

Some companies gained market share from failing competitors and as the economy recovered, they needed capital for growth. Church & Dwight (a manufacturer and marketer of personal care, household, and specialty products under the Arm & Hammer brand name and other trademarks) had grown by acquisitions. It had acquired 14 key brands in 2001–2007, and that strategy required cash and financial strength. The company also had substantial debts that needed to be serviced, causing a determined emphasis on finding free cash flow and debt reduction opportunities rather than simply reducing costs.[103]

Material Flow Begets Cash Flow

Although companies' supply chain operations do not typically make financial headlines, they have three significant effects on cash flows and working capital requirements. First, DPO (days payables outstanding) are unpaid bills to suppliers and represent a de facto loan of cash from the supplier to the company. Second, DSO (days sales outstanding) are customers' unpaid bills and represent a de facto loan of cash from the company to its customers. Third, DIO (days inventory on-hand) is cash tied up in inventory. Companies can reduce their working capital levels through paying suppliers later (increasing DPO), accelerating the collection of customer payments (reducing DSO), or reducing inventories (reducing DIO). A spring 2009 survey found that 55 percent of companies extended payment terms with suppliers (DSO), 25 percent worked to accelerate customer payment terms (DPO), and 44 percent worked on reducing supply chain wide inventory (DIO) as part of their efforts to manage working capital.[104]

Terms of Endearment: Reducing Working Capital

Prior to the financial crisis, many salespeople paid little attention to customers' payment terms. That left their companies with high DSO and high working capital requirements. The recession made companies more aware of the costs of giving away working capital via generous terms. Many of them looked to reduce DSO by improving customers' compliance with payment terms. Companies scrutinized actual payments relative to contractual payment terms, realizing that payment terms in reality were longer than specified in the contract—especially with customers strapped for cash who tried to delay payments. When Nypro compared its actual DSO to its contractual average, it found that its average contractual DSO was 52 days but the actual average payment was received 65 days after delivery. The company started focusing on chronically late customers in order to decrease this average.

Similarly, the financial crisis also led companies to scrutinize supplier payment terms. For example, in the past, Nypro let each of its plants negotiate and manage supplier payment terms, but that practice resulted in a wide range of 30- to 75-day terms. During the crisis, Nypro created global supply contracts with its top 50 suppliers and worked on lengthening its payment terms. Nypro had some success because its financial stability and reputation for consistent and timely payments made suppliers more willing to extend the terms.

Nypro's program was part of a larger effort to create a cash-neutral supply chain, adding discipline to incremental activities that might consume cash or capital. For example, Nypro started performing a capital and cash-flow analysis of all new programs, including large sales quotes, so that the company didn't take on projects or sales commitments that it couldn't afford. This analysis included the capital, inventory, terms, and ROAE (return on average equity) implications of any new program or quote. By incorporating cash and capital analyses at that level, the program managers and salespeople became aligned with the company's financial goals.

Cash neutrality also affected on-going supply chain activities. If the company faced a unilateral increase in DSO on the customer side, it passed that increase through to the DPO and the supply side. Keeping the terms matched on both sides avoided unexpected demands for cash to support supply chain operations. Nypro also rented equipment for flexible capacity rather than buying all the equipment needed for the upside estimates of demand. That way, if demand failed to materialize, Nypro didn't have surplus capacity on its books. In total, Nypro freed up $100 million in cash from the beginning of the financial crisis to October 2009.

Too Much Junk in the Trunk: Reducing Inventory

A January 2010 survey found that 60 percent of companies had reduced their inventory levels throughout 2009.[105] Both Church & Dwight and Limited Brands worked to become more demand-driven with leaner inventories. In fact, Church & Dwight started measuring inventory in terms of dollars rather than weeks to emphasize the financial burden of inventory rather than inventory's role as a buffer. The company reduced inventory through improved sales-and-operations-planning (S&OP) processes, tightened safety stock requirements, integrated raw materials planning, and consignment-at-vendor optimization. The company also paid special attention to slow-moving and remnant inventory, the size of which grew during the downturn, as a result of the drop in demand as well as the shifts in demand patterns. This emphasis helped improve other financial variables such as write-offs and capital tied up in warehouse space.[106] Between 2006 and 2009, Church & Dwight reduced remnant inventory from 12 percent to between 4 and 5 percent.

Relative Credit Quality in the Supply Chain: Winning the Battle and Losing the War

Strategies to reduce working capital requirements can have unintended effects. Lengthening payment terms to suppliers meant that those suppliers' financial situations worsened. Too-low inventories of material and parts reduced a company's buffers to any supply hiccup. And low inventory of finished goods could reduce the company's level of service, straining its relationships with customers. Even tightening payment terms and cutting down on the time until the company got paid (cutting down DSO) carried a risk, especially during the downturn, that customers would demand better prices or other extra services in return for cutting DSO or take their business to suppliers who offered longer payment terms.

Advance Auto Parts (AAP), a Fortune 500 automotive retailer of parts, accessories, and maintenance items, was careful about reworking terms with suppliers. An improved, longer DPO for AAP meant a worse DSO for its suppliers. AAP saw this as a zero-sum game or worse. A company could readily optimize itself into a worse position by being too aggressive with longer DPO terms. First, if AAP's supplier had to borrow extra cash because of lengthening payments, those borrowing costs would appear in the supplier's prices. And if the supplier had a worse credit rating than AAP, then the supplier would pay more for one day of the supplier's DSO than AAP would pay for one day of its DPO. Second, longer payment terms to suppliers could increase the risk of a supplier bankruptcy. AAP devised an innovative supply chain financing program to address this issue.

AAP did very well during the crisis; although many consumers stopped buying new cars,[107] most still had a car, and those cars needed maintenance. The maintenance needs of the aging fleet meant good times for car part retailers such as AAP.[108] While Chrysler begged for a government bailout and slipped into bankruptcy, AAP had little trouble obtaining credit on favorable terms.

The company had many small suppliers that make automotive replacement parts, including ones that supplied the struggling OEMs. Given the small size of the suppliers and the turmoil in the automotive industry, the suppliers were hurting for cash but couldn't borrow at affordable rates, if they could borrow at all.

AAP crafted a supplier financing program[109] with some financial institutions in which the financial institution paid the supplier's invoice at a discount on quick terms—as short as 20 days. But rather than use a discount factor based on the supplier's credit rating, the program used AAP's much better credit rating. This rate was about half the one the most suppliers could have gotten on their own. The result was that suppliers became willing to offer AAP significantly longer payment terms—as much as 240 days. At the end of this much-extended payment term, AAP paid the invoice amount to the financial institution.

AAP noted three key details that were needed to make the program work. First, AAP inspected incoming goods in a timely fashion to certify the invoice to the bank, making the supplier eligible for quick payment. The 20-day early payment terms reflected the minimum time that AAP needed to ensure the quality and correctness of the order. Second, careful documentation also ensured that AAP had the necessary audit trails and Sarbanes-Oxley compliance.[110]

Third, AAP worked with its outside auditor and rating agencies to ensure that the program would be counted as accounts payable and not ordinary debt on the company's balance sheet. The reasoning worked, because the financing was directly tied to transactions between AAP and the suppliers. Moreover, the supplier (not AAP) controlled the duration of the "loan" because the supplier decided when to ask the bank for the money.

The three-way financial relationships in the program helped all three participants. AAP got longer payment terms, which let the company conserve cash without incurring more debt on its balance sheet. The program also reduced AAP's supplier risks because it helped improve the financial strength of the suppliers. The supplier got paid quickly but also had flexibility to manage cash coming from outstanding receivables on favorable interest-rate terms. Suppliers were not forced to use the program or pay any fees for unused borrowing. The financial institution earned interest through the difference paid to the supplier and the amount paid by AAP. The mutual benefits of the program enabled AAP to attract several financial institutions to the program as well as a large number of its top suppliers.[111]

When Black Swans Drop In

Some types of very rare, high-impact disruptions lead to novel responses, such as a clever way to create a beneficial relationship between a company, its cash-strapped suppliers, and risk-averse bankers. Other types of disruptions, however, have less idiosyncratic causes and more frequently felt effects. For these kinds of disruptions, companies can prepare options prior to the disruption that accelerate recovery and mitigate impact. Many of these preparations also help when some unpredictable phenomenon hurtles the company, industry, or the economy toward a crisis.

6

AN OUNCE OF PREPARATION

The likelihood that a specific high-impact disruption will take place at a particular time at a given location is very small. However, the probability that something significant will happen somewhere, sometime during a year and disrupt a multinational company with dozens of facilities and many thousands of suppliers across the globe is not small at all. "I have 14,000 suppliers. I guarantee that with 14,000 suppliers, at least one of them is not performing well today," said Tom Linton, chief procurement and supply chain officer at Flextronics.

One role of risk managers is to prepare options for crisis managers and their teams. An option represents the right, but not the obligation, to take a certain action. The type of option discussed here is not a financial option but rather a so-called *real option* or investment that gives crisis managers a tool or capability that they can use, at their choosing, in case of a disruption. To use a trivial example, when a firm invests in fire extinguishers in a building, it, in effect, acquires the option to use them in case of fire.

Building a resilient enterprise involves two broad categories of options: building *redundancy* and building *flexibility* of supply chain assets and processes. A related group of options, beyond the design of the supply chain itself, includes operational response capabilities: the specialized places, people, and processes needed to deploy redundant and flexible assets during a crisis. Companies such as Walmart, Cisco, and Intel develop response capabilities by creating a set of special plans, designated people, dedicated places, and specific processes to accelerate and coordinate an effective and efficient response.

REAL OPTIONS: THE VALUE OF PREPARATION

The concept of a financial stock option provides a way to think about the value of preparing for disruption response. Real options are tangible assets that give the owner of the option the right, but not the obligation, to do something.[1] For example, the extra inventory in a warehouse or the spare capacity in a factory is a real option stemming from supply chain design; the owner can use that spare stock or extra capacity during a supply disruption or a surge in demand. Similarly, crafting a well-documented business continuity plan to deal with a certain type of disruption allows crisis managers to activate that plan when the need arises.

Options Valuation

Real options have two defining elements: a known upfront cost of creating the option (e.g., the capital cost of spare factory capacity or the cost of training and drilling) and an unknown payoff that is contingent on some uncertain future event (e.g., the value of business continuity if the redundant or flexible capacity is needed). The mathematics of real options weighs the uncertain benefits of being able to use the option in the future against the certain costs of creating it in the present. The model considers the statistical likelihood of the benefit over time and the cost of the money over the time period when the option is available. (Chapter 14 contrasts and compares real options vs. insurance coverage.)

The analytical methods to evaluate real options are beyond the scope of this book,[2] but the general results are clear. If the likelihood of needing an option is high enough or the payoff from having the option, relative to its cost, is high enough, then the option will be worth the investment. Most crucially, the value of having an option increases if volatility increases, be it demand volatility or supply volatility (e.g., if the world has more disruptions or if the company is more exposed to these disruptions), then real options such as spare capacity become more valuable. In contrast, if there were no disruptions or unexpected demand fluctuations, there would be no value to investing in optional capabilities that never get used.

Naturally, good preparation involves a portfolio of options, including extra inventory, capacity, and sources of supply, or having the flexibility to change production schedules, input materials, and shipping lanes. Redundancy and flexibility extend into the supply chain. "You need to create fungible capacity among your network of suppliers so that you can absorb spikes in demand. You have to have a prequalified set of suppliers whom you can ramp up or down as needed," said Martha Turner, vice president at management consultancy Booz & Co.[3] In addition to creating options with ordinary supply chain assets, companies can also create specialized assets in the form of disruption management tools. Having options in place can increase an enterprise's resilience by reducing the time to recovery, mitigating customer disruptions, and avoiding negative long-term consequences.

Real Options in Action

When Superstorm Sandy threatened the East Coast, AT&T sent in the COWs—which stands for "cell on wheels"—special truck trailers that can erect a high-capacity cellular network station anywhere, anytime. The self-contained trailers include multibeam antennas on a telescoping tower, a power generator, network equipment, and cooling equipment. Different COWs offer different functions, such as 5- and 18-beam cell towers, mobile command center, and microwave backhaul for relaying the combined traffic from the cellular signals to a distant high-capacity Internet connection.[4] The company also has a fleet of smaller COLTs (cell on light truck) that use a satellite up-link to provide service.

If a natural disaster strikes, AT&T can send in these vehicles to immediately restore cellular service while the harder job of repairing downed cell towers and power lines takes place. "We designed the trailers so that the stuff in the central office is exactly the same equipment you have on the trailers that we pull around. We can pull these trailers anywhere. Put them in a parking lot and that parking lot becomes our central office," said AT&T's director of network disaster recovery Robert Desiato.[5] In the case of Superstorm Sandy, the company had five days' warning of the impending storm and could reposition its nationwide fleet of COWs to be ready to serve any areas hit by Sandy.

Yet COWs are not just for handling disruptions during a disaster. In 2012, AT&T sent nine COWs to Indianapolis for Super Bowl XLVI to help support the massive surge in cellular use that occurs when 85,000 fans, press, staff, and players inundate the stadium and surrounding area.[6] The company deploys COWs to sporting events, festivals, large public gatherings, or any time the company expects a localized surge in demand for cell phone usage. An event like Superstorm Sandy creates both a supply disruption and a demand surge. The storm knocks out power and cell towers at the same time that call volumes increase two to four times over normal daily averages, according to Tim Harden, president, Supply Chain and Fleet Operations for AT&T Services, Inc. Whether it's Superstorm Sandy or Superbowl Sunday, these purpose-built assets provide AT&T with an option to deliver needed bandwidth where demand outstrips supply regardless of the reason.

REDUNDANCY: OPTIONS FROM A LITTLE BIT EXTRA

Redundant amounts of standard supply chain assets such as inventory, production capacity, and multiple facilities offer an obvious option for crisis managers. Such assets require no additional expertise to create and no qualitative changes to operational processes. They only require the willingness to invest in creating and maintaining spare amounts of familiar assets, giving crisis managers the option of utilizing the extra assets to mitigate the effects of a disruption.

A First Line of Redundancy: Extra Inventory

"During the hurricane period in central America, we ensure we have more stocks in the region by applying a so-called hurricane factor in our safety stock levels," said Frank Schaapveld, senior director supply chain Europe, Middle East, and Africa (EMEA) for medical-equipment maker Medtronic.[7] Extra inventory of both finished products and parts can be utilized immediately after a disruption. Even if the inventory is not sufficient to cover the entire time-to-recovery, it allows crisis managers to "catch their breath" and organize for response—continuing operations while collecting data from suppliers, consulting with customers, and launching various recovery efforts.

All companies hold some inventory to cover both the average level of demand between regular cycles of manufacturing and shipments (cycle stock) and to handle routine fluctuations in supply and demand (safety stock). The mathematics of inventory management helps companies estimate the amount of cycle stock that balances the economics of production and transportation vs. the cost of holding inventory, as well as the amount of safety stock that is needed to provide a given level of customer service in the face of uncertain demand, as discussed in "The Story of Inventory" in chapter 1. In addition, work-in-process inventory is the stock held while the parts or products undergo some process, such as during shipment or conversion.

At its core, inventory provides a decoupling function between links in the supply chain. The traditional view of inventory management is that cycle stock allows each stage in the supply chain—such as ordering, production, or distribution—to operate at its own optimal rate, creating optimal order size, manufacturing batch size, and shipment size in accordance with the parameters of that activity. Safety stock allows for decoupling of activities from random variations. Thus, for example, distribution centers hold inventory in order to decouple the manufacturing process from random customer demands and manufacturing plants hold parts inventory to protect against variation in the inbound flow of parts. These operational safety stock sizing decisions generally assume a normal distribution of statistical variations and the ready possibility to reorder more product at any time.

In addition, companies may keep extra inventory for mitigating larger disruptions that could have a significant effect on operations. Such extra inventory also fulfills a decoupling function: isolating the company's customers from a disruption. Whether a company chooses to hold these extra inventories depends on the value-at-risk, the cost of holding enough inventory to cover the value-at-risk, the cost/possibility/timing of procuring alternate supplies in the event of a disruption, and the likelihood of a disruption. Holding inventory to protect against large-scale disruptions may not be cost-effective because a long-duration supplier failure would require a large amount of extra inventory. In addition, the low frequency of large-scale disruptions means that such extra inventory will have to be carried for a long time before its value is realized, if ever.

The Hershey Company is the largest chocolate manufacturer in North America. It operates two plants next to each other in Hershey, Pennsylvania, and thus may be vulnerable to a local disruption. To mitigate this risk, the company keeps six months' inventory of milk chocolate in giant blocks (so as to minimize the amount of chocolate subject to oxidation) in a refrigerated warehouse.[8] Most companies cannot afford to have six months' worth of parts, raw materials, or finished products. Yet, long and complex supply chains may have many points where inventory accumulates and can be used during a disruption.

A Chain Full of Hidden Inventory

GM faced a potential disruption of catalytic convertors when a maker of the ceramic honeycomb substrate inside the convertor suffered severe yield problems. Some 40 percent of the delicate honeycombs were being scrapped, which meant that there wasn't enough supply to cover demand. This capacity bottleneck was rooted deep in a multitier supply chain, in which a Tier 4 supplier made the substrate, Tier 3 suppliers coated it with the catalyst, Tier 2 suppliers installed it in a metal shell, and Tier 1 suppliers assembled it into a complete exhaust system.

GM averted a disruption to car production by accelerating the manufacturing and shipment processes along the three-month catalytic converter supply chain. It also identified inventory hidden in manufacturing work in process (WIP), in safety stock held at various upstream echelons, and in products in transit. Each tier along the chain had these hidden inventories and, in total, these inventories could provide weeks, even months, of supply during the crisis. The three-month cycle time from substrate to vehicle meant there was three months' of catalytic convertor inventory in various states scattered across the chain.

According to Fred Brown, GM's director of assembly and stamping in the global supply chain organization, the company worked to accelerate each stage and each shipment, reducing the cycle time down to less than one month. Although it was more costly to run fast and lean, accelerating the cycle let GM access two months' worth of converters that were in WIP inventories along the chain. This covered the production shortfall while the substrate maker fixed its yield problems. Once the yields improved, the substrate maker produced extra substrates to refill the buffers in the chain and return to the standard three-month cycle time.

Similarly, other companies, even those with lean supply chains, have also found hidden inventories in long global supply chains that could be used to mitigate disruptions. Intel, for example, weathered the impact of the 2011 Japanese tsunami, in part because of these hidden inventories diffused across its otherwise lean supply chain.

Note, however, that disruptions that take place "downstream" in the supply chain, in other words at an OEM plant or at a Tier 1 supplier, will have fewer opportunities to find "hidden inventories" and to accelerate the flow of materials and parts. In the case described above, GM was able to take advantage of hidden inventories and accelerate the flow exactly because the disruption was four tiers deep in the supply chain, and three months removed.

Upper Limits on Inventory

Whereas cycle stock and traditional safety stock can be modest in volume in a lean supply chain, the extra inventory required to cover high-impact disruptions may be quite large if the time-to-recovery is long. In addition, as mentioned above, the rarity of such disruptions means that these large inventories have to be carried for a long time. Consequently, such redundancy is too costly in most situations.

Furthermore, some materials might be subject to hazmat (hazardous material) regulations that impose added costs or restrictions on large inventories. When Intel faced a potential disruption in high-grade hydrochloric acid supplies, it struggled to find a facility willing to store four months' supply of the highly corrosive acid (see chapter 7). Finally, the inventoried items might have a limited lifespan. In some industries, such as fashion and high technology, goods become obsolete quickly—newer and better models become available, reducing the value of the items in stock. In other industries, such as chemicals, food, and pharmaceuticals, materials have shelf-life limits, noted Tim Hendry, Intel's vice president and director of fab materials. Whether because of cost, regulatory edicts, market forces, or material properties, there are practical limits to the amount of inventory that many commercial enterprises can keep.

Perhaps the highest cost of extra inventory—a factor that the Toyota Production System (TPS) brought to light—is the cost of quality issues. Faster inventory turns in lean systems accelerate the detection and mitigation of product defects and lapses in quality. In a traditional first-in-first-out make-to-stock inventory management system, defective parts arising from a defective manufacturing process may go undetected until those parts work their way through the inventory "pile" and make it into production or sale. In contrast, faster turns mean faster detection, learning, and improvement, which are keys to the concept of *kaizen* (continuous improvement), which is part of the Toyota Production System. Thus, although added inventory can allow a company to keep satisfying customers' demand after a disruption (at least for a time), it increases costs and introduces product quality risks.

Other Kinds of Redundancy

Redundancy comes in many forms. Having two suppliers with different risk profiles introduces redundancy—giving the company the ability to use materials or parts from whichever supplier is not disrupted. However, in many cases additional suppliers come with additional costs because each supplier provides a smaller volume that offers less opportunity for economies of scale and amortization of fixed costs such as tooling, engineering, and contract management. When a disruption at a wheel parts supplier forced GM to source parts from multiple suppliers, costs climbed as each one was handling a small part of the business (see chapter 11). In addition, suppliers may be reluctant to share innovation with the OEM when they know that the OEM also works with their competitors. Finally, in high-tech, automotive, aerospace, chemicals, and other industries, the introduction of more than one plant making a certain material complicates engineering and quality assurance processes.

Cisco considers both dual manufacturing sites and the qualification of alternate sites when assessing the resilience of new suppliers associated with new products. This assessment, together with the supplier's inventory levels, capacity reservations, manufacturing rights, and other mitigation measures, contributes directly to Cisco's own Resiliency Index (see chapter 7). This index is a scoring mechanism used at Cisco for all new product introductions.[9]

In addition to inventory, companies might have redundancy in their own production facilities and production capacity. For example, Medtronic opened a second distribution center in Europe after a risk assessment revealed that having only one distribution center posed too much risk.[10] A company might also build and use more than one factory site for the same product line rather than a single factory location. Naturally, the decision to operate with multiple sites has many implications beyond resilience—the addition of a plant or a warehouse will affect costs, taxes, local employment, corporate social responsibility exposure, and customer service levels.

THE ULTIMATE REAL OPTION: FLEXIBILITY

Flexibility is a strategy for increasing the number of potential uses for a given asset. This applies equally to production lines that can be configured to manufacture several products, the use of retail stores for e-commerce, or the cross training of employees so they can be moved between tasks, as needed. Plants, for example, can be either specialized (one location can produce only one product from one set of parts) or flexible (each plant can produce many different products from many different sets of parts). Flexibility enables resilience. If one asset or supplier becomes disrupted, other flexible assets can be redeployed to produce, store, or move the product handled by the disrupted asset.

Flexibility and redundancy complement each other. Redundancy—in particular extra inventory—provides near-instantaneous coverage, but only for a finite duration. Flexibility can cover longer duration disruptions with a shift in asset deployment but may take time to implement. Thus, redundancy provides time for organizations to "fire up" their flexible assets by reconfiguring equipment, repurposing machinery, contacting alternate suppliers, reassigning personnel, shipping raw materials to the back-up facility, and so forth. Both redundancy and flexibility are means to reduce the white-space gap between the moment of disruption and the beginning of recovered production, service, and supply.

Flexible Manufacturing: The Option to Make Anything

Flexibility ensures that when the chips are down, they are not down for long. For example, a 2003 tornado ripped the roof off of P&G's Pringles chips plant in Jackson, Tennessee. The damage threatened the snack supplies of the company's United States, Latin American, and Asian customers. Fortunately, P&G had a second plant in Mechelen, Belgium, that also could make Pringles. P&G ordered extra raw materials with an accelerated lead-time, boosted production in Belgium, and also tapped European inventories to help cover the shortfall in US production.

Flexing the remaining capacity did take some work, however. Only two packing lines in Belgium could run the Asian SKUs as a result of case-count differences (14 vs. 18 units per case). And a special quality assurance team had to be formed to oversee production of the unique flavors needed for Japanese products. Overall, the Belgium plant delivered 18.6 million cans of crispy chips, and P&G discovered some opportunities to improve its supply chain.[11]

Full flexibility—being able to make anything anywhere—is usually prohibitively expensive or infeasible. The natural and economical specialization of machine tools and labor imply that full flexibility is too costly. Yet research shows that a company can achieve extremely high levels of flexibility at the enterprise level with only a modest amount of flexibility at the plant level.[12] The strategy requires that each plant be able to make just two different products but arranging this flexibility in a special way.

For example, imagine having four factories, A, B, C, and D and four products, 1, 2, 3, and 4 with a particular pattern of flexibility: factory A can make products 1 and 2; factory B can make products 2 and 3, factory C can make products 3 and 4, and factory D can make products 4 and 1. If factory B gets disrupted, threatening deliveries of products 2 and 3, then both factories A and C can chip in to cover for the loss of factory B. Even if factory C is already running at capacity, it can still take over production of product 3 by shifting C's responsibilities for product 4 to factory D. As long as some spare capacity exists somewhere in the network, production can be shifted. By creating a "daisy chain" of product assignments to factories, the company can literally shift production around the network and create a system that is flexible enough to make every product even if one facility is disrupted.

Flexibility requires some amount of system-wide redundancy. Assuming in the example above that each factory has the same capacity and that product demand is the same, this flexibility strategy would require each factory to boost production by about 33 percent on the average to cover for the disrupted fourth factory. Of course, part of the benefit of such an arrangement is that the extra capacity is needed on the average and not necessarily in each plant. As with the case of surge capacity at second-source suppliers, a company might use overtime, an additional shift, or might delay routine maintenance to boost production on a temporary basis.

Flexible Distribution Networks: Emergency Realignment

Walmart's wide selection and everyday low-price strategy depends on the smooth functioning of its distribution network. Walmart has 158 distribution centers (DCs) in the United States, with each DC serving about 90 to 100 stores within a 200-mile radius.[13] If a distribution center goes down on account of weather, natural disaster, power outage, or other problems at the facility, then timely replenishment to that DC's regional network of stores would stop. To prepare for these types of emergencies, each DC has two or three nearby DCs that are designated as back-ups. If one DC goes down, an emergency realignment of the service areas of the backup DCs fills in for the disabled DC.

This flexibility requires that Walmart have some spare capacity in each DC so that it can continue to serve its original region while also contributing to serving the region that has a disabled DC. Although a simplistic analysis would suggest that each of the two or three backup DCs would need between 33 and 50 percent extra capacity to make up for a 100 percent loss of another DC, the required redundant capacity is much smaller. First, each backup DC can increase its output through overtime and extra labor. More important, the dense DC coverage means that as the backup DCs devote a fraction of their capacity to serving the region of the missing DC, a shortage may take place for the regions served by the backup DCs. But those DC also have backup DCs who can help to make up any capacity shortage of the original backup DCs.

As part of its desire to provide faster and same-day service to its customers, Amazon embarked in 2011 on an ambitious program of building dozens of fulfillment centers around the United States. While intended to support its aggressive service level targets, the large number of facilities naturally allows the company to back up each one in case of a disruption, adding to Amazon's resilience.

Risk Pooling: Aggregation Aids Mitigation

Risk pooling is a statistical phenomenon by which flexible systems have lower volatility risks than do specialized systems. For example, Dr. Pepper Snapple Group (DPS) built its Victorville, California, plant with flexible bottling lines that can each handle both cold- and hot-fill products, including carbonated soft drinks, energy drinks, teas, juices, and bottled water. Moreover, each line can handle different container sizes.[14] The flexibility to make different products on the same equipment enables risk pooling—a reduction in overall risk or volatility by aggregating across multiple risks or volatilities.

Demand volatility of the individual bottle sizes and flavors is high owing to fickle consumer preferences, retailer promotions, seasonality, and weather. If each variety and size of beverage used a different bottling line, utilizations of each line would also be very volatile and many lines would be idle much of the time while others ran out of capacity. Yet, demand volatility for beverages overall is much lower—people drink something every day—so that each day the demand for a given flavor or type may be down while another one is up. On average, such random variations tend to cancel each other out and consequently the volatility of utilizing a flexible bottling line will be lower than the volatility of the demand for each flavor or size.

Risk pooling works especially well with product variants that are negatively correlated; if people buy more of a certain brand of breakfast cereal on a given day, chances are that sales of a competing brand will be lower. The total sales of breakfast cereals, however, will be less volatile from one day to the next than the sales of any given brand. This is also the reason why central holding of inventory in distribution centers reduces the overall levels of inventory required to serve retail stores subject to random demand variations. Even if purchases are independent, risk pooling reduces the amount of inventory required to provide a given service level. For independent and identical retail outlets, the required inventory will be reduced in proportion to the square root of the number of outlets served. (Of course, concentrating many assets in a single facility creates a different risk.)

Risk pooling is primarily a strategy to reduce operational demand volatility. But it is also an element of flexibility that can be helpful during times of disruption. For example, if a major natural disaster creates a surge in demand for bottled water, or if an equipment failure at a flavoring supplier prevents making some products, Dr. Pepper Snapple can shift production quickly at modest cost.

Flexible Inventory: Postponement

Postponement is a manufacturing strategy and a supply chain architecture in which a particular intermediate product can be quickly customized into any one of many different finished goods. It involves a design of the product and the production process so that the point of differentiation is delayed as much as possible. Rather than hold extensive inventories of each finished product variant, the company holds inventory in an unfinished intermediate state and performs the last step (customization) when it gets a firm order or when demand is more certain. The benefits of postponement arise from the mathematical fact that the required safety stock inventory of the unfinished product is relatively low as a result of risk pooling—the inventory of unfinished product benefits from the averaging of the demand for all the variants. The customized product can then be made to order or very close to the selling season when demand projections are relatively accurate.

Companies that have used postponement strategies include HP (printers customized for different countries),[15] Reebok (sports fan apparel customized to various team stars),[16] many automotive manufacturers (using the same "platform" for several models), Bic (retail packaging postponement),[17] paint manufacturers (cans of paint customized to different colors), and many others.

Although postponement is primarily a way to handle demand-side risks, it also can help during a supply disruption. Having inventory of semifinished products means that the finished product can be allocated to the most important customers in case of a shortage.

Range Forecasting: Quantifying Flexibility

Range forecasting is also a way for managing volatility in the supply chain, especially on the demand side. "Everyone is worried about supply risk, but what is worse is demand risk," said Charlotte Diener, senior vice president for global supply chain operations at On Semiconductor. On Semiconductor faced a serious problem when a customer forecasted high demand that never appeared. "We were ramping up our capabilities and our production, and our customer's forecast dropped like a rock," she says. "In one month, it looked like we had less than a week of product supply, and at the end, we had more than 40 weeks of supply." Now, the company uses range forecasting to manage the risks.[18]

Rather than estimate a single number for the expected demand or the number of items to be manufactured, a range forecast includes two or more estimates spanning the likely range of values for the demand, such as a high, medium, and low value. Understanding the range lets a company estimate how much flexibility it really needs and enables it to manage the volatility with a robust plan. More important, it "socializes" the company to expect changes and react to them—be they demand volatility or supply disruptions.

Companies can also use range forecasts to establish contingencies with suppliers. For example, HP uses range forecasts to establish a flexible portfolio of contracts with suppliers for each new product. HP will contract for parts based on the "low" estimate (which HP is sure it can sell) using guaranteed-purchase contracts to get a low price for the guaranteed volume. For the medium-level of estimated demand—which may be the expected demand—the company uses flexible terms in the supply contract. That is, HP tells the supplier that the supplier will get orders for some quantity between the low and high estimates, with no guarantee that anything will actually be purchased. Such contracts involve specifications of optional increased quantities with the associated payment terms and sometimes capacity-option purchases. For the highest estimate, HP does not contract with any supplier. Instead, if demand is very high, the company will use existing suppliers and the spot market. Even if the spot market price is quite high, the high demand for the product will ensure that the volume of sales provides sufficient margins.[19]

Similarly, Jabil Circuit, Inc., uses flexible supply contracts that might specify a +25 percent capacity boost with a one-week notice, and a +100 percent boost with four weeks' notice. The most important lever for increasing supply chain flexibility is supply assurance, sought by 72 percent of global executives in a 2011 survey.[20] The survey found that companies with flexible supply chains worked with key suppliers to develop a preferential delivery schedule in case of capacity constraints. They also collaborated to have processes with a maximum of both upward and downward flexibility so that suppliers become more comfortable with fluctuations, which may be due to forecast errors, demand surges, or supply disruptions.

READY FOR THE WORST: BUSINESS CONTINUITY PLANS

General Dwight Eisenhower, supreme commander of Allied Forces in World War II and the 34th president of the United States, said,

"In preparing for battle I have always found that plans are useless, but planning is indispensable."[21] Business continuity planning (BCP) is a process for preparing disruption responses. "The collective Intel response underscores the importance of creating and sustaining a well-prepared response and recovery capability. Speed is vital," said Jackie Sturm, Intel's vice president and general manager of global sourcing and procurement about Intel's response to the 2008 earthquake in Sichuan near Intel's Chengdu facility.

When the Going Gets Tough, the Tough Use Playbooks

Since 2008, Cisco has created 14 supply chain incident management playbooks. The playbooks—Cisco's term for BCP—cover relatively high-likelihood disruptive events. The company's attitude toward the playbooks is, "if you get caught twice, then shame on you."[22] The playbooks vary across locations, depending on the types of disruptions typically experienced at those locations. For example, Texas has tornados whereas Thailand has monsoons and floods. According to research by Cranfield University's Uta Jüttner, the top contingencies covered by BCP include loss of IT (91 percent of organizations surveyed have plans covering that), followed by fire (68%), loss of a site (62%), employee health and safety (52%), loss of suppliers (43%), terrorist damage (37%), and pressure group protest (22%).[23]

Cisco creates a new playbook by pulling together relevant elements of existing playbooks and using supply chain risk management (SCRM) analytics and know-how. After each incident, Cisco reviews its response and the responses of suppliers to collect the lessons and improve the playbook (or create a new one) for the future. After the Thai floods of 2011, for example, Cisco looked at how suppliers handled the floods (e.g., how they moved delicate test equipment to the second floor or built barriers around key buildings) and incorporated those tactics into its flood playbook.

Cisco's playbooks list the types of questions vital to answer in a crisis, such as how many suppliers are in the region, what parts or products they make, how they could be affected, whether there are backups for the suppliers, and how to assess the actual impact on the ground. The playbooks also contain templates, checklists, and other materials to assist in managing and mitigating a disruption.

Similarly, Medtronic uses action-oriented BCP based on checklists. Each checklist item includes a task, its status, the people responsible, the timing of the task, and optional supporting documents.[24] Medtronic's planning process stresses the information, people, and actions required for recovery and continuity. The information flow elements of its BCP ensure the right people learn of the event as soon as possible via a mass notification system and that people working on continuity have the information they need to do their jobs.[25]

The philosophy behind Medtronic's business continuity plans is to enable the company to operate at a predetermined, minimum capability/service level and meet demand during a disaster.[26] Because Medtronic's medical device products are crucial to the health of patients, continuity of supply is essential. Each of Medtronic's plans addresses a worst-case scenario because a large disaster requires as much planning as possible in order to accelerate the response. Lesser disasters can always use a subset of the plan. As imperfect as plans might be, planning helps companies think through and predetermine how they might react to disruption, who should be involved in the response effort, and what assets should be prepared ahead of time.

Supply Me Your BCP

Medtronic also expects suppliers to create and maintain Medtronic-specific BCPs and to be able to show their BCPs to Medtronic on request. The company expects each supplier's approach to business continuity to include a plan of action, a checklist of activities, communication plans, escalation procedures, and the organization of teams, roles, and responsibilities. Medtronic expects suppliers' plans to address the recovery time needed for a variety of business interruptions, contact information for key locations, and a supply chain assessment of risks to equipment, material, supplied components, and labor.[27] Similarly, the 2013 Business Continuity Insights Survey by consulting firm PwC found that 64 percent of respondents are involving critical suppliers in their organizations' business continuity management programs.[28]

In the same way, Cisco expects suppliers to use BCP and asks them about specific continuity assets, such as backup generators (and fuel), fire protection and sprinkler systems, IT recovery strategies, and overall site recovery plans. Cisco's goal with these supplier requirements is to help a supplier site better understand how to recover the site quickly. Cisco also asks for the supplier's expected time-to-recovery. If Cisco finds gaps in a supplier's BCP, it works with the supplier via Cisco's supplier commodity managers.

Playbooks to the People

The primary value of a BCP is realized only when people get to exercise it. Like Cisco, Juniper Networks created a series of business continuity plans to cover disruptions linked to facilities, locations, suppliers, and geopolitical events. As Steve Darendinger, vice president of worldwide procurement at Juniper Networks described it, each BCP is encoded in a PowerPoint presentation that can be pushed to employees' computers wherever they are. The plans also fit on a USB thumb drive for physical distribution if computer networks are not available. Juniper created online video training courses for its BCPs and by 2012 had trained about 75 percent of its worldwide operations staff in the use of the BCPs. Other companies, such as Medtronic, use third-party incident management software to distribute BCPs to stakeholders when they need them.

The Bigger Picture: From BCP to BCM to ERM

At Medtronic and other companies, business continuity plans are part of a larger effort of business continuity management (BCM). BCM is the overarching process of planning, disseminating, executing, and refining BCPs. In turn, BCM is a subset of enterprise risk management (ERM). BCM tends to focus only on operational risks such as disrupted supply, production, distribution, and service. ERM considers operational risks plus many other risks such as financial risks, regulatory risks, competition, customer disruptions, talent risks, product quality, intellectual property risks, compliance risks, corporate social responsibility risks, and others.[29]

Whereas BCM arises out of an organization's internal motivation to maintain continuity, ERM has some external drivers for its adoption and structure. The US Sarbanes–Oxley Act of 2002 requires companies listed on US stock exchanges to manage risks,[30] especially those risks associated with financial reporting and compliance. In particular, section 404 of the law requires a top-down risk assessment of financial reporting controls, risks of material misstatements, entity-level controls, and transaction controls.[31] Although the law is focused on financial and accounting risks, Sarbanes–Oxley encouraged the adoption of ERM standards such as COSO[32] and ISO 31000,[33] which were then applied to other enterprise risks.

PEOPLE: IN CASE OF EMERGENCY, PLEASE CONTACT _____

In his book *Only the Paranoid Survive*, Intel cofounder Andrew Grove wrote, "You need to plan the way a fire department plans. It cannot anticipate where the next fire will be, so it has to shape an energetic and efficient team that is capable of responding to the unanticipated."[34] Walmart, GM, Intel, and Cisco all stress the importance of preparing *who* should be on the team that handles a disruption. That means preparing contact lists, predefining likely roles, and training and drilling so that people can quickly step into their emergency roles. "We focus on the people we need for disaster recovery and this will be based on their experience," said Frank Schaapveld, senior director supply chain Europe, Middle East, and Asia for Medtronic.[35]

Who's on Deck and Who's in Reserve

Part of business continuity planning involves preparing people before trouble hits. As John O'Connor, Cisco's senior director of supply chain transformation, said about risks that have unknown durations and impacts, "You need to work with response playbooks that identify critical infrastructures and stakeholders."[36] For example, within two days of the Japan earthquake in 2011, Cisco's team members used their playbooks to structure and staff their "war room." The playbooks define the key contacts related to various types of incidents and the structure of each function.

Because large-scale disruptions are rare, most disruption team members have other day jobs until something happens. Even in the largest companies, only a few staffers work full-time on disruption-related activities such as monitoring, risk analysis, planning, and the preparation and execution of drills and training exercises. For example, Cisco's incident management team comprises nine full-time dedicated personnel out of a staff of almost 70,000.

If an event reaches what Cisco calls the "activate" threshold, the company pulls people from among a pre-identified list of 100 to 150 "volunteer firefighters" who are on call but have other jobs. The company builds a response team and orchestrates cross-functional mitigation of the events.[37] This pre-identified list is similar to GM's list of people tapped for the 2011 Japan crisis and later ones—the company learns from each disruption who has the breadth of skills and mental toughness for crisis response.

Similarly, Walmart has a small permanent staff plus pre-identified members of a set of emergency support functions that include emergency management, transportation and logistics, merchandising and replenishment, facilities, power, security, corporate affairs, and corporate giving. At Medtronic, the key people in the extended business continuity team align with three types of activities that tend to occur in a crisis: first response, salvage and recovery, and resumption of operations.[38] The primary response personnel include facility-level emergency responders and corporate-level HR and communication people. The salvage and recovery team includes disaster-specific personnel in IT recovery, materials salvage, freight, distribution, and customer service. Medtronic's resumption personnel are mainly affiliated with manufacturing operations and distribution center operations.

Supply Chain Contacts

Following the 2008 Sichuan earthquake, Cisco realized it needed to include key external players like contract manufacturers and logistics partners in its incident management teams.[39] Similarly, Mark Cooper, Walmart's senior director of global emergency management, mentioned that the company's emergency operations center has seats for key outsiders, such as the Red Cross and Salvation Army, who help Walmart understand the community's needs.

Cisco and other companies also compile suppliers' contact information, ensuring they know whom to call if something goes wrong. Yet these contact lists have one minor and one major problem. The minor problem is that turnover and promotions of workers at suppliers mean that names of contact lists go stale over time and a company must periodically refresh the list (typically, once every six months). The larger problem is that these contact lists are shallow—they include mostly Tier 1 suppliers but rarely go deeper. Yet a substantial portion of supply chain disruptions originate deeper than Tier 1.[40] For example, data from the nonprofit supply chain auditing group, Sedex, shows that noncompliance incidents per audit are 18 percent higher at Tier 2 suppliers and 27 percent higher at Tier 3 suppliers compared to Tier 1 suppliers.[41]

PLACES: EMERGENCY OPERATIONS CENTERS

In the heart of Walmart's Bentonville, Arkansas, headquarters sits a mostly empty room. At first glance, it could be a break room with a dozen tables and about 50 chairs. Tabletop placards for different Walmart groups seem to hint at assigned seating for an upcoming luncheon. Yet the people and the luncheon never seem to come. Further scrutiny suggests a more utilitarian purpose, because every spot at the table has a tangle of power cords and computer connections at the ready. On the walls hang big-screen monitors and maps of Walmart's operations. The room is Walmart's Emergency Operations Center (EOC). In the corner, a few staffers monitor global news feeds, weather maps, earthquake reports, and the like. The EOC springs into action when a significant disruption requires a coordinated response. Thankfully quiet most of the time, the room is there when it is needed.

Near the EOC site is Walmart's equivalent of a certified 911 emergency dispatch center. If there's a problem in a Walmart store or facility, anytime and anywhere across the nation, store employees can call this 24 × 7 center. The center can also detect store situations through in-store sensors and remote cameras. Whether as a result of a call from store personnel or through automatic detection, the center can dispatch security, firefighters, medical help, or whatever else is needed. The call center handles 400,000 calls a year—similar to the call volume of the Los Angeles Fire Department. The vast majority of the calls are minor—a leaky roof or a false alarm on a smoke detector. Some of the calls are more serious, but localized—a fistfight in the parking lot or somebody slipped and fell. A few make bigger headlines, such as the attempted knifepoint abduction of a toddler by a deranged person in June 2013.[42] And some are larger-scale problems that require a more coordinated response, such as a regional power outage or a hurricane.

The Local and the Global

Whereas Walmart has one EOC for the entire company at its headquarters, Intel has an EOC at each of its large multibillion-dollar facilities located around the world. Each local Intel EOC has a satellite phone (in case all other communications links break down—see 4) and a set of key response personnel (e.g., security, HR, and environmental health and safety). EOCs in earthquake regions have out-of-building capabilities (tents, portable generators, etc.). In addition to these local physical EOCs, Intel has a Corporate EOC (CEOC) that convenes virtually because Intel's executives are not all based in one location. The CEOC includes experts in engineering, procurement, manufacturing, logistics, and even public relations, and it plays a major role in larger disruptions when Intel must shift resources and activities between sites.

Governments' Business EOCs

"Katrina was a wake-up call to governments [to realize] that they couldn't handle the response themselves," said Lynne Kidder, senior vice president for public-private partnerships at US Business Executives for National Security.[43] In the aftermath of hurricane Katrina and Walmart's efficient restocking of necessary supplies and rapid reopening of stores in Louisiana, US emergency management policy makers realized that the private-sector could—and should—play a key role in humanitarian disaster response.[44] Given the private sector's dominant role in supplying food and other necessities during normal conditions, leveraging private sector supply chains during a catastrophe made sense. The use of private sector inventories and assets by the government, however, required some form of public-private partnership for joint coordination of disaster response efforts. "Every disaster is different and a dynamic situation. We need that ongoing dialogue," said Tina Curry, assistant secretary of California's emergency management agency's Planning, Protection and Preparedness Division.[45] Thus, the BEOC (Business EOC) was born.

A BEOC is the physical or virtual place associated with a local, regional, or federal government EOC that coordinates incident response with companies operating in the communities in the EOC's jurisdiction (such as utilities, retailers, banks, and major employers). For example, the Louisiana BEOC seats 44 people, 40 of whom represent the business community, including trade associations, chambers of commerce, economic development councils, and critical infrastructure operators. "The idea is that every business in Louisiana is represented by someone in that room," said Joseph Booth, executive director of the Stephenson Disaster Management Institute at Louisiana State University.[46] Many states and larger metropolitan areas have BEOCs or a BEOC-like element in their disaster planning. The United States even has a National BEOC at FEMA's (the Federal Emergency Management Agency) headquarters in Washington, DC.[47]

"We began to see that if the businesses don't survive, the community wouldn't bounce back," said David Miller, administrator of the Iowa Homeland Security and Emergency Management Division. "And the businesses saw that if the community suffered, employees couldn't come back to work. So it was in the interest of both to get the whole community back up and running."[48]

The main role of any BEOC is to coordinate and manage a two-way flow of information. The BEOC improves the situational awareness for businesses in terms of the status of infrastructure and community needs. "We want to prevent the government from deploying food and water to areas where there's already service in place," said Andres Calderon, associate director of the Stephenson Disaster Management Institute. The BEOC also improves situational awareness for government in terms of private-sector resources such as which stores are open or closed so government aid can focus its efforts on under-served areas. The combination also improves the effectiveness of the response. For example, during Hurricane Gustav in 2008, public-private coordination helped prioritize the reopening of roads and restoration of power in Louisiana so that local restaurants could feed people in shelters. The restaurant-provided meals made good use of the local food supply and distribution resources, avoiding the need for special resources.[49]

PROCESSES: BEING ALERT FOR INCIDENT MANAGEMENT

Many companies have structured processes for responding to disasters, often called *incident management* or *crisis management*. Cisco, for example, uses a six-step incident management lifecycle: monitor, assess, activate, manage, resolve, and recover. The first key step in incident management is the decision whether the event is: irrelevant to the company; a minor, local event best handled by site personnel; or a major event requiring a larger regional or corporate-wide response. Incident management encompasses the decision to activate the EOC, call up the incident management team, and mobilize other corporate resources.

Pulling the Trigger: Going on Alert

Cisco, Walmart, and Intel all use a small number of predefined levels of alerts of increasing escalation. Cisco has four levels of alert status designated L0 through L3.[50] The lowest level of alert, L0, is an "FYI, we're tracking this" message. L1 is for incidents in which an impact is expected but might be minor. L2 is for large incidents that have an estimated impact on the order of $100 million. L3 is for extreme incidents with an estimated impact on the order of $1 billion and greater.[51]

For the most part, these alerts are internal, although the company does communicate with key customers if the customer is concerned about a developing situation (as it did in anticipation of

Hurricane Ike in 2008).[52] During the assessment phase, the company will contact suppliers and logistics operators in the affected region to assess the status of inbound, conversion, outbound, and shipping operations. As the alert levels escalate, companies activate their crisis teams, use their EOCs, and engage senior management in the response.

For publicly held US companies, large-magnitude events may also trigger regulatory reporting of "material events" using the Securities and Exchange Commission's (SEC) Form 8-K.[53] For example, in 2011, Seagate Technologies filed an 8-K report on the impacts of the Thailand floods.[54] Although the SEC lists many specific events (e.g., changes in upper management) that require filing a 8-K report, the guidance for reporting events like supply chain disruptions is vague and contradictory. The SEC leaves assessment of materiality in the hands of the company[55] but discourages "over disclosure" caused by a company's fear of shareholders' suits[56] because investors might get lost in the disclosures.[57] Some companies, such as Medtronic, have defined a series of materiality criteria with thresholds for key impact metrics such as lost revenue, percentage of customers affected, duration of new product launch delays, and extent of production outages as part of the risk-management efforts.[58]

Activating the Crisis Team

Cisco allocates two members of its supply chain risk management (SCRM) team to monitor and assess the potential impacts and risks arising from global events. Cisco pulls in the supplementary staff during the "activate" phase, when the company builds a response team and orchestrates cross-functional mitigation of the events. For example, the trigger for activating the company's SCIM (supply chain incident management) team is when an event might affect shipments and revenues in the next 24 hours. The team then carries out recovery activities to return supply chain operations to normal. Incident-related resource levels drop as the team manages the incident and resolves any disruptions.[59]

At Walmart, Alert level 1 is a base level of activity—the steady drumbeat of minor problems that occur in any large company with thousands of facilities and hundreds of millions of customer visits each month. Alert level 2 is for somewhat larger problems, such as the threat of a tropical storm or minor hurricane. For level 2 events, Walmart puts the emergency support function team members on call and uses virtual meetings to coordinate action. Only if the incident reaches alert level 3 do people come to their preassigned stations at the EOC, staffing it 12 hours per day and holding multi-participant teleconferences at key times. Level 4 is reserved for the worst disasters, like Katrina—those disruptions that damage large areas, close many stores, and require more intensive recovery and humanitarian efforts. These disruptions involve not only a fully staffed EOC 24/7 but also key senior executives.

Like Walmart, Intel also defines multiple alert levels, with level 1 being a minor local blip; level 2 being a modest interruption (e.g., a minor fire at a facility) that's handled by the local facility EOC; and level 3 being a major event requiring CEOC attention. EOCs are a key part of a broader system, said Intel's Jim Holko, program manager, corporate emergency management, "because we have the CEOC structure and because we have the emergency notification system and everybody is trained to do this, we typically get back on our feet really fast."[60]

There's an App for That: Technology and Continuity

"Information and visibility are the backbones of incident response, and these tools have to be in place prior to the crisis," said John O'Connor, Cisco's senior director of supply chain transformation.[61] Information and communications technologies allow for quick coordination of activities. For example, when the ash cloud from the Eyjafjallajökull volcano forced the closure of large swaths of European airspace, EU transportation ministers used video teleconferencing to discuss the issue.[62] The rise of mobile broadband over cellular or Wi-Fi networks changes both the level of transparency and the degree of coordination possible during a disruption. Risk managers can now use mobile apps to plan for and mitigate disruptions.[63] And BCP can be deployed to mobile devices using apps such as PLANet and Quantivate.[64] Organizations can even run a virtual EOC via tools such as WebEOC.[65]

A related technology is cloud computing, in which third-party IT systems host key data or services on off-site computer networks that are independent of the company's potentially disrupted facilities. Cloud-based shared document environments such as Dropbox, Google Docs, and TeamViewer enable connections to remote facilities, to suppliers, and to employees working from home during a disruption.[66] Anyone can access these cloud resources from anywhere in the world. For example, Medtronic uses externally hosted business continuity and incident management systems.[67] "If the location is impacted, then we have a plan which allows people to work from home. We have already changed our policy so that everyone has laptops instead of desktops and we have a system whereby people know they should stay at home, log in and wait for instructions," said Medtronic's Schaapveld.[68]

Although these technological options benefit from the natural flexibility and robustness of Internet-based networks, such systems still depend on functioning telecommunication links and electrical power. Whether the event was the Japanese earthquake in 2011 or Hurricane Sandy in 2012, many companies cited problems with communications resulting from power blackouts, damaged lines, or overloaded circuits. Walmart has predetermined fallback plans for replenishing stores that cannot communicate their needs to headquarters. Nonetheless, continuous innovations and high-volume manufacturing are bringing down the costs of information and communications technologies, and creating new resilient solutions—for example, a solar-powered Wi-Fi repeater costs only a couple hundred dollars.[69]

Drill, Baby, Drill

On Thursday, October 15, 2009, officials in China noticed an unusual increase in acute respiratory infections in Guangdong Province, Shanghai, and Beijing. By Wednesday, October 21, the Chinese health minister had declared an influenza epidemic in China. Two days later, when the health minister temporarily closed schools and universities in Guangdong Province, Cisco's SCRM team assembled an SCIM (supply chain incident management) team and put it in standby mode, monitoring the situation and assessing risk to Cisco.[70]

As the flu worsened, the SCIM escalated from "standby" to "activated" on Sunday October 25, and the SCRM team conducted a detailed risk assessment of the potential impact of the epidemic on Cisco and prepared mitigation options for discussion on Monday. That Monday, Cisco asked materials managers at select facilities to analyze whether their parts inventory levels were high enough to build up extra finished goods inventory. Cisco then asked certain facilities to ramp up production to maximum overtime levels to create a buffer in case of a plant closure. SCIM members also began contacting suppliers to determine the status of their operations and whether they had been affected by the swine flu outbreak.[71]

On Tuesday, October 27, the World Health Organization (WHO) raised alert levels to phase 4 on its six-phase pandemic alert system. The next day, the WHO upped the alert level to phase 5 as the flu spread. On Thursday, October 29, China's president recommended that all businesses close for five days and told the public to stay home, in an attempt to stem the spread of the virus. Cisco decided to close its Guangzhou site until November 2; fortunately its risk assessment showed that it had enough inventories at that point in time to suspend production for that period without any revenue impact.

The SCRM team's further investigations revealed that although there were serious flu outbreaks in Guangzhou, other cities had no outbreaks. As a result, the SCRM team shifted to monitoring the city-by-city situation rather than relying on the blanket WHO alert levels. Eventually, the authorities realized that this flu was not as deadly as they feared, and businesses, universities, and schools began to reopen. Cisco discontinued its inventory build-ahead efforts, and the SCIM team alert level dropped down to "monitor-only" activities. Although the flu continued to spread around the world, the sense of crisis abated, and Cisco did a postmortem of the event.

In reality, no flu outbreak occurred. The epidemic was all part of Cisco's 2009 annual BCP drill.[72] Cisco holds annual BCP drills to ensure that its plans are actionable and incorporate the lessons from past disruptions.[73] For example, although this drill simulated a pandemic in China, the SCRM team realized that it needed to examine its business in Mexico more closely, given Mexico's rising importance to the company. Cisco works with several dozen supplier and partner sites in Mexico and some of them are in regions prone to hurricanes. The drill prompted SCRM members to discuss proactive steps they could take to ensure continuity of supply if a hurricane hit that region.

Drills such as the ones Cisco undertakes also serve to train people in crisis management: who does what, what to expect, and how to respond. Drills test the efficacy and completeness of a BCP or a playbook as well as the readiness of disaster resources. Companies sometimes uncover significant gaps in their preparedness. When one company simulated an earthquake at headquarters, most of the event went as planned except for one crucial detail. Participants discovered that a key computer server that was essential to 100 percent of the sales of the company had no failsafe outside of the vulnerable headquarters building. Thus, the drill enabled the company to find a gap in its risk mitigation efforts and correct it before a real emergency occurred.

After hurricane Katrina, Walmart's CEO H. Lee Scott Jr. spoke about the value of all these preparations and planning—the development of options for managing disruptions. "We have an infrastructure that allows us to react," he said.[74] As with the example of P&G's Folgers coffee plant (see chapter 4), Walmart began preparations many days before Katrina's landfall. The company loaded 45 trucks full of critical supplies at its distribution center in Brookhaven, Mississippi, and waited for the winds to subside.[75] It managed to reopen 66 percent of its stores in the affected area within 48 hours. Within one week, 93 percent of stores were reopened.[76] Walmart earned high praise for its timely and effective response. "If the American government would have responded like Walmart has responded, we wouldn't be in this crisis," said Aaron F. Broussard, president of Jefferson Parish in the New Orleans suburbs, during a tearful "Meet the Press" interview.[77]

7

CAVEAT EMPTOR

The options for creating resilience mentioned in the first part of chapter 6—redundancy and flexibility—as well the constructs described later in that chapter (business continuity planning, emergency operations centers, and incident management systems) all help organizations respond to and mitigate a disruption after it occurs. In contrast, strategies and processes for managing procurement risks can help prevent disruptions before they occur or detect their onset, enabling effective mitigation. This is especially important given the engagement of off-shore suppliers, driven by globalization, which has increased the risks to supply chain operations.

ASSESSING SUPPLIER RISKS

Supplier risk assessment typically relies on the same triplet of likelihood, impact, and detectability introduced in chapter 2 but focuses on each of a company's suppliers and their inputs to the company. Given that large companies can have thousands of suppliers providing tens of thousands of different subassemblies, parts, materials, software, and services, many companies focus their efforts on "key" or "critical" suppliers, defined by some metric. Supplier prioritization metrics can include the importance of the material to the company, the availability of alternative suppliers, the speed with which a change (in supplier or material) can take place, total "spend" (total amount of money given to that supplier in a time period), supplier location, or a more formal analysis of the supplier's financial contribution to the company's business. The majority of supply-chain risk managers within the companies surveyed by the Business Continuity Institute (81 percent) say they have identified all or almost all of their key suppliers, which is the first step in such an analysis.[1]

Consider the (Sole) Source: Prioritizing Key Suppliers

To cope with the risk of supplier bankruptcies during the financial crisis of 2009, Boston Scientific Corporation, the Massachusetts manufacturer of advanced medical devices, identified which components in its product portfolio came from sole source, single source, dual source, or multi-source suppliers. A "sole source" means that there are no other readily available sources of supply, which may be due to intellectual property issues, technology, a joint venture, or a contract,[2] while "single source" means that other suppliers are available but that buying from only one supplier was done for economic or convenience reasons.

"Some supply chain professionals measure the importance of a supplier by the 'spend',\" said Nick Wildgoose, global supply chain product manager for Zurich Financial Services Group. "Instead, it should be driven from a top-down approach: what is our most profitable product or service and which suppliers do we rely on to drive that."[3] One such example is Cisco's global component risk management (GCRM) process. Although Cisco sells a vast variety of products, a relatively small number of products generates the majority of the company's revenue. These are the most critical products. Cisco makes more than ten thousand products from more than sixty thousand parts sourced from more than one thousand suppliers. Yet some parts—and thus some suppliers—are more critical than others because they are used in those top products or in multiple Cisco products, which are together responsible for a significant fraction of its revenue (or value-at-risk, to use the term defined in chapter 3). GCRM periodically assesses the risk of each such part based on its sourcing status (single vs. multi-sourced), quality history, technology status (legacy vs. new) and lifecycle (new, continuing, end of life).[4] The analysis is used to prioritize and prepare risk mitigation strategies for the risky parts.

Impact, Detectability, and Likelihood

As mentioned in chapter 1, most manufacturers have visibility to their 1st tier and possibly some 2nd tier suppliers, but they have little visibility into deep-tier suppliers. Typically, they do not even know who those suppliers are. Thus, when a deep-tier supplier is disrupted, it takes some time before a company realizes that it has a problem. This is mitigated somewhat, however, by the fact that it will also take time for the disruption to affect the company. Just as the impact of a fracturing fault line ripples outward from the epicenter to more distant locations, the impact of a disrupted supplier ripples outward from the supplier to more distant customers. Parts shipped before the disruption—as well as inventories in every intermediate tier, work-in-process in factories, in transportation conveyances, and finished goods inventories—all mean that the deeper in the supply chain the disruption is, the longer it will take for the company's customers to experience the impact.

Furthermore, once the disrupted supplier recovers, it takes less time to resume production because of accelerated efforts by the supplier and expedited shipping. Thus, the supply chain fills more quickly during recovery than it drained during the disruption. This explains why some of GM's Japanese chip suppliers were down for months following the Fukushima disaster but GM never stopped selling cars.

Detecting deep-tier disruptions quickly is essential. It gives the company time to assess the problem and mitigate the disruption—by finding alternative suppliers, qualifying new materials, or helping the deep-tier supplier to recover. It also gives the company a leg up on competitors in securing supplies. A new breed of software alert tools, such as Resilinc,[5] Razient,[6] and SourceMap,[7] are designed to help companies quickly detect that they have been disrupted somewhere around the globe, and to quantify the potential impact of such a disruption (see chapter 8).

The likelihood of disruption of a given supplier or supplier facility depends on the combined likelihoods of causes such as earthquakes, fires, labor strikes, bankruptcy, and so forth. Boston Scientific uses a *risk wheel* to score event risks and aggregate them into an overall supplier risk probability index. The outer ring lists potential disruptions such as service problems, delivery problems, quality problems, labor strikes, changes of ownership, bankruptcy, and natural disasters. The company scores each supplier on each risk using a qualitative five-level spectrum from green (very low risk) to red (very high risk). The middle concentric ring organizes risks into broader categories of disruptions—such as performance, human resources, financial—with a risk score aggregated from the risk scores of the events in the outer ring. For example, potential quality, delivery, and service problems in the outer ring are aggregated into a "performance" category of risks in the middle ring. The center is the aggregate risk score, called a risk probability index.[8] This probability index is combined with the revenue-at-risk (similar to the daily impact described in chapter 3) for that supplier to determine the total exposure of the company to the supplier under consideration.

As mentioned in chapter 2, disruption likelihood can be estimated using models based on past data, as well as qualitative estimates of political risks, labor relationships, or indicators of financial distress. For its own geographic site selection decisions, Intel also looks at the response times of firefighters and police, which may affect the likelihood of larger losses.

One challenge with assessing location-related supply risks is that supplier master data in SAP, Oracle, or other enterprise requirement planning (ERP) systems generally include only the suppliers' administrative addresses or headquarters. Risk assessment requires knowing the actual operational locations of production facilities, warehouses, and distribution centers. To this end, companies such as Cisco and Intel, as well as third-party alert services, collect data on the suppliers' operational locations, not just on administrative locations.

Why No Supplier Is "Low Risk"

Even suppliers with a low likelihood or low impact of supply disruptions (having, for example, multiple plants or short time-to-recovery), can still present significant risk. This risk arises from the company's exposure to any supplier's corporate social responsibility (CSR) transgressions that could impact the company's brand.

In 2010, Greenpeace attacked Nestle with a video parody of the company's KitKat "give me a break" candy bar ads.[9] The video implied that Nestle was killing orangutans by buying palm oil from suppliers who were destroying Indonesian rain forests.[10] The activist organization launched a boycott of Nestle despite the fact that Nestle does not buy palm oil from any specific plantation but rather in the commodity market and, in the words of Jose Lopez who was responsible for Nestle's manufacturing, "you would have to 'look through a microscope' to find the palm oil in the snack."[11]

Consumer-facing companies are especially sensitive to brand reputation issues, which is why activists typically attack consumer brand companies rather than the suppliers or middle-tier B2B companies that may be guilty of perceived social responsibility misdeeds. For example, Forest Ethics has a long-running campaign to force companies to avoid buying diesel fuel supplied from Canada's tar sands.[12] Although many of the targeted manufacturers and retailers buy no diesel fuel directly because they rely on trucking companies to move their wares, consumer-facing companies are more susceptible to public pressure, demonstrations, and boycotts. "The trucking companies care more about what their customers want than what we want," explained Forest Ethics's US campaign director Aaron Sanger.[13] This issue is discussed in greater depth in chapter 11.

Specific Risk Analysis for Specific Risks

Specific functions within an enterprise may handle specific suppliers' risk assessment tasks, in collaboration with procurement professionals. For example, the finance department typically assesses the financial health of suppliers to estimate the risk of bankruptcy—by using methods similar to the financial risk scoring of customers—in order to decide appropriate payment and credit terms. A manager at an energy company notes that, "before the financial crisis, we didn't have a very professional assessment of our suppliers' financials; now we have a very good system working."[14] Similarly, A. Schulman Inc., an international supplier of custom compounds and resins, gave more finance training to purchasing people so they could incorporate financial measures into supplier evaluations. Boston Scientific created a vendor health program specifically to assess the risk of financial insolvency of Tier 1 suppliers.

A different set of specialists assess suppliers' potential for causing reputation risks resulting from CSR practices, including environmental sustainability, working conditions at factories, the use of forced overtime, the use of child labor, unsafe working conditions, contributions to water and air pollution, and clear-cutting forests. In companies such as Patagonia, where corporate social responsibility is a mission as well as a key element of the brand, the social and environmental responsibility group wields veto power over supplier selection. According to Cara Chacon, director of social & environmental responsibility at Patagonia, during the screening process of 18 new factories that suppliers wanted to utilize in 2013, five were approved, eleven more were approved conditionally (subject to certain commitments for improvements), and two were rejected by Patagonia's CSR group.

Supplier Risks in New Products

Cisco reduces some procurement-related risks in the design stage, before engineers have made final decisions about the materials and manufacturing of a new product. "The resiliency of the product design, and all the elements of the value chain—components suppliers, manufacturing locations, logistics—are being taken into consideration early in the new product introduction process, as early as 18 to 24 months before the customer sees the product," said Cisco's John O'Connor, director of supply risk management at the time.[15] A scorecard-based tool analyzes the proposed bill of materials for 17 risk factors, such as the supplier's time to recover, single-sourced parts, end-of-life parts, the maturity of the supplier's risk management processes, and the robustness of the bill of materials. The tool provides an overall score for the new product as well as specific mitigations that could improve product resilience. The results give development engineers time to consider alternate or more resilient suppliers before the design is finalized.[16]

Cisco treats each new product resiliency analysis as guidance rather than as a mandate. Business reasons might justify using an end-of-life component to create a simple extension of a popular product line. Or Cisco might use a young sole-source supplier for an innovation that can differentiate Cisco's products. Thus, Cisco balances trade-offs between the risks of supply disruption against the growth goals of the company (in other words, the risk of impeding growth). "Thinking about risk early in the product life cycle allows us to take a more aggressive posture about how to control its destiny throughout the product life cycle," said Kevin Harrington, Cisco's vice president of global business operations at the time.[17]

Supplier Risk Scorecards

Some companies pull all these factors together into a multidimensional scorecard. In addition to its risk probability index described above, Boston Scientific Corporation uses ten indicators related to delivery, audits, and quality. The company monitors both absolute levels and rising/falling relative values of these indicators to track trends in the riskiness of key suppliers. Boston Scientific continuously surveys suppliers about their capacity, employee turnover, and the like. The company also uses D&B records to monitor financial problems such as liens, bankruptcies, or judgments against a supplier. Because 90 percent of the medical device company's suppliers are privately held companies, Boston Scientific uses third-party data related to financial risks of suppliers, including PayDex, financial stress score, and commercial credit score. According to Mike Kalfopoulos, senior manager, global sourcing at Boston Scientific, the company uses this scorecard system with only 57 core suppliers, which together affect 75 percent of revenue.[18]

Insurance company Zurich's supply chain risk assessment[19] includes 23 risk grading factors, most of which reflect supply-side risks at three levels: 1) the supply-side industry, 2) the supplier, and 3) the supplier facility. Zurich's assessment uses a detailed risk evaluation of each key supplier. The evaluation includes 77 in-depth questions focused on seven areas: the relationship to the company, quality systems, risk management practices, labor and skill levels, operations details, physical environment, and the supplier's own supply chain.

COMPLEXITY VS. SPEND

Many different risk dimensions can affect procurement strategy, including financial impact, likelihood of disruption, time-to-recovery, and product profit margins. Yet two additional dimensions that are linked to the nature of the supply base offer a useful way to look at the intersection of supply risk and procurement strategy. The first is spend—the amount of money spent per year (or any other time period) on a given part or with a given supplier. A high-spend input could be a bulk commodity or a high-tech, high-value product such as the touchscreen display panel for a cell phone. Low-spend parts might be the screws that hold the product together or be the pressure sensor in a car wheel. Note, however, that value-at-risk can be independent of spend—engine parts costing a few dollars each can halt the production of cars costing tens of thousands of dollars each.

Spend affects the cost-effective or feasible procurement strategies available to a company, owing to two factors. First, spend reflects the cost of inventory—protecting against one week of disruption costs proportionally more with a high-spend material. Second, and most important, the level of spend is a proxy for a metric that is more difficult to estimate: the importance of the company's business to the supplier(s) of the input under study. The company's importance to the supplier affects the suppliers' willingness to mitigate risks or reduce the impacts of disruptions to the company through preferential allocation or expedited recovery processes. Suppliers with whom a company spends a significant amount of money are more likely to collaborate with that company and to take risk-reducing steps, to adopt the company's guidelines for business continuity and CSR, and to give the company priority in the event of a disruption.

The second dimension is the complexity of procuring that input in terms of the effort required to secure second sources of materials or cope with the total loss of the primary supplier. Some materials are simple to procure, such as diesel fuel for trucks, PC hard disks, or 6061 aluminum alloy bar stock, because they are widely available commodities with standardized specifications and multiple suppliers. In contrast, some inputs require much more complex procurement cycles because of coordination with the supplier, engineering time for customized parts, costly validation of samples, auditing of the supplier, and so forth. Inputs such as custom-molded parts, specialized machine tools, ultrahigh purity chemicals, semiconductor chips, and branded ingredients may be expensive, time-consuming, or impossible to second-source. In some cases, intellectual property issues—such as a trademarked ingredient or patented component—preclude a second source, forcing a company to re-engineer its product to use another supplier's part.

These two dimensions are depicted in figure 7.1. The procurement complexity on the vertical axis ranges from "simple" to "complex" inputs. The horizontal axis is the "spend" on that item or with that item's supplier. The 2 × 2 matrix defines four categories of procurement conditions: tactical buys (simple-procurement, low-spend), leveraged buys (simple-procurement, high-spend), critical buys (complex-procurement, low-spend), and strategic buys (complex-procurement, high-spend).

Philips buys directly from about 10,000 Tier 1 suppliers and 30,000 service providers, which motivates the company to prioritize its supplier risk assessment efforts. To this end, it classifies suppliers based on spend, and procurement complexity, measured by factors such as geography, type of relationship, and business risk.

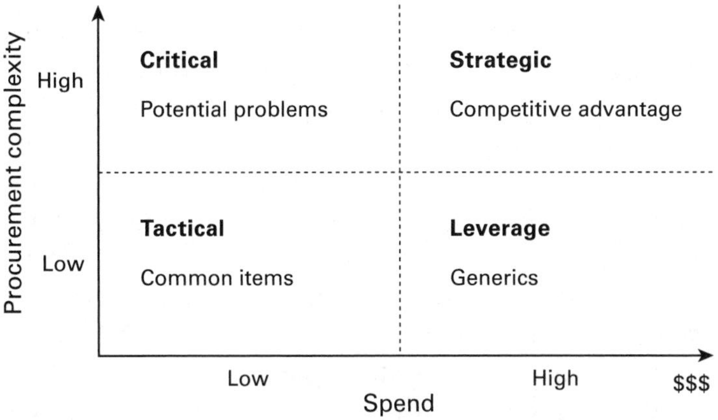

Figure 7.1
Spend/Risk Procurement Matrix

In 2012, Philips identified 497 product and component suppliers and 97 service providers as "risky" using these parameters. These are the suppliers that Philips audits routinely.[20]

Simple to Procure Items

The procurement of simple items includes both tactical buys of low-spend common items and leveraged purchasing of high-spend generic items. In both cases, second sources may be easily obtained. Thus, the main objective during the procurement process is to lower the costs.

Tactical buys refer to common items with low volume and ready availability. Because the volume is low, transaction costs as a percentage of spend are relatively high. These costs can be lowered by using procurement cards, electronic ordering, and consolidation of transactions. Sometimes, common items are managed with supplier-managed-inventory, so that the supplier can spread transaction and delivery costs across several customers.

To both minimize transaction costs and maximize volume discounts of low-spend items, companies may be less likely to second-source common items. They may simply depend on the ease of finding a second source if the first one is disrupted. If the low-spend, simple-to-procure item has a high value-at-risk or a high likelihood of disruption with any given supplier, then companies may hold some additional inventory to cover the modest lead-time required to start deliveries from another source. The inventory costs for a low-spend item will often be lower than the administrative costs of maintaining two simultaneous suppliers.

Leveraged buys refer to high-spend commodities. The main strategy for lowering the costs of such generics is to minimize the total landed costs, namely the cost of the items, including all the associated costs of delivery, service, administration, and so forth. To achieve this, companies leverage the purchasing volumes across all divisions and locations and may even join a buying consortium. If the company has any concerns about the time-to-recovery for a generic item, then it is more likely to pursue second sourcing rather than hold extra inventory. The administrative overhead of a second source may be less than the costs of holding the large amounts of inventory required to cover even a short disruption duration.

Strategic Buys: Fragile Geese That Lay Golden Eggs

"We've got a couple of suppliers where on purpose we have chosen to go mono-source because of innovation capability, price, and business continuity planning, where they can support us from different factories if one goes down," said Klaus Hofmann, senior vice president, global purchasing, at Reckitt Benckiser PLC, a UK manufacturer of household and healthcare products.[21] Some suppliers are "worth the risk" because of the unique products, processes, or services that they bring to the relationship.

Strategic buys are typically items or services that provide a competitive advantage. Companies frequently enter into long-term, deep partnerships with such key suppliers, involving several levels of contact between the organizations. In addition to collaborating on innovation, efficiency, and supply chain performance, these partnerships include joint work on mitigating risks of their codependency. Cisco, for example, works with its top suppliers on "get-well plans" that mitigate a supplier's risks and reduce time-to-recovery. Suggestions to the supplier might include second sourcing in Tier 2, opening alternative manufacturing sites, relocating to lower-risk regions, or accelerating equipment buys so the supplier can recover at an alternative site. "It's not just 'here's the exposure,' but 'here's five ways to diffuse that exposure,'" said Cisco's Harrington.[22] Similarly, Jackie Sturm of Intel said, "We stay very closely connected and so we develop practices and processes together, but we also say that these are going to be preferred suppliers."

Such close relationships involve long-term contracts, sometimes with gain sharing; joint product development and innovation sharing; and even co-investment. At the same time, companies monitor these key suppliers for signs of trouble—the proverbial "putting all the eggs in one basket and then watching that basket very carefully" strategy. "We quickly find out what we can do to help," added Whirlpool's Brian Hancock, referring to the key vendors that Whirlpool monitors.[23]

Critical Buys: Linchpin Makers

"Companies shouldn't overlook the risk of losing a vendor that makes basic yet essential parts. The loss of either could result in a significant supply chain disruption," said Gerry Smith, senior vice president of global supply chain at Lenovo.[24] Low spend is risky with essential materials, especially if it means the company is not an important customer of the supplier.

For example, both GM and Verifone depend on a variety of electronics industry suppliers. But, many of those suppliers pay more attention to cell phone and computer makers who tend to use the latest high-margin products rather than to other users of chips. In turn, vehicle companies such as Caterpillar (construction vehicles) and Deere (farm equipment) feel they play second fiddle to the large automakers who are more important customers to vehicle component suppliers. Even the cell phone makers have a pecking order. Cell phone maker "HTC has had difficulty in securing adequate camera components as it is no longer a Tier 1 customer," one unnamed HTC executive told the *Wall Street Journal*.[25] In essence, every company is a minor customer to some of its suppliers, and that low-spend situation adds to the risk of disruption.

The obvious risk mitigation strategy for critical, low-spend, hard-to-procure items is to keep high inventory. "We now keep some inventory of critical parts, especially electronics, on hand because it's such a long supply chain. In the past, we might have told Mister Supplier to keep all the inventory of little footpads on washing machines, but no longer," said Whirlpool's Hancock.[26] Inventory carrying costs are, by definition, low for low-spend materials, and the strategy does not require supplier cooperation. Furthermore, as the risk varies over time, companies can adjust inventories in sync with the level of risk, such as Medtronic's "hurricane factor" for safety stocks (see "A First Line of Redundancy: Extra Inventory" in chapter 6). The use of inventory to mitigate risk, however, is limited by the shelf-life of the material.

Strategically, critical buys are the riskiest. Dual sourcing may not be viable as a result of the lack of alternatives and the high cost involved relative to the spend. Thus, mitigation efforts should be focused on changing engineering specifications (to avoid uniqueness), thus reducing the complexity and moving the item to the "tactical" quadrant. Cisco, for example, tries to standardize parts, where possible, using its new-product resiliency index. A different mitigation effort can be focused on consolidating procurement in three ways. First, companies can reduce the variety of parts, funneling more business to a critical supplier. "In the old days, 20 washers could have 20 different controls," said Whirlpool's Hancock. "Now you might have only four different controls for 20 models."[27] Second, companies can consolidate buying of the critical part by all product divisions across the company to the same supplier, and also combine the procurement efforts with other companies, creating a buying consortium—thus increasing the spend and the attention paid by the supplier to the company. Third, companies can direct the procurement of other, non-critical parts and materials to the critical supplier, thus making the company a more important customer. All three initiatives serve to move the critical part and its supplier to the "leverage" quadrant. Companies can also couple these approaches with investment, equity stakes, joint innovation initiatives, and other such approaches, thereby moving the supplier to the strategic quadrant.

Long-term supplier agreements help to create commitments for collaboration and mutual survival, according to Lenovo's Gerry Smith.[28] When PC makers faced shortages of disk drives after the Thai floods (see "Highest Bidder" in chapter 3), many of them entered into long-term agreements with Seagate, Western Digital, or both, thus treating them as strategic suppliers. The move was aimed at guaranteeing access to disk drives, even though the long-term agreement curtailed the ability of the PC manufacturers to extract future price concessions.

Similarly, Whirlpool pursued this tack during the 2007–2009 financial crisis. Rather than bidding out freight to get the lowest rates, the company gave more business to a smaller group of transportation carriers and strengthened its connections with them. "In the midst of all this volatility in the housing market and the retail landscape, we can't control the banks, we can't control the economy, but we can control supplier relationships," said Hancock.[29]

MULTI-SOURCING

"We can't rely on one source. We can't tie our future to one solution," said GM's CEO Dan Akerson about GM's chip supply in the aftermath of the Japan tsunami.[30] Yet, multi-sourcing is not always effective, can be costly, and can even increase certain risks. The main alternative is to keep a single supplier and invest significantly in the relationship and monitoring. Relationship investments can include embedding representatives at the suppliers, analyzing the supplier's financial situation in detail, conducting frequent audits, and having a say in the choice of Tier 2 and even deeper-tier suppliers. Sometimes the relationship extends to influencing the choice of the supplier's senior personnel. Deep relationships are typically justified with strategic and, sometimes, critical suppliers. But such deep relationships are expensive; therefore, many companies choose to dual- or multi-source when the option exists, especially with non-strategic products.

Don't Put All the Baskets in the Same Floodplain

Hard disks would seem to be extremely easy items to procure and to second-source. They adhere to well-known mechanical, electrical, and software standards. Although drives do vary somewhat in performance and reliability, they are generally interchangeable for all but the most demanding applications. Moreover, in 2011, the hard disk industry had five large competitive suppliers to handle the volume.[31] But then the rains came.

In March 2011, all regions of Thailand experienced heavy rains of up to ten times the normal level of monthly rainfall. These rains caused local flooding, saturated the ground, and pushed river and reservoir levels to above normal. And that was before the rainy season. Between late June and early October 2011, above-normal monsoons plus five tropical cyclone systems struck Southeast Asia and dumped heavy rains in the highlands of Thailand. Runoff totaling more than a billion cubic meters began draining toward the lowlands of central Thailand. Over a period of weeks, the waters rose, displacing more than two million people, flooding 7,510 factories, and damaging 1,700 roads, highways, and bridges. Some factories were underwater for more than five weeks.[32]

The disaster proved that second sourcing doesn't always mitigate risks. The industrial parks in central Thailand had become a cluster for making hard disks and their components. Four of the five top suppliers of drives (Western Digital, Seagate Technologies, Hitachi Global Storage Technologies, and Toshiba) all had facilities or key suppliers in Thailand. And all four suffered substantial decreases in production capacity after the Thai floods.[33] In aggregate, Thailand provided 45 percent of worldwide hard-drive production, and the 2011 floods disrupted much of that production.[34] As a result, the PC industry faced a 35 percent shortfall in disk supplies in the fourth quarter of 2011.[35]

Concentrated geographic risks can also extend to transportation. Walmart has over 100,000 suppliers well distributed across hundreds of cities in dozens of countries, but the bulk of its imports previously flowed through a very small number of ports on the West Coast, such as the port complex of Los Angeles/Long Beach. The 2002 West Coast port lockout[36] demonstrated the problem of relying on too few ports of entry. Since that time, Walmart diversified its import network to include major facilities at Houston, Savannah, Norfolk, Chicago,[37] and other ports. By 2010, Walmart had configured its inbound shipping so that no more than 20 percent of the company's imports entered through any single port.[38] Moreover, shifting volumes to multiple ports during periods of normal operations enables a faster response during a disruption. A pre-established relationship in the port and having "known shipper" status with local customs authorities helps Walmart push higher volumes through the ports when necessary.

Validating a Second Source: Just-in-Case vs. As-Needed

Whether a company decides to second source "just-in-case" or wait to validate another source as needed depends on the tradeoffs between paying up-front validation costs versus facing potential validation delays during a disruption. The costs of finding and validating a second source may not be trivial. In some industries, such as automotive or medical products, a second source requires regulatory approval. This might require safety tests, such as a series of air bag crash-tests required of one UK carmaker—costing

£30,000 ($48,000) for each crash test—simply because the auto maker replaced the source of the leather in the car's interior.[39] Furthermore, companies may not always have the freedom to decide on the matter. As Tim Griffin, general manager of Flextronics' Milpitas Operations mentioned: for contract manufacturers to add a second source may require approval by customers (the OEMs).[40] Sometimes, as Mike Lypka, GM's director of powertrain/GMCH (GM Corporate Holding) supply chain commented, an OEM might make a directed buy, instructing the Tier 1 supplier to use a specified Tier 2 part, limiting the choices of that Tier 1 supplier.[41]

Other validation tests or regulatory approvals take time, implying that the time-to-recovery could be very long if the company waits until a disruption. For example, testing nylon fuel lines for long-term reliability and safety calls for soaking the candidate plastic tubing in hot fuel for 5,000 hours (seven months) to simulate decades of exposure to fuel.[42] Medical products makers such as Boston Scientific face a 12- to 24-month process for regulatory approval of a supplier's manufacturing facilities. However, many companies found that internal validation processes can be accelerated during a disruption by working overtime and delaying other engineering tasks. After the 2011 quake in Japan, Cisco had to undertake over 900 new manufacturing qualifications related to disrupted parts from 65 suppliers and performed these activities in one-third of the usual time.[43]

Intel's risk management approach uses five levels for analyzing and implementing dual sourcing that help the company modulate just-in-case vs. as-needed tradeoffs. The first level is a paper study that simply assesses the feasibility of using a dual source in case of a disruption. The second level identifies specific potential second sources and evaluates samples from these potential sources. For the third level, the factory samples the potential second sources over time to ascertain their consistency. The fourth level pilots a second source in production. Only the fifth level is a full implementation of dual sourcing that can directly reduce the initial impact of the primary supplier's disruption. The other four levels reduce risk by shortening the company's time to recovery.

Dual- or multi-sourcing didn't help in the case of the Evonik chemical plant explosion (see chapter 4) because no second source in the world had the capacity to make up for the loss at Evonik, which was producing 40 percent of the global volume of nylon-12. High global demand for nylon used in plastic components, carpets, solar panels, and other products meant tight supplies even before the Evonik fire. As mentioned in "Other Kinds of Redundancy" in chapter 6, however, capacity can increase beyond "100 percent" during a disruption through the use of overtime, deferred maintenance of machinery, expedited activities, reformulations, and related actions.

Double-the-Sources, Double-the-Headaches

Both Intel and GM are somewhat ambivalent, even circumspect, about dual sourcing because second sources can increase some risks even as they reduce supply disruption risks. Intel alluded to a kind of alchemy that enables unique, sole-sourced chemicals to do their magic. The chipmaker noted that second sources are never identical, which increases the risks of yield or quality problems. Similarly, GM described the casting of metal as more of an art than a common process, which motivates GM to sole-source certain parts despite the risk.

Chrysler had to recall 30,000 Jeep vehicles because of problems created by its response to the shortage of nylon-12 associated with the Evonik fire. The shortage spurred Chrysler to substitute closely related nylon 6-12 for fuel tank tubes in Jeeps. But the replacement plastic proved incompatible with the existing manufacturing process. Fuel tubes made from the substitute nylon sometimes crimped during use, causing stalls, and even caused one accident.[44]

Second sources, if not identical, also complicate product lines and after-sales support. When the Japan quake cut off supplies of Xirallic, a sparkly paint additive, Hyundai opted to use mineral mica as a similar-looking second source alternative. "It's a more readily available component, not single-sourced as Xirallic," said John Krafcik, Hyundai North America's chief executive. But Xirallic and mica don't look the same. That complicates Hyundai's supply chain and after-sales service. "We actually have to go and rename, recode, and re-specify every paint," Krafcik said. Hyundai dealers and repair shops now must stock both the Xirallic and mica formulations of body paint, increasing the required inventory levels of these paint SKUs.[45]

Corporate social responsibility (CSR) risks are also likely to worsen under multi-sourcing. The more suppliers a company has, the higher the chance that one of them (and it only takes one misbehaving supplier to create a problem) might get caught in a CSR scandal involving environmental, worker rights, or political issues. Avoiding increased CSR risks from multi-sourcing implies adding even more costs to monitoring and compliance. Pharmaceutical maker Pfizer consolidated suppliers because of these compliance reasons: "If you are dealing with several thousand suppliers in 150 countries and you haven't got those controls in place, then your risk as a business increases enormously," said Colin Davies, senior director of procurement at Pfizer.[46] The United Nations Industrial Development Organization noted that larger companies often rationalize their supply chains to a smaller number of large suppliers that are easier to monitor.[47] Supplier relationships require careful management; the more suppliers, the higher the cost of managing those relationships. The intended benefits of diversification of supply sources may decline if the companies are not able to carefully select and monitor each new supplier.

SUPPLIER RELATIONS: SOWING THE SEEDS FOR RESPONSIVENESS

The 2011 Thai floods had a significant impact on the small electric motor industry and illustrate the benefits of good supplier relationships. Verifone, a maker of credit-card processing equipment for retailers, faced a shortage of the small motors used in its credit-card receipt printers. The company attributed getting the part allocations that it needed to its good relationships with its suppliers.[48] In times of disruption, companies often rely on suppliers for surge capacity, expedited deliveries, additional allocations of inventory, or special services such as re-engineering a component to work around a disrupted supply of a deep-tier raw material. Although suppliers certainly have every incentive to recover quickly, they may prioritize their recovery efforts or allocate limited inventory or capacity to different customers. The customer's historic relationship with the supplier (as well as the spend and the importance of the customer) affects the supplier's choices. Thus, good supplier relationships can make a difference in times of need.

Fears of Tier 2 Tears: Cascading Requirements

Recall that shortly after the 2011 Japan earthquake and tsunami, GM estimated that only about 390 parts might be disrupted based on GM's knowledge that it had two dozen Tier 1 suppliers in the damaged area. Yet the actual number of affected parts was nearly 6,000, owing to hidden impacts on deeper-tier suppliers into which GM, like many companies, had poor visibility. Similarly, Intel's Sturm said, "We're trying to understand the sub-supply chain wherever it's possible and where our suppliers will share that information." One major challenge is the natural reticence of suppliers because a supplier's suppliers, the materials they procure, and the relationships between the companies are proprietary and are part of the supplier's competitive advantage.

Rather than try to extract sensitive commercial information about the deeper-tier suppliers, some companies are encouraging their Tier 1 suppliers to manage their Tier 2 risks with the intent that Tier 2 suppliers will manage the Tier 3 risks, and so on. Boston Scientific trains Tier 1 suppliers on its supplier scorecard system so they can use the system for their own suppliers. According to Tim Harden, AT&T's president of supply chain and fleet operations, the company "requires Tier 1 suppliers to ensure that they are protected against Tier 2 suppliers' failure." During both the Japanese earthquake and the Thai floods, AT&T avoided disruption because its Tier 1 suppliers had geographically dispersed the next tier of suppliers. Likewise, Tanya Bolden, program manager for the Auto Industry Action Group, said that "auto makers are relying on their large, direct suppliers to 'cascade training on safety and other workplace issues to their subcontractors.'"[49]

Tim Hendry, Intel's vice president, technology and manufacturing group and director of fab materials said, "We're trying to get our suppliers to work with their sub-suppliers on their resiliencies, sitting down and discussing their business continuity plans." Intel's expectations for suppliers' business continuity planning (BCP) include deeper-tier risk assessment by asking suppliers to consider the following questions:[50]

- Have you discussed business continuity with your critical suppliers?
- Do you have contingency plans in place if they cannot deliver to you?
- Are secondary sources available for critical suppliers? How quickly could these be activated during an emergency?
- Do your inventory and spare parts strategies allow sufficient buffer to ensure operations are not disrupted?
- Are engineering workarounds an option for extended supplier outages?

Intel's contracts with suppliers stipulate downtime, process flow, and security requirements,[51] and the company publishes its expectations for supplier BCP.[52] Similarly, to ensure it has the relevant information, Cisco surveys approximately 700 of its top suppliers and partners twice a year on BCP issues.[53]

How to Ensure Less Force Majeure

Many supply contracts include "force majeure" clauses to cover events in which one party fails to perform as a result of natural and unavoidable catastrophes that are beyond its control. A declaration of force majeure lets a supplier avoid breach of contract penalties when faced with so-called acts of God or other overwhelming events. The number of companies reporting force majeure invocations was one in ten in 2009.[54] By 2011, almost a quarter of the companies surveyed had experienced a force majeure disruption in the preceding 12 months. Within the manufacturing sector, the 2011 rate was 44 percent.[55]

Yet companies don't want force majeure to be an easy excuse for suppliers' failures to manage risks. Cisco's contracts, for example, have time-to-recovery requirements that supersede force majeure.[56] And Cisco is not alone; a 2011 BCI survey found that 40 percent of companies were using business continuity issues to negotiate greater specificity in force majeure contract clauses.[57] They are asking their suppliers to use BCP, to commit to recovery times, and are negotiating the types of events excluded or included in force majeure. Even if the disruption is beyond the control of the supplier, customers might expect and require the supplier to recover quickly.

Under applicable contract law and intellectual property rights laws, a customer normally has no rights to make, say, a proprietary chemical or part, even if the supplier were disrupted, bankrupt, or simply decided to stop making the material. To avoid these kinds of situations, Intel negotiates "have made" rights with certain suppliers so that Intel could take the proprietary methods to a second source or use them internally if need be. Although Intel has never had to exercise these rights, such contract terms help motivate the supplier to manage risks more effectively, according to Intel's Sturm. Similarly, Cisco has manufacturing rights agreements with certain suppliers if strategies such as last time-buys (in which the company makes one last buy of all the parts it might need for the life of a product relying on that part or until it can find another source of supply) are not feasible. Under these agreements, if the supplier's financial strength falls below a certain threshold, regardless of the reason for it, Cisco can take control of the operation with other subcontractors.[58]

Becoming a Customer of Choice

"The customer is king" does not prevail in all industries. Powerful companies who previously browbeat suppliers for price concessions are seeing a changing world. "We're operating in a world where suppliers are very powerful. There aren't too many places we can get spare parts for Rolls-Royce engines," said Paul Alexander, head of procurement at British Airways (BA).[59] "Airlines are heavily fragmented—BA has about 2.5 per cent of the industry—and the supply base is often heavily consolidated or monopolistic," Alexander continued.[60] "We're moving into a world of scarcity, particularly because of the growth of India and China." Instead of seeing competition between suppliers, he added, "my biggest challenge is competing with other buyers."[61]

BA's solution is to become the "customer of choice," so that BA gets the best possible treatment. "We aspire to enter a relationship with our suppliers where they value us, where they really want to work with us." BA's goal in an environment of strong suppliers is to "do our very best to make sure that [vendors] know we care, know we value what they do for us and that they actually have a place in fulfilling our customer proposition."[62]

Consumer-facing companies have contributed to the rise of strong suppliers. As consumers rose in power in the supply chain, competition among retailers intensified. Large retailers, such as Walmart and Target, wielded cost-cutting mandates that induced a wave of mergers among consumer packaged goods suppliers, such as Procter & Gamble's acquisition of Gillette in 2005. The same trends took place in the automotive and other manufacturing industries, creating "super suppliers." The driving force was the suppliers' desire to increase their bargaining power with the retailers and OEMs. It was also motivated by the OEMs consolidating their buys in order to better manage their procurement.

Many companies make a point of helping suppliers when possible, in order to cement their relationships. This tactic depends on the supplier's willingness to reveal its problems and its suppliers to the customer, as well as on the customer's relationships with other suppliers. For example, a Ft. Wayne, Indiana, supplier of wheels for GM's full-size pickup trucks ran into trouble with its Siemens logic controllers on the manufacturing line while starting production of a new truck model. The supplier needed to fix the problem and begin production by 10:30 p.m. on a Sunday night to ensure a smooth start. But the small supplier couldn't get timely help from Siemens.

So the supplier called GM for help. Although GM does not use much Siemens equipment in its North American plants, it does in its European plants. Using its strong European relationship with Siemens, GM got help for the wheel supplier, and the problem was fixed. Fred Brown, director, assembly and stamping plants at GM, said "We try to help our suppliers, because it's a win-win. They can't do it alone. In many cases, we do have a lot of influence that we can use to our advantage and their advantage. So, everybody wins."

The irony of multi-sourcing as a risk management tactic is that it may not even reduce supply disruption risks as much as expected because dividing the spend among suppliers reduces the company's importance to those suppliers. "'Customer of choice' is partly about supply security, so you want to make sure that in a crisis situation you are fairly high up in the food chain," said Klaus Hofmann, senior vice president, global purchasing, at Reckitt Benckiser, a maker of household and healthcare products referred to earlier.[63] A Corporate Executive Board survey of senior sales executives validates the merits of the "customer of choice" strategy for risk management, innovation, and cost reduction. The survey found that 75 percent of suppliers say they regularly put most-preferred customers at the top of allocation lists for materials or services in short supply. And 82 percent say that these customers consistently get first access to new product or service ideas and technologies. Moreover, a resounding 87 percent of suppliers offer unique cost reduction opportunities to their most-preferred customers first.[64] A 13-year analysis of supplier relations in the automotive industry found a positive correlation between supplier relations and profits.[65]

A GENUINE PROBLEM WITH FAKES

In January 2013, the Food Safety Authority of Ireland shocked Europe with an analysis of 27 hamburger products, 10 of which tested positive for horse DNA and 23 tested positive for pig DNA.[66] Food, however, isn't the only industry dealing with counterfeit goods. A 14-month US congressional investigation uncovered thousands of cases of counterfeit electronic components for American military equipment.[67] In civilian aviation, about 520,000 counterfeit or unapproved parts make their way into planes each year, according to the Federal Aviation Administration.[68]

Misery over Mystery Meat

Irish officials traced the counterfeit hamburger meat to three suppliers, which led to recalling 10 million burgers from the shelves of prominent European retailers. "Mystery meat" may be an age-old issue, but the rise of low-cost DNA testing threw a bright light on the dark corners of the European beef supply chain. The scandal ensnared name-brand companies at all levels of the food supply chain, affecting at least 28 companies in 13 countries.[69] Consumer packaged goods makers such as Nestle[70] and the Iglo Food Group (maker of Iglo and Birds Eye brands)[71] had to recall products. Horsemeat was found in private label products of retailers such as the UK's supermarket giant Tesco,[72] in IKEA's iconic meatballs,[73] and at Switzerland's Co-op grocery chain, which prided itself on organic, locally-sourced food.[74] It also affected European outlets of fast food chains Burger King[75] and Taco Bell.[76] "It is already clear that we are dealing with a Europe-wide supply network," Owen Paterson, the British environment secretary, told the British parliament.[77]

More disconcerting was the poor visibility that companies—and even food sellers—had over their supply chains. Outsourcing and globalization had created a complex assemblage of middlemen between livestock producers and retailers, making it impossible to track sources, quality, ingredients, and other product aspects that consumers may care about. (The problem is even more acute with CSR practices, as explained in chapter 11.)

In the case of frozen foods maker Findus, the horsemeat originated four or five tiers deep in Europe's food supply chain, making the exact point of fraud hard to determine. The horses were legally processed by abattoirs in Romania but then the meat went through a dealer in Cyprus on behalf of another dealer in Holland, which sent the meat to a plant in the south of France which sold it to a French-owned factory in Luxembourg, which made it into frozen meals sold in supermarkets in 16 countries.[78,79] Somewhere along the chain, someone changed the label from "horse" to "beef."

Romanian officials defended the safety and security of their meat industry—horsemeat being a legal food product in Romania, France, and other countries. The prime minister of Romania, Victor Ponta, stated "the data we have right now do not indicate any violation of European rules by Romanian companies or companies operating in Romania."[80] Sorin Minea, head of Romalimenta, the Romanian food industry federation, said, "They delivered the meat to someone in Cyprus," insinuating that the fraud may have occurred with the middlemen traders further along the supply chain.[81] In other cases, horsemeat was traced to suppliers in Poland[82] and Wales.[83]

The affected companies had to conduct large-scale recalls. Ikea, for example, pulled the potentially affected meatballs from shelves and store cafeterias in several countries and did not restore meatball sales until a month later after it identified the Polish source and changed suppliers. The impact was significant because Ikea sells 150 million meatballs a year. To deal with the reputational damage, IKEA donated 3.5 million servings of "clean" meatballs to European food banks. IKEA spokeswoman Ylva Magnusson emphasized that the meat pulled from the shelves that contained horsemeat "became bio gas."[84] The company also strengthened its standards for all its food suppliers, increased its requirements from suppliers and started unannounced audits of these suppliers.

Flying Fakes, a Herculean Problem

Modern aircraft use so-called glass cockpits with computer display panels to present pilots with a wide range of critical data, such as the heading, attitude, vertical speed, yaw, rate of climb, engine performance, fuel use, route plan, weather, and various warnings. In 2010, a cockpit display panel failed in flight on a C-130J Hercules military cargo aircraft during active duty. The plane's maker, Lockheed, returned the failed display to the supplier, L-3 Display Systems in June 2010. L-3 engineers determined that a Samsung video memory chip had failed, which seemed like an isolated event. Yet five months later, L-3 engineers detected that the in-house failure rate for display panel memory chips—the same chip that failed in flight—had climbed to 27 percent.[85]

L-3 sent the failed chip and inventory samples to an independent lab, which discovered "multiple abnormalities." In particular, someone had "blacktopped" the chips by removing the original markings, repainting the top of the chip, and adding new markings.[86] Further analysis suggested the chips were originally manufactured more than 10 years before, then used, recycled, and remarked as new chips.[87] When asked about the reliability of these old chips, Samsung said simply, "One cannot expect such parts to function properly, or at all.[88]" No one knew the reliability of these old chips because no one knew how the chips had been handled in the intervening decade. Failure of the video memory chips could cause a degraded image, blank display, and loss of data.[89]

L-3 discovered that all of the chips had come from Global IC Trading Co. in California, which had bought the chips from Hong Dark Electronic Trade Co. in Shenzhen, China.[90] The suspect chips went into 400 display units used in C-130Js, C-27J tactical transport aircraft, C-17 cargo aircraft, and CH-47 Marine Corp helicopters.[91] Two other part numbers used in other defense aerospace programs and being supplied by Hong Dark were also found to be fakes. In total, L-3 had bought 30 shipments of electronic parts totaling 28,000 pieces from Hong Dark.[92] Half were suspected counterfeits and the other half had not been tested at the time of Senate hearings on counterfeit parts.[93]

Other defense contractors had bought chips from Hong Dark, too. A total of 84,000 suspect counterfeit Hong Dark electronic parts made it into the Department of Defense supply chain, including chips used in aircraft collision avoidance systems.[94] Nor was Hong Dark the only supplier of bogus parts. A 2012 US Senate Armed Services Committee investigation uncovered 1,800 cases of counterfeiting totaling one million parts. "Our committee's report makes it abundantly clear that vulnerabilities throughout the defense supply chain allow counterfeit electronic parts to infiltrate critical US military systems, risking our security and the lives of the men and women who protect it," said US senator John McCain.[95]

"The global supply chain has resulted in significant efficiencies, but it has also created vulnerabilities to counterfeiters," said Michelle McCaskill, spokeswoman for the US Defense Logistics Agency.[96] Fake electronic components made their way into many types of military equipment, including targeting systems for helicopter-launched Hellfire missiles, mission computers for interceptor rockets, and crucial ice-detection sensors for naval patrol aircraft.[97] "Counterfeit microcircuits put at risk weapon systems and personnel safety," McCaskill said.[98]

Counterfeiters "are starting to be very, very good," said Dr. Simard-Normandin of MuAnalysis, a testing lab in Ottawa. One recent shipment seemed legit. "When we received those chips for analysis, they looked absolutely brand new," she said. But when examined under a special acoustic microscope, "we find they are all cracked and damaged inside. These are chips that have been removed from boards and essentially cleaned up and repainted and resurfaced, and they put a new [serial] number on them, and they are sold as new," Dr. Simard-Normandin explained. "Eventually, they will fail. They are on average of very poor quality."[99] Thomas Valliere of San Francisco-based Design Chain Associates concluded, "There is a huge incentive for unscrupulous people to counterfeit, especially when it is hard to identify counterfeit parts just by looking at them."[100]

Disruptions and End of Life Mean the Beginning of Counterfeits

The majority (57 percent) of counterfeit-part reports from 2001 through 2012 involved obsolete or end-of-life (EOL) components.[101] "The issue of counterfeit parts is just a symptom of a supply/demand imbalance," said Tyler Moore, director of supply assurance at Arrow Electronics.[102] "Obsolete parts have the highest degree of demand and supply imbalance, and because of that imbalance, counterfeiters move into that space," Moore said.[103]

"Obsolete parts are unavoidable, and represent a major element of counterfeit part detection and avoidance," added Rory King, director of supply chain product marketing at IHS Inc..[104] "Industry figures suggest that a single incident of an obsolete part can cause as much as 64 weeks of down time and $2.1 million to resolve," King said.[105] Although many incidences of counterfeit parts might involve less downtime, an important element of risk management is to understand and manage these worst-case scenarios.

When the EU implemented RoHS (Restriction of Hazardous Substances Directive) in 2006,[106] it forced suppliers to discontinue many products. Suppliers cited the RoHS "environmental compliance" as the reason for at least 20 percent of all product discontinuation notices in 2006 and for at least 25 percent of them in 2007.[107] Suppliers found it cost-prohibitive to redesign older parts to eliminate the six RoHS materials: lead, mercury, cadmium, hexavalent chromium, polybrominated biphenyls, and polybrominated diphenyl ether. "If a product is 20 or more years old, you simply can't avoid obsolete parts, which are prime breeding ground for counterfeits," King said.[108] In this case, as in many others, actions (regulatory action in this instance) intended to reduce one kind of risk can increase other kinds of risks.

"The Japan crisis exposed multiple companies in many more industries than ever before to the risks of counterfeit and obsolete parts," King said.[109] Following the earthquake, some disrupted suppliers accelerated end-of-life (EOL) notices rather than spending resources to restore production of aging product lines. And customers, in seeking emergency second sources for disrupted supplies, were forced into the arms of less-known suppliers. "The earthquake showed that any time there is a supply disruption, supply chain behaviors change dramatically, and risk can increase very quickly for all companies," King said.[110] "They (counterfeiters) can operate very quickly. We've seen a lot of reports where they can get these counterfeit products out as quickly as a week," added Chris Gerrish, copresident of Rochester Electronics.[111] "For simple re-marking of devices from one manufacturer to another or from a lower specification to a better part, the technology to do this is easily available and can happen anywhere," said Lim Cheng Mong, RS Components head of electronics marketing for Asia Pacific.[112]

Suppliers Mark the Genuine

To combat the rise of counterfeit parts, the US military started using a marking scheme called SigNature DNA.[113] The process coats microcircuits used in weapon systems with a layer containing supplier-specific sequences of plant-based DNA. The marks cannot be replicated or transferred to other objects. Lab tests can then verify the provenance of the parts.[114]

Marking technologies like SigNature DNA can also be used to link criminals to stolen goods. For example, banks use SigNature DNA in their ink bombs. "In one case, police tracked down a criminal and found loads of money under the floorboards of his home," he says. "Because the money was marked with SigNature DNA, they were able to track it back to about 23 different bank robberies and convicted the man for all of them."[115] Other anticounterfeiting technologies include holographic labels, serialized barcodes, radio frequency identification, tamper-evident seals, and special chemical taggants.[116]

Customers Test for Fakes

After Europe's horsemeat scandal, companies vowed to increase testing. Nestle said it was "enhancing our existing comprehensive quality assurance program by adding new tests on beef for horse DNA prior to production in Europe."[117] Similarly, Birds Eye announced that "going forward we are introducing a new ongoing DNA testing program that will ensure no minced beef meat product can leave our facilities without first having been cleared by DNA testing."[118]

The higher risks of counterfeits among end-of-life and disruption-related procurement suggest the need for more testing of any new second sources in these cases. "If you desperately need parts and you buy them with no reason to trust what they are, you will have to test them both for functionality and for material content," said Michael Kirschner, president of Design Chain Associates.[119] Yet as the Mattel example (see chapter 2) showed, the time pressures of disruption-related procurement also forestall extra testing. That places a premium on prearranging trusted second sources (as discussed in the section titled "Multi-sourcing" earlier in this chapter).

"The safety of products bearing Disney characters and other intellectual property is of crucial concern to us," said John Lund, senior vice president, supply chain management at Disney.[120] The company ensures the safety of its products and the security of its brand with a multifaceted program. "Contractually, Disney requires that licensees and manufacturers comply with all applicable legal and regulatory safety requirements and that they have procedures in place to verify such compliance," Lund said. "Our Product Integrity professionals monitor and confirm that manufacturers and licensees are conducting safety tests by independent, certified third-party testing laboratories or equivalent procedures. They also seek to verify that product manufacturers are complying with and keeping abreast of current and changing product safety standards," he added.[121]

8

DETECTING DISRUPTION

"No matter how you mitigate risk, you're always going to be measured on your reaction time when something occurs, because generally speaking, it's the speed of your reaction that matters," said Tom Linton, chief procurement and supply chain officer at Flextronics, when discussing the 2011 earthquake in Japan. By detecting disruption quickly, a company can respond to disruption quickly. "Who's first to lock in their supply?" Linton asked. Detecting the onset of disruption before it hits gives a company time to prepare.

Detection time is measured from the instant a company realizes it will be hit to the time the disruption actually takes place. Thus, it is the amount of warning time during which the company can prepare for and mitigate the disruption, be it a hurricane or an upcoming regulatory deadline. The detection time can be practically zero—as is the case with earthquakes and fires. It can also be negative when a company realizes it has been hit only after the disruptive event—as is the case, for example, with a latent product defect or stolen intellectual property.

INCIDENT MONITORING: WARY WATCHFULNESS

Companies rely on a wide range of monitoring activities to detect a wide range of potential disruptions. The goal of the monitoring is "situational awareness"—relevant and timely data that reflects risk conditions that might affect the company and its decisions. For companies with global supply chains, this implies monitoring global events. Although monitoring the entire world for any of dozens of kinds of potential disruptions seems like a daunting task, companies can rely on automatic software and devices as well as on monitoring services that convert the flood of raw data into relevant alerts and warnings.

Preparing for a Potential Disruption

In 2008, the Black Thunder mine in Wyoming—the largest coal mine in the United States—planned to install a massive new conveyer tube to move coal to a silo for loading trains. When David Freeman, who at the time was vice president of engineering at BNSF Railway Company, first heard the mine's plans, he wanted to be sure the railroad had input. The mine planned to hire a 2.4 million pound Lampson Translift crane to hoist the 260-foot long, 500,000-pound conveyer tube 150 feet into the air and place it on pylons. The intricate installation process would suspend the tube over three tracks, where eighty BNSF and Union Pacific (UP) trains travel every day carrying almost a million tons of coal to fuel power plants all across the Midwest and the East Coast. Over the course of an average year, one-third of America's transported coal would pass on the rails under that 260-foot long tube as it swung from the crane's cables.

Freeman's job was to review the plans and to ensure close coordination to minimize service interruptions to BNSF's customers. Thus, BNSF and UP halted traffic while the crane was scheduled perform its delicate maneuver on a Saturday in May 2008. Freeman also sent two repair crews with four large D-9 Caterpillar tractors to the site to assist if needed. And he had a team on notice at BNSF's Fort Worth headquarters.

BNSF's readiness made a difference. At 12:30 pm that Saturday, he got a phone call. "They dropped the tube on the tracks," said a stunned onsite worker. The crane doing the heavy lifting had collapsed and the giant tube had fallen directly across all three tracks.[1,2] Three construction workers were injured in the incident.

Freeman and his team immediately flew to the site to help the mine with the response. Given the injuries, the MSHA (the US government's Mine Safety and Health Administration) needed to investigate the accident. The investigators would arrive on Tuesday, three days later, and they had asked that nothing be moved at the site until they completed their investigation. Freeman explained that the delay would affect more than 200 trains, potentially affecting the supply of coal to power plants, and that he had to move the tube as soon as possible. MSHA agreed that BNSF could shift the tube very carefully, as long as it did not disturb any evidence associated with the collapsed crane.

Although moving the huge conveyor tube was daunting, BNSF had experience moving large objects—a derailed locomotive or loaded rail car can easily weigh up to 450,000 pounds. Applying that expertise, BNSF accomplished the move in 21 minutes. After shifting the tube, they were relieved to find minimal damage to the tracks, and trains were soon running normally later that day. By developing contingency plans in advance, BNSF had equipment and personnel ready and on the spot. Once they had gotten permission to move the tube, they could do it promptly with minimal disruption.

The Weather Watchers

In an average year, 10,000 severe thunderstorms, 5,000 floods, and 1,000 tornadoes rage across the United States,[3] not to mention about a dozen named Atlantic tropical storms and hurricanes.[4] The US National Weather Service detects and monitors these storms via reams of data from two weather satellites in geosynchronous orbit,[5] 164 Doppler weather radar sites,[6] 1,500 real-time monitoring stations,[7] and the SKYWARN network of nearly 290,000 trained volunteer severe weather spotters.[8] Nor is the US network unique. Each country and region has its own portfolio of weather-data gathering and forecasting resources.

Because logistics is an all-weather sport, companies tap into data, forecasts, and warnings through a variety of local and national channels. After a surprise blizzard shut down UPS's main air hub in Louisville, Kentucky, in 1994, the company hired five meteorologists for its Global Operations Center.[9] "Our customers in Barcelona and Beijing don't care that it snowed in Louisville. They want their packages," said Mike Mangeot, a spokesman for UPS Airlines. "So we felt the need to have a greater read on the weather that was coming."[10] Jim Cramer, UPS Airlines meteorologist added, "UPS Meteorologists work very closely with the flight dispatchers and contingency coordinators who fine-tune the air system based on weather issues every day."[11]

Facility Monitoring: Who's Minding the Stores

Other data streams come from a company's own assets. Walgreens, like Walmart (see chapter 6), uses in-store sensors to monitor each of its 8,300 US locations. The raw data flows to Walgreens's centralized Security Operations Center (SOC), which handles the retailer's safety, security, and emergency response needs. "In the SOC, we monitor all the burglar and fire alarms in our stores, and, on average, three stores are robbed each day and two stores have break-ins every night," said Jim Williams, manager, Walgreens emergency preparedness and response, asset protection, Business Continuity Division.[12]

Electrical power sensors alert Walgreens to blackouts, which lets the company quickly take steps such as contacting the power company, dispatching generators, or sending refrigerated trucks to recover perishable inventory. Walgreens stores carry both refrigerated foods and temperature-sensitive pharmaceuticals, so faster detection means less spoilage. "The process has saved us over $3.6 million in perishable goods in just one year," Williams said.[13] SOCs and emergency operations centers (EOCs) are on the frontline of detection of disruptions, especially those occurring at the company's facilities.

Keeping an Eye on Government

Changes in government policies affect companies' cost structures, siting decisions, and compliance challenges. Lead time for government regulations varies and can be quite long. For example, US legislation on "conflict minerals" (Dodd–Frank Act section 1502) passed in July 2010 with a nine-month timeline for writing regulations for subsequent years.[14] Conflict minerals include tin, tantalum, tungsten, and gold, which are mined by militia groups (notably in the Congo) using slave labor in war-torn areas and then sold to fund the continued fighting. The US Securities and

Exchange Commission now requires certain public disclosures by publicly held companies relating to conflict minerals contained in their products. Companies had months if not years to prepare for the regulations. Drafting the rules, public comments, and final issuance took until August 2012, with coverage beginning in 2013, and reporting beginning in 2014, nearly four years after the law was passed. Indeed, Flextronics released its Conflict Minerals Supplier Training document[15] in January 2013, specifying suppliers' reporting of the sources of the materials and parts supplied to Flextronics. These reports support Flextronics's own mandatory annual reporting, which was scheduled to commence in May 2014.

Other government actions can hit with little or no warning. When the United States boosted import duties on Chinese tires from 4 percent to 35 percent in September 2009, it did so with only 15 days' notice.[16] Tires that left Chinese ports in early September became instantly one-third more expensive during the long boat ride across the Pacific. Similarly, when the Chinese cut exports of rare earths in late December 2011, the new limits applied almost immediately.[17] About 200 import tariff events take place each year.[18]

Government policies affect a wide range of corporate affairs such as financial reporting, taxation, human resources, workplace safety, product requirements, environmental emissions, facilities, and so forth. At the US federal level alone, the government publishes some 20,000 to 26,000 pages of new or changed rules every year.[19] The job of noticing relevant regulatory changes often falls under a centralized corporate function such as legal, compliance, or ERM (enterprise risk management). [20]

Managing Thousands of Fire Hoses of Event Data

To manage disruptive events, Cisco uses a six-step incident management lifecycle, as mentioned in chapter 6: monitor, assess, activate, manage, resolve, and recover. The company does not try to predict incidents—an impossible task—but focuses on monitoring and early response instead, according to Nghi Luu, Cisco's senior manager, supply chain risk management.[21] Cisco built an incident management dashboard to detect potential disruptions to the top products that make up the majority of Cisco's revenues. The development cost of the dashboard was in the low five figures, and Cisco's investment has been paid back many times over, according to research firm Gartner.[22]

Rather than attempt to monitor all possible events worldwide, many companies subscribe to event monitoring services such as NC4,[23] Anvil,[24] IJet,[25] OSAC,[26] or CargoNet.[27] These services collect incident data, analyze the severity, and then relay selected, relevant alerts to their clients. Different services might focus on different types of threats, ranging from travelers' security (Anvil) to sociopolitical threats (OSAC)[28] to cargo security (CargoNet). Thus, many companies subscribe to more than one service.

In a representative week, a service such as NC4 might issue 1,700 alert messages covering 650 events around the world.[29] Many events seem quite localized, such as a shooting in a mall in Omaha, student demonstrations in Colombia, or the crash of a small plane in Mexico City.[30] Yet if a company has facilities or suppliers in the area, they could easily be affected by lockdowns, blocked roads, heightened security, or the event itself. Most alert software tools offer customization, allowing companies to specify alert thresholds for each type of facility based on event severity and distance from the facility.[31] Cisco, for example, uses NC4 and overlays event data on a Google Earth map to visually highlight the Cisco (and suppliers') locations that are within affected areas. Cisco incident management team members can view events on the map or as a list, and they can assign events to an incident watch list to indicate its severity, status, and potential quarterly revenue impact.[32] Cisco also taps "informal" sources to detect developing problems, including in-country personnel in Cisco's global manufacturing organization, commodity teams, and what it calls "lots of feelers." In many cases, relationships between engineers in trading partners may bring up issues that managers are not ready to discuss, or are even not yet aware of. [33]

Companies including Walmart, Intel, and Cisco noted that multiple functional groups in the organization share incident-monitoring data feeds. The supply chain group might watch for incidents affecting the company's facilities, logistics channels, and suppliers.

At the same time, HR might watch the incident feeds for events that might jeopardize the safety of any employees who are posted or traveling abroad. Finally, corporate finance might monitor the feed for events that affect financial matters, such as exchange rates and credit ratings. Supply chain risk is only one part of the broader security and enterprise risk management picture.

Crying Wolf vs. Missing the "Big One"

When Cisco saw news of wildfires in Colorado in 2012, it wasn't concerned, because it had no manufacturing or suppliers in the area. What the company missed, however, was that the fire affected one of the company's call centers.[34] Detection faces a classic trade-off between two types of detection-error risks. An oversensitive detection system can generate false alerts on benign events too often; an undersensitive system can be too late to recognize important disruptions.

A related issue is comprehension and response. During Superstorm Sandy, for example, governments up and down the East Coast had the same federal data on the storm's track, forecast impacts, and warnings. New Jersey's governor issued a mandatory evacuation of coastal and low-lying areas, but the mayor of Atlantic City did not.[35] Both "detected" Sandy, but the mayor didn't comprehend its significance. At a practical level, detection occurs only if the organization realizes the implications of the event and takes appropriate action. Just as a monitoring system can underdetect or overdetect, so too, the response system can underreact or overreact.

DELAYED DETECTION, ACCUMULATED DAMAGE

Not all disruptions are as visible or instantly news-making as an earthquake or tornado. Some disruptions lurk in the complexities of the materials, components, people, companies, and interactions inherent in supply chains.

Hidden Causes, Invisible Effects

On January 9, 2011, Intel began shipping a new generation chipset called Cougar Point that PC makers would use to connect Intel's newest generation of microprocessors to other devices such as hard disks and DVD drives inside PCs.[36] In mid-January, after making about 100,000 of the chips, Intel began receiving reports of problems.[37] As with any extremely complex product, some rate of failures is expected. PC makers and chip makers track failure rates and their proximate causes. As more failures took place, engineers began to suspect the Cougar Point chip. Although the chip had passed quality assurance and reliability testing, Intel began retesting the chips with intensified stress.[38]

Intel discovered that a design update had introduced a tiny engineering defect into a key transistor that supported four of the chip's six communications channels used in some models of PCs and laptops. One of the transistor's microscopic layers was a little too thin and could fail over time. "On day one or two of using a device with the chip, you won't see a problem," said Chuck Mulloy, corporate communications director for Intel. "But two or three years out, we're seeing degradation in the circuit on ports 2 through 5. We're seeing a failure rate in approximately 5 to 20 percent of chips over a two- or three-year period, which is unacceptable for us."[39]

On January 31, 2011, Intel announced the flaw, shut down deliveries of the defective chip, and started a recall. By the time Intel had traced the defect and comprehended its seriousness, it had shipped eight million Cougar Point chips. More than a dozen OEMs had to halt production of affected models and offer some sort of program of refunds, exchanges, or other remediation for customers who bought computers with the flawed chips.[40] Intel initially estimated that the flaw cost it $300 million in lost revenue and $700 million in added costs for replacing the flawed chips.[41] But Intel's fast response completely mitigated the revenue impact and halved the expected costs.[42]

Events such as product design defects, manufacturing errors, and contamination can create delayed consequences in product performance. In such cases, the effects of the defect may not be readily apparent until the product reaches consumers' hands and is put to use for some time. Moreover, in consumers' hands, products can be used in ways the manufacturer never envisioned and which reveal a safety issue. Such events spawn after-the-fact disruptions, which mean the detection time is negative.

The impact of a defective part or product grows worse with each added day. The higher the level of inventory spread across the supply chain when a defect is finally caught, the more defective units must be scrapped, returned, replaced, or reworked. Naturally, just-in-time production and lean supply chain processes reduce the consequences of these negative-detection-time events. When a flaw is discovered, the affected products already in customers' hands have to be recalled. In addition, the finished goods inventory in retail stores and warehouses has to be returned and fixed. The lower the inventories on the shelves of stores and warehouses, the lower the total costs of sending it back and repairing the defect. Thus, make-to-order, postponement, and just-in-time schemes reduce the consequences of late detection of problems in a finished product.

The Race to Trace

In August 2004, a German clay mine sent a load of marly clay to a McCain's potato processing plant in Holland. Unbeknownst to either the clay company or the potato processing company, the clay was contaminated with dioxin, which is a highly regulated carcinogen. McCain's plant made a watery slurry with the clay and used it to separate low-quality potatoes (which float in the muddy mixture) from denser, high-quality potatoes. Fortunately, the dioxin did not contaminate the processed potatoes, which were used to make French fries and other snacks. Unfortunately, the dioxin did contaminate the potato peels that were converted into animal feed.

Not until October did a routine test of the milk at a Dutch farm reveal high levels of dioxin. Initially, the authorities suspected a faulty furnace as the cause, but further investigation finally uncovered the true cause.[43] "On Nov. 2, 2004, it was confirmed that the potato industry by-product had been contaminated by marly clay used in the washing and sorting process," said Dutch agriculture minister Cees Veerman in a letter to his parliament.[44]

By the time authorities traced the source of the dioxin to the potato peels, contaminated peels had been fed to animals at more than 200 farms.[45] Fortunately, the EU's food traceability rules include a "one step forward and one step back" provision for all human food and animal feed companies.[46] That capability enabled the authorities to trace all the customers of the tainted peels to animal food processors in the Netherlands, Belgium, France, and Germany and on to the farms that may have received the poisonous peels.

Rapid detection and tracing in both directions prevented any dioxin-tainted milk from reaching consumers.[47] Yet detecting the contamination after the fact was cold comfort to the farmers who were forced to destroy milk or animals. Ironically, the reason McCain began using clay in the separation process was that a previous salt-water process had been outlawed for environmental reasons.[48]

When people get food poisoning, health authorities look for commonalities among the victims—did they all eat particular foods of particular brands or from particular restaurants? These analyses take time, delaying the identification of the cause and allowing more cases to occur. To this end, the US Centers for Disease Control and Prevention developed FoodNet, a joint program with 10 states and the US Agriculture Department, to conduct active surveillance of laboratory-confirmed foodborne infections in order to accelerate the detection process.[49]

Other types of events can have negative detection time, too. These include cyber security breaches, embezzlement, IP thefts, disruptive innovation, and CSR risks. If the effects aren't readily visible in the product (e.g., the use of child labor) or the causes aren't immediately obvious (e.g., a mysterious pattern of illnesses), then detection can be delayed. And the greater the delay in detecting effects and tracing causes, the greater the magnitude of the disruption.

The Costs of Inadequate Detection

Even when a company knows of a problem, corporate culture, financial pressures, and wrong incentives can prevent quick actions that would limit the damage. In other cases, legal liability issues may prevent a company from taking action, even when it is not at fault. For example, when two employees of Domino's Pizza created five YouTube videos in 2010 showing them defiling sandwiches (as a prank), the videos went viral and were viewed by over a million people. Although crisis communications experts counsel companies to take immediate responsibility, such a strategy would have exposed the company to liability. Instead, Domino's crafted an NGO-based viral response, but it took 24 hours to craft, leaving the social media world abuzz with speculations and making the brand's recovery longer and more difficult.[50]

Chevrolet Cobalt cars circa 2005 used Delphi ignition switches that were easier to turn than GM had initially wanted. These so-called low-torque switches had a problem. If the driver had a lot of keys on their keychain and went over a big enough bump or hit the keys with their leg, the torque on the key could suddenly jostle the ignition switch from "run" to the "accessory" position. Drivers experienced these events as unexpected stalls, and both GM and the National Highway Traffic Safety Administration (NHTSA) received complaints about the car.

When GM became aware of this cause of stalling, it discussed various options, including redesigning the ignition switch. At that point, the issue was seen as a customer satisfaction issue on the low-margin Cobalt, not a safety issue, which made it not worth solving via more aggressive steps such as a more expensive ignition switch. Instead, GM created a key insert that reduced the torque from the key ring on the key and distributed a technical service bulletin in December 2005 to dealers describing the issue, the key insert, and suggesting that dealers tell customers not to load too much weight on their key rings. GM did modify the ignition switch design a couple of years later and used an improved torque switch during the 2007 model year.[51]

What GM's engineers and even federal safety officials didn't realize at the time was that the defect had more insidious side effects.[52] Although many of the car's electronic systems remained "on" when the ignition switch was in the "accessory" position, the airbag system was de-energized. This was an intentional safety feature to reduce injuries from accidental deployment of airbags in parked cars.[53] But, the side effect turned the problem of the misturned key into a hidden safety problem. If the ignition switch was jostled into the "accessory" position and then the car crashed, the air bags would not deploy.

In 2007, a Wisconsin state trooper reported on an off-road crash of a 2005 Cobalt that killed two teenagers. The state trooper discovered that the ignition was in the "accessory" position and the air bags had not deployed. The trooper even cited GM's technical service bulletin as the likely cause of the nondeployment. The trooper's report went to both GM and the NHTSA, but neither organization realized the implications of that report or subsequent reports of a similar nature.

At many points in both GM's and NHTSA's investigations, key data were never found in all the disparate databases and reports related to automobile performance, defects, complaints, and crashes. GM investigators and attorneys reviewing Cobalt cases were unaware of the state trooper's report for years.[54] At least two investigations by the Office of Defects Investigation at NHTSA found no correlation between the crashes and the failure of air bags to deploy.[55] The complexity of airbag deployment algorithms, the potential for sensor anomalies, the potential for crash damage preventing a deployment, and the off-road nature of many of the crashes made it hard to connect all the dots and easy to explain away the various accidents.[56]

Eventually, the "dots were connected" as a result of a Georgia attorney who sued GM on behalf of a dead driver. The company then recalled the 780,000 cars with low-torque ignition switches in early 2014.[57] By the time of the recall, the defect was linked to at least 13 deaths (according to GM) or as many as 74 deaths (according to Reuters[58]).

The issue sparked congressional investigations of both GM and NHTSA, yet no evidence of a cover-up was found.[59] The matter led to a broader examination of ignition switches and more recalls. Ultimately, GM recalled about 14 million vehicles in 2014 as a result of potentially defective ignition switches.[60] Chrysler had two recalls totaling 1.2 million vehicles with similar problems, although no deaths were linked to Chrysler's ignition switches.[61] The recalls cost GM $1.2 billion in addition to the costs of lawsuit judgments and fines.[62] Between the first week in March 2014, when publicity broke wide open on the GM faulty ignition switches, and the first week in April, the company's market value declined by nearly 8 percent.[63]

MAPPING THE HAPPENINGS: WHERE ARE THE LINKS IN YOUR SUPPLY CHAIN?

Weather, earthquakes, social unrest, electrical blackouts, and government regulations all have a strong geographic element. Mapping the facilities of the company and suppliers is a prerequisite to detecting disruptions linked to geographic causes. Chapter 7 noted that companies like Cisco determine the locations of key suppliers to assess supplier risks. These companies map their Tier 1 supply base using BOM, ERP, and other data. Such location data then feeds into incident monitoring systems.

The Pressure to Peer into the Tiers

Conflict minerals regulations and traceability regulations are pushing more companies toward mapping at least some parts of their supply chains to greater depths. For example, Flextronics and many other electronics companies are using a standard template developed by the Electronic Industry Citizenship Coalition (EICC) and the Global e-Sustainability Initiative (GeSI)[64] for reporting the use of conflict minerals as well as suppliers' due diligence on tracing the sourcing of conflict minerals. That template essentially encourages each supplier to get its own suppliers to fill out the template, too, cascading the analysis all the way to the smelter level and beyond.[65]

Traceability regulations affect many industries. Although conflict metals such as tantalum, tin, gold, and tungsten would seem to be restricted to hard-goods products such as electronics and automotive, even apparel companies may be subject to conflict mineral regulations owing to the use of these metals in zippers, rivets, fasteners, glittery materials, belt buckles, dyes, and jewelry.[66] Other industries face analogous traceability rules on other types of commodities. EU Timber Regulations[67] target illegal logging, affecting the supply chains of construction, furniture, office supplies, and packaging companies. FSMA (the US Food Safety Modernization Act of 2010) includes a mandate that the US FDA create traceability requirements for certain categories of food products,[68] and California's drug pedigree law, set to take effect in 2015, foreshadows traceability regulation in the pharmaceutical industry.[69]

There's an App for Mapping and Detection

Mapping of suppliers and their deeper tiers remains a challenge because of the dynamic nature of supply chains and the proprietary nature of each supplier's relationships with its partners. Moreover, as more companies attempt to map their supply chains, suppliers face administrative costs for responding to multiple requests for information.

Resilinc Inc.[70] of Fremont, CA, exemplifies a new generation of supply chain software and services companies addressing these mapping issues. In 2005, Bindiya Vakil graduated with a master's degree from the supply chain management program at the MIT Center for Transportation and Logistics and went to work managing a program in supply chain risk at Cisco. Five years later, she left to found Resilinc. Her husband, Sumit (also a graduate of the same MIT program) quit his job and joined his wife, first as a software developer and then as the chief technology officer.

Resilinc surveys a client company's suppliers to map them and keeps suppliers' data secure. The surveys cover risk management issues such as supplier facility locations, subsupplier locations, BCP, recovery times, emergency contact data, conflict minerals, and other concerns. Resilinc uses the client's bill-of-material and value-at-risk data to cross-reference parts with mapped locations and identify high-risk parts. The software uses data on the locations producing each part, the parts in each product, and the financial contributions of each product to estimate the value-at-risk of each supplier location via a methodology like that described in chapter 3.

To support real time response, Resilinc scans several event data sources for potential disruptions. The company filters out non-supply-chain disruptions (e.g., residential house fires) and then cross-compares potential disruptions with the known facilities of mapped suppliers. If an event potentially affects a supplier and thus affects one or more of its clients' companies, Resilinc determines which parts and products may be affected as well as the potential value-at-risk and sends an alert about the event to each affected company. During the 2011 Thailand floods, Resilinc helped

Flextronics gain about a week's warning regarding the threat posed by the rising waters.

Other companies offering mapping and detection software (and related consulting services) include Razient Inc. of Miami, FL,[71] and MetricStream of Palo Alto, CA.[72] Several companies providing supply chain event management applications—including Trade Merit Inc.,[73] CDC Software,[74] and Manhattan Associates[75]—have also geared their offerings to risk management. In addition, many consulting organizations have developed supply chain risk management practices, assisting companies in assessing risks and developing prevention and mitigation measures. Examples include PricewaterhouseCoopers,[76] JLT Specialty Limited in the UK,[77] Marsh Risk Consulting,[78] Capitol Risk Concepts Limited,[79] LMI,[80] and scores of others.

Some companies, such as IBM, Cisco, and ATMI, created inhouse supplier mapping applications. However, third-party services such as Resilinc and its competitors reduce the costs of supplier mapping and updating. The reason is that they gather their information primarily through suppliers' questionnaires. Thus, once a supplier fills out a questionnaire, the anonymized information can be used for other customers of that supplier because most suppliers serve multiple industry players. Such a "network effect" reduces the costs of information collection as well as the suppliers' compliance efforts. Similar information-gathering efforts and mapping are also used for CSR applications when suppliers have to comply with codes-of-conduct of their customers.

SUPPLIER MONITORING

With the general shift from local production and vertical integration strategies to globalization and outsourcing comes the need to monitor a global supply base. This monitoring goes beyond the kinds of geographic mapping and incident detection described in the previous section. Companies concerned about supplier bankruptcies, failures in quality, changes in supplier business strategy, and corporate social responsibility try to detect potential problems through comprehensive supplier monitoring.

Watching the Warning Signs

To create a list of warning signs, Boston Scientific queried its materials employees, manufacturing people, outside contractors, and accounts payable staff—everyone who interacted with the supply base. Managers created a list of 20 warning signs and then trained employees to watch for these signs as they visited or interacted with suppliers.[81]

Some of the most important signs included financial telltales such as failure to prepare timely financial reports, multiple adjustments to annual reports, frequently renegotiated banking covenants, deteriorating working capital ratios, and lengthening accounts payable (or check holding).[82] Industry participants in a 2009 MIT supply chain conference on the financial crisis reported, however, that many sources of financial data don't provide timely detection.[83] Financial data may be infrequently collected and is a lagging indicator because it reflects the supplier's previous-year or previous-quarter sales, profits, and debts. The conference participants cited examples of abrupt bankruptcies among seemingly sound suppliers. To collect more timely in-depth financial data, companies wrote contracts that mandated supplier cooperation with audits and timely reporting of key financial metrics.[84]

Another option is the monitoring of news aggregation services such as Lexis-Nexis for indicators of business health.[85] For example, in the two years prior to the bankruptcy of the British retailer Woolworth, the service reported 4,400 news items about Woolworth with the terms "going into administration," "company strategy," "redundancies and dismissals," and "corporate restructuring,"—all clearly indicating turmoil. The number of these news reports swelled six months before the bankruptcy in November 2008. Similarly, the service reported 15,000 news articles mentioning Kodak with the terms "insolvency," "Chapter 11," "law and legal systems," and "spikes in divestitures" in the two years leading up to Kodak's bankruptcy. The frequency of these kinds of articles surged in the final months leading to its bankruptcy filing on January 2012.

Companies can also watch for operational problems at critical suppliers. These include high employee turnover, especially in key positions; failed projects such as acquisitions or new product launches; operating losses and lack of capital investments; and so on.[86] Companies can monitor operational warning signs such as late or missed deliveries, incomplete shipments, quality issues, billing and invoicing errors, and carrier selection errors. These may be signs of corner-cutting, of layoffs, and that the supplier's management is preoccupied with issues other than customer service. "It's all in the data," said one presenter during a 2012 conference at MIT.[87] By monitoring supplier quality carefully, companies can get three to five months' warning of an impending failure and can take steps either to help the supplier or to find alternative suppliers.

The frequency of formal reviews of supplier risks can vary from monthly to annually, depending on the company and the risk profile of the supplier. During the financial crisis, for example, many companies increased the frequency of reviews, especially of weaker suppliers. "The frequency with which we identify the risk depends on what we've classified as risk. For example, we monitor materials on a daily basis, but if we're talking about business continuity planning (BCP), we assess risk on a yearly basis and review it every six months," said Frank Schaapveld, senior director supply chain Europe, Middle East, and Asia for Medtronic.[88]

Trust-But-Verify Monitoring

Detection at a distance has it limits. Surveys and third-party data go only so far in detecting incipient disruptions or disruption-prone suppliers. EMC Corporation uses a "trust but verify" approach to detect emerging risks with suppliers. Trevor Schick, vice president of Global SCM and chief procurement officer at EMC, said that the company deploys 50 people in Asia (where its manufacturing is done) to focus on quality and to identify red flags early. These people visit suppliers, walk the lines, see the warehouses, and speak to the engineers and factory workers. They use a checklist of warning signs such as quality problems, capacity reductions, stopped lines, and excessive inventory. If a supplier is reluctant to let EMC people in the door, then that is a warning sign in itself.

Other companies use similar methods to detect risks in the supply base, but with a focus that depends on the types of risks most salient in their respective industries. For example, Ed Rodricks, general manager, supply chain at Shaw's Supermarkets, said that the grocer's field buyers pay attention to food handling and product quality standards when they visit farms and contract manufacturers.[89] Apparel retailer The Limited, on the other hand, inspects apparel suppliers with an emphasis on working conditions and workplace safety to avoid the use of "sweatshops" or child labor.[90] Ikea, the Swedish furniture giant, employs 80 auditors, performing about 1,200 audits per year at supplier locations, most of which are based on unannounced visits. The audits are focused on environmental sustainability and working conditions. As with EMC, refusal to let the auditors in is considered a violation, triggering an immediate stoppage of deliveries from the supplier. Similarly, chemical company BASF conducts onsite audits of high-risk chemical suppliers to assess environmental, health, and safety issues.[91]

Those Dastardly Detection Defeaters

To monitor the quality of raw materials supplies, many companies use routine laboratory tests to detect low-quality, diluted, or adulterated materials. For example, cows' milk and wheat gluten are tested for protein levels. But the protein test isn't perfect, and unscrupulous suppliers can fool the test by adding melamine—a cheap industrial chemical used in plastics, insulation, and fire retardants.[92]

Unfortunately, melamine causes kidney failure if consumed in large amounts. In 2007, an estimated 14 dogs and cats died in the United States from melamine-adulterated gluten used in pet food.[93] In 2008, six infants died and 300,000 were sickened in China as a result of melamine-laced infant formula.[94] The episode forced regulators and companies to deploy more expensive tests to detect the protein-mimicking melamine. Similar problems with "undetectable" counterfeits were discovered with the anticoagulant drug heparin.[95] On March 19, 2008, the US FDA reported that the contaminant found was "likely made in China from animal cartilage, chemically altered to act like heparin, and added intentionally to batches of the drug's active ingredient."[96]

Chinese manufacturing issues were also identified as the cause in the death of children in Panama and Haiti using drugs that were supposed to contain glycerin but instead contained diethylene glycol, a syrupy poison used as antifreeze.[97] The Chinese authorities and the Chinese companies involved refused to cooperate with the FDA and stonewalled its investigation.

Sometimes a supplier's efforts to elude auditors are simple and crude. Ikea's senior auditor, Kelly Deng, has seven years' experience, and the typical auditor in her office has been on the job for five years. The experience helps her spot telltale signs of violations during her visits—such as a worker hurrying by with a stack of papers. Factory managers may falsify records, she said, and send a worker to take the accurate records out of the building.

ACCELERATING DETECTION AND RESPONSE

Fast detection gives companies time for avoiding impact, preparing for response, or mitigating the consequences. To accelerate detection, companies can collect data more often and from closer to the cause of the disruption. Some supply chain risk services companies are using data mining to predict disruptions even before they happen. For example, Verisk Analytics[98] uses data science to find possible correlations between various incidents and impending geopolitical events that may disrupt businesses.[99]

When Cisco started its monitoring program, it specified an eight-hour response time; then through process improvements such as stationing team members around the globe and using follow-the-sun operations, Cisco was able to cut response time to less than two hours. For example, when a large, 7.8 magnitude earthquake hit Sichuan in Central China near midnight on a Sunday (Cisco headquarters' time), Cisco used team members in Asia for the immediate incident response and was able to shift suppliers and reschedule orders by the end of the following Monday, minimizing the impact on key customers.[100]

Clearing the Tracks with Better Data on Storm Tracks

In mid-April 2012, a massive low-pressure system formed over the central plains of the United States. Its strength prompted the National Weather Service's Storm Prediction Center to issue an unusual multiday advance warning. It predicted a 60 percent chance of severe weather for north-central Oklahoma and south-central Kansas for the afternoon and evening of Friday the 13th.[101] Strong convection and the build-up of ominous clouds promised a busy day for weather forecasters and storm chasers. Government and private weather services watched the skies for the threat of high winds, severe rain, large hail, and tornados. At 3:59 pm, as if on cue, a tornado touched down southwest of Norman, Oklahoma.[102]

Trains and tornados don't mix, and BNSF Railway has thousands of miles of track crisscrossing "tornado alley" in the central states of the United States. BNSF subscribes to AccuWeather, a company that detects, tracks, forecasts, and warns its clients of impending severe weather. AccuWeather uses data from advanced high-resolution Doppler radars to help spot tornados accurately and quickly.[103] AccuWeather detected the formation of the Norman, Oklahoma, tornado 30 minutes before it touched the ground. Using data on prevailing winds and models for tornado behavior, the company forecast the likely trajectory of the twister and warned BNSF that a tornado might cross BNSF's tracks in Norman sometime between 3:50 and 4:30 pm. By the time the tornado thundered across BNSF's tracks at about 4:10 pm, the railroad had had 40 minutes to clear the area of trains.[104]

From an Internet of Things to an Internet of Warning Dings

The declining cost and growing use of technology in the supply chain plays an increasingly important role in managing supply chain risks. For example, FedEx's SenseAware is a flat, hand-sized, red-and-white device that shippers can slip into a box, pallet, or container. The device contains a battery-powered GPS receiver, temperature monitor, pressure monitor, and light sensor.[105] It also contains a cellular data network circuit that can connect to the same ubiquitous cell phone networks used by mobile phones. Periodically, the device "phones home" with data about the package's location and status.

With these data, the shipper, carrier, and customer can detect problems with a package while in transit. The GPS location data can detect misrouting or theft, confirm delivery, and trace a lost package. The temperature data can ensure that temperature-sensitive shipments have not been damaged by freezing or heat during the trip. The light sensor can detect unauthorized access to the cargo (e.g., theft, tampering, counterfeiting, contamination), and damage to light-sensitive cargos, as well as unexpected delays if a time-critical package hasn't been opened.

SenseAware is but one example of a broad trend of the "Internet of Things,"[106] which refers to a growing use of low-cost computing, sensors, wireless data, and Internet connectivity to provide enhanced situational awareness and control. For example, Schneider National, a large American truckload carrier, has GPS/cellular data tracking units on every last one of its 44,000 intermodal containers and van trailers.[107] Tracking and communicating with a moving truck fleet leads to higher utilization, increased driver productivity and lifestyle improvements, fuel cost optimization, better customer service, and more accurate billing.[108] The same sensors also improve freight security by detecting and tracking stolen trailers.

Since the 2005 publication of *The Resilient Enterprise*,[109] cell phones (and cell phone towers) multiplied to serve 85 percent of the world's population, the iPhone arrived, and cellular data networks went through four generations. With 1.4 billion users,[110] smartphones provide an increasingly important data source for detecting and assessing disruptive events. Smartphones typically include a GPS, compass, and a camera,[111] which lets in-the-field supply chain workers or ordinary citizens document and transmit geotagged pictures and data about facilities and events. Real-time damage reports accelerate detection of the extent of disruptions as well as help to assess response needs.[112]

Supply Chain Control Towers

Airport control towers—with their all-weather ability to choreograph the intertwining movements of aircraft on the ground and in the air—provide a natural model for managing supply chains. A supply chain control tower is a central hub of technology, people, and processes that captures and uses supply chain data to enable better short- and long-term decision making.[113] "You can respond much more quickly when your people, technology and systems are in a single location," said Paul McDonald of Menlo Worldwide Logistics.[114]

In 2009, Unilever established an internal organization, UltraLogistik, based in Poland. UltraLogistik operates as a control tower, managing all Unilever transport movements in Europe. Centralizing all transportation procurement and operations (using Oracle's transport management system) yielded cost savings, reduced carbon footprint, and increased visibility, which translates into quick detection of problems. Beyond a single company, one of the main missions of the Dutch Institute for Advanced Logistics (DINALOG) is the "Cross Chain Control Center (4C)." The 4C vision is to coordinate and synchronize the flow of physical goods, information, and finance of several worldwide supply chains relevant to the Netherlands.[115]

Although a supply chain control tower primarily serves day-to-day operations, it sits on the front line for detecting disruptions, handling incidents, and coordinating responses.[116] In that capacity, the control tower is similar to a full-time emergency operations center in that its staff can be the first to notice telltale signs of looming significant disruptions such as unexpected supplier component shortages, problems in the flow of items (e.g., port closures or customs worker strikes), and accidents.[117] It can then respond by rerouting flows, notifying customers, informing company facilities, and so forth.

Good Geofences Make Good Supply Chain Defenses

Dow Chemical tracks the location of rail tank cars using GPS trackers with cellular data connections. If a tank car deviates from its expected route or approaches a heavily populated area, Dow's systems automatically detect it and warn the company, who can then alert authorities of any potential danger.[118,119] Dow Chemical's Railcar Shipment Visibility program is an example of geofencing, which is the creation of a virtual boundary around either a high-value or high-risk mobile asset, or a critical geographic area, along with ways of detecting when the item enters or exits the virtual boundary.

Geofencing can detect negative events such as theft, misrouting, or terrorist hijacking, as well as positive ones such as the arrival of the shipment in port or at the customer's loading dock. Some companies participating in a 2012 MIT industry roundtable on risk management practices[120] were working on combining shipment tracking with dynamic geofences around disruptive events to detect, for example, the real-time entry of an ocean shipment into the path of a hurricane.

Social Media in the Supply Chain

"Every citizen is a sensor," said Brian Humphrey of the Los Angeles Fire Department. Six billion people (out of the estimated seven billion people in the world in 2014) had access to a mobile phone.[121] In fact, more people have access to mobile phones than to working toilets. In addition, 1.7 billion people use social media such as Twitter, Facebook, Instagram, or other country-specific services. The USGS (United States Geologic Service) now monitors Twitter to detect earthquakes. "In some cases, it gives us a heads up that it happened before it can be detected by a seismic wave," said Paul Earle, a USGS seismologist.[122]

Meteorological and geophysical sensors for tornados, floods, tsunamis, and earthquakes offer only a crude proxy for detecting disruption. Just because a quake exceeded some number on the Richter scale doesn't indicate which buildings, logistics infrastructure, or utilities were damaged. Social media channels can provide an informal, real-time damage assessment because the local population will naturally talk about what they felt, what they saw, and the problems in their location.

The United States Army says organizations should encourage people on the scene to send situation information via social media.[123] During Superstorm Sandy, people posted as many as 36,000 storm-related photos per hour.[124] Geotagging of these photos, a common feature built into smart phone cameras, provides the exact time and GPS coordinates of the image for accurate data on the location of the damage (or lack of damage). Services like SeeClickFix encourage citizens to report nonemergency problems to city governments such as potholes, damaged traffic signals, debris on roadways, and other problems, leading to more timely maintenance of the transportation fabric of the city.[125]

Twitcident[126] is a broader monitoring system that analyzes Twitter's social media data stream to detect and monitor disruptive events such as fires, extreme weather, explosions, terrorist attacks, and industrial emergencies.[127] Twitcident uses semantic analysis of messages and real-time filtering to automatically extract relevant information about incidents. The initial system is intended to help first responders,[128] but it could be adapted for commercial use.

After the April 15, 2013, Boston Marathon bombing, the FBI posted photos of the likely bombers on the Internet, unleashing a tsunami of responses. Within minutes, thousands of armchair detectives were scouring the Internet to identify the suspects. David Green, a marathon runner and Facebook user, helped by providing a high-resolution picture of the suspects. Within about 24 hours, one suspect was dead and one was in custody.

Social media data, however, should be used with care. The Internet crowd of terrorist hunters was not equipped to handle allegations with professional care and healthy skepticism. For example, Twitter became rife with rumors that a missing Indian-American student was one of the bombers, flashing the accusation across the Internet, to the dismay of the student and his parents. The rumor subsided only after NBC News contradicted the false reports.

Dell created its Social Media Listening Command Center as a means to detect and respond to problems big and small.[129] The computer maker uses this "listening and responding" program for customer service and support, community-building, and topical discussions.[130] Every day, thousands of Dell customers use Twitter, Facebook, and Dell.com for routine product support. Yet the company also monitors message trends to detect problems such as product defects, negative public relations drives, or an adverse shift in customers' attitudes toward Dell and its products. The company tracks 22,000 mentions of Dell each day. "When you are embedding social media as a tool across virtually every aspect of the company to be used by employees as one of the ways they stay in touch with customers every day, it simply becomes part of how we do business. Listening is core to our company and our values," said Manish Mehta, Dell's vice president for social media and community.[131]

Response-on-Warning: Faster than a Speeding Missile

Detection leads to alerts, and alerts lead to response. When militants in the Gaza strip fire a missile at Israel, the time from launch to impact is very short. Most Israeli citizens live and work within range of Palestinian rockets.[132] That includes Intel's $3 billion Kiryat Gat chip fabrication factory with 3,000 workers,[133] which lies a scant 45 seconds—as the missile flies—from potential launch sites.

Fortunately, radar in Israel can detect the attack and estimate the missile's trajectory within one second[134] and relay the signal to a central monitoring facility that then activates sirens and SMS messaging in the likely target zone. When the sirens blare, Intel's people know what to do. Weekly, monthly, and annual drills have trained them to respond instantly to the warning. They rush to secure locations such as hardened bomb shelters formed from the plant's staircases, reinforced concrete shelters spread in all open places, and hardened basements. (The system is also used to launch interceptor missiles as part of Israel's "Iron Dome.")

Many warning systems include "reverse 911" systems,[135] which can notify wide populations in a plant or an urban area about an impending problem. The systems now rely on mobile technology to reach people wherever they are.[136,137] The USGS tweets for quakes,[138] and its Earthquake Notification Service sends emails and texts messages of quakes to all of its registered users.[139]

Winning the Race between Data and Destruction

In 2003, OKI's semiconductor factory suffered $15 million in damages and 30 days of lost production from two earthquakes near Sendai, Japan. The company then installed a system that used Japan's new Earthquake Early Warning system.[140] Earthquake warning systems can't predict when or where a quake might start, but they can predict when and where the shockwave will go once a quake does start. An earthquake's shockwave radiates through rock at about 3,000 to 6,000 miles per hour,[141] but radio signals from a seismograph and government warning system travel at the speed of light, or 186,000 miles per second. In places like Japan, Mexico, and California, seismologists have deployed real-time warning systems using networks of detectors.[142] For facilities located more than a few miles from the epicenter, the detection signal can arrive seconds or a few tens of seconds before the shaking.

Although a few seconds of warning seems useless in the event of a devastating quake, it can avert some of the consequential disasters. Organizations can use an early warning signal to bring elevators to a halt, close pipe valves carrying hazardous materials, park the heads of hard disk drives to reduce the chance of lost data, shut off heat sources, put industrial processes in safe mode, halt trains, stop traffic from driving on bridges, and alert people to seek shelter.[143] When an 8.0-magnitude quake struck off the coast of Manzanillo, Mexico, officials in Mexico City were able to shut down the Metro system 50 seconds before the tremors arrived. After OKI installed an early warning system, two subsequent earthquakes caused only $200,000 in damage and a total of only eight days of downtime.[144]

The same applies to tsunami warning systems,[145] which can provide minutes or even hours of warning based on fast analysis of seismic activity and deep water sensing of the passing tsunami wave. Moreover, this principle applies across the tiers of a supply chain, in which data about disrupted deep-tier suppliers could flow much faster than the weeks it might take for the absence of shipped parts to be felt at the end of the chain. "Lower-tier suppliers that serve a number of markets often spot shifts in the economy early on—and can warn customers about them," wrote Thomas Choi and Tom Linton.[146] If the data can travel faster than the disruption can, then companies with good "listening" networks can detect disruptions early and prepare to respond before the disruption hits them.

9

SECURING THE INFORMATION SUPPLY CHAIN

The deep and extensive hacking of Sony Corporation in late 2014—stealing Sony's most precious pieces of intellectual property and embarrassing secret email conversations—shows how vulnerable every company is to cybercrime. With the growing reliance on software and communications for global supply chain operations comes growing vulnerabilities in these systems. Since 2004, five key trends have increased the risks of IT-related disruptions to companies' operations. These key trends are: more outsourcing of IT infrastructure to cloud computing, more Internet connectivity of industrial devices, more use of personal devices on corporate networks, more personal data online, and an overall increasing reliance on Internet-connected technologies to run global supply chains.

All of these trends stem from the declining cost and increasing utility of the technology, and they increase the risk of supply chain disruptions resulting from IT or communications failures. In fact, disruptions of information systems and telecommunications consistently rank as the number one or number two most frequent source of supply chain disruptions.[1] These vulnerabilities go beyond accidental disruptions caused by power outages, computer downtime, or software bugs. Intentional disruptions include theft of intellectual property, monetary and reputational damage from theft of customer data, and sabotage of products and manufacturing operations.

CYBERCRIMINALS IN THE SUPPLY CHAIN

"Our operating system was never built for digital security," said an oil industry executive to the US Council on Competitiveness.[2]

"There have been specific cases in which hackers got all the way into the digital process controls. As we've moved into higher levels of digital integration, creating visibility through the value chain, our systems have become electronically linked. Automating oil field production increases the level of exposure as well. And cyber-vulnerabilities create physical security problems. Physical security is enabled by digital security—all physical security-locking mechanisms are now IT controlled. Security has become a strategic issue."

The Devil's in the Industrial Devices

In June 2010, a Belarusian malware-detection firm found a strange new computer worm: a type of malware that spreads independently without user action or knowledge. This new type of computer worm was infecting computers in Iran, and it had a very complex design, used stolen security certificates, employed four previously unknown vulnerabilities, and behaved quite strangely.[3]

Named Stuxnet, the computer worm illustrated a systemic vulnerability of manufacturing systems. Stuxnet spread within networks of Windows PCs via previously unidentified weaknesses in both USB flash memory sticks and in networked printers. This enabled it to spread across an organization, and even to PCs that were isolated from the Internet (so-called air-gapped computers).

But Stuxnet did not attack these PCs. Instead, it looked for any computers that were being used to manage Siemens programmable logic controllers, which are used in factories around the world.[4] When Stuxnet found a connection to an industrial controller, it gathered information about the equipment attached to the controller and could reprogram the controller and turn off alarms. Stuxnet is thought to have been cooked up by US and/or Israeli spy agencies to infect and damage Iran's nuclear weapons program by making Iran's uranium enrichment centrifuges spin out of control.[5]

Given Stuxnet's sophisticated abilities to spread without being detected, it's not surprising that it escaped Iranian detection. After Stuxnet was first reported, Chevron found Stuxnet in its systems, possibly arriving on an infected thumb-drive. "I don't think the U.S. government even realized how far it had spread," said Mark

Koelmel, general manager of the earth sciences department at Chevron. "I think the downside of what they did is going to be far worse than what they actually accomplished."[6] By September 2010, Stuxnet had spread to 100,000 infected hosts in Iran, Indonesia, India, Azerbaijan, Pakistan, the United States, and over 100 other countries.[7]

Nor are Siemens industrial controllers the only ones vulnerable to hackers. Security researchers found major vulnerabilities in facilities management devices that use Tridium's Niagara framework. Niagara runs on some 11 million devices in 52 countries to remotely control electronic door locks, lighting systems, elevators, electricity and boiler systems, video surveillance cameras, alarms, and other critical building facilities.[8] "There are hundreds of thousands of installations on networks, including [Defense Department] installations and Fortune 500 firms," said Billy Rios, coauthor of *Hacking: The Next Generation*, a handbook for security experts.[9] "These customers have no idea they are exposed," Rios continued. For example, Singapore's Changi Airport—a major airfreight logistics hub for Asia—uses Niagara to manage more than 110,000 devices and sensors.[10]

Residents of Great Falls, Montana, got a bit of a shock on the evening of February 11, 2013, when their TVs broadcast an official Emergency Alert System (EAS) message warning: "The bodies of the dead are rising from their graves and attacking the living. Do not attempt to approach or apprehend these bodies as they are considered extremely dangerous." Zombies were in Great Falls! "This was a prank," said James Barnett, a retired Navy rear admiral and partner in the cybersecurity practice at law firm Venable. "But if something was done to try and panic the public—or even worse, to interrupt communications during an actual emergency—that's pretty serious."[11] After the hoax zombie warning, the Federal Communications Commission issued an "urgent advisory" to all television stations, requiring them to immediately change the passwords on all EAS-related equipment, place the devices behind firewalls, and check for bogus alerts.

Examples like Stuxnet, Niagara, and the EAS Zombie hoax illustrate the amount of critical infrastructure that is on the Internet.

In the past, industrial and facility-related devices were relatively isolated from the external environment because they used dedicated and proprietary connections to an organization's computers. But modern machines rely more on open Internet-based connectivity and easy-to-use web-based interfaces that create a double vulnerability. First, hackers can now reach in and access these devices to then monitor or disrupt company activities. But the more insidious vulnerability is that hackers can infect these devices. Thus, a printer can become a host for a computer worm that attacks any machine on the same network as the printer.[12] Malware can even infect smartphone rechargers,[13] keyboards, and computer mice.[14] The problem will only get worse, because by 2015 an estimated 25 billion devices will be on the Internet in what is referred to as "The Internet of Things,"[15] or, more aptly, "The Internet of Everything."

Targeting Supply Chain Partners

During the first half of the 2013 holiday shopping season, US retailer Target enjoyed "better than expected sales," said Chief Executive Gregg Steinhafel.[16] But in the midst of that holiday cheer and ringing cash registers lurked a major cybercrime in progress. During the frenzy of shopping over the Thanksgiving weekend (November 29 was "Black Friday"—the day of the highest shopping volume in the United States) and until the intrusion was detected on December 12, every time a Target customer swiped his or her card, hackers swiped the card number.

This crime began months before and illustrates the security threats latent in supply chains. Extensive analysis by private and public security experts[17] estimated that sometime in September 2013, criminals (probably operating in Russia or Eastern Europe) sent a phishing email to one or more workers at Fazio Mechanical Service in Sharpsburg, Pennsylvania. At least one recipient opened the email, thereby infecting one of Fazio's computers with an off-the-shelf password-stealing program known as Citidel.[18]

That may not seem relevant to the Target story, except that Fazio was a vendor to Target, working on the retailer's HVAC (heating ventilation and air conditioning) systems at Target stores in the western Pennsylvania region.[19] As a vendor, Fazio had accounts on

Target's normal electronic billing, contract submission, and project management systems.[20] The criminals' password-stealing bot gave them access to Fazio's accounts on Target's systems.[21]

Although Target maintained a separation between the vendor portal and its credit card processing systems, the criminals seem to have found a way to breach that firewall and gained access to Target's network of 62,000 POS (point-of-sale) terminals. Sources estimate that between November 15 and November 28 (the day before Black Friday), the attackers successfully installed data-stealing software on a small number of cash registers within Target stores.[22] When the test worked, the criminals rolled out their malware to the rest of Target's POS terminals.

Getting into Target was only half the battle; the hackers also needed to get the stolen data out of the company—an act that can raise alarms. To do this, the criminals commandeered a control server inside Target's internal network to become a central repository for the data taken from all of the infected registers.[23] Beginning on December 2, the attackers used a virtual private server (VPS) located in Russia to download the stolen data. Over a two-week period, they extracted a total of 11 GB of stolen customer information.[24] The data included 40 million credit card numbers as well as nonfinancial data (names, email or physical addresses) on as many as 70 million customers.[25]

The thieves then began uploading blocks of 1 million credit cards at a time for sale at prices ranging from $20 per card to $100 per card.[26] Bank security officials first became aware of the breach through routine monitoring of known black market sites. A bank bought some of their own cards from the thieves and discovered that the common denominator among the cards was purchase activity at Target. The bank alerted federal officials, federal officials talked to Target, and Target uncovered the breach and announced it to the public on December 19.[27]

The crime and the aftermath of the very public, headline-making announcement of the breach hit Target from many directions. "Results softened meaningfully following our December announcement of a data breach," said Target's CEO.[28] Profit in the holiday quarter was nearly halved from a year earlier to $520 million, and revenue slid 5 percent to $21.5 billion.[29] Other damages included: $17 million in expenses (net of insurance payout) at Target,[30] $200 million in card replacement costs for financial institutions,[31] an estimated $1.1 billion for fraudulent transactions on stolen cards,[32] and the potential for up to a $3.6 billion fine for Target for violating PCI-DSS (payment card industry data security standards).[33]

Target's problem was by no means unique in a world of Internet-connected supply chains, outsourcing, Internet-of-Things devices, and cloud-hosted IT systems. Customer data was stolen in 2014 from Home Depot, Goldman Sachs, and many others—in total, 375 million customer records were reported stolen in the first half of 2014.[34] Even the US Department of Homeland Security was hit as detailed records on employees and contractors were stolen from a contractor responsible for background checks.[35] "We constantly run into situations where outside service providers connected remotely have the keys to the castle," said Vincent Berk, chief executive of FlowTraq, a network security firm.[36] Cybercriminals have entered and gained a beachhead inside company networks via video conferencing equipment, vending machines, printers, and even thermostats. Estimates of the percentage of breaches caused by third-party suppliers range from 23 to 70 percent.[37]

Technology Forecast: Clouds with a Chance of Downtime

On August 16, 2013, the unthinkable happened. Google went down.[38] And with it went 40 percent of all Internet traffic.[39] Although Google's systems came back up in only a few minutes, the crash showed just how much of the world depends on this one company's sprawling global network of servers. Beyond its use for Internet searches, many companies use Google's public and corporate services for mail, file storage, collaborative document editing, mapping, navigation, Android smartphones, and more.[40]

Google isn't the only Internet-based service on which people and companies depend. Another key trend affecting the safety of IT systems is the rising use of cloud computing—outsourced software services and data hosted on distributed server systems. Also called software-as-a-service (SaaS), the cloud vendor promises high reliability, low cost, and worldwide access. Although cloud-based systems use geographically distributed data centers and independent server farms to promise extremely high reliability, they can still fail. Microsoft's Azure platform failed twice in twelve months: once over a lapsed security certificate[41] and again because of a rather minor component of its cloud going down, but going down globally.[42]

In other instances, a minor outage cascades into something larger. In April 2011, a minor outage in Amazon's East Coast data center cascaded when systems designed to ensure Amazon's reliability actually clogged the network with what Amazon described as "a re-mirroring storm." A sudden loss of access to data caused automatic data replication across the network, jamming it with data traffic.[43]

Bring Your Own (Infected) Device

Cisco, like many companies, has adopted a BYOD (bring your own device) policy, in which employees use their personal devices instead of company-provided ones. "At the end of 2012, there were nearly 60,000 smartphones and tablets in use in the organization—including just under 14,000 iPads—and all of them were BYOD," said Brett Belding, senior manager overseeing Cisco IT Mobility Services. "Mobile at Cisco is now BYOD, period."[44] BYOD lowers the cost of information technology for Cisco and enables employees to carry just one device of their own choosing. It's a win for both the company and employees, but it's also a potential win for cyber attackers.

"If you get an infected device or phone coming into your business, your intellectual property could be stolen," said Chuck Bokath, senior research engineer at the Georgia Tech Research Institute.[45] For example, mobile versions of the FinSpy/FinFisher malware allow attackers to log incoming and outgoing calls; conceal calls to eavesdrop on the user's surroundings; and steal data such as text (SMS) messages, contact lists, and phone/tablet media (such as photos and videos).[46]

Mobile malware is growing.[47] Malware can infect a smartphone and enter corporate IT systems through several means. The most prevalent vectors for infection are Trojan apps—malware apps masquerading as something the user might want, such as a popular game, a plug-in for playing media, or even a fake antivirus app. Although Apple and Google try to run malware-free app stores, the vetting process may be imperfect. Moreover, the open Android platform lets users "side-load" apps from any source they choose, which makes the platform vulnerable. And if the user "jail-breaks" his or her phone to bypass security systems imposed by the phone maker or cellular service provider, then the phone becomes much more vulnerable. For example, jail-broken iPhones are susceptible to a worm called IOS_IKEE that has the ability to accept remote commands, collect corporate information, and send it to a remote server. [48]

Mobile malware can come in other forms, too. For example, one attack on Android phones comes in the form of an SMS message that appears to be a link for a DHL package tracking message. If the user clicks on the link, the phone downloads malware that steals the user's data and sends infected SMS messages to everyone on their contact list.[49] Malware even came installed on the Android SD cards of Samsung's S8500 Wave and Vodafone's HTC Magic smartphones.[50]

As of 2013, Android devices were the target of 98.1 percent of these malicious programs, owing to the platform's growing popularity and more open app-loading environment.[51] Criminals do follow the path of money. As tablets begin to outsell computers, criminals are building more tools to attack tablets, too.[52]

In 2013, most mobile malware targeted consumers with spam advertising, theft via premium SMS services, theft of banking information, and pay-to-unlock extortion-ware scams.[53] Of concern to corporate and supply chain security are three categories of malware. The first category is systems used in bank account theft, because they can also be used to breach corporate two-factor security systems by stealing SMS messages that contain the second password. The second includes cases in which Android malware was a vector for installing Windows malware: bring-your-own-device can become bring-your-own-virus. Third are more general backdoor malware systems that can be used to eavesdrop and steal mobile device data, including corporate data. "BYOD is a real problem," acknowledged Matthew Valites, Cisco's CSIRT manager for information security investigations.[54]

The Internet of (Insecure) Things

At the 2013 Defcon hacker's conference, two security researchers demonstrated a particularly nasty proof of concept.[55] The researchers showed that they could take over the steering wheel of a Toyota Prius through its lane-keeping and parking-assist software, and they could command the steering wheel to jerk sharply while driving on the highway. They could also apply the brakes or disable the vehicle at any time.

Nor was the Prius the only car they found a way to control. They also found that they could completely disable the brakes on the Ford Escape at low speed. Other hacks affected dashboard displays—changing the speedometer and the odometer, and even spoofing the GPS location of the vehicle. Fortunately, these security researchers were "good guys." In fact, DARPA had funded their efforts to help root out security vulnerabilities in automobiles.[56]

Car makers aren't the only manufacturers who may have to worry. More and more products come with smartphone or direct web integration. Besides the unsurprising range of Internet-connected consumer electronics such as big screen TVs, stereos, gaming platforms, and home automation, is a growing range of connected home appliances such as ovens,[57] crockpots,[58] and washing machines,[59] as well as children's toys.[60] These systems can be breached to allow criminals to control these devices, monitor the home, and access the homeowner's local network. In fact, security analysts uncovered five different vulnerabilities in Belkin's WeMo line of home automation products (light bulbs, light switches, and remote monitoring devices) that could be used for such purposes.[61] Another major flaw was the Heartbleed vulnerability that allowed penetrations of widely used secure networking protocols and went undetected for two years.[62] This vulnerability demonstrated that virtually any smart product might contain an exploitable flaw.

Furthermore, the issue of counterfeit chips discussed in chapter 7 implies that procurement also plays an ongoing role in product security. "As we connect our homes to the Internet, it is increasingly important for Internet-of-Things device vendors to ensure that reasonable security methodologies are adopted early in product development cycles. This mitigates their customer's exposure and reduces risk," said Mike Davis, principal research scientist at the security research firm IOActive.[63]

Finally, as mentioned earlier in this chapter, the Internet-of-Things trend is also invading freight transportation. Tractors, trailers, cargo, and even individual packages can be tracked in real time.[64] Wireless monitoring of axle weight, reefer temperature, and engine performance can certainly improve operations. All these digital links and devices, however, likely introduce unknown vulnerabilities.

AN INFORMATION SUPERHIGHWAY OF CRIME

When researchers at MIT wanted to test the intensity of digital devilry, they simply attached a clean, brand-new computer to MIT's network and monitored all the attempts to access or attack the virgin machine.[65] Within 24 hours, they had logged some 60,000 attempts to breach the machine. Attacks had come from every country in the world with the exception of Antarctica and North Korea. Most disturbing was that many of the attacks had come from other machines inside MIT's network, indicating that they had presumably been infected earlier.

"We are seeing some disturbing changes in the threat environment facing governments, companies, and societies," said John N. Stewart, senior vice president and chief security officer at Cisco.[66] Far more serious than bored teenage vandals or Viagra-touting spammers are the growing risks of deliberate IT disruptions and threats. Hit-and-run malicious pranksters have been supplanted by more malevolent persistent threats tied to organized crime, state-sponsored corporate espionage, and cyber warfare.

An analysis of over 47,000 IT security incidents during 2012 found that 75 percent were financially motivated cybercrimes.[67] Typical targets for these kinds of intrusions include retail organizations, restaurants, food-service firms, banks, and financial institutions.[68] The crimes often involve highly organized, tightly coordinated teams operating on a global scale. For example, criminals stole 1.5 million records from an electronic payments processor in 2008 and made fake ATM cards. They then used the cards during a tightly timed period to withdraw more than $9 million in 49 cities around the world.[69]

A Malware Supply Chain

Malware has matured, literally. Famous computer viruses of the past such as Melissa,[70] the Love Bug,[71] and Bagle[72] were largely the work of mischievous individuals. But what started as a loose assortment of youthful hackers has become an industry with a bona fide supply chain of tool vendors, vulnerability suppliers, data thieves, and distributors and retailers of stolen data.[73] Criminals can now buy "fraud as a service."[74]

Packaged attack kits sell for between $40 and $4,000, with an average retail price of approximately $900.[75] Underground marketplaces and organizations cater to creating and selling vulnerabilities in popular operating systems and software (Windows, Adobe Flash, Adobe PDF, Java, and server software). A vulnerability for a financial site might retail for as much as $3,000.[76] The worst, and highest-priced, vulnerabilities are the so-called zero-day vulnerabilities, which are IT security flaws in a piece of software that have no known countermeasures because no one even knew the vulnerability existed until the attack occurred. Zero-day vulnerabilities that allow a hacker access to any Windows machine anywhere sell for as much as $100,000.[77] Attackers can also rent networks of infected PCs called botnets for $40 per day for launching penetration attacks, distributed denial of service attacks, click fraud, and spam.

Bogdan Dumitru, CTO at BitDefender, an antivirus firm, estimates that between 70 percent and 80 percent of malware now comes from organized, well-financed groups.[78] The sites offering these services are as sophisticated as any e-commerce site. Just click on the malware product you want, pay, and it is on its way to you. There's even the opportunity to buy optional modules, maintenance agreements, and customization from the underground vendors of malware. Of course, malware buyers might well wonder to whom they just gave their credit card details for these services....

It's 10 pm, Do You Know Where Your Data Are?

Google uncovered a cyber-intrusion in December 2009. At first, it seemed to target the email accounts of human rights activists,[79] but further study found that the attack was both deeper and broader. What became known as "Operation Aurora"[80]—named after clues inside the attacker's software—emanated from China and sought proprietary data and software codes from Northrop Grumman, Dow Chemical, Juniper Networks, Morgan Stanley, Yahoo, Symantec, Adobe, and at least 27 other companies.[81,82]

"We have never ever, outside of the defense industry, seen commercial industrial companies come under that level of sophisticated attack," said Dmitri Alperovitch, vice president of threat research for McAfee, Intel's antivirus software subsidiary.[83] Aurora exemplified a new kind of attacker: the advanced persistent threat (APT). Aurora burrowed deep into the networks of target companies, using several levels of encryption and nearly a dozen pieces of malware. "In this case, they're using multiple types against multiple targets—but all in the same attack campaign. That's a marked leap in coordination," said Eli Jellenc, head of international cyber-intelligence for VeriSign's iDefense Labs.[84] "It's totally changing the threat model," Alperovitch added.[85]

Security firm Mandiant uncovered one advanced persistent threat (which they called APT1 and others have called "Comment Crew") that had compromised at least 141 companies spanning 20 major industries. Unlike the Hollywood vision of hackers broadcasting zombie alerts or making laughing skulls dance on their victims' screens, APTs try to stay undetected so they can plunder broad categories of companies' intellectual property over a long period of time. In a report entitled, "Exposing One of China's Cyber Espionage Units," Mandiant stated that APT1 maintained access to victims' networks for an average of a year, with the longest incursion lasting four years and ten months.[86] APT1 searched corporate networks to steal copies of technology blueprints, proprietary manufacturing processes, test results, business plans, pricing documents, partnership agreements, emails, and contact lists.[87] Even the source code of Windows 2000 was stolen from Microsoft in 2004, allowing hackers not only to sell unlicensed software but to analyze the code in order to find new vulnerabilities. In a final ironic twist, malware-infected copies of the Mandiant security report were used in a phishing campaign.[88]

"This is not some 15-year old trying to hack your database to see if he can," said Andy Serwin, adviser to the Naval Post Graduate

School's Center for Asymmetric Warfare and chair of the information security practice at international law firm Foley & Lardner. "This is a large-scale organized effort to steal your company's most valuable information."[89] An analysis of 168 of the largest US companies found evidence that machines inside 162 of them had transmitted data to hackers.[90]

These cyber-espionage risks extend into commercial supply chains and include attacks on the suppliers and partners of large companies. "When we thought of espionage, we thought of big companies and the large amount of intellectual property they have, but there were many small organizations targeted with the exact same tactics," said Jay Jacobs, a senior analyst with the Verizon RISK team. Jacobs found that cyber-espionage breaches were split almost fifty-fifty between large and small organizations. "We think that they pick the small organizations because of their affiliation or work with larger organizations."[91]

Over 95 percent of cases of cyber-espionage attacks originated from China, Jacobs claims.[92] "It is fundamentally important that the American private sector wake up to the fact that dozens of countries—including China—are robbing us blind," said Tom Kellermann, head of cybersecurity at Trend Micro and former commissioner of President Obama's cybersecurity council.[93]

Government-Sponsored Cybercrime and Cyberwarfare

Some analysts allege that governments now back or support some high-profile cybercrime activities. Alleged perpetrators include China (APT1 and Aurora),[94] the United States (Stuxnet, Flame, Duqu, and Gauss),[95] Iran (the Saudi Aramco attacks),[96] Syria (Denial-of-Service attacks on US banks),[97] and Russia (using the "snake" toolkit against Ukraine).[98] Unfortunately, the attacks can be difficult to trace because attackers can use botnets in any country to perpetrate, manage, or route their malicious activities.

These governments have technology resources that dwarf those of organized crime or the average credit card thief. "They outspend us and they outman us in almost every way," said Dell Inc.'s chief security officer, John McClurg. "I don't recall, in my adult life, a more challenging time."[99] Estimates of APT1's current attack infrastructure include over 1,000 servers.[100] Stuxnet may have involved the work of more than 30 coders working for months, if not years, on the worm.[101]

China vociferously denies the allegations that it was behind APT1, claiming that it has been the victim of cyber-attacks, too.[102] "China resolutely opposes hacking actions and has established relevant laws and regulations and taken strict law enforcement measures to defend against online hacking activities," said Hong Lei, a ministry spokesman.[103]

Yet Mandiant traced APT1's high volume of activity and some of its people to the same neighborhood in the Pudong area of Shanghai as a 12-story building housing People's Liberation Army Unit 61398. This building has a special high-capacity fiber-optic communications infrastructure "in the name of national defense" and Unit 61398 has specifically sought to hire large numbers of English-speaking computer security experts.[104] "Either they [the attacks] are coming from inside Unit 61398, or the people who run the most-controlled, most-monitored Internet networks in the world are clueless about thousands of people generating attacks from this one neighborhood," said Kevin Mandia, the founder and chief executive of Mandiant.[105]

The participation of governments marks a dangerous new phase of IT disruptions. "Nations are actively testing how far they can go before we will respond," said Alan Paller, director of research at the SANS Institute, a cybersecurity training organization.[106] Estonia suffered a country-wide Internet blackout on July 15, 2007, that is believed to have been caused by Russia.[107] South Korea suffered a series of cyber time-bomb attacks on banks and broadcasters that may trace back to North Korea's open declaration of seeking online targets in the south to exact economic damage.[108] At oil company Saudi Aramco, 30,000 PCs were destroyed by the Shamoon virus, which may have been created by Iran.[109] "The attacks have changed from espionage to destruction," said Alan Paller.[110]

US defense secretary Leon E. Panetta warned of a "cyber Pearl Harbor."[111] He said: "An aggressor nation or extremist group could use these kinds of cyber tools to gain control of critical switches. They could derail passenger trains, or even more dangerous, derail freight trains loaded with lethal chemicals. They could contaminate the water supply in major cities, or shut down the power grid across large parts of the country."[112]

DEPTH OF DEFENSE

In 2013, a total of 13,073 vulnerabilities were discovered in 2,289 products from 539 vendors.[113] Given all the threats of malware-laden websites, zero-day OS vulnerabilities, phishing emails, infected USB flash drives, insecure suppliers, cell phone backdoors, and dodgy Wi-Fi hotspots used for cybercriminal intrusion, cybersecurity seems hopeless. Yet as leaky as the cybersecurity walls around a global supply chain organization may be, organizations can defend themselves in many different ways.

Killing the Kill Chain

The military uses the concept of a "kill chain" to describe the steps for finding and successfully destroying a target. By analogy, cybercriminals must also accomplish a sequence of actions in order to reach their goals against their target. By understanding those steps in the cybercriminal's kill chain, an organization can defend itself.

Cybercrime, especially the advanced persistent threats faced by corporations, involves seven steps, according to defense technology firm Lockheed Martin.[114] First, the criminal uses reconnaissance methods to research, identify, and select targets. Second, the criminal creates a weaponized deliverable such as an infected Adobe PDF or Microsoft Office document. Third, the criminal delivers the payload via a phishing email, infected website, or USB media. Fourth, the criminal's code will exploit some vulnerability to run that code once inside the target's firewall. Fifth, the criminal will install some kind of remote access Trojan horse software or backdoor. Sixth, the criminal will establish a command and control system to manage their system's activities inside the target corporation. Seventh, and finally, the criminal will pursue nefarious objectives such as collecting and exfiltrating sensitive data, sabotaging the target's systems, or using the target to gain access to another organization.

"We look at what they are trying to do and focus on whatever their objectives are ... and cut off their objectives," said Steve Adegbite, director of cybersecurity for Lockheed Martin.[115] Because criminals must accomplish all seven steps to achieve their objectives, an organization's cybersecurity only needs to thwart the attacker at any one of the steps to prevent or halt the intrusion. The Lockheed Martin approach to cybersecurity is based on depth of defense. For each of the cybercriminal's seven steps, Lockheed Martin deploys a matrix of tools or processes that detect, deny, disrupt, degrade, deceive, or destroy the cybercriminal's attempted actions.[116,117] "I can still defend the doors, but I'm not going to sit there and put all my efforts there," Adegbite said.

Building a Walled Garden

Reducing the vulnerability of a system markedly reduces the rate of cybercriminal attacks on the system. As of mid-2013, Android devices somewhat outnumbered Apple devices by 900 million[118] to 600 million.[119] Yet Android malware outnumbered iOS malware by more than 750 to 1 in 2013.[120]

Security analysts cited two factors that make iOS a harder target. The first is Apple's dictatorial "walled-garden" app model, whereby users aren't permitted to load apps on their iPhones and iPads except via Apple's curated store.[121] In contrast, Android users can freely visit a variety of open market places and "side load" any apps they choose, but they run much higher risks because cybercriminals put infected copies of popular apps on these third-party marketplaces.

The second is Apple's vertical integration and ability to push updates (including security updates) to iOS users.[122] In contrast, Google leaves the updating process to Android device OEMs and cellular service carriers, which leads to delays in updates.[123] In 2014, nearly 90 percent of iOS users were on the latest version of Apple's software, while less than 10 percent of Android users were on Google's latest version.[124] The issue of missed or delayed security updates is far more serious than it seems, because hackers can actually analyze each security update to learn about vulnerabilities in computers or phones that aren't using the latest version.

The walled garden model applies to corporate IT systems as well. A number of technology advances give companies more control over workers' computers and smartphones, such as limiting apps' access to sensitive files[125] or enabling a remote-controlled erasure of stolen or lost devices.[126] Companies can create their own internal app stores that contain only the safest subset of carefully vetted apps. Ongoing efforts are aimed at creating more secure operating systems, application installation systems, locked-down boot systems, email filters, and software mechanisms that "sandbox" potential malware in a limited part of the computer.[127]

Red Team Training to Avoid the Hooks of Phishers

Dr. Zaius is one cute cat, a Turkish Angora with a purple Mohawk hairstyle. He was the lead image in an email sent in 2013 to some 2 million people. The email promised more feline photographic foolery. But recipients who clicked the link—and 48 percent of them did—were disappointed, even chagrined, when all they got was a warning from cybersecurity firm PhishMe Inc. on behalf of their IT departments about the dangers of phishing.[128]

Phishing emails attempt to lure a victim to click on emailed links or attachments with promises of titillating images, hoax messages from package delivery services, threats of discontinued bank services, and the like. Employees remain on the front line of a company's IT security. As software vendors work to patch vulnerabilities in operating systems and software packages, attackers must rely more and more on the users agreeing to open a message or download an app that contains malware.

Over the 2014 Labor Day weekend in the United States naked and seminaked photos of celebrities including Kirsten Dunst and Kate Upton appeared online. Many media outlets put the blame on Apple iCloud storage service, yet the iCloud was not hacked. Instead, a combination of phishing emails or possibly "sniffed" user names and passwords over open Wi-Fi networks allowed hackers to penetrate the account of these celebrities on Apple's cloud storage service and download the private photos.

Brian Fees, chief financial officer of CedarCrestone, a consulting and managed services company, knows all about phishing. He even hired MAD Security to do quarterly red team test attacks to train CedarCrestone's staff. One day, Fees received an urgent email from CedarCrestone's CEO mentioning one of the company's key clients. He immediately opened the attachment and realized he'd made big mistake. The email was actually a hacker's ruse designed to infect the CFO's computer. Fortunately, the ruse was perpetrated by MAD Security using the newer phishing strategy known as spear-phishing. As MAD's managing partner, Michael Murray explained, "We went through their website and figured out who one of their key clients was, and then set up a fake email chain."[129] Red team services such as those offered by PhishMe Inc. and MAD Security help train employees to be aware of the potential untrustworthiness of the emails they receive and to immediately report them.

In spear-phishing, the attacker uses public data (e.g., the web and social media) to construct a realistic and urgent spoof message to the victim. As people share more and more data about their careers, their lives, and their plans via LinkedIn, Facebook, Twitter, and other sites, it becomes easier for determined criminals and cyber-espionage attackers to create realistic messages that seem to come from trusted friends, family, and colleagues from the victim's social network.[130] In 2011, IBM found that spam is declining, but spear-phishing is increasing.[131] A June 2012 study by Deloitte and Forbes Insight ranks social media "as the fourth largest source of risk over the next three years," following the global economic environment, regulatory changes and government spending.[132] Whereas consumer identity theft is a numbers game relying on hit-or-miss generic phishing, corporate cyber-espionage is more likely to target specific individuals in specific companies with spear-phishing.

Automated Stress Testing

"Chaos Monkey" and "Chaos Gorilla" are two mischievous bits of software that try to wreak havoc in Netflix's video distribution systems.[133] But they aren't the product of evil hackers or unfriendly governments. Instead, Netflix itself intentionally attacks its own systems to find and prevent larger vulnerabilities. Chaos Monkey randomly disrupts part of Netflix's network to ensure the company can quickly respond to outages. Chaos Gorilla disrupts entire regions to test Netflix's systems automatic rebalancing of the load without user-visible impact or manual intervention.[134] Testing the system with many small, controlled disruptions helps Netflix find weaknesses and prevent larger, uncontrolled disruptions.

On October 4, 2012, Europe attacked Europe.[135] Yet the attack on Europe's online e-government and financial services was an example of ethical hacking,[136] in which one group is authorized to attempt to breach or disrupt a voluntary target to test the target's ability to withstand some form of malevolent attack. "This was a collective effort with members of the organizations working with a friendly botnet to strike the services of members and point them in the right direction," said Paul Lawrence, VP of international operations at Corero Network Security.[137]

Stress testing can assess the resilience of an organization's infrastructure under DDoS (distributed denial of service) attacks by a nation-state, terrorist group, or extortion group, as well as so-called hacktivist CSR-related attacks. This kind of stress testing uses one or more methods that attempt to disrupt a company's web sites, email, or other Internet-mediated activities by flooding the company with spurious requests, bulky data, or computationally costly commands.[138] "Working together at the European level to keep the Internet and other essential infrastructures running is what today's exercise is all about," said Neelie Kroes, vice president of the European Commission and European Commissioner for Digital Agenda.[139]

Detection: From File Signatures to Behavior Signatures

"Consumer–grade antivirus you buy from the store does not work too well trying to detect stuff created by the nation-states with nation-state budgets," said Mikko Hypponen, chief research officer at Finland's F–Secure Oyj.[140] File signatures (a kind of digital fingerprint used to detect computer viruses) can change often or be previously unseen in the case of well-funded or state-sponsored attacks. Moreover, advanced types of malware can disable or hide from antivirus software via a variety of tactics.

Yet from a kill chain perspective, that attacker's installation of a piece of malware is not the final objective. Although malware might remain hidden, its behavior in a computer or on the network may be quite visible, detectable, and thus defeatable. That's why companies such as IBM and Sift Science are working to automate detection of unusual and potentially malevolent patterns of activity in computers and networks. "You can spot patterns the naked eye would never notice," said Sift Science cofounder Brandon Ballinger.[141]

Defense contractor Lockheed Martin caught an attacker in 2011 by watching its behavior. The intruder had a valid security token—possibly stolen from the token provider—from one of Lockheed's business partners. "We thought at first it was a new person in the department ... but then it became really interesting," said Lockheed Martin's Steve Adegbite. What tripped Lockheed's alarms was that the intruder was attempting to access data unrelated to the work of the user he or she was impersonating. "No information was lost. If not for this framework [Kill Chain], we would have had issues," Adegbite said.[142]

Some of the most vexing risks emanate from within the organizations—disgruntled employees intent on harming their company or enriching themselves by stealing data (à la Bradley Manning, who gave stolen data to Wiki-leaks, or Edward Snowden who shared his NSA-stolen data with media outlets). Yet, as the risks of cyber-attacks proliferate, so do defensive methods. Companies can now easily monitor when any employee attaches a USB device to a computer that has network access or downloads any file, especially "tagged" documents, which then trigger real-time alarms.

Collaboration

Cooperation among victim corporations aids cybersecurity via improved detection, characterization, and elimination of cybersecurity threats. A new generation of detection systems benefit from network effects—the more companies that share intrusion data or allow joint monitoring, the sooner these systems can spot infections and mount preventative countermeasures. "Our biggest issue right now is getting the private sector to a comfort level where they can report anomalies, malware, and incidences within their networks," said Executive Assistant Director Richard McFeely, head of the FBI's cyber-crime efforts. "It has been very difficult with a lot of major companies to get them to cooperate fully," McFeely added.[143]

The idea is to arrive at the same level of cross-learning that systems like the aviation industry's "near miss" tracking provide. Whenever two planes pass too close to each other, the pilots and air traffic controllers involved report the occurrence to the Aviation Safety Reporting System of the US Federal Aviation Administration. The incidents are investigated, and enhanced safety procedures are distributed worldwide. The US system is voluntary, confidential, and run by NASA, which has no enforcement power, contributing to the high rate of reporting. Similar systems are operated by relevant agencies in other countries, such as Canada's Transportation Safety Board, or the UK's Civil Aviation Authority.

The US National Cyber Forensics and Training Alliance (NCFTA) offers a neutral third-party venue for sharing of cybersecurity events, threats, and knowledge. As a neutral venue, NCFTA lets subject matter experts from the private sector, academia, and government collaborate freely. NCTFA also addresses other kinds of illegal activities that have a significant online component, including online sales of counterfeit merchandise and illicit drugs. In Europe, the European Union Agency for Network and Information Security (ENISA) plays a similar role.

Ongoing Defensive Processes

Software vendors and IT security firms continue to find and close avenues of attack. For example, once Stuxnet was detected, its spread was halted by revoking the stolen security certificate used by the worm to masquerade as trusted software.[144] Microsoft then issued a series of patches to close the zero-day vulnerabilities used by Stuxnet to further prevent Stuxnet variants from spreading.[145] At Microsoft, the "Security Development Lifecycle (SDL) was built on the concept of mitigating classes of potential exploits rather than specific exploits, and reducing vulnerabilities to help provide protection against unforeseen threats," said Dustin Childs, group manager, response communications, at Microsoft Trustworthy Computing.[146]

Beginning in 2003, Microsoft designated the second Tuesday of each month as "Patch Tuesday" so that corporate IT security people could plan their testing and deployment efforts for reducing the numbers of vulnerable PCs on global networks.[147] In 2013, Microsoft released 96 security updates (up from 83 in 2013[148]) that covered 330 vulnerabilities.[149] Other software companies such as Adobe, Mozilla, and Oracle also use periodic, scheduled security updates.[150] Yet "patching" brings its own risks of disruption.[151] On more than one occasion, the patch itself has disrupted IT systems by degrading, crashing, or damaging users' PCs.[152,153]

The Cat and Mouse Game

Prevention of shifting threats depends on detection: finding new malware infections and vulnerabilities before they can inflict significant damage, and adjusting defenses to prevent further infections. "In response, attackers continue to evolve their techniques to find new avenues into an organization," said Tom Cross, manager of threat intelligence and strategy for IBM X-Force.[154] "When you know you're the target and you don't know when, where or how an attack will take place, it's wartime all the time," said Arabella Hallawell, vice president of strategy at Arbor Networks, a network security firm. "And most organizations aren't prepared for wartime," she said.[155]

Who's in Charge?

Responsibility for cybersecurity cannot lie with the IT department alone. Most other corporate functions have a role in ensuring cybersecurity. Procurement departments, working with legal professionals, must ensure that supplier contracts include cybersecurity measures, allow for auditing supplier IT security processes, and manage the authorization and de-authorization of supplier employees on the company's networks or portals. Finance plays a role as a result of its expertise in risk mitigation measures and because any disruption is likely to have financial consequences. Human resources must vet employees, train workers on cybersecurity issues, secure employee data, and ensure safe processes when using corporate email, databases, and other resources. Sales, marketing, and investor relations should prepare for communicating any intrusions with customers and investors. To coordinate cyber-defenses across the enterprise, several companies have created a multifunctional council chaired by a chief operating officer or the CEO to oversee, coordinate, and enforce company-wide defenses.

Ultimate responsibility for cybersecurity belongs at the highest level of the organization—those who provide direction and governance of the organization. Thus, the board of directors has a special responsibility to ensure that the company is as protected as possible. Unfortunately, while many board members at large companies are versed in finance, marketing, law, and operations, very few board members are versed in advanced information and communications technologies. A 2014 survey by the Institute of Internal Auditors found that 58 percent of audit executives said the board "should be actively involved" in cybersecurity issues, but only 14 percent said the board was actively involved in these issues.[156]

10

PLANNING FOR SCARCITY AND PRICE SHOCKS

Between 1994 and 2004, the price of diesel fuel varied from week to week by only an average of one cent per gallon. But between 2004 and 2009, weekly price volatility increased as the price of diesel fuel in the United States tripled from \$1.50 per gallon to \$4.75 per gallon and then slumped to \$2 per gallon during the recession, but then rose again during 2011–2013 to around \$4 per gallon.[1] Such rapidly increasing prices created difficulties for supply chain designs and operating strategies that depended on low transportation costs. The markedly increased fuel price affected every company dependent on transportation for supply, internal operations, or distribution.

Nor was fuel the only commodity that experienced significant price increases. Metals, rubber, and agricultural commodities all saw rapid price rises as well as spot shortages, affecting both materials producers and manufacturers. "Commodity prices have gotten more volatile," said Gerard Chick of the Chartered Institute of Purchasing and Supply. According to Mr. Chick, the situation is "potentially fatal for some organizations. Think of airlines procuring fuel—do you go for the long or short term? How do you outguess the market?"[2] Extreme volatility in energy and agricultural prices was ranked as a top-five global risk by the World Economic Forum in 2012.[3]

FUEL PRICE FEVER

The US trucking industry spent \$146.2 billion on diesel fuel in 2008, and the doubling of fuel prices from the prior year induced about a 22 percent increase in total truck transportation costs.[4] As one supply chain conference participant put it, "all hell broke loose."[5] Previously sedate and periodic discussions between shippers and carriers about fuel prices became heated. A 2008 survey found that 35 percent of companies had experienced a supply chain disruption in the prior 12 months because of fuel price increases or shortages.[6] Supply chains that had been optimized for low oil prices came under fierce scrutiny.

Demand Inelasticity

Transportation's key role in global supply chains—and the difficulty in changing shipping distances, shipping volumes, or shipping modes in the short term—exposes companies to fuel price risks. A 1 percent rise in the price of gasoline induces only a 0.034 to 0.090 percent change in gas consumption.[7] These numbers imply that demand for fuel is inelastic, meaning that even small disruptions in supply can have a major effect on prices—a 1 percent drop in global supply can potentially induce an 11 to 30 percent rise in fuel prices. (And prices plummeted as supply from new North American sources flooded the market in 2014 and 2015.) Although only a limited response to a rising fuel price is possible in the short term, transportation demand is more elastic in the long term because shippers can change, for example, facility locations and suppliers, while carriers can purchase more fuel-efficient assets or even change the fuel type on which their vehicles run.

The 2008 energy situation was a perfect storm comprising three factors.[8] First, growth in the developing world was creating rising energy demand. Second, price elasticity of demand in the United States and other developed countries was dropping such that even a large spike in oil prices would not blunt near-term demand.[9] Third, oil production was stagnating as the rate of new production capacity failed to keep pace with demand. "I don't think anybody really knows where fuel prices are going in the next three months," said Southwest Airlines CEO Gary Kelly to analysts in 2008. "All I have to do is look back at the last three months and the three months before as evidence of that," Kelly explained.[10]

Large increases in the price of such a crucial raw material make it difficult for companies to make decisions related to costs and prices. Violent swings in fuel and electricity costs create a "supply chain whiplash," said Rick Blasgen, president of the Council of Supply Chain Management Professionals.[11] Fuel price increases also affected the vehicle mix of automobile makers. General Motors, for example, had expected about 27 to 28 percent of consumers to pick the six-cylinder variant over the four-cylinder variant of one of its cars, but the surge in fuel prices meant that only 2 to 10 percent picked the bigger engine, requiring unexpected changes to manufacturing schedules, supplier agreements, inventory levels, and related factors, according to GM's manager of vehicle scheduling, Annette Prochaska.[12]

Response: Go Slow and Full

Companies mitigated some of the impacts of high fuel prices in the short term by diverting shipments to less fuel-hungry modes and less fuel-intensive operating strategies. UPS saw its customers shift some of their business away from minimizing inventory levels to minimizing transportation expenditures. Where possible, companies shifted from just-in-time supplies to using full conveyances; deploying inventories to multiple distribution centers close to customer locations; and shifting to slower, more fuel-efficient transportation modes (air to truck, truck to rail, and international air to maritime). The extent of such changes is limited, however, because they may require adjustments to other operational parameters such as inventory policies, order patterns, delivery commitments, and production schedules.

Limited Brands offered mode choice to its retail customers, and 60 percent of them took advantage of the cost savings offered by a slower mode. Overall, the apparel company's international shipments mix changed from 35/65 percent ocean/air to 60/40 percent ocean/air.[13] Limited Brands also curtailed prolonged design cycles to reduce last-minute air shipments. Adidas consolidated orders where possible and held retailers to minimum order sizes to reduce the impact of transportation costs on the costs of its shoes. Several companies used advanced Transportation Management Systems to improve mode selection by optimizing the transportation choices in real time, such as creating "milk runs" instead of using less-than-truckload transportation, or by delaying some shipment tendering until the last minute to create bigger, more cost-efficient shipments.[14]

The shift from air to ocean helped companies cope with higher transportation prices, but, as mentioned above, it involved many other operational changes. An additional challenge was the relatively lower delivery time reliability of ocean shipping vs. air (or rail shipping vs. trucking). In response, some ocean carriers created enhanced door-to-door service offerings with delivery guarantees. APL, a large ocean carrier, for example, offered a guaranteed on-time freight ocean product, taking control of the inland logistics in addition to the ocean portion.[15]

The Mother of Invention

The proverbial saying, "necessity is the mother of invention" (the Latin *mater atrium necessitas*) is sometimes ascribed to Plato's *Republic* but most likely was added by a translator in the 15th century. Regardless of who said it, the surge in fuel prices created a surge in necessity and a surge in innovation related to fuel-saving technologies. An exhaustive study of major US trucking fleets, by the North American Council for Freight Efficiency, found that the fuel-saving technologies with the fastest adoption included trailer skirts, use of synthetic transmission oil and synthetic transmission fluid, and installing speed limiters.[16] On the average, the use of these technologies reduced the annual fuel costs per truck by $7,200, which is over 10 percent of the average annual fuel cost.[17]

The same trends were seen in other transportation modes. For example, ocean carrier Maersk commissioned the development of new ships dubbed Triple-E ("Economy of scale, Energy efficient and Environmentally improved," according to Maersk). The Triple-Es—the largest container ships in the world (as of 2013)[18]—can carry 18,000 TEU (twenty-foot equivalent unit) of shipping containers while consuming 35 percent less fuel per container than the contemporaneous 13,100 TEU vessels. The savings come from a combination of the Triple E's size, innovative hull design, twin-skeg ultralong stroke propulsion system, and its advanced heat recovery system.[19]

In the air, Boeing developed the 787 aircraft to be 20 percent more fuel efficient than the 767 aircraft it replaces. The savings come from using lighter materials (including 50 percent composites and 20 percent aluminum), new engines, lighter-weight batteries, and electrically powered systems (instead of pneumatic systems that bleed high pressure air from the engines and rob the airplane of thrust).[20]

What Goes Up May Come Down

Big pickup trucks have always been big fuel guzzlers. Ford embarked on a complete redesign of its big F-series pickup truck, the best-selling vehicle in the United States for 32 years running (1982–2014), to use a lighter-weight all-aluminum body. Ford spent $3 billion and took nearly five years of intensive design, prototyping, testing, retooling, and retraining to develop the innovative truck. Ford even had to help train independent auto repair shops on how to work on the new aluminum bodies. The resulting vehicle was exactly what Ford had hoped for. The new truck weighed 700 pounds less than the prior model, could tow up to 11 percent more, and got up to 20 percent better fuel economy.[21]

Just as Ford released its new aluminum F-150 full-size truck in late 2014, however, crude oil prices slumped, falling from $115 a barrel in June 2014 to $69 in December of that year. Gasoline prices in the US dropped below $3 a gallon and even fell below $2 a gallon in some locations such as Texas and Oklahoma.[22] During November 2014, sales of gas-guzzling SUVs and trucks surged[23] as consumers were less concerned about fuel economy. Oil prices continued to collapse and on March 17, 2015, the price of West Texas Intermediate crude fell below $43 a barrel.

For Ford, "the world seems to have fundamentally changed from when the product was first planned," said Barclay's senior analyst, Brian Johnson, to the *Wall Street Journal*. "Getting a premium based on future lifetime fuel-economy savings isn't going to happen."[24] The price reversal can be a disruption to those companies that make large strategic investments to benefit from high prices. Thus, many US shale oil producers were expected to default in 2015. As James Wicklund, managing director of energy research at Credit Suisse said, "The [oil] producers with the most debt are at the most risk."[25]

A RAW DEAL ON RAW MATERIALS

Whereas energy price risks have an impact on multiple aspects of virtually every company's supply chain, specific material price risks affect only specific supply chains. Yet, despite the specificity of material price disruptions, their impacts may be quite common. A 2008 Aberdeen survey found that 49 percent of companies had experienced a supply chain disruption in the 12 months preceding the survey because of raw materials price increases or shortages.[26] High technology supply chains, especially, depend on a very large number of commodities and unusual chemical elements. "Twenty or thirty years ago electronics were being made with 11 different elements. Today's computers and smartphones use something like 63 different elements," explained Thomas Gradael, a professor of geology and geophysics at the Yale School of Forestry and Environmental Studies.[27]

Of Rare Earths and Precious Metals

Rare earth elements (REE) are a set of 17 metals that play a crucial role in many automotive, electronic, and high-tech applications. Rare earths go into iPhones, wind turbines, solar cells, jet engines, fiber optics, hard disk drives, compact fluorescent bulbs, and many other products.[28] In 2007, the metal *europium* (an REE) cost $300 per kilogram.[29] By 2010, that price had more than doubled to $625; in 2012, it surged to $3,800.[30]

The average Ford car contains about half a kilogram of rare earths scattered in the vehicle's sensors, electric motors, displays, and catalytic converter. In 2002, those rare earths cost only about $10 per car. As of 2012, they cost $100. New electric cars require even larger amounts of rare-earth materials in their batteries and electric motors—about $1000 per car (in 2012 REE prices).[31]

Although the scarcity of rare earths or precious metals may not be surprising, other base metals, such as aluminum, titanium, manganese, and cobalt, could see worsening imbalances of supply and demand in the future.[32] Such imbalances may create disruptions because some countries' supply chains can be heavily dependent on imports. For example, the United States is more than 90 percent import-reliant for many minerals, such as manganese (100%), bauxite for aluminum (100%), platinum (94%), and uranium (90%).[33] Other material scarcity stress points in global supply chains include indium (used in computer display panels), silicon (chips and solar power), and wood fiber (paper, furniture, and biofuel).[34]

Shortages and significant price shocks can take place in many types of commodities, even ordinary ones, as a result of a confluence of events. For example, between 2006 and 2012, corn prices tripled,[35] affecting food prices, meat prices (for corn-fed animals), sugar prices (derived from corn syrup), and ethanol prices (biofuels derived from corn). High food prices can also lead to social unrest (see chapter 12).

Scarcity and price spikes can also hit manufactured goods. After the 2011 Thailand floods, prices for large-capacity hard disk drives for servers and high-end desktops rose by double- or triple-digit percentages. "We're looking easily at $75 more per computer," said Matt Bullock, chief technology officer at Nova Mesa Computer Systems. "This is just one more factor that will separate the strong from the weak," added David Milman, CEO of Rescuecom, which builds and repairs PCs. Also, during 2006, the prices of very large truck tires quadrupled because of the booms in mining, construction, industrialization in emerging markets, and US defense needs in Iraq and Afghanistan. "Right now the entire mining industry is going berserk, and we're feeding into it," said Michael Hickman, owner of H&H Industries, one of the United States's largest retreaders of used mining tires, whose company tripled its work force between 2004 and 2006.[36]

Of course, a sharp drop in the price of any commodity, while a boon to customers, can threaten manufacturers. Just as the price of crude oil slumped in the second half of 2014, the price of other commodities, such as copper, lead and nickel, fell between 2011 and 2014.[37] Nomura gold analyst Tyler Broda estimated that 15 percent of global gold miners would be under water given the 2013 slump in gold prices. "Any company that hasn't been focused on efficiencies and costs for the last three to four years is going to fail in this market," said Gavin Thomas, chief executive officer of Sydney-based gold miner Kingsgate Consolidated Ltd.[38] Primary materials producers often have expensive capital assets and large debts, making them susceptible to bankruptcy if the price of the commodity falls below their costs of production.[39]

Commodity price increases can lead, indirectly, to other supply chain problems, such as theft. For example, in 2012, thieves stole 359 ingots of copper, each weighing over 800 pounds, from a mining facility in Arizona. The criminals tried to smuggle the $1.25 million in copper to China but were interdicted at the Port of Los Angeles. In addition, shortages of high-tech manufactured products create strong incentives for counterfeiting, as discussed in chapter 7.

Resource Nationalism

In July 2010, China restricted exports of rare-earth elements. Its chokehold on 95 percent of the world supply of REE basically cut off many companies that make products using these materials.[40] In response, the United States lodged a formal protest with the World Trade Organization (WTO). EU trade commissioner Karel De Gucht said, "China's restrictions on rare earths and other products violate international trade rules and must be removed. These measures hurt our producers and consumers in the EU and across the world, including manufacturers of pioneering high-tech and 'green' business applications."[41]

China countered that the move was to conserve natural resources and protect the environment, which was devastated by mining.[42] Yet restricting exports also serves China's strategic economic development plans by ensuring that Chinese makers of rare earth–containing products get preferential allocations of scarce supplies. This helps China develop into a maker of high-value goods.[43] Although some viewed China's requirement for environment permits as a thinly veiled scheme to prevent exports, it should be noted that refining rare-earth minerals does produce a witch's brew of toxic and radioactive byproducts. In fact, radioactive wastewater leaks contributed to the shutdown of the largest rare-earth mine in the United States in 2002.[44]

China's rare-earth export policy was but one of many examples of resource nationalism in which governments restricted the availability of commodities produced within their borders. Besides export restrictions, special taxes on mining are another kind of resource nationalism. Countries that announced or enacted increases to taxes or royalties during 2011 and 2012 include major producers such as Australia, China, the Democratic Republic of Congo, Indonesia, Ghana, Mongolia, Peru, Poland, South Africa, and the United States.[45] Governments' rationale for these actions include Australia's desire to reap higher tax revenues from surging commodities prices,[46] Indonesia's strategic intentions to move the country up the value chain,[47] and China's desire to ensure that its local industries have access to sufficient supplies.[48]

INPUTS' PRICE AND AVAILABILITY RISKS

Companies can mitigate the risks of scarcity and price shocks with specific procurement practices. For short-term protection, companies can create buffer stocks. For example, following Hurricane Katrina—which knocked out 95 percent of oil production in the Gulf of Mexico and induced a 40 cent per gallon fuel price spike[49]—UPS began building 1,200 underground automated storage tanks in the United States that it could tap in the event of another hurricane.

When the Rate Is Against You

With global supply chains come the risks of fluctuations in foreign exchange (FX) rates. A company might be buying raw materials in US dollars, paying for labor in Thai baht, and getting customer revenues in euros. "When the dollar slips in value, as it did sharply in 2008, US companies sourcing and operating internationally in countries with currencies appreciating against the dollar can face rising material and shipping costs as well as increasing labor costs," explained Tim Dumond, corporate advisory and restructuring services principal.[50] Naturally, when the dollar appreciates in value, companies with US operations are at a disadvantage in export markets. For chemicals giant BASF, even a one-cent shift in the US dollar/euro exchange rate has the potential to add or subtract €50 million in annual earnings.[51] These exposures are significant enough that over one quarter of executives in a 2011 World Economic Forum survey cited currency risks as triggers of global supply chain disruptions ahead of the risk of energy shortages, labor shortages, and pandemics.[52]

Hedging and Long-Term Contracts

"Our goal in hedging currencies and commodities in our auto manufacturing operations is to lock in some near term certainty for the revenues and costs of our vehicle production worldwide," said Neil Schloss, vice president and treasurer of the Ford Motor Company.[53] A company can avoid price surprises for fuel, commodities, and exchange rates by negotiating long-term, fixed-price contracts denominated in the company's preferred currency. But if a company's suppliers refuse to accept those terms, then the company can use financial derivatives (so called because these contracts *derive* their value from the performance of the underlying commodity). One type of derivatives contract locks in a fixed price, while another allows the company more nuanced control over exposure to a range of price changes. Derivatives tend to be highly leveraged, such that small amounts of corporate capital can control large positions in futures contracts.

With the first type of hedging, the company uses forward contracts in the financial markets to buy (or sell) the same or a related commodity on some future delivery date but at a fixed price. Through this hedge, the company can keep its floating price relationship with its preferred suppliers while creating a financial position in the futures markets that offsets the fluctuations in commodities costs from those suppliers. For example, BASF uses derivatives to hedge the risks of price increases in raw materials including crude oil, oil products, natural gas, precious metals, and electricity. The company also uses financial derivatives to manage foreign currency risks, interest rate risks, and sales price risks for agricultural products.[54] A 2010 survey by the Association for Financial Professionals found that 72 percent of organizations with exposure to foreign-exchange risks hedge their exposure.[55]

In the second strategy, companies buy and sell options, which are contracts that give the option-holder the right, but not the obligation, to buy or sell a commodity at a given price regardless of the prevailing market price. This creates an upper (or lower) bound on the effective price of the commodity. For example, a company might buy *call* options at 20 percent above the current base price on a key material to limit the possibility of high cost of that material. If the price jumps higher than 20 percent above the base price, the company can exercise the option and pay just 20 percent above the base price (even if the prevailing price has doubled). But if the future price falls or only rises 10 percent, then the company would not exercise the option but would buy the key material at the prevailing price. Similarly, a producer of a commodity might use *put* options that set a floor price for its goods. Using options for hedging protects the company while still preserving the chance that if prices move favorably, the company can benefit from the price changes.

Although options sound like they have no downside, they do have significant upfront costs. Options expire on a certain date and are worthless if the price does not move past the threshold defined by the option. In that regard, options are like insurance—the company pays a premium for a contract and the contract covers the risk of a price change event if the event occurs. Options are particularly useful during volatile times, and naturally they are more expensive during such periods. They are also costly if the company wants to avoid even small exposures to price fluctuations, and if the company needs price protection over a longer duration.

Derivatives contracts are assets on a company's balance sheet that can create financial risks even as they mitigate supply risks. After Southwest Airlines bought futures contracts to cover much of its fuel needs, it enjoyed a $511 million gain in early 2008 when fuel prices surged. But when the financial crisis hit and fuel prices plummeted later in 2008, the value of those futures contracts plummeted from $6 billion to $2.5 billion, forcing the carrier to take a $247 million one-time charge and declare its first loss in 17 years.[56] Similarly, the large decline in the price of fuel at the end of 2014 caused Delta Airlines to project a $1.2 billion write-off as a result of fuel hedging, while American Airlines, which does not hedge fuel prices, was set to enjoy windfall profits as a result of the lower fuel price.[57] By the same token, a hedged supplier of a commodity foregoes the windfall profits that would occur if prices increase. Some oil producers lost out on potential high profits during the early 2008 surge in oil prices.[58] Moreover, derivatives positions may require cash collateral to create and maintain the hedge.[59]

Yet, both sides to a futures contract can avoid significant losses albeit forgoing windfall gains. The supplier ensures that its sales price is not lower than its cost, and the buyer ensures that its costs are no higher than its selling price. "I'm just trying to ensure we know what our costs are. We know when we quote a price to a customer that we've locked in our profit," said Gary Wool, chief financial officer at Preferred Plastics & Packaging.[60] To the extent that a company optimizes its operations based on a certain price of fuel, then futures contracts can ensure that the price of fuel the company uses will not deviate from that price regardless of the market price. Despite Southwest's roller-coaster experience with hedging in 2008, it continued to buy derivatives to lock in fuel prices up to four to five years into the future.[61]

Localizing Production

"The weak U.S. dollar [during 2009] has made it more competitive for foreign companies to do business in the U.S.," said Jeff Olin, national managing partner of International Tax Services at Grant Thornton.[62] Speaking about the company's LEAF electric vehicle program, Nissan's CEO, Carlos Ghosn said, "When we started the offensive on the LEAF, it was back in 2006, 2007, where the yen to the dollar exchange rate was about 110. When we started selling the LEAF, the dollar to the yen was about 80, which, obviously, we had to absorb more than 25 percent over cost, compared to what we were planning. Not because our guys did not work well, but because we had a major element in the competitive environment, which played against us." To cope with exchange rate risks, the company started producing the LEAF in the United States and will also be producing it in Europe, thus matching manufacturing costs to selling prices. "The trajectory of localizing production, cutting the cost, reducing the cost, is going very well," the CEO said.[63]

Exchange rates, however, are not the only rationale for locating manufacturing closer to the demand, or reshoring. Rising wages in China, higher fuel prices, better operational controls, and proximity to customers also motivate a return of manufacturing from distant shores. High fuel prices motivated Stonyfield Farms to consider moving sourcing and manufacturing closer to the point of consumption to minimize total transportation requirements.[64] A 2012 survey found that more than a third (37 percent) of large manufacturers were planning or considering reshoring to the United States.[65] These considerations change direction with the strength of the US dollar in 2015 and the collapse in the price of the euro.

Vertical Integration: Procure the Producer

Delta Airlines made an unusual move to protect itself against large increases in the spread between the cost of oil and the cost of jet fuel, known in the oil industry as the *crack spread*. In 2012, the airline bought an oil refinery in Delaware for $150 million, spent $100 million upgrading the facility to increase jet fuel production, and is buying crude oil directly.[66] Delta expects the arrangement to save about $300 million annually[67] on the airline's $12 billion cost of fuel. Moreover, by trading the gasoline and diesel fuel that's coproduced by the refinery for more jet fuel, Delta will acquire 80 percent of its fuel needs at a discount. CFO Paul Jacobson said Delta expects the deal "to be accretive to Delta's earnings, expand our margins, and to fully recover our investment in the first year of operations."[68] Some companies in other commodity-intensive industries, such as steel, have chosen vertical integration to address price and availability risks of raw material such as coal and iron ore.[69]

Yet, like most other risk mitigation strategies, vertical integration may swap one supply chain risk for another (possibly smaller one), as well as involve unexpected costs. Delta's vertical integration strategy brought it some of each. Hurricane Sandy delayed the start of the acquired refinery, and a gasoline-production outage created early losses for the project.[70] With vertical integration, Delta may be less exposed to global jet fuel price increases but more affected by its own local refinery's facilities risks. Analysis of vertical integration in the steel industry finds similar risk issues, especially because mining iron ore is a far riskier business than steel making.[71]

TURNING DOWN THE VOLUME ON PRICE INCREASES

Companies can respond to scarcity and price increases of inputs in a variety of ways. In the short run, a company might absorb such a disruption by using inventories or hedging. But large or long-term scarcity or price disruption requires larger or longer-term supply chain changes. Three strategies with respect to input materials can reduce the impacts of long-term scarcity and price increases: efficiency, substitution, and recycling. All three materials strategies displace primary resource consumption and reduce pressure on primary supplies.

Efficiency: Use Less, Pay Less

Efficiency is the first input-material strategy for reducing the impact of price spikes. When palladium prices spiked in the late 1990s, catalytic-converter makers found ways to use less of the precious metal. Thinner coatings reduced the amount of palladium per converter, and less-polluting engine designs reduced the need for large convertors.[72] The price spike also encouraged investment in the efficiency of palladium-refining processes. For example, Norilsk Nickel, a major producer of palladium, invested in improving its metal recovery from ores, resulting in increases in production efficiency.[73]

When bunker fuel prices doubled in 2008, ocean carriers started using slow steaming to reduce fuel consumption. The strong relationship between speed and drag means that most transportation modes use less fuel at lower speeds. Running vessels more slowly can save owners significant outlays. For example, operating a 12,000 TEU container ship at 18 knots instead of 20 knots can reduce the fuel consumption by almost 30 percent.[74] Of course, spending more time at sea offsets some of these savings—a trip from the port of Shanghai to the port of Rotterdam takes 28 days at 20 knots vs. 25 days at 18 knots, a 12 percent increase in the labor and asset costs.[75] The higher the cost of fuel the more the savings on fuel justifies the added expense of a longer journey time. By late 2011, 75 percent of carriers surveyed by Man Diesel and Turbo SE had implemented slow steaming.[76]

The same physical phenomena that cause ocean ships' fuel consumption to climb rapidly with speed also affect other transportation modes. Thus, carriers in other modes have looked at slowing down as a fuel-saving strategy, such as by using speed limiters on trucks. Limiting a truck's speed to 65 mph, instead of 75 mph, saves 15-20 percent on fuel over a trip.[77] In fact, the US 55 mph limit on highway speed was originally enacted during the 1973 oil price spike and supply disruptions (limiting truck speeds to 55 mph would save almost 30 percent in fuel). Aircraft also consume less fuel at lower cruising speeds and can optimize fuel use through management of the vertical flight profile, as well as other operational enhancements.

Slow steaming's longer transit times affect the supply chain, though. More than half of shippers (52 percent) cited increased inventory levels (cycle stock) and the related holding costs as the main effect of slow steaming. The second impact cited was customer service levels owing to the difficulties of supplying parts as fast as customers asked for them. In addition, companies had to adjust production scheduling to account for the longer lead times.[78] On the other hand, ocean carriers have become more reliable than in the past because the slow speed allows for buffer time in transit. This can mitigate somewhat the effects of slow steaming on another inventory element: safety stock.[79]

Substitution and Flexibility

Substitution is a second strategy for reducing price risks by reducing exposure to the risky commodity. In the face of scarcity or surging prices, companies seek technological innovations that use cheaper materials to substitute for the more expensive ones. For example, one of the largest uses of rare-earth metals is in ultrastrong magnets, which are used in everything from disk drives to automobile power windows, electric car motors, and wind turbine generators. Given the large increases of REE prices and their availability risk, wind turbine makers are looking at new generator designs that don't need rare-earth magnets, substituting other electronic technologies to reduce use of these materials.[80]

In fact, price increases can reach a tipping point that causes permanent change. In 1980, Zaire, now known as the Democratic Republic of the Congo, had only 0.06 percent of the world's population but produced 40 percent of the world's cobalt, a metal used in steel, magnets, and other applications. A revolution in Zaire in 1980 caused cobalt prices to spike six-fold and made cobalt-based magnets too expensive. Some magnet makers went out of business. The one-time price spike created a permanent dislocation, however. Magnet buyers and surviving magnet makers made material substitutions and never went back to using cobalt, even when cobalt prices returned to normal.[81] Ironically, the substitute magnet material was neodymium, which is one of the rare earths that spiked in price in 2010.

Companies can also substitute fuels. For example, the growing supply of natural gas made available by hydraulic fracturing of shale formations in the United States decreased prices of that energy source. Those falling prices have encouraged trucking companies and truck makers to switch from diesel to natural gas. Switching fuels can require substantial upfront capital investments that are then repaid through lower ongoing fuel costs. For example, Waste Management is buying compressed natural gas-fueled garbage trucks[82] that cost $30,000 more per truck, but then save the company $27,000 a year per truck in fuel costs.[83] "The economics favoring natural gas are overwhelming," said Scott Perry, a vice president at Ryder Systems Inc., in 2012.[84] Even with the low crude oil prices, by the end of 2014 natural gas prices[85] corresponded to about half the price of diesel fuel.[86]

In some cases, companies can flexibly substitute commodities at will. For example, companies can use flexible fuel vehicles that can run on either diesel or LNG. Kathryn Clay, executive director of the Drive Natural Gas initiative of the American Gas Association, says, "The new technology is really game changing because the trucker can run on either fuel."[87] Similarly, both palladium and platinum can be used in automotive catalytic convertors, industrial process catalysts, and jewelry. Users of these metals switch between the two depending on their relative prices.[88] To respond dynamically to price changes, companies can pre-identify, when feasible, substitute materials at the outset and design product variants for different raw materials to give themselves flexibility in the event of a disruption in the source of one of the materials.

Flexibility through substitution helps ensure continuity of supply, which a 2011 PWC survey found to be the most important lever for supply chain flexibility.[89] In the survey, 71 percent of respondents were working on setting up flexible production and assembly facilities—capable of using various factor inputs—when prices or availability change.

Recycle Materials to Create a Secondary Source

Recycling is a third strategy for reducing scarcity and price risks. An MIT study of the platinum market found that recycling can play a role in both lowering prices and stabilizing the price of this precious metal.[90] Three factors help recycling reduce risks of availability and price increases. First, recycling creates a new, diffuse source of the commodity that is independent of the factors that induce price increase in the primary supply, such as geopolitical instabilities. Second, for many materials, recycling consumes less energy than does primary extraction and refinement. This uncouples, to some extent, the price of the material from energy price increases. Third, recycling stabilizes prices because in times of short primary supply, recyclers can more quickly increase recycling capacity than miners can increase primary supply.[91]

As a material's price rises, the economic motivations for reclaiming the material from industrial and postconsumer sources increase. For Johnson Controls, the benefits of recycling automotive batteries are obvious: up to 80 to 90 percent of the lead used to make batteries can come from recycled content, providing a significant price advantage and protection from availability risks. To collect the batteries after use, the company encourages retailers, mechanics, and even junkyards to hold on to the batteries consumers leave behind. The batteries are collected either when new ones are delivered or on special runs.[92]

Similarly, specialized e-waste recycling efforts target the recoverable materials in consumer electronics. Intel, for example, works with PC makers to ensure that recyclers can reclaim the valuable metals and materials in chips and electronic equipment. Dell had by 2014 already recycled a billion pounds of electronic waste toward its stated goal of 2 billion pounds. The company partnered with Goodwill Industries to enable electronic waste recycling at 2,000 Goodwill sites in the United States.[93]

Recycling has other benefits beyond mitigating price risks. It also is an environmental sustainability initiative (see chapter 11) that can also reduce disposal costs. Recycling can often take advantage of empty backhaul capacity for the reverse logistics that move recovered materials from retail outlets upstream.

Although recycling may be easier than developing new primary sources, it faces technological, social, and regulatory challenges. First, recyclable materials tend to be commingled with other materials in the end product, creating physical challenges in separating the desirable recyclable materials from each other and from waste materials. For example, a personal computer contains a wide range of different materials[94] such as plastics, metals, lead, gold, and rare earths that are physically and chemically intermingled. Second, cultural and social norms create barriers in the form of consumer habits, market resistance, and transaction frictions in getting discarded goods to a pickup point and recycling center. The Japanese carefully recycle 77 percent of their plastic waste, while Americans recycle only 20 percent of their plastic.[95] Third, regulatory policies might have unexpected (and unintended) consequences on recycling. For example, the US Toxic Substances Control Act (TSCA) creates a compliance burden for companies attempting to recycle electronic waste.[96]

SURCHARGES: TRANSFERRING THE RISK TO OTHERS

A company can transfer its price risks to its customers via a surcharge linked to the price of the risky commodity. When oil prices surged, many transportation providers—including trucking companies, ocean carriers, and air carriers—levied fuel surcharges that were separate from the baseline. In addition to fuel and energy surcharges, suppliers have also added surcharges for steel,[97] copper, rare earths,[98] helium,[98] and other commodities.

The Magic Formula

Adding a surcharge can solve the problem of risks latent in the conflicted time frames between long-term, fixed-price supply contracts sought by customers and the short-term commodity price volatility that can wreck the finances of suppliers. To solve this conflict in a "fair" way, the contract for the product or service would have two components. First, the contract includes a baseline, long-term, fixed price that covers known costs such as equipment, maintenance, and labor, as well as baseline costs for the risky input element at some pre-agreed "peg" or baseline market price. Second, the contract specifies a surcharge price component that references an independent price index, the peg price, and an escalator (the amount the cost of the product or service escalates for each dollar of price increase in the price index). The index comes from an impartial third party—for fuel in the United States, truckers and shippers commonly use the US Energy Information Administration's weekly regional survey of fuel prices.[100] The escalator reflects the amount of the risky commodity consumed by the product or service, such as fuel consumed per mile, steel used per screw, or the amount of plastic in a bottle. Commercial real estate leases have long included detailed terms for a base rent plus a litany of escalators and pass-through costs for power, water, taxes, gas, inflation, and all sorts of other special charges.

The escalator term is especially important because it controls the amount of risk transfer. If the escalator is too low, the supplier is still exposed to some price risks. If the escalator is too high, the supplier profits from high commodity prices while the customer sees excessive price increases. The correct value of the escalator is determined by the amount of resource used by the supplier and its efficiency. In the case of fuel surcharges, it's the fuel efficiency of the truck (or other transportation mode)—how much fuel is used per mile traveled (including the effects of empty miles). In the case of materials surcharges (e.g., the price of screws vs. the price of steel), the value is determined by the material content of the part (which is the weight of the part plus scrap minus any recycled or reworked scrap). For example, if the global price of steel increases by 10 percent, and the net steel content in a screw amounts to 40 percent of the screw's cost, then the price increase should be 4 percent.

Perceptions of Fairness

Suppliers and customers often bargain vigorously over the particulars of risk transfer mechanisms. Discussions at a supply chain roundtable at the MIT Center for Transportation and Logistics during 2008 revealed that many shippers felt gouged by transportation carriers' surcharges through two mechanisms. First, shippers thought that while the price of fuel in the surcharge formula was tied to a government index, the index did not reflect the carriers' actual fuel costs. Carriers could buy diesel fuel in bulk and therefore pay less than the index price. Moreover, motor carriers can use the 1,000–2,000 mile range between refueling to exploit regional variations between fuel prices and buy fuel at lower-than-index prices. Also, carriers can hedge fuel costs. Thus, although fuel prices may rise at the pump (and on the fuel price index used to calculate the surcharge), the carriers' actual cost of fuel might be lower. While shippers applauded carriers' efforts to minimize fuel costs, they wanted to see those savings reflected in the transportation price.

Second, shippers thought that carriers, especially in airfreight, were selectively timing the surcharge for the carrier's benefit. Shippers felt that airlines were quick to add a fuel surcharge when fuel prices rose but seemed slow in reducing the surcharge after fuel prices dropped. Shippers noted that after fuel prices dropped to presurcharge levels, air carriers were still charging 12 cents more per pound shipped. Yet the story may not be so simple, because airlines buy fuel on contracts that may be a year out, so their average cost of fuel might remain high even after a price drop. (Of course, this also means that surcharge increases should lag fuel price increases.) According to Tom Linton, chief procurement and supply chain officer at Flextronics, in some cases the buyer may want to audit the supplier's processes before agreeing to an escalation clause.

Finally, while suppliers seek to protect themselves from significant cost increases of key inputs, customers want to motivate suppliers to reduce consumption of the risky commodity, such as by becoming more efficient, substituting another input, or recycling, as mentioned in the previous section. Customers may not want the surcharge to insulate the supplier from commodity price increases so much that the supplier has no incentive to invest in efficiency.

MANAGING PRICE RISKS

Although managing commodity risks does parallel the methods for managing other causes of supply disruptions (see chapters 3 and 7), it differs in four key areas. First, commodity scarcity risks are not tied to specific suppliers, which means dual sourcing offers little benefit because the source of the risk is broader than any given supplier. Second, unlike earthquakes or accidents, commodity price volatility events are global, not local occurrences in the sense that the price of the commodity might surge or plunge on global markets affecting all users regardless other location or choice of supplier. Third, salient information about the risk might not reside in the bill of materials (BOM) because the underlying types and amounts of commodities used may not be defined for any but the most trivial parts. Complex parts (e.g., a door assembly or circuit board) may contain a multitude of materials that are not called out on the OEM's BOM. Only the deeper tier BOMs might have the raw materials listed. Fourth, scarcity risks can arise from demand growth or spikes in unrelated industries, thus putting the cause outside the supply chain of the company.

Assessing Exposure to Risk

The first step in estimating the potential of price and availability risks is to identify what commodities prices the company may be exposed to and the amount of exposure. Whether this is easy or difficult varies by material and its uses. For example, when Ford analyzed the effects of rare-earths price volatility on vehicle costs, it took 18 months to find all the rare earths used in its cars, because Ford doesn't purchase rare earths directly.[101] In addition, rare earths comprise more than a dozen different elements, with a great many obscure applications in sensors, electronics, displays, motors, and catalysts. One tricky aspect of this step is finding hidden consumption or dependencies deeper in the supply chain—materials required by suppliers that aren't in the supplier's products but are used in their processes. The most common hidden commodity is energy used in production and transport; many key metals such as aluminum, gold, and copper require substantial amounts of energy to refine, which makes their prices sensitive to surges in oil and energy costs. They may also be indirect materials such as cleansers, catalysts, or materials used by manufacturing processes but not present in the finished product.

Ironically, deep-tier or indirect commodities exposures can imply that financial hedging makes a company's financial statements more volatile, even as the hedging makes their cash flows and ultimate costs-of-goods less volatile. For example, Ford hedges various metals that go into the components that it buys from its suppliers. Yet because Ford does not buy these metals directly, it is prohibited under accounting rules from designating the hedges as an offset to specific costs. Under these rules, to the extent that the market value of so-called nondesignated hedges fluctuate, Ford must declare the gain or loss immediately, which causes Ford's earnings to appear to fluctuate.[102]

Understanding Each Commodity's Risk

The second step is to identify causes of risk based on factors such as the origins of the raw materials, total known reserves of raw materials, and trends in demand. Price volatility events don't follow power laws like earthquakes and accidents do. Instead, they are driven by patterns of supply and demand, mismatches in the growth of the two, and the effects of inelasticity that can amplify small changes in supply or demand into large changes in price.

For example, the fact that China provides most of the world's rare earths (and magnesium) brings risks of resource nationalism that could (and did) constrain supply and cause a price spike. Some materials are sourced from one limited geographic area, such as South Africa, which provides most of the world's platinum. This creates exposure to natural disasters or political upheavals that could threaten supply and cause price spikes. Even if the commodity comes from many geographic sources (e.g., oil), price inelasticity can imply large global effects from modest local disruptions. Demand trends can drive risks, too. Prices for copper, for example, rose fivefold between 2003 and 2008, slumped by two-thirds during the financial crisis and then rose again to record levels after the crisis only to drop by one-third toward the end of 2014.[103]

Companies can also face causes of price or availability risks that come from outside their industry. For example, Tyson raises and sells chicken as well as other food products. Corn, soybean meal, and other feed ingredients account for 71 percent of the cost of growing a chicken. Prices of these grains fluctuate wildly with the vagaries of weather and farming. Yet the company also cites the renewable energy industry as a contributor to grain price risk because ethanol and biodiesel makers compete with Tyson for grain supplies.[104]

Price risk might have some natural bounds or cycles. Trends in price can affect supply (e.g., motivating development of new sources of supply) and demand (e.g., motivating efficiency or substitution). Many basic materials are under long-term price pressures because of the inexorable economic growth in demand and the environmental difficulties in developing new supplies. At the same time, speculation about increasing commodity prices can lead to short-term price bubbles in commodities, which, in turn, leads to hoarding, causing artificial shortages and further escalating prices. But then after supply catches up with demand, the price collapses as the bubble bursts and the hoarders dump their stockpiles. The behavior of suppliers, middlemen, and customers amplifies volatility up the supply chain in a bullwhip effect, exacerbating price volatility in commodities including rice, cotton, copper, oil, iron, and steel.[105] Other materials, such as natural rubber, can be easily substituted and might cycle up and down in price with less likelihood of severe prolonged shortages.

Assessing Mitigation Options

The third step is to choose among many strategies for coping with price risks. These can include: minimizing consumption of the commodity subject to price risk; transferring price risks to suppliers by negotiating long-term fixed-price contracts; transferring price risks to customers via surcharges; assuming price risks via flexible operations; and hedging price risks in the financial markets or with physical inventories. Part of this assessment considers the time required for the company to mitigate the problem, as is the case with any other disruption. This can include lead time to create new primary supplies (e.g., new mines or factories), time to convert to using recycled material, or product development times that would reduce consumption of the scarce material or allow substitution of materials.

In assessing these options, a company estimates the extent to which cost increases could be passed on to customers (via surcharges or price increases), to suppliers (via long-term fixed-price contracts), or to other third parties (via hedging). Whereas restaurant chains such as Morton's Steakhouse or Capital Grille in the United States can raise prices modestly, McDonald's cannot, because McDonald's customers will notice if their Big Mac is priced a few cents higher. Passing price risks to a business partner such as a supplier or B2B customer involves negotiation and depends on the relative strengths in the relationship and whether the partner's business model can manage the risk. A company might also use hedging in the financial markets, assuming that the scarce commodity, or a related commodity, trades on these markets.

Ford's commodity price risk mitigation strategy varies by material. Ford uses derivatives hedging for materials such as precious metals, aluminum, and copper that have a deep and liquid financial hedging market. The company uses long-term fixed-price contracts to lock in the price with suppliers for materials such as plastics and steel where derivative markets are not fully developed or available.[106]

The various hedging strategies work on different timescales and can complement each other. For example, in the short term, surcharges are adjusted "automatically" based on the underlying index. Of medium duration, financial hedging strategies generally cover months or a few years at most. Ford's hedging of commodities, for example, covers a maximum of two years.[107] A 2011 survey found that 62 percent of companies hedge foreign exchange risks on a horizon of 12 months or less.[108] Other strategies may take much longer because they involve more substantive changes in products, processes, and facilities. For example, physical foreign exchange hedging by building plants on different continents and matching production with sales takes years. Similarly, substitutions of basic commodities, such as switching from steel to aluminum or from diesel engines to electric drivetrains, take time because of the nontrivial changes in product design and manufacturing.

11

SHIFTING ETHICS, RISING BARS

A single indelible image, such as that of a very young Pakistani boy sewing a Nike soccer ball for reportedly six cents an hour,[1] can change public sentiment overnight. The 1996 image on the cover of *Life* magazine led to a "Boycott Nike" campaign, and the company lost more than half its market capitalization in the ensuing year. It took the company six years of demonstrated corporate social responsibility efforts to regain the lost value. Nor is Nike's case unique. For example, when insurance company Aon introduced its company's reputational risk coverage, CEO, Greg Case, said, "Eighty percent of Aon's business clients will suffer an event that will cause them to lose more than twenty percent of their value every five years."[2]

Warren Buffett said, "It takes 20 years to build a reputation and five minutes to ruin it. If you think about that, you'll do things differently."[3] Much of the value of modern multinational companies is tied to their brands. In 2002, *BusinessWeek* estimated that more than 50 percent of the market capitalization of companies such as Coca Cola, Disney, and McDonald's is contributed by their brand, leading to multi-billion-dollar estimates of the brand value.[4] Many of these companies believe internally that the figure is much higher.

A company's reputation can affect consumer demand, the supply of job applicants, and investor sentiment.[5] Reputational risks can also create direct financial risks. A spate of suicides at Foxconn forced the company to raise wages, which led to the stock losing half its value.[6] And, in April 2010, Goldman Sachs lost 12.6 percent of its market value when the Securities and Exchange Commission

(SEC) announced a fraud investigation that month. (The investigation was dropped in 2012 when the SEC concluded that "there is no viable basis" for the prosecution[7]—but the reputational damage was done.)

In the wake of the BP Horizon drill rig disaster in April 2010—which was being managed by a BP contractor—BP lost $53 billion in market capitalization. Three years later, the stock was still 30 percent lower than its value on April 2010, just before the disaster, even though its profit margins were higher, demonstrating that it still suffered from brand degradation.

Many potential reputational risks lurk in global supply chains. These risks include labor and sourcing practices of suppliers, the natural resources footprint of the supply chain (energy, carbon, water, mineral, emissions, etc.), and the perceptions of product safety that are often due to product ingredients used by suppliers, as well as suppliers' material sourcing and manufacturing methods. More often than not, NGOs and the media will attack Western brand owners, especially those that sell to consumers, owing to their greater vulnerability to corporate social responsibility (CSR) charges—even if they have no knowledge or direct control over deep-tier suppliers. Consequently, beyond ensuring their own CSR practices, many companies spend significant effort to enforce a code of conduct on their suppliers.

OF SWEATSHOPS AND DEATH TRAPS

On April 24, 2013, horrific images saturated news outlets as over 1,100 bodies were pulled from the collapsed eight-story Rana Plaza garment factory in Bangladesh.[8] Muhammad Yunus, the Bangladeshi Nobel laureate, wrote that the disaster was "a symbol of our failure as a nation."[9] Rana Plaza wasn't an isolated incident. Six months before the Rana Plaza disaster, a fire at a different Bangladeshi garment factory, Tazreen Fashions, killed 112.[10] Events in Bangladesh put a tragic human face on repugnant conditions deep within some companies' global supply chains.

Paralleling the gruesome search for bodies under the rubble of Rana Plaza was the search for the Western companies behind the orders for the garments made in the collapsed factory. Most companies denied using the suppliers who were operating in the structurally unsound building where employees were forced to work despite large cracks appearing in the walls on the previous day. Ultimately, name-brand companies such as Benetton, Mango, Bon-Marche, Primark, and The Children's Place acknowledged their current or past use of the suppliers operating in the collapsed structure.[11] Nor was worker safety the only social concern in Bangladesh. When Pope Francis learned that Bangladesh's minimum wage was only $40 per month, he said, "This is called slave labor."[12]

Many companies simply didn't know which suppliers they were using, given the murky web of brokers, contractors, and subcontractors operating in countries like Bangladesh. For example, when the Tazreen Fashions factory burned, Walmart firmly believed it was not involved. More than a year prior to the fire, Walmart had banned Tazreen Fashions from its approved supplier list after auditors hired by Walmart inspected the factory and declared Tazreen to be "high risk." But one of Walmart's other authorized suppliers subcontracted with another authorized supplier and then that subcontractor shifted the work to Tazreen.[13]

Revelations of substandard working conditions can disrupt a company's operations in at least three ways: consumer revulsion disrupts demand, worker unrest disrupts supply, and regulatory changes can affect costs. "Companies feel tremendous pressure now," said Scott Nova, the executive director of the Worker Rights Consortium, a factory-monitoring group based in Washington, DC.[14] And he added, "The apparel brands and retailers face a greater level of reputation risk of being associated with abusive and dangerous conditions in Bangladesh than ever before."[15] "Worker safety and worker welfare have now been brought into the forefront," declared a top adviser to Bangladesh's prime minister.[16]

Worker Safety

After years of unsafe automobile wheel hub polishing practices, a massive dust explosion killed 75 workers and injured another 185 at Kunshan Zhongrong Metal Production Company on August 2, 2014. Chinese officials blamed the chairman of the factory and local regulators for the severe safety lapses.[17] Yet China Labor Watch, an NGO dedicated to workers' causes, also blamed GM, because the car maker used car wheel maker Citic Dicastal Wheel Manufacturing Co., the world's biggest aluminum alloy wheel hub producer, and Citic Dicastal used Zhongrong.

In response to the accident, GM president Dan Ammann offered his condolences but also said, "Our tier-one suppliers on a global basis are required to make sure that they are sourcing from suppliers that are implementing the right safety standards."[18] China Labor Watch took issue with GM's efforts to distance itself from unsafe deep-tier suppliers, saying that GM "has a duty to ensure safe production in its supply chain, and it shares responsibility for this deadly explosion."[19]

In addition to the criticism, the event created physical disruptions in GM's supply chain. GM had to find alternative suppliers and incurred significant added expenses as a result of unconsolidated purchases from multiple alternative suppliers as well as expediting shipments to avoid disrupted production of cars. Deliveries were further threatened when Chinese authorities closed some 268 factories without warning as part of a crackdown on dust-related safety lapses.[20]

The challenge GM faced was familiar to many other companies—a failure by a small, deep-tier supplier in a distant developing country can tarnish the OEM's global brand. To outward appearances, Citic Dicastal has been a good Tier 1 supplier to GM since 2003.[21] Citic Dicastal had even won a *supplier of the year* award from GM in 2010.[22] "Citic Dicastal's own factories are clean and well-organized," said a middleman who had done business with Citic Dicastal but who also noted, "their external suppliers are small businesses with awful working conditions."[23] Zhongrong had been inspected by the government, but Liu Fuwen, a worker at Zhongrong, said, "If government officials came to inspect the factory, management would ask the workers to clean the dust before they arrived."[24]

Disney may be one of the most reputation-sensitive companies in the world, with a corporate unit devoted to brand management that is responsible for both brand development and its protection.

Disney products and services are synonymous with happy families, the innocence of childhood, and wholesomeness. That image must extend to Disney's supply chain as well. "Our goal is to have a supply chain that mirrors Disney's own desire to operate as a responsible business," said John Lund, Disney's senior vice president, integrated supply chain management.[25] "We must rely more heavily upon our licensees and vendors to help ensure working conditions that are consistent with Disney's standards," added Josh Silverman, executive vice president for global licensing for Disney Consumer Products.[26]

Nearly two months before the Rana Plaza collapse, Disney ordered an end of sourcing from Bangladesh and four other countries (Pakistan, Belarus, Ecuador, and Venezuela) based on audits and personal visits by senior executives. The company told the affected licensees that it would pursue "a responsible transition that mitigates the impact to affected workers and business." It implemented a year-long transitional period to phase out production by March 31, 2014.[27]

Others may follow Disney's departure from Bangladesh. If that happens on a large scale, it will severely damage the country's social and economic fabric. Garment manufacturing employs 3.6 million workers in Bangladesh. The United Nations Research Institute for Social Development said that, for many women, "working in garments, for all its many problems, was a better way to make money than what one had done in the past."[28] Well-intentioned actions can have unintended consequences.

Blood in the Supply Chain

In April 2009, John Prendergast, a human rights activist who had worked for the Clinton White House, the State Department, and UNICEF prior to founding the Enough Project,[29] sent a letter to leading electronics firms, including Intel, HP, Motorola, and AT&T.[30] The letter warned these companies that four metals (gold, tantalum, tin, and tungsten) used in electronic products may have been mined under conditions of coercion and violence in the eastern region of the Democratic Republic of Congo (DRC). These minerals were *conflict minerals*, akin to blood diamonds. That is, militants and terrorists were forcing citizens through violence, rape, and other atrocities to mine the ore to help finance wars. The Enough Project sought to cut off indirect Western funding of the conflict by convincing companies not to buy conflict minerals. The reputational threat to the companies receiving the letter was clear.

Springing to Action At Intel, the letter first arrived on Gary Niekerk's desk. Niekerk, Intel's director of global citizenship, called an internal meeting with the VP of Intel's Materials Group. The first question was, "Are we actually using these conflict minerals?"[31] No one at Intel knew, because Intel itself didn't buy these metals directly; the minerals are merely raw ingredients used in parts Intel bought from other companies.

Next, Intel asked its suppliers, such as suppliers of capacitors, about the sources of their metals. "About 30–40% of suppliers responded that they didn't know," Niekerk said. "A similar percentage said 'we don't do that' but had no supporting evidence for that statement, and the rest didn't respond at all."[32] The minerals entered Intel's supply chain somewhere, many layers deep in the complex web of suppliers that ultimately leads to an Intel processor.

Niekerk saw that determining the provenance of the minerals would be difficult. The team presented its findings to Intel's Chief Operating Officer. "He went ballistic," Niekerk recalled, "saying this was unacceptable. He wanted to see a roadmap tracing the source for every metal." What's more, the COO put a stake in the ground. "I want to know by when we can say we are 'conflict free,'" Niekerk said, quoting the COO.[33] The team faced a daunting task, having to go many levels deep into its supply chain to identify the exact sources of these minerals.

Given the enormity of the task, the team decided to focus first on the roadmap for one metal, tantalum. The electronics industry consumes 60 percent of the world's tantalum supplies, but only 36 percent of the world's tin, and a mere 9 percent of the world's gold. Intel mapped the flow of tantalum from mines to smelters to customs agencies to supplier to supplier to supplier, downstream in the chain and finally to Intel. The mapping effort helped the company see that the relatively small number of smelters could be the logical focal point for controlling the source of ore. Smelters are also the last stage in the supply chain where the source of the ore could be identified. "Once it's turned into a bar of something, you can't trace the source," Niekerk said. "But as an ore, you can trace it. So we focused on smelters."[34]

Identifying smelters of tantalum was one thing, but getting their cooperation in identifying their ore supply sources and then convincing them not to purchase conflict minerals was another. The logical strategy for controlling conflict minerals was to create a pool of certified smelters who ensured the provenance of the ores they bought. Two issues made this difficult. First, it required certifying smelters around the world, including those outside the conflict-affected region. Second, these smelters sat six or seven layers deep in Intel's supply chain, which is far outside the usual span of business relationships and the normal influences that buyers have on their suppliers. Why would a Brazilian tantalum smelter care about Congolese ore or about an American chip-maker that's not the smelter's customer?

Between a Rock and Hard Place Worse, there were early unintended consequences in trying to block conflict minerals. Some smelters' initial response was to simply cease buying all minerals from Congo, but such a broad-brush approach was neither ethical nor effective. "We got letters from the Congo and NGOs saying that there are 100,000 artisan miners in the Congo trying to earn money to eat," Niekerk said, pointing out that not all of the miners work for the militants.[35] In the DRC in particular, mining is one of the two primary sources of income available (farming being the other.) "Putting a de facto ban on materials out of the Congo means that good people might starve," said Niekerk. Damaging the legitimate economy of the country would only fuel further unrest.

So the problem became much more complicated. "I went back to the NGO, saying we're doing what we can, but is it better or worse?" Niekerk said. With atrocities on one hand and starvation on the other, "doing the right thing" became much harder.

To be even more precise about the origin of the ore, Intel mapped over 90 percent of its microprocessor supply chain, identifying 130 unique smelters. Intel employees toured mines with NGOs and followed the journey of the minerals. As of May 2012, Intel employees had conducted more than 50 on-the-ground smelter reviews, visiting 13 countries in person to gain a firsthand understanding of the issues. These reviews helped Intel understand the unique operating characteristics of each smelter and determine the current gaps in their abilities to trace the source of ore from specific mines and countries. For example, some smelters had documentation indicating the country from which a mineral was shipped, but not documentation on the actual country from which the ore was originally mined. This is a critical issue because metals (especially gold) can be smuggled into other countries. "Just because it shipped from Rwanda doesn't mean it didn't originate in the Congo," Niekerk said.

To motivate smelter cooperation with the certification program, Intel realized it would need to work with other companies in the electronics industry. As large as Intel might be, it represents a minuscule fraction of the demand of conflict minerals, especially tin, tungsten, and gold. As such, Intel, by itself, couldn't drive change. To create a critical mass of material buyers, Intel helped found the Electronic Industry Citizenship Coalition (EICC). As of May 2015, the EICC consisted of some 102 member companies, including chip-making equipment suppliers, chip-makers, contract manufacturers, and electronics OEMs.[36] EICC works to promote social, ethical, and environmental responsibility in the electronics supply chain.

Creating the EICC had additional benefits, such as avoiding problems that the apparel industry had faced with its suppliers in developing nations. "What happened in the apparel industry was that Nike was doing one thing, another company was doing something else—suppliers had many different [social responsibility] codes they had to meet. So we in the electronics industry came together through EICC to develop one code," Niekerk said.

As part of an effort to help artisan miners in the DRC, Intel worked with the US Department of State and the US Agency for International Development to establish and fund the Public-Private Alliance (PPA) for Responsible Minerals Trade. This PPA has three objectives, as outlined in an Intel internal May 2012 white paper titled *Intel's Efforts to Achieve "Conflict-Free" Supply Chain:*[37]

- to assist with the development of pilot supply chain systems that will allow businesses to source minerals from mines that have been audited and certified to be "conflict-free"
- to provide a platform for coordination among government, industry, and civil society actors seeking to support conflict-free sourcing from the DRC
- to establish a website designed to serve as a resource for companies seeking information regarding how to responsibly source minerals from the DRC.

Intel also learned that smelters were reluctant to participate in the smelter certification program (abbreviated CFS, for conflict-free smelter) owing to its costs. To address that issue, Intel worked to simplify and standardize the process to reduce the smelters' costs of participation. It also established a modest fund ($150,000) to help defray validation costs and bring more smelters into the program. When a smelter successfully completes the CFS audit, the fund reimburses the smelter for half of the initial audit costs, up to $5,000. Intel partnered with HP and GE Foundation to engage RESOLVE, a Washington, DC-based independent NGO, to implement and manage this fund.

The advantage of focusing on smelters as the linchpin in stopping conflict minerals is that if the smelters do their jobs, then the downstream users of the minerals don't need to change anything as long as they use a certified smelter. The aforementioned Intel white paper set a 2013 goal to eliminate conflict-sourced tantalum in all its microprocessors. Next, Intel tackled gold, tin, and tungsten. These conflict minerals involve even broader coalitions. For gold, for example, Intel started talking with multinational gold mining and refining companies, large and small jewelry manufacturers, and retail chains, as well as the World Gold Council, bullion exchange markets, and the Chinese government. Intel is working on these issues proactively, to fix problems before they become a brand or PR issue. In January 2014, Intel announced that its entire 2014 line of microprocessors would be free of all four conflict minerals.[38]

Rising Awareness Leads to Regulation At the time Intel began its efforts to understand and cut down on conflict mineral use, the US government had also begun considering the issue. In August 2012, the US Securities and Exchange Commission implemented rules outlined in the 2010 Wall Street Reform and Consumer Protection Act (aka *Dodd–Frank*) to require public companies to disclose whether they use conflict minerals.[39] The issue became a matter of regulatory compliance, rather than CSR. Public companies began tracking conflict mineral compliance and surveying suppliers to get conflict-free certified sources of these metals. The regulations also spurred numerous third-party software, service, and consulting firms to offer products and services.

Ethical Manufacturing and Sourcing

Marks & Spencer's "Ethical Model Factories" program used three training activities to improve workers' lives, pay, and productivity. Marks & Spencer focused on productivity because that is what enables the retailer to pay higher wages and address corporate social responsibility issues without losing competitiveness. In less than six months, M&S trained over 6,000 Bangladeshi workers on employee rights. The company also trained 130 supervisors and middle managers on HR policies and procedures, industrial relations, and behavioral skills. The company is replicating this training across other factories in Bangladesh, India, and Sri Lanka.[40] As with the conflict minerals issue, apparel companies face a trade-off between using suppliers with unacceptable working conditions versus leaving the region, thereby creating severe job losses. In the conflict minerals case, the solution was an effort to identify the offending mines, so that smelters could keep socially responsible mines in business. For apparel companies, the solution was training workers and managers, as well as working with local governments to improve working conditions, safety, and pay.

Although Disney left Bangladesh and four other countries, it continued production in Haiti and Cambodia, but only in factories cooperating with the Better Work program.[41] This program, created by a partnership of two NGOs, works with government officials, factory owners, and labor groups to ensure safe and decent workplace conditions. "Disney has sent a strong message to the excluded countries that if they're willing to take responsibility for labor standards, Disney will take another look at them in the future," said Dan Rees, director of Better Work.[42] Other companies, including Cadbury, Office Depot, Mars, and PepsiCo, are working with Europe-based Supplier Ethical Data Exchange (Sedex)[43] to create consistent labor standards and efficiencies throughout global production sites.

The "fair trade" movement arose from concerns that smallholder farmers don't receive a fair price for their goods, which led to the development of a fair trade label and certification.[44] Fair trade covers 16 product categories, such as bananas, coffee, cocoa, cotton, fresh fruit, spices, tea, and wine, as well as sports balls and gold.[45] Fair trade goes beyond factory workers to include self-employed producers, such as farmers and crafts-workers. The certification has been shown to improve retail sales among well-to-do consumers.[46] Most studies demonstrate that the majority of consumers, however, are not willing to pay more for products manufactured in socially responsible conditions, but CSR failures can be punished in the market place.

Benefits to the Brand and Bottom Line

As of 2015, the main benefit of these ethical working conditions programs is brand protection. These efforts ensure that companies are "doing the right things" and therefore are not likely to be targets of NGO attacks or negative media coverage. In addition, companies have claimed to gain other tangible benefits from their efforts—mainly in employee relationships and pride. Marks & Spencer, for example, reported an 85 percent reduction in absenteeism in its suppliers' factories and a 65 percent reduction in factory staff turnover six months after implementing its Ethical Model Factories program. When Coca-Cola worked with its bottlers, co-packers, and suppliers on its Workplace Rights Policy (WRP), it found that 86 percent of sites reduced overtime, 36 percent improved quality, and 18 percent had lower staff turnover.[47] "A company that cheats on overtime and on the age of its labor, that dumps its scraps and its chemicals in our rivers, that does not pay its taxes or honor its contracts, will ultimately cheat on the quality of its products," declared Walmart's then-CEO, Lee Scott, in 2008 to suppliers in Beijing.[48]

TRAMPLED BY FOOTPRINTS: SUSTAINABLE SUPPLY

Companies face CSR risks that are due to their own environmental footprints as well as to those of their suppliers and service providers. Even when the problem is with a supplier buried in the deepest tiers of the supply chain, the brand owner is the one vulnerable to reputational and brand diminution. Concerns about carbon footprint (greenhouse gases), water stress, and the stripping of natural resources ranging from fish to trees present both reputational risks and operational risks of supply disruptions.

The Tide Against Carbon Dioxide

The burning of fossil fuels for transportation, power, and heat is a source of greenhouse gas emissions, which is thought to be the main contributor to global climate change. Reducing energy consumption has been the focus of many companies' CSR activities because such *eco-efficiency* initiatives also lead to cost reductions. These CSR actions are considered to be "low hanging fruit" for companies to act upon because they reduce environmental impacts while cutting costs.

Some energy-saving innovations require minimal upfront investment. UPS's routing software, for example, shaved 20.4 million miles from its routes in 2010 while delivering 350,000 more packages than the previous year. It also reduced annual CO_2 emissions by 20,000 metric tons.[49] Office supply retailer Staples implemented speed limiters on its delivery vehicles, restricting their top speed to 60 mph. The fuel savings paid for itself in only 1.5 days and saves $3 million annually.[50] It cost the company only $7 to reprogram each truck, and the time lost to lower speeds was offset by the time gained from fewer fuel stops.[51]

Brand protection and environmental sustainability issues drove Coca-Cola to develop bottles that include 30 percent plant-derived resins and recycled plastic rather than being 100 percent oil-based.[52] The same considerations also drove detergent manufacturers Procter & Gamble and Unilever to develop concentrated detergent formulas that use smaller containers, thereby saving on material and energy involved in packaging, transportation, handling, and storage.[53]

To focus their efforts and create accountability, companies set targets and metrics for carbon footprint reductions. Staples, for example, committed to a 50 percent reduction in total carbon footprint from its 2010 levels by 2020[54] through efforts in transportation, buildings management, energy sourcing, and product sourcing.

Water, Water Everywhere, but Not a Drop to Drink

"Water is to Coca-Cola as clean energy is to BP.... We need to manage this issue or it will manage us," said Jeff Seabright, vice president of environmental and water resources, Coca-Cola Corporation.[55] Protests at Coca-Cola's 2007 shareholder's meeting—regarding bottlers' depleting and polluting of drinking water resources—persuaded several colleges and universities in the United States not to renew contracts to buy Coke.[56] According to the World Economic Forum's Council on Water Security, nearly 800 million people lack access to safe drinking water, and 1.7 million people die every year as a result of unsafe water.[57] These economic, social, and environmental problems lead to intense environmental scrutiny of companies that use water in products or for industrial processes.

The paradox of water is that it is priceless in both senses of the term: being essential to life and yet often considered an unpriced resource in that users can legally pump or divert unlimited amounts of water from lakes, rivers, and aquifers. The Coca-Cola Company and other soft drink makers faced accusations and lawsuits in India over perceived monopolization of this life-giving resource. "While we are not even close to being one of the largest users of water, we are certainly one of the most visible, and have been subject to criticism that we are depleting groundwater aquifers in the State of Kerala," said Coca-Cola's chief executive officer E. Neville Isdell in a May 2007 address to the Nature Conservancy.[58]

Water is unlike many other commodities because of the subtle difference between consumption and use. Whereas most commodities are consumed and thus, by and large, removed from sources of supply, many applications for water only "borrow" the material. Applications such as washing and sanitation merely borrow water for a time and then return it for treatment and reuse. AB InBev said this crucial difference can create perceived problems for companies that seem to be heavy water consumers but are only using and then recycling large amounts of water, thereby having little real impact on the total water supply.[59] In announcing Coca-Cola's worldwide initiative to conserve water resources, CEO Isdell said, "Essentially the pledge is to return every drop we use back to nature."[60] The company plans to be water-neutral by 2020.[61]

Growing populations, urbanization, and climate change threaten water supplies even more. Water-related issues are likely to change companies' decisions on manufacturing locations and supply chain networks. "If the communities around ... our bottling plants do not flourish and are not sustainable, our business will not be sustainable in the future," said Coca-Cola's CEO.[62]

Sustainable Harvest: "No Fish, No Fishsticks"

A significant risk is that unsustainable practices will lead to a collapse of ecological and economic systems. "If there aren't fundamental changes in agriculture and fishing, then we won't have a business worth being in within one to two decades," said Antony Brugmans, former chairman of Unilever. "No fish, no fishsticks," he said.[63]

Clear-cutting forests is another example of short-term overharvesting of a resource that is not renewable unless performed with special care and renewable methods. When Dogwood Alliance and ForestEthics, two NGOs, wanted to promote sustainable forestry, they looked at the forestry products supply chain and chose the target for their protests carefully. They didn't go after the harvesters who cut down the trees. They didn't go after the various makers of forestry products, such as lumber companies or paper makers. These upstream companies lie hidden to most consumers.

Instead, the NGOs targeted Staples, a $25 billion retailer of office products. The NGOs called Staples the "Tree Cutter Team" and created a "Stop Staples" campaign.[64] Although Staples didn't control harvesting practices directly, the NGOs wanted Staples to use its buying power to influence suppliers' practices. Staples provided a highly visible leverage point for the NGOs. Although Staples and its suppliers adhered to every official law, the law wasn't good enough for activists. In response, Staples decided to buy products only from NGO-approved suppliers, such as those certified by the Forest Stewardship Council.

Similarly, IKEA works to ensure that its 1,600 suppliers in 55 countries only use wood from legally harvested sources and not from protected forests. One of the main foci of IKEA's code of conduct, known as IWAY, includes sustainable forestry practices, in addition to quality, safety, and social standards that are a prerequisite for being a supplier to IKEA.[65]

Recycling: From Rubbish to Resource

Reusing, recovering, and recycling of materials offers obvious strategies for reducing environmental impacts. Interface Inc., which designs, manufactures, and sells carpets, redesigned both its carpet and its carpet supply chain so that it could create "the industry's first completely closed loop carpet recycling system."[66] The company designed its carpets to be made of interchangeable square tiles with randomized patterns, so the tiles could be installed in any orientation and so an old carpet could be refreshed simply by replacing a few worn squares. In addition, the carpets are made from recycled material and are designed to be easily recyclable. To that end, the company changed its business model from selling the carpets outright to a lease plus maintenance contract model that includes replacing and recycling worn carpet squares.[67] Each square of recovered Interface carpet is taken to a specialized facility where it is recycled into new carpet squares. Old carpet fibers become new carpet fibers. Old carpet backing becomes new carpet backing.[68]

As another example, Staples provides convenient recycling drop-off bins for toner and ink cartridges in its stores, resulting in a 73 percent rate of recycling. Overall, the United States recycles about 60 percent of office paper, yet Japan recycles 80 percent.[69] As mentioned in chapter 10, recycling can also create an alternative source of supply, thereby mitigating scarcity and price risks.

Closing the loop in the supply chain to enable more recycled materials in consumer products involves improving the fraction of municipal waste streams that are recycled. A consortium of nine companies including Walmart, P&G, and Goldman Sachs created the Closed Loop Fund. The Fund offers zero-interest rate loans to municipalities and private entities to develop more recycling infrastructure and services. These loans would help waste stream collectors and processors to reduce landfill fees and add revenues from the sale of recycled raw materials. At the same time, the resultant increased supply of recycled raw material would enable companies to offer more products with more recycled content.[70]

Material Benefits: Lower Footprint = Lower Costs

P&G's redesign of liquid laundry detergent to a 2X concentrated formula reduced packaging by 22 to 43 percent, which amounted to a savings of 70 million pounds of plastics and corrugate. The smaller bottles also saved the company 60,000 truckloads and 5 million gallons of diesel fuel per year.[71] Marks & Spencer, for its part, has improved energy efficiency (25%), and cut waste (34%) through a comprehensive portfolio of sustainability activities that they call Plan A[72] "because there is no Plan B for the one planet we have."[73]

Eliminating non-value-adding activities not only improves manufacturing but also reduces resource consumption, carbon footprint, and waste-stream emissions. CNH Global NV, Fiat's agricultural and construction equipment subsidiary, described a massive effort at the company to create world-class manufacturing. The effort helped everyone across the Fiat Group. It brought standardized processes to chaotic craft-driven Italian manufacturing plants and brought efficient automobile manufacturing processes to CNH's agricultural and construction equipment manufacturing lines. Along the way, the company eliminated the equivalent of 10 warehouses of inventory, minimized material handling, and reduced trucking—all with strong environmental sustainability benefits as well as cost reductions.[74]

(MIS)PERCEIVED RISKS OF PRODUCTS

More and more companies are facing social concerns and activism over the potential safety of legally saleable products. This issue goes beyond the long-running campaigns against products like tobacco, alcohol, and firearms. Many are products like fast food, snacks, or soft drinks that can be safely enjoyed in moderation but are too often overconsumed. Others are foods containing potentially controversial ingredients such as genetically modified organisms, trans fats, or artificial colors. Some include products that use very small, legal amounts of known toxins, such as mercury in light bulbs and batteries. Another set of concerns revolves around *how* the raw materials are produced, such as (the above-mentioned) conflict minerals, dolphin-safe tuna, or cruelty-free cosmetics. A PwC survey of consumer and retail supply chain executives found that product safety topped their list of concerns about supply chain integrity.[75]

Reducing Waists: The War on Obesity

When independent film-maker Morgan Spurlock wanted to tackle the issue of obesity, he picked McDonald's as the villain in his award-winning 2004 movie, *Super-Size Me*.[76] The company has been a lightning rod for nutrition activists and consumer watchdogs. It did not help that in December 2013 it was revealed that McDonald's own employee website labeled McDonald's food as unhealthy.[77] Groups such as Corporate Accountability International have long-running campaigns attacking the Ronald McDonald clown mascot, restaurant playgrounds, and Happy Meals as predatory marketing to children.[78,79] The Center for Science in the Public Interest (CSPI) sued McDonald's over toys in Happy Meals, saying, "In time, the practice of using toys to market junk food will seem as inappropriate and anachronistic as lead paint, child labor, and asbestos."[80] McDonald's also faced a multiyear class-action lawsuit alleging the company made people fat.

Over the years, McDonald's has improved both its menu and consumer education. The company reduced the portion of fries in the Happy Meal and added sliced apples to trim the number of calories by 20 percent. McDonald's also added fat-free chocolate milk and low-fat 1 percent milk in September 2011.[81] In addition, it is working to reduce sodium by 15 percent by 2015. "We're proud of the changes we've made to our menu," said retiring chief executive Jim Skinner. "We've done more than anybody in the industry around fruits and vegetables and variety and choice."[82] The company also began posting calorie counts on all its menus, saying,

"We recognize customers want to know more about the nutrition content of the food and beverages they order."[83]

To prove that McDonald's food is not intrinsically fattening, a science teacher in Iowa ran a test. He repeated Spurlock's approach and ate only food from McDonalds for 90 days. The only difference was that he had his students design a balanced meal plan with 2,000 calories per day and recommended allowances for protein, carbohydrates, cholesterol, and several other nutritional guidelines. The result: his cholesterol dropped and he slimmed down by 37 pounds. His mission was to show students that it's how you eat—not what or where you eat—that matters most.[84]

These steps toward a healthier menu[85] face a gulf between consumer preferences and nutritionist recommendations. Only 11 percent of parents chose apples over French fries for their kid's Happy Meals in a study by Yale University's Rudd Center for Food Policy and Obesity.[86] And when McDonald's experimented with eliminating French fries from Happy Meals, parents complained. "That's what we've really felt all along, that ultimately, it's a parent decision to make about their child's well-being," said Danya Proud, a spokeswoman for the company.[87]

Similarly, prominent sellers of soft drinks have attracted negative attention in the wake of rising rates of obesity and diabetes. Added to the negative publicity about sugary drinks was a controversy over whether high-fructose corn syrup—often used in drinks—created higher risks of metabolic disorders than other types of sugar.[88] As with many health and social issues, the attention also spurs politicians and activists to shift the line of regulation with new prohibitions or taxes, such as New York City's proposed ban on large cups and bottles of sugary drinks[89] or a penny-an-ounce tax on soda.[90]

Fear of the Unknown

Whereas many examples of attacks on companies' behaviors involve incontrovertible cases of waste, environmental damage, or risk to human life, some may be driven more by fears rather than evidence. That's especially true of GMOs (genetically modified organisms), also known as "frankenfoods" by their detractors.

GMOs include crops such as nutritious varieties of rice,[91] corn that reduces the need for pesticides,[92] herbicide-resistant soybeans that enable farmers to reduce productivity losses from aggressive weeds,[93] and drought-resistant corn.[94] These GMOs are beneficial to farmers and consumers because they are designed to "resist insecticides and herbicides, add nutritional benefits, and improve crop yields to increase the global food supply."[95] Americans have been consuming genetically modified food for decades, yet despite lack of any scientific proof, many consumers, NGOs, and governments claim that GMO foods have unknown negative effects on public health and the environment.

GMO foods have the added potential to reduce world hunger by increasing yields and crop resilience to variable weather conditions.[96] In fact, the Chinese government has been pushing genetically modified food in an effort to increase food resources in that country.[97] Yet many countries, especially in Europe, ban them entirely. US researchers argue that the GMO ban represents one of the biggest science communications failures in history, allowing what is essentially an unfounded conspiracy theory to spread worldwide,[98] leading to dire consequences for both food security and environmental sustainability. Companies like Monsanto have to navigate not only the various regulatory regimes around the world but also the array of rumors, political agendas, and cultural biases in every country where they conduct business.

Traceability and Trace Ingredients

Many other risks associated with social and health trends have motivated companies to tighten control of their supply chains and demand better transparency from ingredient suppliers. The 50 percent rise in the percentage of children with food allergies between 1997 and 2011 motivated heightened concern about ingredients.[99] It also spurred a change in food labeling laws in 2004 to include explicit listings of allergens.[100] The labeling laws forced companies to document not only allergens in all the primary ingredients (e.g., diary in milk chocolate) but also all the potential trace ingredients introduced in facilities that make multiple products (e.g., a milk chocolate bar made in a facility that also makes candy with peanuts). The ability to document trace ingredients and factory handling practices can have a beneficial side—companies can use it to serve niche diet markets such as vegan, kosher, and halal foods.

MANAGING CSR RISKS

Environmental and sustainability problems can endanger a company's "social license to operate"—that is, the ongoing approval and support of the local community, stakeholders, and customers—if the company is seen utilizing unfavorable practices. Avoiding CSR pitfalls may be particularly tricky as a result of the capricious nature of the "court of public opinion" and the nature of CSR.

The Moving Line of Risks

In an ideal world, companies and people would know exactly what is expected of them. Most laws define a so-called bright line between legality and illegality, making the requirements relatively clear. Each government sets minimum legal standards for a multitude of supply-chain-related practices such as product safety, natural resource usage, labor conditions, minimum wages, factory emissions, and waste disposal.

The sensibilities of civil society, however, ride on the more capricious winds of public opinion. Changing public sentiment, social activists, and gotcha-journalists can strike without warning, magnified by viral social media, and following no legislative calendar or judicial due processes. The court of public opinion is far less predictable than the court of law. Over time, various issues such as child labor, pollution, fair trade, emissions, and forestry practices can quickly surface into the public's awareness; raise the bar of tacit expectations, and damage companies who are found retroactively guilty of not living up to citizens' moving line of sensibilities.

Nike became a case study in worker mistreatment despite having invested in local factories in Pakistan, bringing much-needed jobs to a region that did not have many, and paying prevailing wages. Yet, it offended the sensibilities of Western consumers.

And the line never stops shifting. "After many of the world's leading electronics companies rose to the challenge of phasing out their worst hazardous substances, we are now challenging them to improve their sourcing of minerals and better managing the energy used throughout the supply chain," said Greenpeace campaigner Tom Dowall.[101] Furthermore, a company's own capabilities and CSR activities create a moving line of expectations, too. Walmart's highly acclaimed post-Katrina response set the expectation that Walmart will mount the same or better response in future natural disasters. Similarly, Coca-Cola faces pressures from African AIDS/HIV groups to help distribute AIDS/HIV medications owing to the efficiency of Coke's soda distribution operations throughout the continent.

The Nature of the Beast

From the standpoint of procurement and supply chains, CSR attributes may be among the hardest to measure. Consumers make purchasing decisions based on four categories of attributes in a product.[102] The first category is *search* attributes—obvious tangible properties like size, color, leather seats, and price—which consumers can search for and personally evaluate without ever buying or using the product. The second category is *experience* attributes that can only be judged by the consumer after buying the product—qualities like seat comfort, ease-of-use, and friendly after-sale support. The third category of attributes is *intrinsic credence* attributes,[103] which are inherent to the final product but which cannot be readily evaluated by the average consumer, even after buying and using a product. Intrinsic credence attributes include the chemical content of the paint on a toy or the nutrition content of a food item; evaluating them requires specialized equipment and capabilities not widely available. The fourth category is *hidden credence* attributes arising from the history or provenance of the product but which are not inherent or detectable in the final product. These include many important CSR-related attributes such as carbon footprint, fair trade, suppliers' environmental records, child labor, animal cruelty, and sustainable agriculture. Consumers have little ability to evaluate such attributes because they are not part of the products.

The problem of verifying hidden credence attributes is not only faced by consumers; companies grapple with it as well. Such attributes are difficult to measure because the underlying processes often take place outside the boundaries of the company and no test on inbound or outbound material can detect them. In many cases, it is NGOs, social activists, or investigative journalists who trace the output of a sweatshop forward to a major brand owner. The reason is that these groups are on the ground in developing countries, are trusted by many local groups, and can get the data and evidence more readily than the brand owner who has to trace inbound materials back to all the many suppliers that might be involved.

Uncovering the processes behind a product can be a Herculean task, as Intel's search for conflict minerals described above shows. In fact, the use of SigNature DNA described in chapter 7 is an example of the defense industry turning a hidden credence attribute (supplier authenticity) into an intrinsic attribute (DNA code). Similarly, carbon labels or fair trade labels on products turn hidden credence attributes into search attributes for consumers.

Managing risks linked to hidden credence CSR attributes implies controlling the behavior of suppliers, suppliers' suppliers, and deeper tier suppliers. Companies impose codes-of-conduct on their supply chain and use certification processes to ensure the integrity of their suppliers. Auditing and field-visits ensure that suppliers have adhered to the code of conduct.

Partnering with the Canary in the Coal Mine

In a major initiative launched in July 2011, Greenpeace targeted leading apparel brands over issues of water pollution with its "Detox" campaign. For example, in targeting retailer H&M, Greenpeace protestors in 12 countries spent a week plastering huge "Detox our future!" and "Detox our water!" stickers on the chain's shop windows. They also targeted H&M on social media channels such as Twitter and Facebook. As a result, H&M agreed to eliminate toxins and publicize information about chemicals being released from its suppliers' factories.[104]

Greenpeace and other NGOs play several roles in CSR risks. They are often the primary agitators for social and environmental change. They police the actions of companies or their suppliers and attack perceived transgressors with bad press, boycotts, and protests. They are also on the ground in many developing countries and are the first to detect CSR problems. As a result, some companies seek to partner with NGOs who can provide local insights, advice on sustainability priorities, and possible solutions based on what other companies are doing. Such partnerships also provide a level of authenticity to the company's efforts, helping it deflect criticisms. Some NGOs, such as the Forest Stewardship Council, also oversee certifications that can affect a company's products or supply chain activities (e.g., packaging).

In 1999, Unilever, which has long been committed to CSR, sought out Oxfam International and created a strategic partnership to research Third World poverty in Unilever's supply chain.[105] Oxfam is known for its attacks on multinational corporations, and Unilever is a €40 billion multinational giant in the food and consumer goods industry. The collaborative efforts focused on Unilever's supply chain in specific countries.[106] For example, a joint study released in January 2013 regarding Unilever's workers in Vietnam highlighted both Unilever's commitment to workers' rights and its failings in guarding those rights. It gave the company a roadmap for improving the situation. Both the frankness of the report and the roadmap have probably averted an NGO attack and have given Unilever time to improve the situation.

In some cases, companies and NGOs form joint organizations. For example, Carbon Canopy is a group comprising both companies (including Staples, Home Depot, Domtar, and Columbia Forest Products) and NGOs (including Dogwood Alliance, Rainforest Alliance, Environmental Defense Fund, and the Forest Stewardship Council) that is working to improve forestry practices among the large numbers of small landowners in the southern United States, thereby helping the corporate participants with their environmental sustainability efforts.[107]

Changing Metrics for a Changing Climate

Rising awareness of climate change is motivating some companies, who are committed to cutting their carbon footprint, to use environmental impact metrics. Walmart is measuring and managing its greenhouse gas (GHG) emissions with a goal of cutting 20 million metric tons of emissions from its global supply chain by the end of 2015.[108] To achieve environmental goals, companies use an array of environmental KPIs (key performance indicators), including fleet fuel efficiency, percentage of recycled materials, and water use. For example, AB InBev and Coca-Cola measure water use efficiency—the liters of water needed to make a liter of beer[109] or soda,[110] respectively. Effective KPIs are defined at multiple levels, such that at each level a set of metrics corresponds to what management at that level can influence. Each level can then be aggregated upward, leading to the metrics that reflect the organizations' goals.

Baxter Inc., the medical products and medicines giant, began measuring greenhouse gas emissions in 1997. Baxter assigned its GHG emissions to the scope 1, scope 2, and scope 3 designations defined by the Greenhouse Gas Protocol,[111] which is the most widely used international accounting tool for measuring emissions.[112] In this framework, scope 1 emissions come from the organization's directly owned and controlled internal operations; scope 2 comes from indirect emissions caused by purchasing electricity, energy, and heat for internal operations; and scope 3 are all indirect emissions caused by suppliers, service providers, and the use of products sold.

Baxter divided the total emissions into three categories of sources: upstream (scope 3), Baxter internal (scopes 1 and 2), and downstream activities (scope 3). In turn, each of the three categories included between two and eight subcategories that could be separately measured and managed. For example, the upstream category included everything Baxter buys from suppliers. This category had eight subcategories: purchased goods and services, capital goods, fuel and energy-related activities, upstream transportation and distribution, waste treatment, employee business travel, employee commuting, and upstream leased assets. Each of these categories was measured using relevant KPIs that the managers in charge of these categories could control. In total, the company manages its GHG emissions across 15 subcategories.[113] By including scope 3 emissions created by both suppliers' production of materials and customers' use of Baxter's products, Baxter acknowledges that it has some indirect influence on those emissions through the company's product design and supply chain management decisions.

To implement a comprehensive change, many organizations resort to triple bottom line goals—financial, social and environmental—instituting new performance metrics for managers. A well-formed environmental goal includes some dimension of sustainability (e.g., carbon footprint), a target value (e.g., 20 percent reduction), and a timeframe (e.g., from 2015 to 2020). A fleet manager might be measured on empty-miles percentage, a factory manager might be measured on raw material scrap rates, and a retail network manager might be measured on the balance of low-footprint (ocean) versus high-footprint (air) replenishment orders.

Mapping: Tracing the Footprints

"We know we cannot raise the bar on social, environmental and economic rights among suppliers if we have incomplete knowledge ... and have therefore made significant investment in the traceability of our products and our ability to collect performance data," said a spokesperson for Marks & Spencer.[114] As mentioned before, it is difficult for most companies to know who their deep-tier suppliers are, and even if they do, the companies have little influence over them. For example, when the environmentalist group Forest Ethics was pressuring Target Stores to avoid fuels derived from Canadian tar sands, the retailer noted that it doesn't buy fuel; it doesn't even own trucks. In contracting with outside carriers, the retailer has limited visibility and limited control over the fuels used.[115]

In 2013, Starbucks bought coffee from about 120,000 coffee farms. To ensure that it buys ethically-grown coffee, Starbucks subscribes to C.A.F.E (coffee and farmer equity) practices, developed jointly with Conservation International.[116] Starbucks ensures that farmers meet its standards by gathering information on each farmer, including the geocoding of every plot, the identities of owners and workers, and information about the farming practices, including landscaping and biodiversity.[117] According to Kelly Goodejohn, Starbucks's director of ethical sourcing, the company employs 25 audit and verification organizations to visit and collect information regarding each farm. SES Global Services, out of Oakland, California, manages the quality and the integrity of the verification process. "They act as a second party to us that has oversight over the third parties," added Goodejohn.[118] The information is stored in a continuously updated database that is used for benchmarking across the farms, developing metrics, and improving farm practices.

The Complete Picture

Accounting for environmental impact can be complicated and counterintuitive. Consider, for example, the "eat local" mantra, based on the fact that local sourcing reduces the carbon footprint of food transportation. But transportation is, in many cases, only a small fraction of the total carbon footprint for food production and delivery. An analysis of the CO2 emissions from US milk production found that only about one-quarter (27 percent) of the carbon footprint comes from transportation. Factors such as inefficient production could make local milk less sustainable than milk transported from more efficient but distant producers.[119]

In some cases, the complex realities of resource use in different geographies create counterintuitive recommendations. Consider a seemingly simple choice for a UK company of buying either local UK-made recycled paper or imported Swedish-made virgin paper. Local recycled paper clearly saves on transportation and trees. Yet the carbon footprint of virgin Swedish paper is actually lower than the UK recycled paper, owing to the UK's reliance on coal-fired power plants vs. Sweden's use of nuclear and hydroelectric power to manufacture paper.[120] Similarly, oranges grown in Brazil might have a higher water footprint than oranges grown in Spain, but Brazilian oranges may have a lower environmental impact on water stress owing to the rainy climate and abundance of water in the citrus regions of Brazil.[121]

Only a full life cycle assessment (LCA) can account for the entire impact of a product or a process. But an LCA requires a significant amount of data and effort. In January 2006, Tesco CEO Sir Terry Leahy announced that the supermarket chain would find or devise "a universally accepted and commonly understood measure of the carbon footprint"[122] for every product Tesco sells. The company would assess each product's complete lifecycle, from production to consumption, and label each product it carries with its total carbon footprint. Unfortunately, Tesco found that the LCA required so much work that the grocer could create only 125 labels per year, out of the approximately 50,000 SKUs it carried. By 2011, Tesco's carbon label program was quietly unwound. A full LCA for each product proved too difficult to complete.

PREVENTING DISRUPTIONS TO THE BRAND

While many companies engage in CSR activities out of the sincere belief that it is "the right thing to do," one of the justifications vis-à-vis shareholders is that these activities can help protect the brand against would-be detractors and negative publicity. In other words, they help the company lower the likelihood of disruption from these kinds of threats.

Listening for the Negative Buzz (and Responding)

"Social media has shrunk the timelines," which "are now much faster and more global," said Dr. Deborah Pretty, a principal at Oxford Metrica, a UK-based research firm that analyzed reputation risk events. A company can either "be a winner, or a loser," she said.[123] Since reputational danger can lurk deep in the supply chain, anywhere around the globe, and because social sensibilities are not well defined, companies need to be constantly vigilant. It behooves them to "listen" to the social media "buzz" to detect problems. Coca-Cola, Cisco, Dell, and many other companies monitor sites like Facebook, Twitter, and many blogs in order to stay ahead of developing issues.[124]

Other companies use social media more actively. Zurich Insurance Company's Linda Conrad mentioned the positive side of social media, which enables companies to not only detect emerging brand risks but also to address them before they grow.[125] For example, one airline monitors Twitter for negative mentions of its name, and if the person tweeting is a frequent flyer on the airline, it intervenes to solve the problem or make amends, thus hoping to turn the negative sentiment into a positive one and retain an important customer. Similarly, a hotel chain cross-references a person's social media Klout[126] score upon check-in. Customers with a high Klout rating get free upgrades. Finally, a consumer products company tracks comments on social media to drive product innovation. For example, upon hearing of complaints about reading in bed, the company designed a backlight product. Chapter 8 discussed how companies monitor real-time and emerging risks.[127]

Bridging the Economy and Earth's Ecology

The Chicago school of economics argues that companies have one goal—profit—and only one fiduciary responsibility—to their shareholders. This view permeates judicial interpretations of directors', officers', and companies' obligations to shareholders, although companies retain some breadth of discretion to achieve nonfinancial goals without legal repercussions. When a conservative shareholder group attacked Apple's spending on renewable energy and demanded Apple invest only in measures that were profitable, CEO Tim Cook responded angrily: "When we work on making our devices accessible by the blind, I don't consider the bloody ROI." Cook added that the same goes for environmental, health, and safety issues. "If you want me to do things only for ROI reasons, you should get out of this stock," he said. Apple shareholders voted down the conservative group's resolution to force Apple to disclose the costs of its investments in tackling climate change.[128]

As mentioned earlier, some CSR activities can align with financial goals of increasing profits and shareholder value. These activities primarily include energy-saving actions, material conservation, and recycling. They also include optimizing delivery routes (recall the UPS example in the section "The Tide Against Carbon Dioxide," above), installation of renewable energy sources where it makes sense, and a myriad of other "small" eco-efficiency efforts that can lead to reductions in carbon footprint and save money. For example, Marks & Spencer reported that a collection of sustainability efforts delivered £70 million in net benefits in 2010 and 2011 alone.[129]

But many companies are looking beyond the short-term financial bottom line in managing their operations, in response to social pressure or adverse media coverage. For these companies, sustainability involves a stakeholder-focused, long-term approach to managing a corporation. Although diverting attention from the financial bottom line would seem to threaten profits and shareholders, limited MIT research suggests that, in some cases, the opposite may be true in the long term. Comparing GM vs. Toyota, United Airlines vs. Southwest Airlines, and Boeing vs. Airbus reveals an interesting pattern. In each of these three pairs of companies, the first company of the pair espoused short-term financial goals thought to be aligned with shareholders and the second company espoused longer-term goals more aligned with multiple stakeholders. And yet, the shareholder-focused companies returned only 3 percent annually to their shareholders, while stakeholder-focused companies returned nearly 14 percent to shareholders over almost three decades (1981–2009).[130] While far from conclusive owing to the small number of companies analyzed, the pair comparison was deep and detailed. A broader study of 275 Fortune 1000 firms found that the top 50 on sustainability measures delivered 38 percent higher shareholder returns over five years than did the bottom 50.[131]

This research suggests that companies may actually be more valuable in the long term with a broader view than if the financial bottom line is their only concern. This paradox seems to arise because satisfied customers, employees, suppliers, and communities may be more likely to have more productive relationships with a stakeholder-focused company, which, in turn, leads to higher profits and more satisfied shareholders. Kevin Wrenn, vice president of PC business and operations at Fujitsu Computer Systems Corp., referred to the balance of sustainability and financial performance as the task of "bringing economy and ecology in harmony."[132]

Puma, the German sportswear company, initiated a comprehensive approach to balancing environmental sustainability and financial performance. It published an *environmental profit and loss statement* (EP&L) in 2012. The report estimates the costs to the planet by accounting for the ecosystem services that a business depends on and the cost of direct and indirect environmental impacts to the business and its suppliers. The EP&L allows for year-over-year comparison in terms of a single metric. Puma's 2010 report detailed a total environmental impact of €145 million. Interestingly, only 6 percent of the impact was attributed to Puma's operations; the rest came from its supply chain partners (the analysis went as deep as Tier 4 suppliers).

Finally, several jurisdictions recognize and permit a form of incorporation that has both financial and social goals. These include benefit corporations (B Corp) and low-profit limited liability companies (L3C) in the United States, and community interest companies (CIC) in the United Kingdom.[133] Such companies formally declare that their goals are broader than just shareholders' financial returns and that the company considers society and the environment in its decision making. These companies are then free from the legal fiduciary responsibilities to only maximize shareholders' value. Instead, they can also include social responsibilities in decisions and can attract funding from socially conscious investors.

12

ADAPTING TO LONG-TERM CHANGE

Certain types of disruptions arrive as long-term shifts, not transient shocks. These shifts lead to a permanent change—a new normal—for the company's environment, its supply chain, markets, factors of production, society's expectations, or regulatory frameworks. Some trends affect the viability of specific industries. For example, trends such as the declining use of previously successful products and shifts in norms include the use of landline phones,[1] smoking[2], men wearing hats,[3] fans attending baseball games,[4] or people playing golf.[5]

Other trends have broader effects on multiple industries as well as supply chain structures. These trends include the rise of megacities, the growing middle class in developing countries, the growing use of e-commerce and omnichannel retailing, the aging populations in the developed world, global climate change, the demand by civil society for corporate social responsibility, the rise of Africa as a place of business, and the availability of new energy sources in the US and elsewhere based on new extraction technologies.

Although a trend like an aging population or new energy sources might be obvious, companies face significant uncertainties regarding both the best response to the trend and the timing of that response. In many cases, there are "good" reasons not to respond immediately, such as uncertainty about the validity of the trend or short-term financial pressures that forestall any long-term investment required to adjust and respond.

Another factor that distinguishes long-term shifts from other fast-acting risks is the potential upside opportunities embedded in such trends. The long-term nature of these phenomena means that companies have opportunities to adapt and even create a competitive advantage relative to less-prescient or less-responsive competitors. Indeed, the challenges lie in deciding how and when to invest in response to these trends.

Although the number of medium- and long-term trends is large and varied—including shifting markets, societal expectations, migration patterns, regulations, and natural phenomena, among many others—this chapter is focused on one irrefutable trend, one trend under some debate, and one trend that is not usually thought of as a trend.

THIS OLD COUNTRY: AGING DEMOGRAPHICS

Much of the developed world is aging. In the United States, someone turned 65 years of age every 12 seconds during 2010.[6] The fastest-growing demographic in the United States, as a percentage of the population, is the "over-85" age group. By 2025, the percentage of the population over age 60 is forecasted to be 25 percent in the United States and Asia, and 30 percent in Europe.[7,8]

The strength of this trend varies by country. Japan is especially hard hit as a result of its very low birth rate, long life expectancy, and anti-immigration culture and policies. Not only will Japan's population skew much older, but its total population is expected to shrink by 30–40 percent in the coming decades. China is suffering the consequences of its one child policy: by 2044, China will have more people over age 60 than the United States has in total population.[9] As the Chinese working-age population shrinks markedly, its vaunted low-cost manufacturing position will come under increasing pressure.[10] Other locations, such as southern Europe, have low birth rates, too, but they have high rates of immigration from within and from outside the EU to compensate (although such immigration sometimes creates social and political tensions).

Aging demographics will have a multitude of economic effects that affect supply chains, including a dearth of workers for physical blue-collar jobs; different demand patterns (consuming fewer products and more services, especially healthcare); and significant declines in asset utilization as populations shrink. All these changes imply the rise of new markets, shifting locations for manufacturing centers, and changes to the supply networks connecting the two.

Elder-Economics

The demographic trends of an aging population will affect the composition of consumer households and the patterns of consumer demand that determine freight flows. High divorce rates among older couples[11] (dubbed *the 40-year itch*[12]) as well as the discrepancy between male and female longevity will lead to more people living alone, especially women. In 2013, 42 percent of US women over 65 were living by themselves. In Denmark, the figure was 52 percent.[13] Smaller households skew the retail merchandise mix toward smaller package sizes and smaller store formats, closer to where people live. In fact, Walmart, Target, and other retailers are already building small-format urban stores.

Aging in place may demand an increasing amount of home delivery and in-home services. Moreover, these delivery workers may do double duty by helping put away the delivery, install the product, train consumers in its use, and even provide supplementary home healthcare services. About 70 percent of Americans live in suburban and rural areas, and they plan to continue living there as they get older. These areas rely on personal automobiles for transportation, which becomes problematic as people age. The low density of these consumer locations and the elderly's needs for added services present both risks and opportunities for retailers and logistics service providers.

Blue Collar, Grey Hair

As the baby-boom generation in the United States ages, as China's work force diminishes, and as Japan and some European countries contract, one can expect a relative shortage of working-age adults. Deere, Caterpillar, and Toyota have already seen disruptions in their labor supply, as well as the loss of knowledge when experienced workers retire. In particular, companies lose knowledge of how to handle rare events when long-time workers retire.

Despite the lackluster economy of the early 2010s and high unemployment among younger workers, transportation companies in the United States were still facing shortages of truck drivers. This may be a sign of things to come, as these companies hire more elderly drivers who are on their second or third careers. On the positive side, many older adults will work longer past traditional retirement age to stay active, do meaningful work, and enjoy social interactions—money came in only fourth on the list of reasons why workers between age 66 and 70 keep working past retirement age.[14] The implications for logistics companies include the need to accommodate a "graying" transportation and warehousing workforce and an influx of women into the field. Warehouse operators or motor carriers who can adjust over time to accommodate a 5′2″ (157 cm) 60-year-old female worker will be in a good position to meet their future labor needs.

HOT (AND COLD) AND DRY (AND WET) WITH A CHANCE OF CLIMATE CHANGE

The year 2013 marked the 37th consecutive year of global temperatures above the 20th-century average.[15] These higher temperatures—and the likelihood that the climate will change further by growing hotter on average but also more volatile—pose some known and some unknown risks for companies and their supply chains.

Most mainstream scientific bodies agree with the UN's Intergovernmental Panel on Climate Change (IPCC) and its five reports regarding the existence and causes of global warming. Although some climate change impacts seem undeniable, some respected scientists question the cause of climate change, arguing that it may be natural or unknown.[16] Others question the projections on the basis of the inaccuracies of the underlying models. Long-range forecasting models contain many uncertainties about the rate of change, magnitude of change, and geographic pattern of changes.[17] For example, the latest IPCC report shows that despite the 12 percent increase in atmospheric CO2 since 1990, the temperatures that were predicted to rise between 0.2 and 0.9 degrees Celsius rose by only 0.1 degrees, a figure that was not statistically different from zero.[18] At the same time, scientists, activists, and policy makers still push for mitigation measures. For example, Connie Hedegaard, the European climate action commissioner said, "Let's say that science, some decades from now, said 'we were wrong, it was not about climate,' would it not in any case have been good to do many of the things you have to do in order to combat climate change?"[19] Others, such as former US secretary of state George Shultz, argue that while climate change and its causes may be less than certain, the consequences are so dire that current decarbonization initiatives should be thought of as "buying insurance against a catastrophe."[20] Such uncertainties present companies with a dilemma: when and how much should they invest in mitigation measures given the uncertainty?

Climate change brings four categories of potential supply chain disruptions. First is a long-term trend toward higher effective energy costs owing to regulations or other schemes to limit the world's carbon footprint. Second are potential disruptions to operations and logistics resulting from rising sea levels (which may affect coastal cities that house the majority of the world's population and seaports) or declining river flows, which affect waterborne transportation and agriculture. The third category is increased prices of climate-sensitive commodities such as food, wood-derived packaging materials, and water. Such changes raise the risks of related social and political disruptions as well a threat of drastic regulations. Fourth are reputational disruptions for companies perceived to have high environmental footprints who are operating in areas where NGOs, the media, and public opinion are concerned about climate change. In that sense, it does not matter whether company leadership believes that climate change is real, or whether human activities caused it—as long as public opinion believes it, companies have to at least be seen as aligned with the concerns of their customers. Price and availability risks, and reputational risks are described more fully in chapter 10 and chapter 11, respectively.

Underlying Cause

Greenhouse gases (GHGs) such as carbon dioxide (CO2) and methane (CH4) are believed to contribute to global climate change.[21] These gases trap heat in the atmosphere, thereby increasing temperatures but also potentially accelerating the evaporation of water and the formation of storm systems. This link between emissions and climate puts a bulls-eye on the use of fossil fuels in transportation, industrial production, and energy generation. The total set of GHG emissions associated with a product, process, company, or country define its carbon footprint.

In May 2013, atmospheric CO2 reached 400 ppm.[22] This concentration is about 42 percent higher than the preindustrial level, and it continues to rise at an accelerating rate as a result of the growth of many developing-world economies. Capping CO2 levels at twice the preindustrial level, which they may reach in 2050—let alone reducing them—will require aggressive reductions in fossil fuel consumption. Climate change won't hit suddenly, however. "The math shows that we have 40–60 years left," MIT professor (and the US secretary of energy) Ernest Moniz warned in 2007, "but making a change requires a 50-year planning horizon, so we need to start making changes now. The reason for the time delay is scale—the oil business operates on a trillion-dollar scale ... and will take a long time to replace."[23]

The Rain in Spain May Fall Nowhere Near the Plain

One of the impactful risks created by climate change is supply disruption based on scarcity of water. Scientists expect climate change to affect patterns of rainfall and snowfall,[24] with some areas growing much drier under the confluence of less moisture and more heat. Water shortages would have an impact on agriculture, cities, and a wide range of production processes that consume large amounts of water. Affected water-using industries include food and beverage makers as well as a surprising range of other industries such as semiconductor makers, textiles, and electric power plants.

In November 2011, barge traffic on Europe's Rhine was disrupted by drought and low river levels that were 1.5 feet below normal.[25] Shippers were restricted to lightly loaded barges to avoid grounding.[26] "It's too difficult for ships to move in such low waters. Businesses are being damaged, companies are having to load 4,000 tonne capacity ships with a mere 1,000 tons of goods," said Ralf Schäfer of the Waterways and Shipping Office for Bingen, Germany.[27] Barges handle 11 percent of ton-miles of freight in the

United States[28] and 5–6 percent in Europe,[29] and they are an especially fuel-efficient means of moving large amounts of freight. But barges require sufficient water levels.

Water scarcity will be exacerbated if upstream water users monopolize the limited rainfall or snow melt, leaving downstream agricultural users and cities even drier. Such an action took place when Switzerland restricted water flow to the Rhine after a dry year. This restriction caused the water level to fall, limiting barge traffic on the river and forcing large bulk shippers, such as chemical manufacturing giant BASF, to divert shipments in and out of its mammoth industrial complex in Ludwigshafen to rail and trucking. The result was increased shipping costs, lower customer service, new hazards along the land routes, and higher GHG emissions. BASF depends on river barges for 40 percent of its incoming and outgoing goods,[30] making the company dependent on river levels.

The rise of megacities and urbanization adds to the long-term risks of disruptions in agricultural commodities. The conversion of farmlands to urban developments reduces the amount of land area under cultivation. In fact, the Chinese government is so alarmed about not having enough arable land to feed its population that during 2013 and 2014 it has been buying large tracts of land in Brazil, thereby causing Brazilian land prices to rise considerably, despite a severe drought, which usually causes arable land prices to plummet.[31] In addition, urbanization in developing countries is creating worker shortages in rural areas. For example, Indonesian officials are worried about the nation's food production because the country's youth have left rural areas for cities, and farmers are aging and retiring.[32]

Rising Seas, Falling Rivers: Tripping Up Shipping

Much of the world's trade travels on the oceans between port cities that are, by definition, at sea level. Some predictions of climate change hint at a 13 to 94 centimeter (5 to 37 inch) rise in sea level by 2100.[33] Such a rise could threaten port infrastructure as well as the civilian populations and industry that surround major ports. Storm surge disruptions may grow increasingly likely in major ports such as Shanghai, Rotterdam, and Osaka.[34] Shanghai, the largest container port in the world since 2010,[35] is the most vulnerable major city in the world to serious flooding.[36]

With the higher probability of storms comes a higher probability of disruptions to operations and logistics. Volatile weather played a major role in the 2011 Thai floods, described in chapter 7, that caused significant supply chain disruptions in the computer and automotive sectors. A drought in 2010 in Thailand drained reservoirs and caused $450 million in crop damage.[37] Memories of the drought made Thai authorities hold back water when the rainy season began in 2011, rather than steadily releasing the water in anticipation of future heavy rains.[38] When a series of tropical storms hit Thailand in late 2011, the reservoirs had no spare capacity to absorb the added water and were forced to dump the flood waters on the heavily industrialized central floodplains of the country.[39]

Not all the impacts of global warming are negative for supply chain operations, though. For example, if the thick ice layer covering the Canadian Arctic Archipelago melts, then maritime shipping between Asia and Europe will be 2,500 miles shorter via the so-called Northwest Passage, and Alaskan oil could be moved quickly to the eastern United States and Europe.[40]

Climate Change Begets Regulations and Societal Pressures

Limiting the rate of climate change will require significant reductions in the emissions of GHGs or increasing the absorption or sequestration of greenhouse gases. Because transportation generates 28 percent of all GHG emissions in the United States,[41] supply chains are likely to come under continuing pressure to change to fuel-efficient modes, replace fossil-fuel-powered conveyances, minimize the ton-miles of goods movements, and pay for carbon sequestration or climate change mitigation.

Fuel taxes, emissions restrictions, and cap-and-trade schemes all raise the effective long-term cost of fuel and therefore of transportation, thereby increasing the costs of operating global supply chains. High transportation costs can also push companies toward using slower, bulk modes of transportation (e.g., barge and rail instead of trucking). (See chapter 10, "Efficiency: Use Less, Pay Less.")

Finally, climate change and related commodity cost increases may affect the political stability of countries and regions. One of the contributing causes to the multicountry upheaval of the 2011 Arab Spring was a 43 percent spike in food prices between 2009 and 2011. UN research suggests that food riots are much more likely when the food price index hits 210[42]—the index hit 228 in 2011.[43] Of course, climate change was only one of the elements contributing to the rise in food prices, the other important one being misbegotten climate-change-related ethanol policies in the United States.[44] Price hikes in key food staples have led to riots in many developing countries, such as the 2006 and 2012 riots over corn prices in Mexico[45,46] and the 1998 riots over cooking oil in Indonesia.[47]

IN WITH THE NEW, OUT WITH THE OLD

In a 1963 speech about Charles Darwin's seminal work *On the Origin of Species*, Professor Leon Megginson of Louisiana University said: "It is not the most intellectual of the species that survives; it is not the strongest that survives; but the species that survives is the one that is able best to adapt and adjust to the changing environment in which it finds itself."[48] Every year, companies introduce new products and processes and retire old ones. When competitors introduce superior products, higher capabilities, and better processes, companies can lose market share, experience a drop in revenues, and face existential risks if the companies fail to adapt quickly.

Fall of a Leader

Nokia was a leading example of a successful organization in my book *The Resilient Enterprise* in 2005.[49] When a Philips chip factory in New Mexico suffered a fire in a cleanroom in 2000, Nokia was the first of Philips's major customers to detect the severity of the problem, mobilize resources to fix it, secure alternative supplies, and recover. In contrast, Nokia's direct competitor, Ericsson, also used Philips but was much slower in detecting the problem and much less effective in responding. The resilient Nokia thrived whereas the less-responsive Ericsson suffered a US$2.34 billion loss and was forced to merge its mobile handset business with Sony.

For many years, Nokia dominated the cell phone market with a wide range of innovative handsets. Then, in 2007, Apple introduced the iPhone. In the beginning, Apple was no threat to Nokia. In 2007, Apple sold 3.7 million iPhones[50] while Nokia sold 435 million phones,[51] including 60 million smartphones.[52]

Over time, Apple's minimalist touchscreen design proved extremely popular and became widely copied among devices such as Google's Android system, the Blackberry Z series, and Microsoft Windows 8 devices. Moreover, Apple created a marketplace to connect a supply chain of app developers to consumers through Apple's easy-to-use media distribution channel, the iTunes store. Initially, the app store had only a few apps, and the app model was unproven.[53] But, over time, Apple's popularity grew, although it was a relatively slow process. Even three years after the iPhone's introduction, Nokia smartphones were still outselling Apple iPhones 2 to 1.[54] By 2013, however, Nokia's smartphone share had dropped to less than 3 percent.[55] In that year, Nokia sold its handset business to Microsoft.[56] It was blindsided by the iPhone in a classic case of disruptive innovation.

Nor was Nokia the only company to miss the disruptive threat of the iPhone and phones like it. Microsoft's share of the mobile market dropped from 42 percent in 2007 to 3 percent in 2011.[57] Blackberry's worldwide market share likewise toppled from 44 percent in 2009 to less than 2 percent (including less than 1 percent in the United States) by the end of 2013, even after the introduction of its new models and new touchscreen operating system in 2012.

Why Disruptive Innovation Is So Disruptive

In theory, Nokia should have maintained its market dominance. It invested heavily in research and development and, in 1999, it even invented a phone very similar to what Apple would release seven years later. Nokia's prototype had a touchscreen display set above a single button. In demos, Nokia's chief engineer at the time, Frank Nuovo, showed how the phone could be used for ordering products online, locating a nearby restaurant, or playing a game. "We had it completely nailed," Nuovo said.[58] Finally, Apple was late to the market. "There are already big companies that dominate the space," Bloomberg's Matthew Lynn wrote, reviewing the iPhone at its introduction.[59]

Why didn't Nokia beat Apple? Three types of issues often occur with disruptive innovations: the new product seems inferior; the new product does not seem to address any known unmet consumer needs; and the new product lowers the average profit margins for the incumbent.[60] All these issues kept Nokia from launching a touchscreen phone.

First, Nokia, other incumbents, and technology pundits judged the iPhone to be markedly inferior to existing smartphone designs.[61] The iPhone failed Nokia's five-foot "drop test" for measuring durability. The iPhone used the slow 2G network compared to Nokia's fast 3G phones. Worse, the iPhone had high manufacturing costs and sold at a very high price point of $499, even with a two-year contract. In "Four Reasons Why the Apple iPhone will Fail," influential technology blogger Hung Truong wrote, "Right now, you can get a T-Mobile MDA smartphone for $0 after rebate. The mass market is not willing to pay this much for a phone."[62] The people who could afford iPhones already have "phones from their employers," wrote Rory Prior on January 12, 2007's Think-Mac blog.[63] "These integrate with their various enterprise systems (Exchange, MS Office, IM, etc.) and, while they might be tempted buy an iPhone, the cold hard realities of non-replaceable batteries, no third party software, lack of blessing from the IT department, and the suckiness of onscreen keyboards will keep them tied to their existing Windows Mobile smartphones," he predicted.

Second, disruptive innovations often don't appear to address any customer-perceived shortcomings of existing products to offset their inferiority on other dimensions. That is because the invention does something entirely new or outside the usual needs of the incumbents' customers. Prior to the iPhone, no smartphone user was complaining about the inability to swipe to move pages or delete emails. No one asked to be able to pinch to zoom images on the pre-iPhone smartphones in 2007. No one clamored for an app store. Most incumbents use market research to find out what customers want, missing the opportunity for true innovation. As Henry Ford is quoted as saying, "If I'd asked customers what they wanted, they would have said 'a faster horse.'"

Third, an incumbent would have to disrupt its own business by investing money in making its own offerings obsolete[64]—something that is difficult for corporate boards and Wall Street to stomach. In 2006, Nokia's CEO Olli-Pekka Kallasvuo merged the R&D units of smartphones and basic phones together. As a result, engineering teams vied against each other for resources and, as typically happens, profitable high-revenue current product lines won out against speculative high-cost new products. A new one-button touchscreen phone represented a risky new playing field and Nokia, the leader in the current market, had no reason to disrupt itself.

The same logic caused the Detroit automotive companies to yield market share to Japanese automakers. One of the key phenomena that make disruptive innovations so insidious is that what seems to be an inferior product at its introduction (e.g., a keyboard-less smartphone or a tiny subcompact car) becomes a superior one over time as a result of market acceptance of the new product's unique abilities (e.g., the minimalist iPhone design or the fuel economy of the subcompact car) as well as incremental improvements to the innovation. Thus, Detroit ignored the first subcompacts but then the Japanese introduced compacts and then midsize cars to the market. At each step, the American companies focused on the high-end, profitable part of the market. With each market segment relinquishment, the average profit per product sold by the American firms went up, supporting the decision. In the end, the Japanese introduced the Acura, Lexus and Infinity as well as full size SUVs and trucks, bringing the Detroit automakers to their knees. Of course, the Koreans (Samsung and Kia) are doing this to the Japanese; and the Chinese (e.g., Geely) may be doing the same to the Koreans. Similarly, US steel mills faced the introduction of the mini-mills; and IBM suffered at the dawn of the personal computer age.

Process and Efficiency Innovations

Disruptive innovations are not always products: they can be process or efficiency innovations, too. Innovative processes can allow companies to sell the same product at a lower price, offer more variety, or provide a different user experience—all of which can disrupt competitors. Although traditional retailers previously believed that Amazon's website was an inferior shopping experience to their stores, Amazon's huge selection, low prices, customer reviews of products, and good customer service drove multiple retail stores out of business. Amazon started with books, a product in which most titles sell at extremely low rates in any given town or city, meaning that books often sit on the shelf for long periods and most titles never make it to local bookstores.

In contrast, nationwide, centralized shipping from a warehouse took advantage of risk pooling, allowing Amazon to have "the largest bookstore on earth" in terms of the number of titles in stock. Amazon also avoided the high cost of retail space and retail employees. Amazon's customer reviews and "click to look inside" feature gave consumers the information they needed to purchase obscure titles. As Amazon moved from books to high-tech gadgets, toys, and other products, many traditional retail chains collapsed, unable to withstand the onslaught. Yet brick-and-mortar retail still retained one advantage—shoppers in a store could get products immediately, but shoppers on Amazon had to wait one or two days for delivery.

The rise of ebooks enabled instant gratification via downloads to PCs, tablets, smartphones and Amazon's own Kindle devices—people did not even need to drive to the mall to get a new book. Then, in 2013, Amazon began offering same-day delivery as well as in-person payment and returns in some markets. As previous barriers to online purchasing fade away, more traditional retailers may be disrupted.

Amazon is also in the process of disrupting the publishing industry by offering authors a path to direct electronic and on-demand publishing, cutting traditional publishers out of the process. The new process dramatically reduces the time from manuscript submission to publication and lets authors take a much larger fraction of the sales proceeds. A similar revolution has affected the music and movie distribution businesses, with a shift toward independent productions and digital downloading over physical manufacturing, distribution, and retailing of CDs or DVDs.

Another notable process innovation was the postponement process developed by Dell, Inc. In the early 1990s, Dell perfected its direct sales model for PCs and servers. The company kept no inventory of finished goods but rather took orders over the Internet, letting customers customize the configuration they wanted and see the prices of alternative configurations. Dell then quickly built the specified machine and sent it to the customer in a few days. In bypassing retail channels, Dell was never stuck with outdated PCs. It was able to lower prices as component prices deflated, and it could offer many more product variants than any physical retailer. Dell's innovative process gave it increasing market share and a negative cash conversion cycle (Dell got paid by its customers before it had to pay its suppliers for components).

Yet innovation does not guarantee permanent competitive advantage. In the 2000s, the environment changed as the PC industry matured and shifted from a race for the latest desktop technology—which Dell was well suited to deliver—to an emphasis on inexpensive laptops and netbooks. Longer product lifecycles and reduced numbers of product configurations let Dell's competitors build computers overseas at low cost and use low-cost ocean shipping.[65] Computers became a basic commodity found at low-cost retailers such as Costco and Walmart.

Dell was late to react to the shift, and the company's attempts to cope with the change paralleled Detroit's delayed reaction to low-cost Japanese cars, except that Dell used outsourcing. Dell began outsourcing more and more of the low-value segments of its business—motherboard and computer assembly, supply chain management, and finally the design—to ASUSTek in Taiwan.[66] At each stage, outsourcing to ASUSTek made financial sense because it improved Dell's profitability (costs declined yet revenues stayed the same). At the end of the progression of seemingly rational decisions, ASUSTek started offering better computers to retail chains such as Best Buy at low costs that Dell had difficulty matching.[67]

Innovation as a Lateral Disrupter

The impacts of disruptive innovation can spread beyond the innovator's competitors and even beyond the innovator's industry. Amazon may deliver a lot of products, but it doesn't deliver fresh hot pizza (yet). But Amazon and other e-retailers are implicated in the

2011 (and then again in 2014) bankruptcy of the 800-restaurant pizza chain Sbarro. Although Amazon and Sbarro don't compete, Sbarro depends heavily on foot traffic in shopping malls at their food court outlets.[68] Between 2010 and 2013, foot traffic in US shopping malls dropped by half—a trend blamed in part on rapidly growing e-commerce.[69] The same trend contributed to the 2014 bankruptcy of another food court denizen, Hot Dog on a Stick.[70]

Other types of innovations can occur far upstream in the supply chain but trickle down to disrupt downstream companies. For example, many industries depend on the electronics suppliers, and those electronic suppliers have a wide range of customers in different industries outside the consumer electronic industry. For example, Verifone uses microelectronics—similar to those used in the cell phone industry—inside its point-of-sale terminals. GM makes cars with a wide variety of microprocessors for controlling vehicle systems as well as providing in-dash navigation and driver controls. BASF, the German chemical manufacturing giant, creates and operates complex, high-reliability industrial controller networks in its chemical factories.

Whereas the microelectronics suppliers innovate rapidly to serve the shifting and fickle needs of consumer electronics, not all electronics customers want to abandon last year's chips for this year's crop. Verifone's pace of product turnover is linked to retailers' multiyear capital expenditure plans for point-of-sale systems. GM's multiyear process for designing and producing new car models plus its five-year warranty on all vehicles means that GM may need continuity of parts supply for more than a decade. BASF has a safety-driven policy of "three generations behind" in its IT implementations on production systems because the company wants the reliability and safety of tried-and-true chips, rather than incorporating the latest. All three companies share a common supply chain risk caused by upstream innovation. Their chip industry suppliers change products and design strategies much more frequently than Verifone, GM, or BASF would like.

"We're watching that industry very, very carefully," said Patrick McGivern, senior vice president of global supply chain of Verifone, "because the cell phone guys are driving a lot of it. And then the cell phone guys move on to a different strategy. So we're watching to see, will this industry even be here five years from now? Because it's critical to what we have." The risk is that cell phone makers might move away from the current technology and abandon certain suppliers who are crucial to Verifone. Such suppliers may not survive the loss of their biggest-revenue customers, leaving Verifone without critical components.

Companies with long product lifespans or long-lived assets (e.g., cars, aircraft, factories) that use short-product-lifecycle goods (e.g., microelectronics) have two ways of coping with this obsolescence risk. First, some procure last-time-buys once a problem is identified; that is, they purchase months' or years' worth of future product demand and spare parts. Second, in some cases, companies can base their products on modular architecture, in which some components can be based on a faster design cycle, matching the suppliers' cycle time. A third, future alternative may involve the use of 3-D printing, which would allow suppliers to keep the digital plans for a product and produce it in small quantities on demand after the end of mass production. Customers might negotiate "have-made" rights or escrow rights to the design to ensure ongoing supply even if the original supplier chooses to discontinue production.

The Sharing Economy

In October 2007, Brian Chesky, a recent college grad, abandoned his job hunt in Los Angeles to stay with a friend in San Francisco.[71] Unemployed, Chesky couldn't help his friend pay the rent—until the roommates had an idea. They noticed that a large industrial design conference had come to San Francisco and overwhelmed the local hotel market. Many hotels were sold out and the remaining few rooms had exorbitant prices. The quick-thinking roommates laid out some inflatable mattresses, dashed down to the grocery store to buy some bacon and eggs, and turned their apartment into a bed and breakfast at $80 dollars per person per night. They called their little foray in the hospitality industry an "AirBed and Breakfast" and made enough money to pay their rent.

Realizing that others might want to offer these same services, they launched AirBnB, an online hub for home sharing that by the end of 2013 reached 10 million guest stays.[72] These forms of "sharing" are becoming more prevalent in other areas, too. Sharing options include car sharing services (Zipcar, RelayRides, Car2go), alternative taxi services (Lyft, Sidecar, Uber), bike sharing (Hubway, Zagster), household goods sharing (Snapgoods, ShareSomeSugar), tools (The Southwest Portland Tool Library), and clothing (Tradesy, SwapStyle).

Direct consumer-to-consumer, "sharing economy" businesses blossomed in the wake of the second-hand economy that grew tremendously with the Internet. Small second-hand stores and lowly "want ad" circulars were supplemented by Craigslist, eBay, Secondhand Mall, Secondhand.org.uk, and dozens of others. Lingering financial hardship among consumers following the 2008 financial crisis both created a supply of stuff to rent or share and created demand from consumers looking for cheaper alternatives than full-price retail products and services. An Internet-spawned ethos of person-to-person "sharing" rather than buying, and an increasing willingness to connect to strangers, further enabled this trend.

These sharing companies threaten to disrupt existing rental firms (e.g., hotels and taxis) as well as product manufacturing companies (e.g., reducing demand for new cars). With 600,000 properties in 200 countries in its listings,[73] AirBnB is larger than all but the four largest hotel chains in the world.[74] RelayRides competes with rental car companies at 229 airports in the United States.[75] Rather than pay to park at the airport, consumers are paid to offer their vehicles while they travel or when they don't need the car.

Some companies are embracing the trend. Driven by environmental sustainability, Patagonia partnered with eBay in a campaign to encourage consumers to buy used Patagonia garments instead of buying new ones. While seemingly cannibalizing its own sales, the campaign cemented Patagonia's environmental bona fides, reminded customers of the sturdiness of Patagonia products, and lowered the resistance to purchase new garments by pointing out their resale value.

New Metrics for New Ideas

Unlike a sudden and localized disaster that captures instant headlines, disruptive innovations emerge slowly and gather force over time. Whereas a hurricane makes landfall at a particular instant,

Nokia's experience with the iPhone shows that disruptive innovation has no obvious onset date. Whereas a hurricane exhausts itself in a brief but furious few days of wind and rain, disruptive innovation creates a permanent shift in customer demand and market structure that sparks the need for long-term adaptation by companies. One way of motivating such long-term changes in any organization is by changing the key performance indicators (KPIs) used to assess and reward workers' and managers' activities. Such KPIs drive behavior, because "what gets measured gets managed."

Most companies recognize the potential advantages of innovation, such as reducing the chances of being disrupted, increasing the chances of taking market share from competitors, and being among the first to take advantage of long-term trends. While the uninitiated might imagine innovation as a serendipitous light bulb turning on when inspiration strikes the inventor's mind, innovation can actually be reduced to a methodical process of generating and evaluating potential concepts. To manage this process, leading companies use innovation-related KPIs to measure and manage the rate of new product and process development. Innovation metrics can track the inputs to the innovation process (e.g., spending on R&D, percentage of employees contributing ideas), the process of bringing innovations to market (e.g., new product development cycle times, ramp-to-volume cycle time) and the outputs of the innovation process (e.g., number of patents, number of new products, percent of revenues derived from new products).[76]

Jeff Murphy, an executive director at Johnson & Johnson, noted that the adoption of innovation metrics should follow the steps of the deployment of an innovation strategy.[77] Early metrics track engagement, training, and participation of people at the beginning of innovation activities. Next, additional metrics measure the growing or accelerating pipeline of projects. Finally, a company with a more mature innovation strategy would measure end-goal attainment, such as revenues from new products. Yet the Nokia example shows that the sheer quantity of new products may not be sufficient if the company is too protective of profits from existing product lines. New market entrants, having no incumbent products to protect, can disrupt an otherwise innovative market leader.

SCENARIO PLANNING

"We tend to overestimate the effect of a technology in the short run and underestimate the effect in the long run," said Roy Amara, a researcher, scientist, and past president of the Institute for the Future.[78] Scenario planning is a way to avoid these kinds of long-term forecasting missteps associated with thinking about long-term trends, long-term risks, and strategic responses. Rather than attempt to forecast the likelihoods of changing technologies, political realignments, urbanization, or any other trend, scenario planning asks managers and executives to envision a divergent set of "what-if" futures and how those different realities might affect the company.

Scenario planning complements business continuity planning (see chapter 6). Although both start with a "what if" and are intended to help an organization prepare for risks, the two methods differ on goals and timescales. Whereas business continuity planning tries to create ready-to-execute plans to return the organization to predisruption levels of performance, scenario planning tries to create a plan for adapting to permanent changes in the definition of performance. Whereas business continuity planning handles transient events (e.g., a hurricane), scenario planning handles long-term trends (e.g., a world where almost everything is made by in-home 3-D printers). Finally, whereas business continuity planning aims to mitigate disruptive threats, scenario planning handles both threats and opportunities. Scenario planning is not unlike the war gaming done by military planners who try to envision various new threat scenarios and play out how the military might handle them. Similar approaches are also used by political scientists in developing long-term foreign policies.

Creating Scenarios[79]

An organization begins the scenario planning process by identifying the fundamental question it wants to address. For example, in its 1997 scenario planning exercise, UPS asked "What is UPS's global business in this ever-changing competitive environment?" And in 2010, UPS did a new scenario planning exercise with the focus of "What is the future of UPS's world market and major regional markets in 2017?" In 2010, Cisco asked, "What forces will shape the Internet between now and 2025?"[80]

The next step is to create or select some scenarios. Because scenario planning is meant to spark new thinking about different futures, the effort typically involves multiple mutually exclusive and very divergent scenarios. For example, UPS in 2004 considered four scenarios derived from quadrants defined in terms of the degree of openness in business models (proprietary vs. collaborative) and the business environment (harmonious vs. chaotic). Cisco's 2010 effort looked at four scenarios culled from eight possible scenarios defined by divergent possibilities in the world's level of Internet infrastructure density (limited vs. extensive), patterns of innovation (incremental vs. breakthroughs), and Internet user behavior (constrained vs. unbridled).[81] The different scenarios are not just some quantitative percentage-point variations up or down from an expected forecast. Instead, they are qualitatively different environments.

A well-crafted scenario needs to seem possible (even if it may be unlikely), be internally consistent, and spark strategic discussions about how the company might change to survive and thrive in that new future. Each scenario should be rich in story-like details, such as by providing example news stories from that future, so that the participants feel immersed in that future world. For example, Sainsbury and Unilever, working with Forum for the Future, developed four "consumer futures" scenarios. In each scenario, they gave a seven-year timeline of key developments, postulated trends on ten metrics, portrayed dozens of hypothetical products, described key elements of living and shopping in that possible world, and gave a hypothetical day-in-the-life of a customer called "Suzie's shampoo story."[82]

Thinking in Possibilities Rather than Probabilities

Next, the organization considers the implications of each scenario using structured and unstructured discussions guided by the purpose of the scenario planning effort and the nature of the organization. For example, a National Cooperative Highway Research

Program project at MIT's Center for Transportation and Logistics examined implications of four scenarios for future freight flows in the United States with a number of states' departments of transportation.[83,84] With each scenario, the discussions were structured around five specific types of impacts on the flow of freight. These included the volume of freight, the value density of the freight, the origins, routings, and destinations. The researchers also used a coarse-grained geographic model of the freight infrastructure of the country. During one part of the effort, the United States was segmented into five seaport zones, four regional highway corridors, four rail corridors, four aggregated airport zones, two land-port borders, intermodal, inland waterways, and "other." Some discussions considered the impact on various categories of freight infrastructure such as gateways (airport, sea port, etc.), connectors (intermodal connection, short-line rail, secondary road, etc.), and corridors (highway, Class I rail lines, etc.). In the case of the future of freight flows project, the goal was to answer the question, "Where should investments in freight transportation infrastructure be made today [in 2011] for the year 2040?" Recommendations took the form of investment in capacity in different modes as well as restructuring initiatives such as creating freight-only lanes.[85]

Because many scenario planning efforts look years or decades into the future, the discussions often center on long-term strategy and capital investments rather than tactical responses. Because of the uncertain nature of the distant future, scenario planning does not attempt to estimate precise quantitative implications. Instead, it looks at qualitative differences and similarities in the organization's potential response or adaptation to the different scenarios. One of the most valuable benefits of scenario planning exercises is to widen managers' perspectives and socialize the organization to future possibilities that may be very different from the present.

Building Detectors for Long-Term Shifts

Detection plays a key role in turning scenario planning from a tabletop exercise into a risk management tool. For example, UPS's scenario planning exercise in 1997 made the company aware that it lacked a branded consumer-side outlet. When UPS identified an opportunity to remedy this, in 2001, it bought Mail Boxes Etc.'s network of over 4,000 retail shipping outlets for $191 million from MBE's struggling parent company. UPS's move forced FedEx to pay—some say overpay—$2.4 billion to purchase the smaller 1,200-outlet network owned by Kinko's. The point was that scenario planning made UPS aware of possible shifts and opportunities that it could act on when the time was right.

Different scenarios call for different detectors. A scenario that postulates a dramatic rise in the costs and social unacceptability of long-distance transportation, for example, might affect a company's long-range supply chain network planning and capital expenditures. Detectors for this scenario might monitor fuel prices, regulatory events, and social activist trends that seem to be reinforcing the locavore movement. If triggered, the company might, for example, delay investment in a centralized manufacturing and distribution systems in favor of local production for local customers.

Shifting Economic Scenarios

Scenario planning can help companies think through the implications of projected economic trends. For example, consider the potential for reshoring—moving manufacturing back from Asia to North America and Europe. The rationale for this seems quite plausible, as Tom Linton, Flextronics's head of procurement and chief supply chain officer, mentioned at a presentation at MIT.[86] As labor costs rise in China, companies may leave China in favor of Mexico to be closer to the US and Canadian markets. Given NAFTA, leveraging Mexican labor may give a significant advantage to North America and will reduce transportation costs as well. Indeed, PricewaterhouseCoopers estimates that lower American energy prices could result in one million more manufacturing jobs as firms build new factories in the United States.[87] Finally, new trade agreements in Latin America may reignite the growth of this continent and increase trade with the EU. At the 2013 Business Summit of the Community of Latin American and Caribbean States with the European Union, Latin American leaders committed to open trade and signed a joint declaration with the EU to embrace international trade.[88] US companies might use reshoring as a competitive advantage to offer lower lead-times, better service, and a "made-in-America" branding.

Yet as plausible as this logic sounds, it's not guaranteed. Other events might forestall reshoring, such as a (futuristic) direct China-US rail link via the Bering Strait,[89] unrest in Mexico,[90] regulation of fracking,[91] or antibusiness regulations in the United States.[92] Even if China becomes too expensive, companies might move to other low-cost countries, such as Vietnam, Myanmar, or any of a number of countries in Africa. Furthermore, the Chinese market itself is expanding and offering more local opportunities. Thus, a bet on massive reshoring might be a risky move.

That's where scenario planning can help. The purpose of scenario planning isn't to forecast whether reshoring will happen or not, but to help a company think through the implications of very different futures such as a reshoring renaissance in the United States vs. an even greater dwindling of US manufacturing. In thinking through these issues, companies can create detectors or sensors for the tipping point if the world starts trending toward one scenario or the other, to be ready to take advantage of whichever trend takes hold.

Of course, successfully detecting a qualitative change in the environment may not guarantee a successful response to that change. As the discussion of disruptive innovation implied, companies build portfolios of valuable assets (e.g., factories, products, brands, processes, core competencies), which they then utilize to generate profits and which tend to constrain the company's choices. Companies are naturally loath to abandon these assets, even if a competitor's innovation or an environmental change threatens to obsolete them. Scenario planning can't guarantee a correct decision, but it can help a company think through large-scale changes, possibly even before it commits to building assets that it might later need to abandon.

13

FOR WANT OF A NAIL

"The world is so connected that the feedback loops are more intense," said Ellen Kullman CEO of DuPont.[1] She explained, "Our supply chains are global. Our financial markets are global. So uncertainty in one part of the world infiltrates all parts of the world. These days, there are things that just come shooting across the bow—economic volatility and the impact of natural events, like the Japanese earthquake and tsunami—at much greater frequency than we've ever seen."[2] A flicker of power can reveal the fragility of a company's supply chain: a 70-millisecond power dropout at Toshiba's Yokkaichi memory-chip plant in late 2010 affected the world's supply of NAND flash.[3]

Whereas Japan's 2011 earthquake, tsunami, and nuclear reactor disaster disrupted hundreds of businesses and affected many companies' supply chains around the world, the March 31, 2012, fire at Evonik's factory (See chapter 4) was tiny by comparison and strictly localized. One part of one factory in one town had a fire. Less than a day later, the fire was out. Yet the effect of the Evonik fire was significant—at GM, supplies of 2,000 parts were jeopardized, which was one-third as many parts as were disrupted by the far larger Japanese disaster. The impact of Evonik fire was so large because all of those GM parts required nylon-12 plastic, which suddenly became scarce.

DIAMONDS ARE A SUPPLY CHAIN'S WORST ENEMY

When the Allies wanted to stop the German war machine in WWII, they bombed the ball bearing factories around Schweinfurt, because almost all of Germany's tanks, warships, and airplanes relied on Schweinfurt's ball bearings. Knocking out a single key supplier to many industries would do the greatest damage to those many downstream industries.[4]

The archetypal diagram of a supply chain shows a fan of suppliers feeding the company in an inverted "tree structure." (See figures 13.1 and 13.2.) Each OEM or brand owner has many suppliers, and each supplier has many other suppliers, and so on. The diagram seems to imply robustness, with many alternative suppliers across the tiers. But, unbeknownst to the OEM or brand owner, some supply chains show a different pattern, with a single supplier deep in the chain—such as the Evonik chemical factory or Schweinfurt ball bearing plant—playing a keystone role. Instead of a fan, the shape is more of a diamond, in which the OEMs and many of their suppliers are dependent on that one provider.)

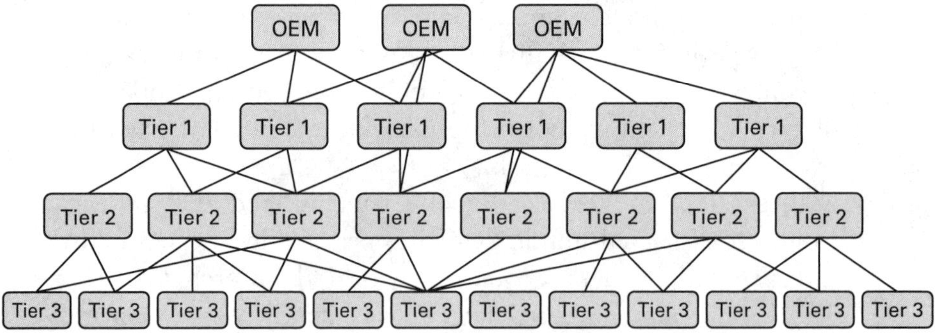

Figure 13.1

An industry supply chain schema

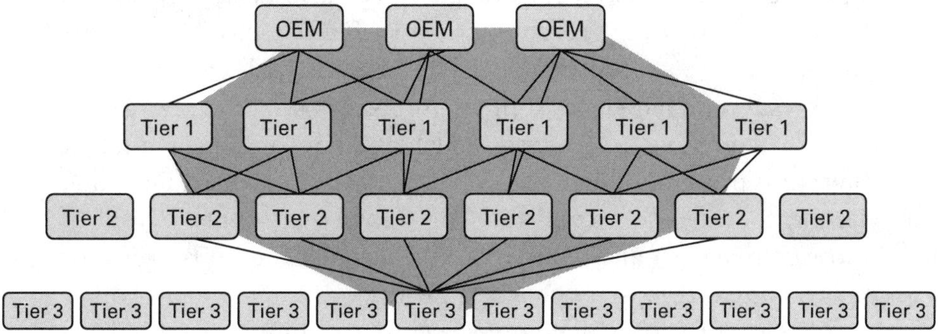

Figure 13.2

A "Diamond"-shaped supply chain schema

Deep-Tier Diamonds

Silicon chips may get all the glory as the premiere technology that powers laptops, tablets, and smartphones, but the unassuming black plastic packaging around the silicon chip is also a work of the highest technologies. Whereas the first integrated circuits (ICs) had perhaps a dozen or so pins connecting them to the circuit board, current-day microchips can have over 500 connections using a tiny grid of solder balls embedded in a thin substrate.[5] That inscrutable density of connections requires high-tech materials such as bismaleimide triazine (BT), an epoxy resin that is strong, thermally conductive, and able to hold extremely tight tolerances over time and temperature variances.

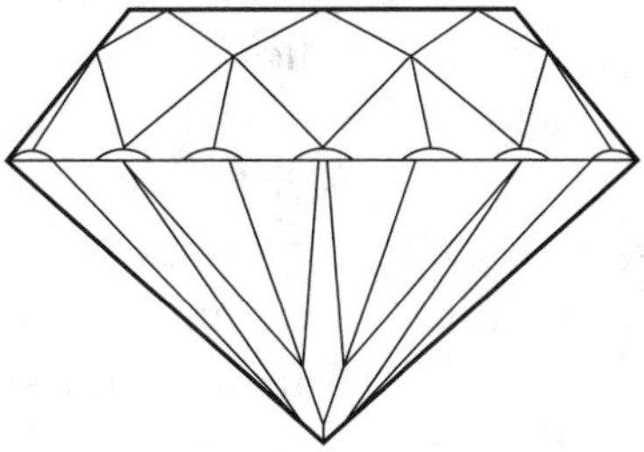

Eighty percent of the world's supply of BT comes from Mitsubishi Gas Chemical's (MGC) Fukushima facility in Japan.[6,7] The 2011 Japan quake changed that. "Our contacts in Asia suggest one of the bigger problems may actually be the growing shortage of BT," said Craig Berger, an analyst with investment bank FBR.[8] A prolonged shutdown of MGC's factories after the earthquake caused bottlenecks in the worldwide IC assembly industry supply chain.[9] Lead-times for IC substrates grew to the 75–125-day range.[10] A company such as Apple or Samsung might buy chips from more than a dozen different chip makers, including second sources and second fabs for many components. Yet all of those chip makers and alternative suppliers depend on BT, most of which comes from that one MGC facility.

BT wasn't the only diamond-structure disruption of specialized materials exposed by the Japan quake. Disruptions in the supply of Xirallic, a sparkly pigment made in Japan by Merck, affected manufacturing of certain colors of luxury cars at Toyota Motors, Chrysler LLC, GM, Ford Motor, BMW, VW, Audi, and other car makers.[11] Lithium ion batteries require PVDF (polyvinylidene fluoride), and 70 percent of the global supply came from one factory in Fukushima province. Although the plant survived the quake, the tsunami devastated the nearby port that was critical to supplying raw materials to the plant.[12] Other supply chain diamond structures revealed by the Japan quake included high-purity hydrogen peroxide used in chip making, and EPDM (ethylene propylene diene monomer) used by car makers in rubber gaskets and seals.[13] "What we've found is that in Tiers 3 and 4, the convergence of underlying raw material supply starts to become really significant," said Jackie Sturm, Intel's vice president and general manager of global sourcing and procurement.[14]

Diamond structures can also create widespread quality risks. In 2005, contaminated Teflon made by DuPont was coated on sockets supplied by Federal Mogul and assembled into diesel injection pumps produced by automotive Tier 1 supplier Robert Bosch. Automakers including Audi, BMW, and DaimlerChrysler had to stop their assembly lines and recall vehicles when the defect came to light.[15] Similarly, when Takata, the world's third largest automotive airbag manufacturer, had a problem with improperly manufactured airbags in 2013, the result was a recall of more than three million vehicles worldwide by Toyota, Honda, Nissan, and Mazda.[16]

In 2014, NHTSA forced an expansion of the recall to include 15 automobile manufacturers, and some US lawmakers called for a criminal investigation by the US Department of Justice.[17]

Few people have heard of Sunland Inc., a $55 million processor of organic peanuts and other nuts. Yet when the company's only factory in the small town of Portales, New Mexico, became contaminated with salmonella,[18] the hidden role of this small food processor was revealed. Sunland wasn't just the maker of some minor off-brand of peanut butter; they were a supplier to dozens of prominent brands.

The recall began with just two peanut butter products from US retailer Trader Joe's but then grew to encompass over 300 products from 36 brand-name companies. The recall hit a number of "healthy" manufacturing and retail brands, such as Whole Foods, Earth Balance, Newman's Own Organics, and Cadia All Natural,[19] as well as more mainstream brands such as Harry and David, Target, and Stop & Shop. And it wasn't just jars of peanut butter but also cookies, snack crackers, brownies, nut mixes, and even ice creams that were recalled. Sunland's products sickened 42 people in 20 states.[20] The direct costs of the recall were $78 million; yet the estimated costs to American peanut-containing product makers was $1 billion, including growers and product makers unaffiliated with Sunland.[21] Deep-tier diamond structures reside in many industries, and a small problem with a niche supplier can reverberate far and wide.

From Eruption to Disruption: Europe Gets Grounded

In April of 2010, a modest-sized ice-capped volcano named Eyjafjallajökull in southern Iceland roused from a 187-year slumber. When blazing hot lava hit the volcano's ice and water-filled caldera, the mixture flashed explosively into ash-laden steam that rose high into the atmosphere. The prevailing winds carried the thick gray-brown ash cloud southeast.

European aviation authorities grew concerned as the ash cloud drifted toward the continent and the UK. If a jet aircraft flew through the ash cloud, the ash could damage the plane's engines, sand-blast the cockpit windows, and damage aircraft instruments.

As a precaution, civil aviation authorities shut down portions of European airspace, starting with Norway. The closures expanded and shifted over a six-day period as the eruption continued and shifting winds pushed the ash in different directions. Major airfreight hubs such as Heathrow, Amsterdam, Paris, and Frankfurt were closed for up to five days.[22]

The last time a volcano shut down European airspace was … never. Although volcanoes, primarily in the Pacific Rim, had in the past caused trouble for individual aircraft and particular air routes, they had been localized incidents easily handled by detouring around the affected area.[23] Companies, however, weren't prepared for an event that shut down every airport and every carrier over a large region. For example, FedEx's contingency plan for a closure of Paris was to use Frankfurt, but Frankfurt was closed, too.[24]

"There's a major disruption of the supply chain," said Paul Tsui, vice chairman of the Hong Kong Association of Freight Forwarding and Logistics."[25] In the UK alone, airfreight provides 25 percent of all imports[26] and 55 percent of exports to non-EU countries.[27] Although some airfreight might not be particularly time-sensitive (e.g., jewelry), many categories of freight are (e.g., perishable foods, vaccines, emergency spare parts, surgical instruments, and components for JIT manufacturing).[28]

"It's a terrible nightmare," said Stephen Mbithi, the chief executive officer of the Fresh Produce Exporters Association of Kenya.[29] During the six days of airport closures, thousands of tons of fresh flowers rotted in storage units and warehouses, representing a loss to the Kenyan economy of $3.8 million per day,[30] which represents about 3 percent of Kenya's daily GDP.[31] "Cow food, that's about all we can do with it now," concluded Kenneth Maundu, general manager for Sunripe, the Kenyan produce exporters.[32]

Migros, the Swiss supermarket chain, noted disruptions in supplies from the United States (green asparagus), Iceland (cod), and Southeast Asia (tuna). Italian exporters of mozzarella and fresh fruits lost about $14 million each day that flights were grounded.[33] The Federation of Hong Kong Industries said hotels and restaurants in Hong Kong had shortages of French cheese, Belgian chocolates, and Dutch fresh-cut flowers.[34] UK grocery stores ran out of presliced fruit and tropical fruits like pineapple.[35] For many retailers of perishable goods, airfreight to or from Europe was a diamond in their supply chain structure—a chokepoint in transportation that affected all of them.

To meet delivery commitments, air couriers routed some airfreight through Spain and Turkey.[36] Similarly, some freight forwarders chartered flights to southern European airports like Barcelona and then transported goods by road to northern Europe.[37] "The cost is doubling," said Tiku Shah, owner of Sunripe in Kenya. "But we don't have a choice. If we don't have product on the shelves, our customers will look for alternatives."[38] The bulk of European airfreight was grounded as carriers suspended delivery time guarantees and stopped accepting European airfreight.[39]

The International Air Transport Association (IATA) estimated that the Icelandic volcano crisis cost airlines more than $1.7 billion in lost revenue in the six days after the initial eruption. At its worst, the ash cloud grounded 29 percent of the world's scheduled air travel and caused the cancellation of some 107,000 flights over an eight-day period.[40] The disruption of passenger air travel would seem to mean little to the airfreight industry, except for the fact that most airfreight actually ships in the bellies of passenger aircraft.[41] In total, global cargo flights were down over 15 percent in April, proving that the post-disruption rebound did not make up for the losses.[42]

In many cases, the declared value of the airfreight belied the importance of the shipments to the recipient—an issue discussed in chapter 7. Nissan's inability to fly $30 air pressure sensors from Ireland to Japan kept the car maker from producing $30,000 Nissan Murano SUVs.[43] Three BMW plants in Germany couldn't get inbound parts from Asia.[44] And an inability to ship transmissions out of Europe disrupted production at BMW's US factory.[45,46]

Airfreight isn't the only vulnerable mode, and volcanoes aren't the only risk to bottleneck transportation routes. The Rhine River carries 16 percent of Germany's trade.[47] Recurring droughts,[48,49] an overturned barge in 2011,[50] and finding unexploded bombs from WWII[51] have all created constrictions in freight volume on the river. In the United States, a quarter of all rail traffic and half of all intermodal rail traffic passes through Chicago. If the weather misbehaves, such as during the 1999 blizzard, then Chicago chokes. "The traffic just kept coming and coming and coming," said David Grewe, a supervisor for Union Pacific Railroad. "We basically waited for the spring thaw."[52]

Labor, a Striking Chokepoint

When 400 unionized shipping clerks walked off the job at the Port of LA and Port of Long Beach on November 27, 2012, it set off a cascade of effects. Ten thousand dockworkers in a sister union refused to cross the clerks' picket lines, and 10 of the ports' 14 terminals shut down.[53] "We estimate that the two ports handle about a billion dollars' worth of cargo a day," said Art Wong, spokesman for the Port of Long Beach. "Three-quarters of the port complex is shut down, meaning $760 million a day worth of goods are just idled." Over the eight days of the strike, those 400 disgruntled workers held up an estimated $6 billion in shipments and threatened 20,000 jobs.[54]

The effects spread beyond the ports. President Matthew Shay of the National Retail Federation called on President Obama to intervene and end this work stoppage. Shay added, "The work stoppage not only impacts retailers but is also affecting their product vendors—many of which are small businesses—and other industries like manufacturers and agricultural exporters that rely on the ports."[55] Jonathan Gold, vice president for supply chain and customs policy of the National Retail Federation, added: "These retailers will also face unanticipated costs. The ocean carriers will charge a $1,000 congestion fee per container for every day they are at sea... The truck drivers ... transporting the containers, will not get paid...."[56] After eight days, the two sides reached a tentative agreement and the ports reopened.[57] But the effects spread beyond the eight days. "Typically, what we hear from our retailers [is that] for every day of a shutdown, it takes two to three days to clear," Gold said.[58]

Labor unions covering key infrastructure or industries have the potential to create systemic risks, as was the case during the 2002 West Coast Port Lockout that shut down all the port along the US Pacific Coast. The rapidly growing damage to the US economy caused then-president George W. Bush to intervene, invoking the Taft-Hartley Act of 1947 to force open the ports.[59]

COLLATERAL DAMAGE

"The disasters in Japan and Thailand this year [2011] were the worst hit that CBI [Contingent Business Interruption] coverage ever took," said Volker Muench,[60] head of corporate underwriting property at Allianz SE's industrial-insurance unit. CBI covers the collateral damage caused by supply chain disruptions by underwriting some of the business losses incurred by companies indirectly affected by a disaster. "If a factory burns down, that's only one claim in property insurance, while the same incident could potentially disrupt the supply chains of hundreds of companies if the factory supplies essential goods to other companies," said Jochen Koerner, a member of the executive board of insurance broker Marsh & McLennan Co.[61] Apple alone filed a $500 million interruption claim after the Japan quake because of interruptions in supplies of flash memory, DRAM, and digital compasses three weeks before Apple was to launch its iPad 2.[62]

Disaster Sprouts for Veggie Growers

When a rare and particularly virulent strain of E. coli bacteria infected some residents in Northern Germany and some European tourists, government investigators rushed to identify the source of the outbreak. The frantic search for the cause depended on very sick people's fuzzy memories of where they had eaten and what they had eaten. The first cases appeared on May 2, 2011; during a two-month period, some 3,100 individuals suffered from bloody diarrhea, more than 850 got hemolytic uremic syndrome, and 53 people died.[63] In addition to a large number of cases in Germany, health officials discovered victims in Britain, Denmark, France, the Netherlands, Sweden, and Switzerland, all involving people who had traveled to Germany. "Our absolute first priority is to clarify the source of the outbreak because, if we can't do that, we're not going to win back consumer confidence," said Roger Waite, a spokesman for Dacian Ciolos, the European agriculture commissioner.[64]

Based on victims' reports, salad topped the menu of suspects. The Robert Koch Institute advised consumers to avoid raw vegetables.[65] Supermarkets all over the continent drastically cut their orders for tomatoes, lettuce, and cucumbers that people wanted to avoid, causing significant losses for European farmers. On May 26, the Hamburg Institute for Hygiene and the Environment found three cucumbers from Spain that tested positive for E. coli.[66] As a result, Germany, Denmark, the Czech Republic, Luxembourg, Hungary, Sweden, Belgium, and Russia banned Spanish cucumbers.[67] The effect was swift and devastating. Spanish farmers lost €200 million a week as some 150,000 tons of unwanted Spanish fruit and vegetables (not only cucumbers) piled up each week, according to FEPEX, Spain's fruit and vegetable export body.[68] Asked about the scope of the slump in demand, Jorge Brotons, FEPEX president, said: "Almost all Europe. There is a domino effect on all vegetables and fruits."[69]

When further tests showed that the E coli found on Spanish cucumbers did not match the strain behind the outbreak,[70] the German agriculture secretary Robert Kloos admitted: "Germany recognizes that the Spanish cucumbers are not the cause."[71] Yet German officials continued to advise consumers to avoid eating raw tomatoes, lettuce, and cucumbers, causing the slump to hit farmers in other countries, too. Victor Miranda, a grocer in Paris, said, "Even if the cucumbers are from France and not from Spain, nobody wants to eat them."[72] Koos De Vries, a Dutch cucumber grower, said, "From a business point of view, it's a catastrophe for us."[73]

When authorities finally found the true cause, they discovered that it had nothing to do with any kind of Spanish produce or any other growers' tomatoes, lettuce, and cucumbers that so many people were warned to avoid. Instead, the E. coli contamination was finally traced to a small producer of organic sprouts in Germany.[74] The warm moist environment of the seed-sprouting trays proved ideal for E. coli growth. Yet the farmer denied that his farm could be the true cause,[75] because he didn't use any manure-based fertilizers that might introduce E. coli to his sprouting houses. And he was right that it was not the fertilizer. Further analysis traced the E. coli to fenugreek seeds imported from Egypt and substandard sprout seed production practices in Egypt.[76] Yet vindication was cold comfort for all the cucumber and salad ingredient producers in Spain and across Europe who were brought to the edge of bankruptcy by the scare and erroneous government warnings.

Two elements were responsible for the collateral damage in this case. First, public fear led to overreaction fueled by unsubstantiated media reports, because fear "sells." The second element was hasty government actions, under pressure to quell these fears. But the German Government and the EU are not the only governments to over-react in haste. A substantial portion of the economic damage following the 9/11 terrorist attack was caused by the United States government closing the borders, stopping the flow of parts and products to and from Canada and Mexico. Similarly, most of the economic damage caused by the 2001 UK foot and mouth disease outbreak, was caused by the UK government closing the countryside, bringing the travel and tourism industry to a halt and causing losses that were higher than the damage to the agricultural industry.

No Disk Supply = No Chip Demand

When floods inundated hard-disk makers in Thailand in 2011, neither Intel nor its suppliers were flooded. In fact, Intel stood to gain because the company sold SSDs (solid state disks), which compete with hard disks for mass storage solutions in PCs, laptops, and servers. "We'll be using this as an opportunity" to increase sales of solid-state drives, Intel's chief financial officer Stacy Smith told analysts.[77]

But the shortages of disk drives hit PC production. In the fourth quarter of 2011, the PC industry faced a 35 percent shortfall in disk supplies.[78] "The floods in Thailand have had an impact on the supply of hard disk drives and as a result [on] the PC supply chain," Smith said in a conference call with analysts. "We've seen a drop in orders for microprocessors in the fourth quarter."[79] Intel lost about $800 million in revenue for the fourth quarter 2011 relative to expectations.[80,81] "We found with Thailand that for want of a nail a kingdom can be lost. So for us, even though our production might continue, if other critical components to our customers can't ship, like a hard drive, then everybody stops," said Intel's Jackie Sturm.[82]

What a Pain in the Acetonitrile

Collateral damage can spread across industries. Acrylic and ABS (acrylonitrile-butadiene-styrene) are very popular plastics used in carpet, cars, electronic housings, and small appliances. When the financial crisis struck in 2008, demand for acrylic and ABS plummeted. Both plastics are made from acrylonitrile, a colorless liquid with a garlic-like odor made by reacting ammonia with propylene gas. As demand for these plastics dropped, global production at acrylonitrile plants dropped by 40 percent.

Acrylonitrile synthesis also creates a sister chemical, acetonitrile, as a byproduct. For every 100 liters of acrylonitrile, the chemical maker also gets about two to four liters of acetonitrile. Some chemical plants simply burn the byproduct as fuel for the factory. But a few companies extract the acetonitrile, purify it, and sell it for a host of minor applications, including as a solvent used in research labs and in quality assurance testing in the pharmaceutical industry.

When acrylonitrile production plummeted, the acetonitrile supply went with it. Moreover, the Chinese restricted production during that same time in order to reduce air pollution for the Beijing Olympic Games, and Hurricane Ike knocked out a Texas supplier.[83] "The market is beyond short," said Jerry Richard of Purification Technologies, a Chester, Connecticut-based firm that buys acetonitrile in bulk, purifies it, and sells it to laboratory chemical suppliers. "You have people scrambling around trying to get material. My phone is ringing off the hook," Richard added.[84] Many industries are cross-coupled by deep tier suppliers in ways they don't understand, increasing the chance of collateral damage from remote events.

NO SYSTEMIC SUPPLY CHAIN RISKS

In addition to its horrendous human toll, Hurricane Katrina also knocked out 20 percent of the US supply of coffee just as demand was ramping up for the holiday season. Hurricane damage closed P&G's Folgers plant in New Orleans for more than three weeks as the company worked to restore the factory and its supporting infrastructure (see chapter 6). Yet, US coffee drinkers never saw a shortage—other manufacturers were able to fill the gap. In fact, the Herculean efforts of Procter & Gamble to restart the plant were motivated by the reality that competitors were there to take up the slack.

A true systemic risk is the risk of a collapse of an entire industry or an industrial system. The term is typically used in finance to indicate a global financial system collapse, such as almost occurred during the 2008 financial crisis when credit dried up worldwide. It is also, however, used in reference to a regional event such as the 1997 Asian financial crisis. A systemic risk in supply chains can be defined as a disruption that brings an entire industry to a halt, resulting in consumers not being able to buy an entire category of products.

Throughout the many disruptions described in this book, end consumers remained largely insulated even as supply chain professionals agonized over how to recover from earthquakes, floods, hurricanes, and all the natural and man-made insults that supply chains endure. Even the largest disruptions—such as the March 2011 Japanese tsunami, the 2011 Thailand floods, or the 2008 financial crisis—had well-contained impacts. Some colors of cars might be delayed, prices for hard-disks might increase, or some companies might disappear. Yet, by and large, retailers' shelves and dealers' showrooms remained well stocked with all the goods that consumers have come to expect.

Thus, it's hard to conclude that modern global supply chains show evidence of true systemic risks. Companies have developed efficient response mechanisms, and the same globalization trends that could create disruption risks for specific companies that use suppliers from faraway lands may also contribute to the prevention of systemic risk by spreading manufacturing capacity around the globe. Most important, global capacity for manufacturing and distribution is large, and while it is crucial for any company to prepare and respond effectively to disasters, there are always others ready to take its place if it fumbles.

Globalization's Hidden Inventory

Verifone's point-of-sale credit card readers use many of the same kinds of electronic components found in laptops and cell phones. That includes the intricately designed board-to-board connectors that route delicate digital signals to and fro inside the devices. After the 2011 Japan earthquake, Verifone faced shortages of these connectors because the big PC and smartphone makers had more clout to commandeer supply. But Verifone wasn't disrupted because it found inventories in the gray market, at distributors, and on the spot market.

The same global coupling that makes many players sensitive to a disruption also means that many players around the globe might have hidden inventories. Competition causes suppliers and distributors to be responsive to customer demand. Given the volatility of both supply and demand, companies are motivated to hold safety stock. Long supply chains also imply days or weeks of inventory in the form of goods in transit. And the same IT and telecommunications infrastructure that supports global supply chains helps companies scour the globe for these hidden pockets of supply.

GM's handling of the catalytic convertor production problems (see chapter 6) illustrates another hidden type of inventory in global supply chains. GM used the inventory latent in three tiers of intermediate suppliers and interconnecting transportation links to buffer a disruption at the deep-tier supplier. Each company in a deeply tiered supply chain might be quite lean, yet the sheer number of companies along the chain holding inventory in low-value form, awaiting value-added steps—plus the large amounts of product flowing through long global supply lanes—lead to a high aggregate level of inventory in the system. This inventory may be hidden, but it's there in an emergency.

Innovation under Stress

When the Evonik fire created a shortage of the precursors to PA-12 plastic (see chapter 4), many competitors of Evonik and of the PA-12 plastic derived from Evonik's chemicals rushed to the foreground. Makers of other polyamides (PA) or nylons touted their products. DuPont offered its Zytel and Hytrel brands of nylon.[85] Arkema, Rhodia, BASF, Netherlands-based DSM, and DuPont offered PA-12 derived from castor bean oil as a green alternative to Evonik's petroleum-derived PA-12. Evonik itself offered nylon 6/10, nylon 6/12, nylon 10/10, nylon 10/12, and biobased Vestamid Terra as alternatives.[86]

The acetonitrile shortage, discussed earlier, spurred innovation among both customers and producers of the chemical. Some acetonitrile users found workarounds, such as alternative solvents,[87] and others changed their testing processes to reduce acetonitrile consumption per test.[88] Through multifaceted modifications of the process, one supplier helped customers reduce run time by over 50 percent and reduce acetonitrile consumption by over 75 percent.[89] Ineos Nitriles, producer of acrylonitrile and acetonitrile, found a way to adjust the reaction conditions during the production of acrylonitrile and increase its acetonitrile coproduct yields by 50 percent.[90] If necessity is the mother of invention, then disruptions create a lot of inventive new parents.

So Many Modes, So Many Lanes

Vistakon, a Johnson & Johnson subsidiary that makes contact lens products, has factories in Jacksonville, Florida, and Limerick, Ireland. The 2010 Iceland volcano severed Vistakon's usual airfreight distribution flows from Ireland to Asia. But the company found many ways around most of the disruption. It used multiple tactics, such as expediting orders from Jacksonville to Tokyo, trucking 60 pallets of contact lenses under the English Channel to Spain for a flight to Singapore, and chartering a cargo ship from Dublin to Tokyo in case the ash cloud lingered.[91]

Similarly, Dutch mail and express group TNT rapidly switched from its usual air hub in Liege, Belgium, to an air gateway in Madrid.[92] BMW was trucking transmissions to Spain in hopes of flying them to South Carolina.[93] Even with airports and air space closed over broad swathes of Europe, companies found ways to move goods.

Growing Maturity of Enterprise Risk Management

The 2005-2015 decade has seen a growing awareness of the need for systematic enterprise risk management (ERM) practices. In the wake of the 2001 Enron accounting scandal in the United States, the Sarbanes-Oxley Act of 2002 pushed companies to adopt more formal risk management procedures by requiring a top-down risk assessment and improved internal risk controls. The ERM Initiative at North Carolina State University has traced the rising adoption of ERM with annual surveys beginning in 2009.[94] In 2009, only 8.8 percent of companies claimed to have "a complete ERM process." By 2013, the number had risen to nearly one quarter (24.6 percent).

ERM is becoming more standardized, too. In 2004, COSO (Committee of Sponsoring Organizations of the Treadway Commission) expanded its corporate accounting risks framework to encompass enterprise risk management. The original COSO framework arose to manage financial controls, accounting audits, and associated compliance risks. The core of the new expanded framework is known as the COSO cube,[95] which segments risk management activities on three dimensions: risk management components, risk management objectives, and entity/scope levels. Specifically, the objectives include strategy and operations, in addition to reporting and compliance.

In 2009, the International Standard Organization (ISO) published the ISO 31000 standard for risk management.[96] Unlike COSO, ISO 31000 encompasses both negative and positive excursions in possible future events, scenarios, and conditions. Furthermore, in addition to ISO 31000, ISO maintains a host of related standards that address specific categories of risks such as ISO 28000 (security risk management systems for the supply chain), ISO 27001 (information security), ISO 26000 (social responsibility), ISO 14000 (environmental management), and ISO 9000 (quality management).[97]

These and other risk standards establish a top-down governance structure with internal feedback loops to manage risks as well as the risk management process. It begins at the board level. The initial component of the ISO 31000 framework calls for a "mandate and commitment" by the board. The board has overall responsibility for risk management, ensures that risk management is embedded into all processes and activities, and reviews the organization's risk profile. The board helps define the organization's risk appetite and manage serious crises. According to PwC's *2014 Annual Corporate Directors Survey*, risk management expertise ranked as the fourth most important attribute of board members, behind financial, industry, and operation expertise but ahead of international, technical, marketing, and legal expertise.[98] Similarly, companies providing a "formal report to the board describing top risk exposures at least annually" have risen from 26.3 percent in 2009 to 47.5 percent in 2013.[99]

Darwinian Winnowing Begets Systemic Strength

The stories in this book demonstrate that individual companies are vulnerable to supply chain risks. While the strong companies can survive and even thrive as a result of preparation and effective disruption management, many others lose market share, lose money, suffer brand diminution, and even go out of business as a result of a disruption in their supply chains. Yet industries as a whole seem to be very robust, and examples of *systemic supply chain risk* are relatively absent from history.[100] The answer to this seeming paradox is that *systemic resilience* exists *because* specific companies are vulnerable and because they operate in a competitive marketplace.

To understand this phenomenon, one can go back to the theory of evolution. Individuals compete for survival, and the weak ones fail. It is the fear of failure during competition that ensures that each element of the system keeps innovating and striving, thus making the winners and the entire system stronger. Therefore, with each disruption the survivors become stronger and more resilient, in the same way that the surviving species are those that are flexible and can adapt.

In his book *Antifragile*, Nassim Taleb[101] uses the restaurant industry as an example. Individual restaurants are among the most failure-prone businesses—about 60 percent fail in the first three years.[102] In highly competitive New York City, about 80 percent of restaurants fail in the first five years.[103] Despite the high rate of disruption of individual restaurants, however, diners can always find a good quality restaurant in New York City. In fact, the quality of many New York City restaurants is exceedingly high.

Corporations and their supply chains also compete with each other. When disruption strikes a company's manufacturing facility or one of its suppliers, that company may go out of business. But because competitors rush in to take market share, the industry as a whole remains very robust. Furthermore, the surviving players learn from the experience of the failing company as well as from their own efforts. They strengthen their defenses, improve their processes, and become less likely to fail during the next disruption.

SIGNS OF EMERGING SYSTEMIC RISKS (MAYBE)

"There's no reason to think the trend towards more unforeseen events [affecting supply chains] is going to end," said Bo-Inge Stensson, vice president for purchasing at SKF, the biggest maker of industrial bearings in the world.[104] History cannot be a definitive guide to the future because the worst earthquake, flood, or industrial accident ever could always happen tomorrow or at some other point in the future. The disruptions of the past have known and bounded magnitudes, but the magnitudes of future events are unknown and unbounded. The properties of the power law distribution discussed in chapter 2 imply that as time marches ever onward, new opportunities for more, bigger, or worse disruptions appear. This property of the bounded past and the unbounded future is why world records are broken (in the future, somebody will run faster, jump farther, or lift heavier than anybody before).

For example, Eyjafjallajökull was a modest eruption by volcanologists' standards and even by Icelandic standards. Katla, a larger mountain near Eyjafjallajökull, might be awakening, and its last eruption produced five times as much ash as did the 2010 eruption of Eyjafjallajökull.[105] Other Icelandic volcanoes have produced 100 times the expelled material and erupted for months on end.[106] The largest volcanic eruptions in world history were 1,000 times larger. Many locations have latent risks for very large disruptions. Seismologists' models suggest that massive earthquakes are "overdue" in places such as California,[107] the Pacific Northwest coast of the United States,[108] Tokyo,[109] and even London.[110]

Financial advisors often utter a common refrain that "past performance is no indication of future performance." In that sense, the fact that past disruptions did not create systemic shortages is no guarantee that the future holds no surprises for the global supply chain systems. Even though the probability of systemic supply chain disruption may be very small, several trends hint at a nonzero probability of future systemic risks. These include the concentration of suppliers, new material requirements, contagion among supply chains inside and across related industries, and the geographical clustering of sources of supply.

Growing Global Diamonds

After a 1997 fire destroyed the Aisin factory that made proportional valves for car braking systems, all Toyota automotive manufacturing plants in Japan ground to a halt. Interestingly, however, no other car company in Japan was affected because Aisin belonged to Toyota's *keiretsu* (i.e., a close affiliation of suppliers with that one brand). Reliance on a single supplier and a JIT manufacturing system made Toyota fragile to Aisin's disruption.

Ten years after the Aisin fire, a 6.8 magnitude earthquake in central Japan severely damaged the Kashiwazaki City plant of Riken Corp., a supplier who made piston rings and other automobile components. Again, Toyota was forced to shut down all 12 of its domestic assembly plants. But Riken's failure also caused the immediate shutdown of eleven other major Japanese automotive and truck companies, including Nissan, Mitsubishi, Mazda, Suzuki Motors Corp., and Fuji Heavy Industries Ltd. This disruption of just one supplier of a $1.50 part forced the closure of nearly 70 percent of Japan's automobile production.[111]

The increased fragility of the Japanese automakers was due to the gradual dissolution of the keiretsu system (in which each supplier kept a strong relationship with only one OEM) to a more open, best-of-breed procurement strategy, in which all suppliers compete to sell to all OEMs and each OEM picks among all suppliers. For example, Toyota spun off Denso Corporation in 1949 but retained the supplier in Toyota's keiretsu for many years. Today, however, Denso supplies most of the automotive, trucking, and heavy equipment companies around the world and has revenues exceeding $40 billion. Similarly, General Motors and Ford spun off their Delphi and Visteon units, respectively, with the expectation that these large suppliers would serve all the automotive companies. Around the world, the level of vertical integration (either via keiretsu cross-holdings like Denso or captive suppliers like Delphi) decreased.

This movement, in part, was due to the desire to create competition among suppliers (rather than be tied to internal capabilities), thereby reducing the costs of parts and subassemblies as well as tapping into more innovation from across the supply base. The result put significant cost pressures on suppliers, culminating in several bankruptcies, such as Delphi's in 2005. Retailers were also growing in size during the same period, and giants like Walmart, Target, Tesco, and Carrefour were pressuring their suppliers to reduce prices.

Although suppliers did grow by serving multiple customers, the pricing squeeze caused them to merge and grow even larger in order to strengthen their ability to withstand OEM's cost-cutting pressures. Suppliers such as Riken worked to improve efficiencies and economies of scale—including Riken's decision to locate all of its factories in one strategic (but earthquake-prone) location.[112] Hitachi, Mitsubishi Electric, and NEC Electronics merged their capacity to produce automobile microcontrollers into a single keystone facility, run by a company named Renesas, which was heavily damaged in the 2011 quake.[113,114] Furthermore, as suppliers grew, they were able to invest more in research and development, and start to offer more specialized, innovative, and unique parts to their customers. For example, Bosch was founded in 1886 as a maker of ignition systems and grew into a $65 billion German automotive conglomerate with 350 subsidiaries supplying most automotive OEMs with electronic and electric components, gasoline and diesel fuel systems, car multimedia, control components, steering technology, and many other systems.

Suppliers' consolidations and their expanded capabilities are increasing the risk of "diamond structures" in supply chains. In other words, a large fraction of a specific industry may depend on a single keystone supplier, who may be buried in a deep tier of the bill-of-materials. This keystone supplier may be disrupted as a result of a strike, sabotage, financial distress, or cyber-attack, thereby affecting its entire operation, even though it may have multiple plants. Such a failure may create a systemic risk for that industry—affecting all consumer-facing enterprises, be they OEMs, brand owners, or retailers.

Supply Contagion and Interdependency

It's not every day that the CEO of one major company makes an impassioned plea for a government bailout to save his fiercest competitors. Yet that's exactly what Ford CEO Alan Mulally did in front of the Senate banking committee on November 18, 2008. He said, "If any one of the domestic companies should fail, we believe there is a strong chance that the entire industry would face severe disruption. Ours is in some significant ways an industry that is uniquely interdependent—particularly with respect to our supply base, with more than 90 percent commonality among our suppliers. Should one of the other domestic companies declare bankruptcy, the effect on Ford's production operations would be felt within days, if not hours. Suppliers could not get financing and would stop shipments to customers. Without parts for the just-in-time inventory system, Ford plants would not be able to produce vehicles."[115]

"Our dealer networks also have substantial overlap. Approximately 400 of our dealers also have a GM or Chrysler franchise at their dealership. The failure of one of the companies would clearly have a great impact on our dealers with exposure to that company. In short, a collapse of one of our competitors here would have a ripple effect across all automakers, suppliers, and dealers—a loss of nearly three million jobs in the first year, according to an estimate by the Center for Automotive Research," Mulally concluded.[116]

During the financial crisis, Ford did far more than just send its CEO to Washington to lobby for support for competing OEMs. Ford reached out to other automakers to explore "how we could work together where legally permissible to prevent a collapse of the supply chain," said Ford spokesman Todd Nissen.[117] Concerns about antitrust issues caused GM to decline to participate.[118] In the end, Ford, Toyota, Honda, and later Nissan agreed to coordinate their efforts to support suppliers that were critical for each OEM.[119] According to *Detroit News* automotive reporter Bryce G. Hoffmand, "It was like Protestants and Catholics coming together to work on a downtown redevelopment plan for Belfast."[120] In Europe, a similar collaboration took place with BMW, Audi, and Mercedes jointly aiding several suppliers with money and other support.[121]

Yet Mulally may have been wrong in his belief of being "uniquely interdependent." The contaminated peanut scare and German E. coli cases showed the interdependence of food producers in which quality failures at one producer can severely disrupt the sales of all producers. The acetonitrile/acrylonitrile case shows the interdependence between the housing and pharmaceuticals industries. It also demonstrated the fragility of coupled production, in which a manufacturing process creates two or more different commodities simultaneously. If demand for one commodity drops, then supply of the other commodity falls, too. Issues such as rare earths, conflict minerals, and RoHS-obsolete[122] parts create interdependence among many companies, industries, and regions.

Finally, the economic events of 2008 proved that the global financial system was the biggest diamond of them all. Most companies discovered just how dependent they were on their suppliers of capital—the banks—to support themselves, their suppliers, and ensure customer demand. Ultimately, government bailouts did avert a systemic cascading failure in the banking system and major industries. Yet the trillions of dollars handed out to support the weakened firms left a bitter taste in voters' mouths and the unanswerable question of whether another financial crisis would prompt a similarly lavish bailout.

Industrial Clusters

"Why do we put all our suppliers on a little island in the Pacific where it rains and floods nine months of the year?" asked a representative of a technology company at a supply chain risk management conference. A 40-mile stretch of Taiwan—from Hsinchu to Taipei—designs and fabricates almost a quarter of the world's integrated circuits. Taiwan is also home to almost 70 percent of the world's IC foundry capacity as well as most of the global capacity for packaging and testing integrated circuits. A 1999 earthquake gave a taste of the effects of a disruption in this key region: the spot-price of computer memory climbed fivefold all over the world, disrupting operations at many electronic suppliers and hampering the launch of certain Apple laptops. The World Bank rated Taiwan as the most vulnerable place for natural hazards, with 73 percent of its land and population exposed to three or more hazards.[123]

Similarly, Japan makes 100 percent of the world's supply of protective polarizer film for LCD displays, 89 percent of aluminum capacitors, and 72 percent of silicon wafers.[124] Four companies in Japan have a near-monopoly on digital compasses—the tiny magnetic field sensors that sit inside almost every new phone, tablet, laptop, and navigation system device.[125] Recall the damage to the disk drive industry in Thailand because of the fact that the country contributed almost half the world's disk drives and most of it was disrupted during the 2011 floods. North Korea's belligerent stance toward South Korea threatens 78.5 percent of the global DRAM capacity.[126]

Much as Silicon Valley is a cluster of information technology companies, Hollywood is a cluster of entertainment companies, and Cambridge, Massachusetts, is a cluster of biotechnology research, so is Northern Taiwan a cluster of chip fabrication and testing and Thailand a cluster of disk drive manufacturing. The long-term trends toward global procurement from "best of breed" (best-performance/least-cost) suppliers were paramount in creating concentrations of suppliers in industrial clusters around the world. Moreover, governments have been pursuing industrial cluster strategies, seeding certain industries and fomenting the self-reinforcing positive feedback loop of industrial agglomeration in order to grow these economic clusters. A positive feedback loop occurs because the bigger the cluster becomes (i.e., if more companies of the same industry agglomerate in a certain geography), the more attractive the cluster becomes to even more companies, and thus it keeps growing. Clustering has caused the concentration of specific manufacturing (and service) industries in specific locations around the globe. (The mechanisms and impacts of industrial clusters are described in my 2012 book, *Logistics Clusters*.[127])

Clustering increases the vulnerability of companies that rely on cluster members as suppliers or customers. The reason is that disruptions that affect a cluster—such as earthquakes, volcanoes, labor unrest, or political instability—hit many companies in the same industry at once, making it more difficult to find alternative sources of supply when all the industry players are scouring the globe looking for the same things. "The floods in Thailand in the fall of 2011 showed us how dangerous it is when a component that is needed at manufacturing facilities around the world is mainly procured from only one region," said Martin Bellhäuser, head of governance framework, at Siemens.[128]

Yet, the feedback loops and the success of governments' cluster strategies are likely to lead to further geographic concentration of supply sources, thereby leading to possible future vulnerabilities.[129] "Many organizations are more or less forced to put all eggs in one basket because of the clusters of suppliers for various goods around the globe," said Damien Pang, regional manager, claims, at Allianz Global Corporate & Specialty Asia/Pacific.[130]

The Best Decisions Can Create the Worst Outcomes

When Queen Elizabeth asked why nobody had foreseen the 2008 financial crisis, a group of economists and constitutional experts explained, "Everyone seemed to be doing their own job properly on its own merit. And according to standard measures of success, they were often doing it well. The failure was to see how collectively this added up to a series of interconnected imbalances.... Individual risks may rightly have been viewed as small, but the risk to the system as a whole was vast."[131] This pattern of locally correct decisions but globally perilous consequences is the epitome of systemic risk and global vulnerability.

This pattern of individual decisions vs. shared consequences is often referred to as the "tragedy of the commons," a term coined in 1968 by ecologist Garrett Hardin[132] based on a concept first articulated by William Lloyd in 1833.[133] Lloyd envisioned a pasture open to multiple cattle herds. Each herd owner has an incentive to add more and more animals even if the growing herds degrade the quality of the pasture. The benefit from each extra animal goes directly to the herder whereas the cost of the impact on the pasture is everybody's problem. The herds keep growing because all the herd owners behave in the same way. At some point, however, the pasture turns to dust and everybody loses. Thus, while each individual entity "does the right thing" in its own best interest, the common ecosystem can fail, to the detriment of everyone.

Bullwhip dynamics, discussed in chapter 5, exemplify this kind of systemic risk created by individual companies each making the best local decision. A bullwhip can form if demand volatility affects each company's rational ordering and inventory decisions in ways that create even higher apparent demand volatility in the next upstream tier. Volatility can amplify to irrational levels in the deeper tiers of a supply chain.

My Risk vs. Our Risk

After Superstorm Sandy, AT&T sent signal-measuring vans around New York City. But AT&T didn't check only its own performance; it checked the performance of other cell phone providers, too. AT&T was concerned about relative performance, wanting to ensure that it wasn't lagging relative to the other carriers as had been reported. AT&T found negligible differences in performance of the wireless networks, said John Donovan, AT&T's technology chief. [134]

Similarly, the 2011 Japan quake made the head of operations at Blue Coat, a manufacturer of electronic Internet equipment, realize how exposed the company was to Asian suppliers, especially if a major disruption hit the southern Chinese province of Guangdong. "I'm not sure what we'd do," he said. "The only compensating factor is that all our competitors would be in the same position."[135]

Tom Linton, chief procurement and supply chain officer at Flextronics, likewise said, "There will always be risks in supply chains, and the best you can do is really manage them well. The difference between winners and losers comes from an analogy. If you look at sports like soccer or football, the best coaches of all time only won 60 percent of their games. The best baseball players of all time only bat 0.400. So the best you can hope for in supply chain management is to beat the average."[136]

In all three cases, the focus is on risks relative to competitors, rather than absolute risk avoidance. From the point of view of a company, this is a rational choice. A company can never know exactly how much it should invest in disaster recovery and resilience, because this includes preparations for low-probability, high-impact events and unknown-unknown black swans. Thus, one benchmark for "enough" investment in preparedness is the "industry standard"—doing what competitors and others in the industry are doing. Consequently, although all companies may have similar levels of preparation, none of the companies may be prepared for unforeseen, extremely large, industry-affecting disruptions.

The Collective Fragility of Individual Business Continuity Plans

At a 2012 MIT roundtable on ocean freight transportation,[137] forty participants discussed their companies' plans for handling potential labor strikes at US East Coast ports. More than half of the participants planned to divert shipments to Canada, Mexico, and the West Coast if the East Coast was closed.

The ocean carriers at the meeting, however, cautioned that all these diversion plans might not be viable because of port capacity limits at the time. None of the diversion options was through a very large port, and many ports had limited spare capacity. For example, Prince Rupert in Canada had only one open berth per week at the time. Moreover, even if the diverted ships could dock, there might not be dray chassis, long-haul trucking, and rail capacity to move the containers from the diversion ports to their final destinations. Diversions to Mexico and Canada might also face congestion or delays at the border. At the time, the Panama Canal was congested on both sides, so diverting from coast to coast could be problematic. To the extent that multiple companies create contingency plans that all tap the same resources, those contingency plans could readily fail if the plans need to be simultaneously activated.

The Whack-a-Mole Game of Risk Mitigation

Many of the common risk mitigation strategies described in this book have side effects that increase other kinds of risks. For example, a very large number of companies use dual sourcing or multisourcing to mitigate the incontrovertible supply interruption risks of sole sourcing. Yet multisourcing increases the risks of CSR issues by increasing the number of suppliers; a CSR failure at just one supplier will diminish the company's brand. Moreover, second sourcing with competitive bidding can weaken the finances of both suppliers and increase the risks of supplier bankruptcies.

Southwest Airlines flies only Boeing 737s, a decision that reduces a wide range of operational risks such as the availability of air crew and spare parts. Yet if some design defect were uncovered in the 737, the entire airline might be grounded. Standardization, consolidation, and risk pooling can all help manage some types of risks, but they introduce vulnerable single-points-of-failure into the organization.

Similarly, added inventory can provide redundancy but may also mask quality problems, hamper their detection, and increase the costs of fixing them. Even hedging—a risk mitigation tactic—can backfire when prices or exchange rates do not move as forecasted. "It's like you can't win," said Betsy J. Snyder, an industry analyst with Standard & Poor's Ratings Services when discussing Southwest Airlines's loss on its fuel hedging practice (see chapter 10). "People bother you when you don't hedge, and when you do, and prices go down, you get hit."[138]

Finally, risk management costs money and time. Those resources may be a very sound investment based on any reasonable analysis of the cost of risk management versus the expected value of averted disasters, mitigated consequences, and retained market share. Yet investing in risk management generally implies investing less in other areas—such as R&D, marketing, capacity, and talent—which can also carry risk. At some level, risk mitigation is like a whack-a-mole game: a company can beat down one type of risk only to have some other type of risk rise.

What Does Not Kill Me

The Eyjafjallajökull eruption and air travel disruption led to numerous projects to improve European air traffic control, refine volcanic ash flow models, create a better warning system, and learn how to avoid ash clouds in flight.[139] And Walmart's experiences with post-hurricane recovery led to more than a 3X improvement in the efficiency of its response. Better staging of inventory and a mobile command center help the retailer quickly serve post-disaster customers without excessive costs. Chapter 4 described how companies learn from disaster, and chapter 6 described how companies learn from drills.

Supply chain risk may be growing as a result of increasing globalization, product specialization, supplier consolidation, industrial clustering, and lean supply chain processes, but companies are also improving their abilities to handle large-scale disruptions such as those that faced Japanese suppliers, Thai factories, or Evonik. Furthermore, governments at all levels are partnering more with companies to prepare for crises. And the collaborative framework evident in the automotive industry during both the 2008 financial crisis and the Evonik fire proves that companies can, under grave circumstances, collaborate with competitors to avoid potentially systemic disruptions. "Big ones" have happened in global supply chains, and "bigger ones" may occur at any time. The future will determine whether companies have learned sufficient lessons from past disruptions or whether some hidden fragility or coupling induces a systemic impact.

14

WHY RESILIENCE?

All organizations face risks simply by virtue of operating in an uncertain world. Furthermore, most observers agree that "for a business to survive, growth is an imperative, not an option."[1] Yet growth, especially, brings added risk as a result of the increased uncertainties that come with new products, customers, geographies, or strategies. The three areas of investment in risk management and resilience—detection, prevention, and response—help reduce the duration, likelihood, and magnitude of disruptions. Yet these three elements do more than directly address risks—they also indirectly add value to the organization in other ways.

In discussing the benefits of enterprise risk management (ERM), Steven Dryer, managing director at Standard & Poor's (S&P) noted, "In many cases, senior executives introduced ERM as a compliance exercise and hence are more likely to focus on ERM's loss-avoidance features and less likely to see ERM as an opportunity in managing uncertainties of both negative and positive directions."[2] In contrast to the compliance-oriented view of ERM, more advanced companies realize that managing risks can also help increase performance on many operational, competitive, and financial dimensions.[3] Investments in resilience and risk management may seem like conservative, risk-avoidance initiatives, but these processes can enable a company to be less risk averse and bolder in pursuing growth, despite the added risk and uncertainty.

PREPARING FOR RESPONSE

Resilient companies invest in specific response strategies, such as Cisco's playbooks mentioned in chapter 6, to cope with relatively high-likelihood, identifiable risks. Yet, as also described in that chapter, companies also have to prepare for unforeseen or unknown types of disruptions, by creating a set of general processes to deal with any business interruption. Companies prepare to respond by creating assets such as emergency operations centers (EOC), business continuity plans (BCP), or drilling staff in disaster scenarios.

Response and Flexibility

"No plan survives first contact with the enemy," the 19th-century German field marshal Helmuth Von Moltke is credited with saying.[4] Thus, military organizations have to invest in readiness and prepare to respond to the unexpected.

When hurricane Katrina veered toward New Orleans in August 2005, the United States Coast Guard (USCG) was ready to respond. In fact, the USCG leapt into action days before the hurricane struck. When the commanding officer for Coast Guard Sector New Orleans, Captain Frank Paskewich, saw that Katrina "was making a beeline for New Orleans ... from that point on it was ready, set, go."[5]

On August 26, three days before the storm made landfall in Louisiana, the Coast Guard began implementing its Continuity of Operations Plan, in which Sector New Orleans relocated to Alexandria, Louisiana, and Coast Guard District 8 Command shifted to St. Louis. "We wanted aircraft on both sides of the hurricane-hit area," said Captain Artie Walsh, head of the district's search and rescue office. "We had units scattered all over ... because we were afraid if we had one safe haven or two ... we'd lose our resources," said Captain Robert Mueller, the deputy Sector New Orleans commander.[6]

At the same time as aircraft, vessels, and personnel near New Orleans and the Gulf Coast were leaving the most dangerous spots, the Coast Guard was pulling pilots, swimmers, flight mechanics, maintenance workers, and support personnel from all over the country toward the area, including 40 percent of its nationwide helicopter fleet.[7] Rear Admiral Duncan planned to reenact the movie *Apocalypse Now* with Coast Guard helicopters. "I wanted to darken the sky with orange helicopters. ... If [people] feel that they need help, I want them to see an orange helicopter somewhere overhead that they can wave at and we'll come get them, and frankly we did that."[8] During four days in Katrina's aftermath, the US Coast Guard rescued 33,500 people (compared to an annual average of "only" 3,500 rescues for the entire United States),[9] and delivered tons of supplies to the devastated communities.

While the USCG responded quickly and effectively, the Federal Emergency Management Agency (FEMA) was widely criticized for being late to respond, unprepared, and ineffective.[10] This was despite FEMA holding a five-day disaster simulation of a hurricane hitting New Orleans only a year earlier.[11] In an after-action analysis, the Government Accountability Office (GAO) said, "Precisely identifying why the Coast Guard was able to respond as it did may be difficult, but underpinning these efforts were factors such as the agency's operational principles. These principles promote leadership, accountability, and enable personnel to take responsibility and action, based on relevant authorities and guidance."[12]

The Coast Guard, unlike FEMA, the National Guard, and many other Federal agencies, is a frontline organization with the authority to act even before the higher-ups know that action is needed. Yet the most important aspect of that difference is that a culture of empowerment—granting authority to people to do what is needed—extends down to all levels of the Coast Guard. For example, when a junior-level pilot flying a C-130 on an environmental inspection mission arrived in New Orleans, she noticed a problem: search and rescue helicopters could not communicate with local officials on the ground. Rather than continue with her official mission or ask what to do, she immediately created an airborne communications platform for the area to help coordinate helicopter flights and get people to safe landing areas and hospitals.[13]

Other organizations, such as Zara, the Spanish fast fashion retailer, also have a speed of response that is the mark of any flexible organization. Zara empowers its designers to make decisions without going up and down the corporate hierarchy. For instance, when one of Zara's 300 designers noticed a blouse Madonna wore at the beginning of her 2005 concert tour, he realized that his customers would love the singer's look. Unlike other retailers that require extensive preparations, market research, and the permission of senior managers before approving a new look, Zara's designers can freely tap inventories, redesign garments, authorize manufacturing (by trusted local seamstresses who can quickly sew the pattern), and then ship the new clothing to stores. In this particular case, Zara designed a Madonna-inspired blouse and got it into stores in only three weeks, before Madonna finished her tour.[14]

The Paradox of Standards

After investigating the USCG response to Katrina, the GAO also concluded that "another key factor was the agency's reliance on standardized operations and maintenance practices that provided greater flexibility for using personnel and assets from any operational unit for the response."[15] As Captain Bruce Jones, commanding officer of Air Station New Orleans, said, "The fact that you can take a rescue swimmer from Savannah and stick him on a helicopter from Houston with a pilot from Detroit and a flight mechanic from San Francisco, and these guys have never met before and they can go out and fly for six hours and rescue 80 people and come back without a scratch on the helicopter—there is no other agency that can do that."[16] Paradoxically, structure and standards can create flexibility and agility, not rigidity and sluggishness, when well-trained teams have the authority to adapt their training to new situations. "That's the nice thing about the Coast Guard; we don't really need to talk a lot ... a couple words pass between a couple of sailors and the job gets done," said CWO3 Robert David Lewald, commander of a Coast Guard construction tender.[17]

The use of standards to create flexibility for response is not unique to the USCG. For example, Southwest Airlines uses only Boeing 737 aircraft (see chapter 13). This means that any mechanic can service any plane and any pilot can fly any airplane in the fleet, allowing for quick recovery from weather, congestion, and other disruptions that bedevil an airline. Similarly, the standard procedures used by UPS in their unloading, sorting, and loading operations allowed UPS to recover quickly from an ice storm that shut down Louisville, Kentucky, in 1996. The storm closed all roads, and Louisville workers were not able to come to work at the airport, where Worldport—the US hub of UPS air operations—is located. But UPS was able to fly workers from other parts of its vast empire to Louisville and, because the operations are standardized, these outside workers could operate the hub.[18] Coupled with empowerment, standards are the key to flexible operations—they allow for risk pooling of assets and surge capacity while empowering frontline responders to improvise when the conditions change.

In tandem with standard procedures, the USCG culture permits flexibility by personnel, which was evident in the improvisation of rescue techniques described by Lieutenant Iain McConnell: "At first we used basket hoists for most survivors, but then the swimmers found that the quick strop hoist technique was quicker so that was an improvisation, and the whole swinging-like–a-pendulum-to-get-a-swimmer-up-onto-a-balcony-underneath-a-roof, that's definitely something you don't practice," he said,[19] and then added, "Yes, a lot of improvisation. But in general that's what Coast Guard aircrews do best." The flexibility of the Coast Guard stems from trusting people to do the right things, giving them the authority to take action, and not putting too many bureaucratic hurdles in their way.

Response Investments

Organizations such as Walmart and UPS invest in response procedures and assets because they serve customers everywhere, including locations with high likelihoods of disruptions from hurricanes, snowstorms, and other natural disasters. Many multinational companies have facilities and suppliers around the globe in vulnerable areas. While the probability that a particular disruption will strike a particular location at a particular time is very small, the likelihood that *some crisis* will happen *some place* at *some time* is significant. Consequently, such companies can justify investments in EOCs and BCP.

If and when disruptions occur, preparations for response pay off in terms of both accelerated recovery and mitigated impacts. In other words, the option to use risk assets is exercised (see chapter 6). To the extent that emergency response and business recovery teams are active the minute a disruption hits, recovery can begin immediately, shortening the duration of the disruption. Preorganized teams, precreated plans, a preconfigured "war-room," and prestocked recovery supplies all help accelerate response.

Each disruption also offers a learning opportunity. As Mark Cooper, senior director of Walmart's emergency management, commented, lessons from Katrina and other storms helped Walmart improve the efficiency of its response by a factor of three or four. A robust EOC and drilled recovery process help the company reopen its stores faster and at lower cost than before.

AN OUNCE OF PREVENTION

The Coast Guard is geared for response because it can't prevent the incidents to which it must respond. Most companies, however, can take steps to reduce the likelihood of disruptions.

When the Stakes Are High

Inattentive or sloppy processes have dire consequences for companies in high-risk industries. In December 1984, a leak of methyl-isocyanate from Union Carbide's plant in Bhopal, India, killed 4,000 and injured over 500,000. Some sources put the death toll much higher.[20] Union Carbide never recovered from this horrific tragedy.[21] Less than a year later it was the target of a hostile takeover by GAF Corporation, which forced it to divest many of its most profitable divisions.

As mentioned in chapter 11, BP lost $53 billion in market capitalization in the wake of the Horizon drill rig explosion in April 2010. Four years later, in August 2014, the stock was still more than 30 percent lower than its value at the beginning of 2010.[22] By 2014, the company had paid $27 billion in cleanup costs, fines, and settlements, with some cleanup liabilities and many court cases still pending.

The failure to imagine and model the consequences of coseismic coupling in the faults around the Japanese islands off the coast of Fukushima (see chapter 1) resulted in significant damage to the nuclear reactors from the 2011 tsunami. Water flooded the plants and the reactor control systems. With no backup ability to dissipate heat, the cores overheated, causing explosions and nuclear meltdowns. The incident raised energy costs in Japan as the government started turning away from reliance on nuclear power. It also raised energy costs in Germany, where the government closed all of its old nuclear power reactors and decided to phase out the remaining ones by 2022. As a result of the increased energy costs, numerous energy-intensive German manufacturers have diverted many of their capital investments out of Germany.[23]

BASF buys, handles, manufactures, and ships a wide array of chemicals, many of which are highly flammable, highly toxic, or both. To ensure the safety of its workers and the citizens living near its plants, BASF's risk prevention culture spans the entire organization from the board of directors to frontline employees.[24] Relying on standard procedures, the company uses a risk management process manual and a set of standardized evaluation and reporting tools based on the 2004 COSO II (the Committee on Sponsoring Organizations, Treadway Commission) framework.[25] While the board of directors approves investments in risk management, the company delegates the management of specific risks to local business units. BASF develops models for all manner of potential industrial accidents, down to the failures of individual pumps, valves, and tanks.[26] BASF's culture of prevention means it biases its assessments toward worst-case risks. If a type of event (e.g., an explosion in a mixing tank) can produce various levels of severity at different probabilities, BASF uses the worst-case risk class to decide the level of prevention efforts.

Mark Twain once wrote, "Man is a creature made at the end of the week … when God was tired."[27] Indeed, the vast majority of safety incidents are due to human error.[28] To reduce the rate of human error, BASF trained more than 10,000 employees in process safety and more than 47,000 employees in compliance in 2013.[29] The training also addressed prevention of cybercrime and the protection of knowledge and sensitive information.

To create a global safety culture, BASF emphasizes visible leadership and open dialogue, as well as many prevention-related KPIs such as the lost-time injury rate, number of accidents, and product spillage.[30] As of 2012, the company had about half the lost-time injury rate of other safety-oriented chemical companies[31] who are members of the Responsible Care Global Charter.[32]

BASF's culture of prevention extends beyond safety and compliance risks. "We try to prevent unscheduled plant shutdowns by adhering to high technical standards and continuously improving our plants," BASF wrote in its 2013 annual report.[33] The prevention of downtime extends to procurement decisions. The company assesses critical paths in the flow of materials and adds capacity to ensure it has supply alternatives, according to BASF's Dirk Hopmann.

Other companies face less tangible but no less dangerous potential disruptions that drive them toward prevention. As mentioned in chapter 11, Disney's image means everything to the company. Approximately $29 billion of the company's value is ascribed to its brand.[34] With Disney's emphasis on children and families, the company is especially concerned with preventing social responsibility risks. Consequently, it is selective about the countries from which it sources and with whom it does business. For example, Disney won't buy from eight countries including Sudan, Iran, and Burma because of the difficulty in ensuring acceptable working conditions.[35]

Reduced Insurance Premiums and More

Reducing the likelihood of disruption also reduces the likelihood of payout by the company's insurers. When Microsoft builds new data centers or other key facilities, it uses HPR (highly protected risk) standards by working with engineers from its insurance company, FM Global.[36] Achieving HPR certification requires design and operating features that reduce the risks of fires, floods, and seismic damage through prudent site selection, material selection, protective features, equipment redundancies, and proper attention by personnel.

HPR sites have one-quarter the probability of loss and one-tenth the average gross loss compared to non-HPR sites,[37] which translates into lower insurance premiums. Microsoft uses estimated economic value to quantify the value of investments in risk management. "So far in fiscal year 2009, which goes through June 30, FM Global has calculated more than US$1.8 billion in risk improvements," said Susan Shaw, senior risk manager at Microsoft.[38] The model-based calculations included factors such as potential losses, deductibles, and premium savings over the life span of the building to offset the added construction costs.

Although HPR is primarily about minimizing property losses, it also reduces the likelihood of business interruption. For example, to achieve HPR at a new data center, Microsoft divided the space in half with a fireproof wall so that the maximum foreseeable loss is only half the facility and the surviving half can maintain uptime for customers. "With data centers, the scale of the loss involves more than just property. It's losing credibility with the public, and losing standing in the technology community," said Shaw. "One thing that's not insurable, and that I've taken into account, is reputation risk. There's a tie-in between managing reputation and managing any kind of risk—in this case property, including business interruption," Shaw concluded.

Prevention and Response

Prevention and response are complementary aspects of risk management, and different companies may emphasize different investments in one over the other. Prevention efforts reduce the likelihood of events that would need a response. In contrast, response capabilities allow companies to accept certain risks by relying on their mitigation prowess. Neither approach suffices on its own because of the uncertainty involved. Prevention cannot avoid all disruptions, and response capabilities can't mitigate all impacts to an acceptable level. The balance between the various investments is company- and facility-specific, and it depends on the tradeoff between the cost-of-prevention and the cost-of-response.

Finally, as companies and industries become safer, the marginal cost of the next safety measure increases and the marginal value of preventing the remaining extremely rare events drops. Such an effect may be starting to happen in the airline industry, in which some question whether postcrash airline location monitoring measures proposed in the wake of the disappearance of Malaysia Air 370 are worth the costs, given the rarity of such events, and the possible use of the investment to enhance air safety measures that may have higher expected benefits.[39]

DETECTION

Vigilance entails investments in monitoring current events, surveying suppliers, visiting supplier facilities, "score-carding" inbound shipments for quality, analyzing natural hazards models, and other data-gathering and analysis activities. Companies can use the resulting knowledge of risks and events to prevent and respond to them.

The Value of Detection for Response

Rather than wait for executives to hear the news during the morning drive to work, Cisco's incident monitoring process runs 24 × 7, with personnel around the world in different time zones. Cisco combines monitoring with an escalation process that guarantees a two-hour response time. During the 2011 Japan earthquake that occurred at 9:46 pm Cisco headquarters' local time, the company detected and understood the significance of the event within 40 minutes and had escalated it to senior management 17 minutes later.[40]

Even before a natural disaster strikes, companies such as P&G and Walmart use the detection lead time to marshal resources for the postdisaster recovery. If a company detects an imminent disruption it can, for example, relocate assets and inventory out of the disaster zone, perform controlled equipment shutdowns to avoid machinery damage or hazmat release, address social activist issues before they go viral, or start backup systems. For example, as mentioned in chapter 8, OKI Semiconductor Company avoided about $15 million in losses by using systems that detect earthquakes and provide a few seconds or minutes of warning.[41] Timely detection also helps limit the impact of hidden disruptions such as contamination, counterfeiting, and cybercrimes in direct proportion to the reduction in the duration of the damage.

Early detection can also provide competitive advantage in constrained-supply scenarios. In 2013, Juniper Networks got an urgent notification from Resilinc's monitoring service. A key supplier of memory chips had had a fire that would affect 21 parts. Within a couple of hours, Juniper had analyzed the issue and, according to Juniper's Joe Carson and Dmitri Kamensky, secured alternative supplies at prices that were substantially less than what slower-acting companies paid. A study of nearly 4,000 European firms found that companies in more competitive situations were significantly more likely to be vigilant.[42] Some companies are always looking for trouble.

The Value of Detection for Prevention

Early detection can also be an important factor in preventing disruptions. Detection of a potential problem as a result of, say, deteriorating labor relations at a supplier, parliamentary debate regarding drastic government regulations, or increasingly negative buzz about a supplier on social networks allows the company time not only to prepare mitigation activities, but also to counteract and possibly avoid a disruption. Alternate suppliers can be contacted, resources can be used to lobby governments, or the causes of negative buzz can be redressed.

Detection for prevention extends into the supply chain. In tandem with the proliferation of NGOs and media watchdogs, many companies are working hard to ensure that not only they but also their suppliers do not cause CSR, safety, or quality-related disruptions (see chapter 7). For example, the Ford Code of Conduct[43] mandates ethical conduct and high social responsibility standards at suppliers in every country where it does business. Furthermore, the code requires that "all Company personnel must report known or suspected violations of this Policy through the established reporting channels. The Company prohibits retaliation against anyone who in good faith reports a violation."[44]

Audits provide value in three areas. First, audits help detect specific problems in specific suppliers. Disney's audit checklist, for example, includes 75 questions covering issues such as working conditions, underage labor, fire safety, worker freedoms, and healthcare. Second, audits provide insight into country-level trends, which may help detect risks and also highlight business opportunities hidden in those trends. Third, audits have a direct preventative value in addition to detecting risks, because suppliers are likely to take proactive steps to avoid unfavorable audit reports.

At some companies, this kind of detection extends to the deeper tiers. For example, Intel tries to get potential suppliers to reveal their own suppliers early in the relationship, in order to detect potential risks and assess vulnerabilities. Intel does not always succeed, because of suppliers' reluctance to share competitive secrets. Yet the company has been a leader in the tracing of conflict minerals, which required understanding of its supply chain to the deepest tier (sometimes down to Tier 6 or 7).

The Value of Learning from Near-Misses

Detecting minor events that did not cause a disruption but could have is one way to detect, prepare for, and prevent larger disruptions. The aviation industry has long recognized the wisdom of learning from mistakes and minor incidents, even when they do not cause an accident. The Aviation Safety Reporting System (ASRS) collects and analyzes voluntarily submitted, confidential aviation incident reports to identify systemic or latent errors and hazards and to alert the industry about them. The ASRS receives more than 30,000 reports annually and issues directives on a regular and as-needed basis. Most aviation experts agree that these efforts have resulted in an ever-increasing level of civilian airline safety as system operators increase their vigilance by recognizing more conditions that can lead to disasters.

Hospitals use a similar "near miss" analysis system of reporting, investigating, and identifying vulnerabilities to root out medical mistakes. Likewise, BASF insists on timely recording of any safety-related incidents, including near-misses, that could indicate a vulnerability.[45] Industrial accidents follow a power law distribution, as described in chapter 2, which implies that organizations can use data on the frequency and impacts of small events to predict the likelihood and impacts of much larger events. This analysis of small events helps detect and prioritize risks that could potentially produce unacceptable disruptions.

INVESTING IN RESILIENCE

No company takes on additional risks for the excitement of the exposure, peril, or potential liability. Yet, as mentioned above, risk is part of running a business, and it goes hand-in-hand with growth.

To prosper, companies must grow; and to grow, companies have to manage the risks and uncertainties inherent in taking on new initiatives where less is known.

Many companies see risk management as just another cost with no sure benefit. In the words of a transport manager, "It takes resources away from what our core business is."[46] An unused EOC seems like squandered office space and corporate resources. Drills take time away from day-to-day operations. Extra inventory is expensive. The perception of waste can seem doubly true with prevention strategies, because they intentionally seek to ensure that nothing ever happens. Yet investments in resilience can provide value, directly and indirectly, as well as support growth.

Resilience vs. Insurance

Traditionally, organizations estimated the value of investments in resilience in terms of the avoidance or reduction of losses created by disruptions. *Prevention* reduces the likelihood of disruptive losses, *response* reduces the consequences of disruption, and *detection* improves the effectiveness and timeliness of prevention and response. Each "it-could-have-been-worse" event is tallied as a win for these kinds of investments.

For example, Cisco created a database of risk mitigation efforts and subsequent disruptive events. In addition to helping the company track its risk mitigation efforts, the databases let Cisco tally the direct value of those efforts.[47] By documenting the improvement in recovery time resulting from its risk management processes, Cisco tracks impacts that it avoided, such as lost revenues, late shipments, and other critical business metrics.

In many ways, this approach looks at spending on resilience in the same way that the company looks at spending on insurance: companies buy it because they feel they have to, even though a direct return on insurance premiums can be measured only when a disaster strikes.[48] Under this view, therefore, the ROI of resilience is only measured in terms of how much it reduces the likelihoods and consequences of disruptions. This view, however, misses many other advantageous aspects of investments in resilience.

Resilience is superior to insurance for four primary reasons. First, insurance offers only financial indemnification, whereas resilience also helps avoid the loss of trust or reputation incurred if a company fails to fulfill its commitments to its customers. Second, insurance often covers only named hazards, but resilience can also cover unknown, uncertain, and acts-of-God events. After the 2010 Iceland volcano eruption, insurance companies denied business interruption claims—even for airlines and airports—because the volcano caused no physical damage that would create the basis for a claim.[49] Third, insurance is an adversarial transfer of risk and faces uncertainties in pay-outs, whereas resilience is an internal capability aligned with the business. In its annual report, Intel notes that one of its risk factors is that "one or more of our insurance providers may be unable or unwilling to pay a claim."[50] The exact wording of a policy and the legal interpretations of that wording affect whether a particular incident creates a valid claim.[51] Finally, the biggest difference is that resilience can bring competitive advantages even if no disruption ever occurs, because resilience can improve both top-line and bottom-line performance.

A Better Brand: New Business

At 6:30 pm on December 6, 2004, a fire broke out on the 29th floor of the 45-story La Salle Bank headquarters in Chicago. Smoke inhalation and other injuries afflicted 37 people but, fortunately, no one was seriously hurt as 500 people evacuated the smoke-filled building. Some 450 firefighters worked to subdue the fire that raged for five hours and caused $50 million in damage to the historic Art Deco building.[52]

Even as firefighters were arriving and bank workers were evacuating, the company activated its crisis management plans at 6:45 pm via a pre-established emergency conference call. At 8 pm, the crisis management team held the first meeting and all department-level business continuity plans were officially initiated. A disciplined approach to crisis team meetings kept them short and on track as the teams determined how to handle the damage to headquarters.

LaSalle Bank's mantra became "business as usual" and at 7:30 am the next morning, the bank opened. Some 750 workers went to prearranged backup sites and 400 others telecommuted from home. Constant customer communications, including a telephone system that automatically forwarded customer calls to relocated workers, assuaged any anxiety about the bank's ability to keep going. Throughout the crisis, the bank worked to avoid conflicting stories coming from different people at the bank and from city officials. Journalist reports in the local, national, and banking industry press highlighted La Salle's resiliency. By continually making clients aware of what was happening, the bank succeeded not only in retaining its current customers, but actually signing several major commercial customers after the fire. These large commercial customers cited LaSalle's resilience and continued customer service throughout the disruption as the reason for the business.[53]

Higher Sales: Pop-Tart Sales Pop

When hurricane Sandy threatened the East Coast in 2012, Walmart already knew what to do. In 2004, Linda Dillman, chief information officer, claimed that "we have gathered so much historical data, we've decided to anticipate what will happen in a given situation instead of waiting for it to happen, and then reacting."[54] From previous hurricanes, Walmart knew that people stock up on bottled water, tarpaulins, spotlights, and manual can openers. They also buy seven times the usual volume of strawberry Pop-Tarts. Headquarters alerted Walmart stores in the path of Sandy to pre-order these popular items in advance of the storm, as well as to order other in-demand products like Armour Vienna sausage, Spam, and hardy fruit, such as apples. The company also prepared for replenishment of after-storm cleanup supplies, such as mops and chainsaws. And just as important as deciding what inventories to push forward to boost prestorm and poststorm sales were the inventories that Walmart pulled back. Walmart knows people stop buying meat and other highly-perishable goods for fear they will spoil without power for refrigerators.

The data management systems that Walmart used to prepare for disasters are the same ones that help it prepare for seasonal changes, major holidays, and other fluctuations in demand. The same tools that help the company track the effects of summer weather on soft drink demand can track the effects of bad weather on bottled water demand, too. Walmart's everyday inventory management system tells it which store has what goods, which store sold what, and which distribution centers are carrying what. Walmart's trucks are equipped with onboard computer and communication systems that let shipments be redirected at any time. Resilience during a disruption and responsiveness in daily operations are two sides of the same coin.

Responsiveness to Disruption Creates Agility in Operations

Some companies use their response to crises to make improvements to everyday operations. The 2008 financial crisis hit many companies, including P&G's feminine care division. "Obviously we weren't happy about the drop in business," said Stefan Brünner, the division's Budapest plant manager for manufacturing in Europe, the Middle East, and Africa.[55] Rather than just cut costs, the company launched an aggressive recovery program to transform the supply chain. "We saw this as an opportunity to focus on improving some supply chain fundamentals and emerge from the recession in a stronger position," said Brünner.[56]

P&G tightened internal and external integration, including greater collaboration with key suppliers. It developed rapid product changeover capabilities to launch new products in order to reignite growth. As a result, the company increased manufacturing productivity by 20 percent, reduced regional inventory by 18 percent while keeping customer service levels high, cut material lead times by as much as 50 percent, accelerated new product launches, and dropped total delivered costs by more than 12 percent.[57]

When Intel uncovered a defect in its new Cougar Point chipset in 2011 (see chapter 8), it had to make six million replacement chips as fast as it could. Intel used an internal discussion forum called "Output Max" to expedite production and distribution. The response taught Intel how to go faster when needed. It reset expectations for what could be done when speed is the top priority. Intel now calls it "Cougar Point speed." The event was a key part of Intel's ongoing evolution to ever-greater speed and agility. "As fast as we did Cougar Point, you always find a way to do one more thing like take four hours out of manufacturing to make an earlier flight," said Frank Jones, Intel's VP and general manager, customer fulfillment, planning, and logistics.[58]

At Caterpillar, visibility tools help the company become more responsive when managing disruptions or day-to-day operations. "I can see everything in motion," said an expert from Caterpillar.[59] "Now I can respond effectively to disruptions, see how the network is flowing, see delays and the costs they incur. I can manage a single disruption like a port labor strike." Those same tools can also tune the company's network. "I can optimize because I can see everything. That allows me to drive better predictability. And I couple that with analytics to figure out what dials and levers to adjust to make improvements. That gives me a much better supply chain," said the same expert.[60] The company's efforts are paying off, and Caterpillar rose two places in the 2013 Gartner Supply Chain Top 25. Resilience during a disruption and agility in normal operations are both benefits of the same investments in better visibility and management of uncertainty.

At an MIT supply chain conference during the financial crisis, several companies cited a rise in positive communications and the benefits of collaboration created by response efforts.[61] The financial crisis brought dramatic changes in consumer behavior and threatened the survival of key players in companies' supply chains. Not only did internal departments work together more (sales, supply chain, and finance) but externally, third-party logistics providers (3PLs) and even competitors worked together. In a survey of 650 executives regarding BCM's benefits beyond incident management, 56 percent (the highest number in the survey) reported improved cross-functional understanding and working within and outside the organization as a collateral benefit of BCM.[62]

After 9/11 revealed the vulnerability of Manhattan skyscrapers, the risk management group at a leading Wall Street financial services company concluded that the entire staff needed the ability to work from home. But upper management balked at the cost of supporting tens of thousands of telecommuters. The risk management group then partnered with HR and repurposed the project as a diversity and inclusion initiative that would allow mothers to stay with their babies and empower disabled employees to stay active. Identifying an HR benefit aided the effort to gain approval of the resilience project.

Coping with Booms Is Like Coping with Dooms

"Risk can also be the inability to capitalize on an opportunity," according to Boston Scientific.[63] Companies can face surges in demand during economic recoveries, competitor disruptions, and new product launches. For example, when Starbucks launched its breakfast sandwiches, it estimated a low, medium, and high forecast for the expected demand. The actual demand was 200 percent higher than the highest forecast, requiring Herculean efforts to satisfy customers.

Intel's "Output Max" discussion forum helps the company maximize the output of its manufacturing lines to deal with disruptions as well as with unexpected demand for new products. If resilience is the ability to bounce back from downside events, it also provides the ability to bounce forward for upside events.

Detection speed plays a key role in the competitive advantage of Takeda, a mid-size pharmaceutical firm. Like many companies, Takeda integrates internal information with external data obtained from a third-party service provider, but just gathering the data isn't sufficient. "Speed of response is quite important so we do not miss any business opportunities," said Hiro Fukutomi, managing director, Takeda UK.[64] "The competitive advantage derives from the measures you take out and how quickly you react to the information out there," said Axel Mau, chief financial officer for Takeda's German subsidiary.[65] For example, if the company hears of a competitor's planned product launch in a particular region, Takeda crunches the numbers in real time and "right away, the sales force can put efforts in that region to hold the market share or increase it. If you have to wait a month before we have an analysis—as we'd sometimes have had to in the past—then it's rather difficult," Mau explained.[66]

Taking Stock in Resilience: Attracting Lenders and Investors

After a five-year implementation of rigorous, holistic risk management practices, Canadian utility Hydro One received a favorable credit rating by both Moody's and Standard & Poor's. Credit analysts specifically cited the company's efforts at risk management in granting the rating, which gave Hydro One a lower cost of capital on a $1 billion loan.[67] During the 2008 financial crisis, creditors and credit rating agencies came to realize that the likelihood of a borrower repaying a loan depends intimately on the borrower's likelihood of surviving disruptions. Rating agencies such as S&P began to explicitly analyze a company's enterprise risk management to assess its risks and preparedness.

The rating agency's analysis of creditors' ERM takes into account an organization's risk management culture and governance, risk controls, emerging-risk preparation, and strategic management.[68] Although S&P does not attempt to estimate all the likelihoods and impacts of supply chain disruptions, it does consider four broad factors: country risks, industry risks, operating risks, and governance. The analysis takes into account factors such as the dependence of the organization on a small number of key facilities, the financial resources to absorb calamities, and the company's sensitivity to industry-specific disruptions—such as airlines' vulnerability to terrorism or agribusiness' vulnerability to commodity prices.[69] The analysis results in a one-to-four rating of weak, adequate, strong, or excellent, which modulates the company's credit rating and cost of capital.[70]

Two cross-sectional studies find a correlation between risk management practices and financial performance. A large-scale survey and analysis in 2012 of more than 500 firms affiliated with the Federation of European Risk Management Associations (FERMA) contrasted the five-year financial performance (2004–2011) of those companies with "advanced" risk management practices versus those with lower levels of maturity in risk management. Advanced firms had nearly double the five-year revenue growth rates (16.8 vs. 8.9 percent) and more than double the five-year EBITDA growth rates (20.3 vs. 8.9 percent).[71] A 2005 Conference Board analysis of companies with advanced ERM likewise found they had statistically significant higher profitability and lower earnings volatility.[72]

Have Your Cake and Eat It, Too

Resilience has something in common with quality. Quality investments cost money, which seems to imply a choice between low cost with low quality and high cost with high quality. But a key insight from the quality movement pioneered by the Toyota Production

System is that letting defects corrupt a product is even more costly than ensuring the quality of the raw materials and processes. Avoiding a defective part is cheaper than fixing a defective car.

Similarly, resilience—developing prevention measures, response alternatives, and detection systems—costs money, which seems to imply a choice between fragile efficiency and expensive robustness. Yet fragility may be more expensive than resilience. Done right, resilience investments can have a positive return.

The proverbial "an ounce of prevention [or preparation] is a worth a pound of cure" remains in force. Yet, as mentioned above, this view is too narrow in tallying the returns of resilience investments. Resilience is more aligned with the cost and growth goals of a company than the intuitive cost vs. resilience would suggest. For example, according to 36 percent of executives in an international survey, BCM also provided process optimization through analysis and greater understanding of end-to-end dependencies and key activities.[73]

As with quality, investment in resilience can pay off through faster recovery times, lower impacts, and the many indirect advantages discussed above. Yet, the best level of investment is unclear. A company can overinvest in quality—creating a car that needs no maintenance, lasts for a long time, but is very expensive. Similarly, building heavily fortified factories, monitoring every supplier action, and using only suppliers with perfect financials may be possible but would be expensive. Furthermore, it may stunt growth by deterring procurement from innovative but higher-risk suppliers.

The proper level of investment in resilience varies from company to company and industry to industry. Proper investment levels are relative to the risks, which depend not only on geography, industry, position along the supply chain, and strength, but also on customer support and the company's general reputation. For example, when Nike was accused in the 1990s of running sweatshops and employing child labor in Pakistan, its sales and market value plunged. In contrast, when worker suicides at a supplier highlighted poor working conditions in Apple's supply chain, the company weathered the storm and suffered no loss of sales. Apple most likely owes this to the loyalty of its customers and the aura of its brand, something that not many other companies can count on. For many companies, the best level of investment in resilience might be gauged relative to the competition. In a race to be the least disrupted and the fastest to recover, it may pay to spend just a little bit more on resilience than peer companies spend, regardless of whether the industry tends to spend high or low.

Risk-Versed, Not Risk-Averse

One common, yet erroneous, assumption is that managing in a risky world requires being a stodgy, conservative organization. If anything, the opposite is true—stodgy, conservative organizations may be deficient at managing risks. In a study of decision making during extreme events, one financial services organization manager admitted, "[We are] an older organization. Decision-making is slow and restricted to a few senior managers. We need considerably quicker responses to crises and to do things at multiple levels, but it doesn't happen. For example, after the 7th July terrorist attack in London, we had no capacity to make quick decisions and we couldn't get statements to the media as quickly as we would have liked."[74]

S&P's Dryer writes that a "successful risk culture begins with fostering open dialogue where every employee in the organization has some level of ownership of the organization's risks, can readily identify the broader impacts of local decisions, and is rewarded for identifying outsize risks to senior levels. In such cultures, strategic decision-making routinely includes a review of relevant risks and alternative strategies rather than a simple return-on-investment analysis."[75]

Toshiba's subsidiary Westinghouse Electric is extremely conservative, as one would expect of a company that makes and services nuclear reactors. "We don't train people to take risks, we train them not to," said Stephen R. Tritch, chief executive officer of Westinghouse Electric.[76] Yet the parent company also wanted growth, which required Westinghouse to branch out, be creative, and try new things, which meant taking risks. The company took a "fast, small bets" approach, in which engineers and managers could learn more about customer needs even if they didn't win every contract. The company started taking business risks such as hiring twenty engineers from a competitor and opening an office for a new line of business before they had any contracts to justify the expense.[77]

As a result, Westinghouse won new business, including business in a market the company had previously left to competitors, and in a new area: developing new methods to repair an alloy used in old reactors.[78] By 2013, Westinghouse's revenues reached a record $5 billion,[79] up from $2 billion in 2004,[80] in spite of both the global recession and the aftermath of the 2011 Fukushima disaster on the nuclear industry. "Today, we have a sense of energy about growth that we didn't have before. Five years ago, the idea was if we stuck to our knitting, but stayed flat, that was success. I don't think anyone here sees that as success anymore," concluded Nick Liparulo, then head of the company's engineering services.[81]

Resilience in a Dynamic Global Economy

Resilient companies embody the Nietzschean adage that "what does not kill me makes me stronger" by being learning organizations. Each and every event, drill, near-miss, or scenario planning contingency expands the awareness of the company and adds to its repertoire of responses. For example, every year, Starbucks reviews the prior year's events from around the globe and estimates the top risks for the coming year. This triggers a set of planning and preparation activities. Those abilities of sensing, reacting, and adapting help the company thrive in a complex, dynamic, global economy.

The rise in global competition means that, as Andy Grove, former Intel CEO said, "only the paranoid survive."[82] The Internet enables customers and consumers to find the winning product offering in virtually any product category, and global supply chains deliver those winning goods at unprecedented scale. Moreover, financial pressures on companies from shareholders and cost-cutting customers will continue to push companies toward lean, just-in-time operations rather than just-in-case redundancies such as extra inventories and spare capacity. Thus, a supply chain disruption can mean an existential threat to the unprepared.

At the same time, the world seems to be experiencing an accelerating rate of large-scale disruptions and unimagined "unknown unknowns." The threat seems unlikely to abate given long-term trends such as the increase in the world's population coupled with the burgeoning billions of consumers who are straining the earth's resources.[83,84] Furthermore, such pressures are also responsible for political upheavals, security concerns, and economic crises. The concentrated economic density created by the migration of people into crowded urban agglomerations also contributes to the rise in economic losses with each new natural disaster.

The rate of "creative destruction" is climbing. Perhaps one of the greatest and least appreciated threats to any company is the self-imposed peril of stagnation in a world obsessed with both the next big thing and annual cost reductions. Companies need to constantly seek growth, if only to replace products and business lines that have become obsolete in the face of global competition, technological advances, changing corporate social responsibility standards, or regulation.

Thriving—indeed even surviving in this environment of flocking black swans and creative destruction—will depend on resilience. Companies can even exploit risks, such that "disruptions" can bring an increase in their sales, market share, and profits. Disruptions can also create opportunities to implement significant changes (such as improving organizations and processes) that are not possible when there is no "burning platform." An especially well-prepared and responsive company can be ready to supply what other less-prepared companies cannot. By being more resilient than competitors, better at preventing disruptions, more effective at mitigating impacts, and faster at managing scarce postdisruption supplies, a company can dominate its industry.

A company that can detect, prevent, or respond to natural, accidental, and intentional disruptions can make the most of its winning products by ensuring continuity of supply. Resilience helps companies compete—even in the face of true unknown-unknown disruptions—by imbuing an organization with the vigilance, responsiveness, and flexibility to detect and respond to unexpected events quickly and effectively. And resilience is more than just a way to bounce back. The activities that create resilience also improve collaboration, coordination, and communications in both directions of the supply chain, making it a strategy for bounding forward into a future rich with possibility.

Notes

Preface

1. http://www.wto.org/english/res_e/booksp_e/world_trade_report14_e.pdf.

Chapter 1

1. http://www.researchgate.net/profile/F_Yamazaki/publication/237704747_New_development_of_super-dense_seismic_monitoring_and_damage_assessment_system_for_city_gas_networks/links/00463527b593f7a46b000000.pdf.

2. http://www.geonami.com/tohoku-earthquake-geophysical/

3. The magnitude of earthquakes, as measured by the seismic moment (a very low frequency component of the energy) goes up by a factor of $10^{1.5}$, which equals 31.6, for every step on the scale. Thus, a magnitude 4 earthquake is actually almost 32 times more energetic as a magnitude 3.

4. David Cyranoski, "Japan up to Failure of Its Earthquake Preparations," *Nature* 471 (2011): 556–557.

5. http://earthquake-report.com/2012/03/10/japan-366-days-after-the-quake-19000-lives-lost-1-2-million-buildings-damaged-574-billion/

6. http://www.nature.com/news/2011/110329/full/471556a.html

7. Cyranoski, "Japan up to Failure of Its Earthquake Preparations," pp. 556–557, 2011.

8. David McNeill and Jake Adelstein, "The Explosive Truth Behind Fukushima's Meltdown," *The Independent*, August 17, 2011.

9. Mike Weightman, "Japan Earthquake and Tsunami: Implications to the UK Nuclear Industry," Interim Report, Office for Nuclear Regulations, May 2011.

10. Tokyo Electric Power Company, "The Evaluation Status of Reactor Core Damage at Fukushima Daiichi Nuclear Power Station Unit 1 and 3," November 30, 2011.

11. Geoff Brumfiel and Ichiko Fuyuno, "Japan Nuclear Crisis, Fufushima's Legacy of Fear," *Nature* 483 (March 2012): 138–140.

12. http://en.wikipedia.org/wiki/Fukushima_Daiichi_nuclear_disaster

13. http://www.forbes.com/sites/jeffmcmahon/2011/03/28/epa-expect-more-radiation-in-rainwater/

14. Japan Ministry of Economy, "Trade and Industry, Forecast and Measures for Future Electricity Supply and Demand in TEPCO Areas," http://www.meti.go.jp/english/electricity_supply/pdf/20110325_electricity_prospect.pdf

15. Suvendrini Kakuchi, "Energy Savings 'Setsuden' Campaign Sweeps Japan after Fukushima," *Guardian*, August 22, 2011.

16. Chikako Mogi and Yoshifumi Takemoto, "Nuclear Shutdown to Threaten the Japanese Economy," Reuters, June 24, 2011, http://www.reuters.com/article/2011/06/24/us-japan-energy-idUSTRE75N1TD20110624

17. http://en.wikipedia.org/wiki/Japanese_reaction_to_Fukushima_Daiichi_nuclear_disaster r

18. http://en.wikipedia.org/wiki/Energy_in_Japan

19. Tsuyoshi Inajima and Yuji Okada, "Nuclear Promotion Dropped in Japan Energy Policy after Fukushima," Bloomberg.com, October 27, 2011.

20. http://www.bbc.co.uk/news/world-asia-17967202

21. http://www.jaif.or.jp/english/news_images/pdf/ENGNEWS02_1344213298P.pdf

22. http://www.bloomberg.com/news/2014-05-29/nuclear-free-japan-faces-prospect-of-power-shortage-in-heartland.html

23. http://www.intel.com/content/www/us/en/jobs/locations/japan/sites/tsukuba.html

24. Interview with Jim Holko, program manager of Intel's corporate emergency management, July 31, 2012.

25. Interview with Jackie Sturm, vice president, technology and manufacturing, and general manager of global sourcing and procurement at Intel, July 31, 2012.

26. Interview with Jeff Selvala, director, assembly test global materials at Intel, August 13, 2012.

27. http://www.eetimes.com/document.asp?doc_id=1258973

28. http://www.eetimes.com/document.asp?doc_id=1259019

29. See http://www.shinetsu.co.jp/e/news/back_shinetsu2011.shtml for a series of 11 status reports.

30. http://www.shinetsu.co.jp/en/news/archive.php?id=286

31. Shin-Etsu, "Shin-Etsu Group current situation impacted by the 2011 off the Pacific Coast of Tohoku Earthquake" (5th report), http://www.shinetsu.co.jp/en/news/archive.php?id=265

32. Interview with Jackie Sturm, July 31, 2012.

33. http://www.logility.com/blog/chris-russell/july-2012/not-so-hidden-inventory

34. Interview with Jeff Selvala, August 13, 2012.

35. Ibid.

36. Interview with Jackie Sturm, July 31, 2012.

37. https://www.semiconportal.com/en/archive/news/main-news/110414-electricity-saving-25percent-summer.html

38. Interview with Jackie Sturm, July 31, 2012.

39. A full supply chain includes not only the "inbound" network of suppliers of all tiers and service providers but also the "outbound" network of distribution infrastructure, customers, and return/repair/disposal infrastructure.

40. https://www.apple.com/supplier-responsibility/our-suppliers/

41. Yossi Sheffi, *Logistics Clusters: Delivering Value and Driving Growth* (Cambridge, MA: MIT Press, 2012).

42. http://www.wto.org/english/res_e/booksp_e/wtr13-2b_e.pdf

43. In 2013 the largest container vessels were the Maersk Triple E. http://www.maersk.com/innovation/leadingthroughinnovation/pages/buildingtheworldsbiggestship.aspx. In 2015, the largest vessel was the Chinese CSCL Globe, with capacity for 19,000 standard containers. http://www.bbc.com/news/uk-england-suffolk-30700269

44. http://www.worldshipping.org/about-the-industry/liner-ships/container-vessel-fleet

45. Robert Charette, "This Car Runs on Code," *IEEE Spectrum*, February 1, 2009, http://spectrum.ieee.org/green-tech/advanced-cars/this-car-runs-on-code

46. http://www.embedded.com/print/4219542

47. http://www.mobile-tex.com/trends.html

Chapter 2

1. Leo Tolstoy, *Anna Karénina*, translated by Nathan Haskell Dole (New York: Thomas Y. Crowell & Co., 1887).

2. http://www.actuaries.org/HongKong2012/Presentations/MBR14_Philip_Baker.pdf

3. Alan Punter, "Supply Chain Failures," Report 2013, Airmic Technical, http://www.airmic.com/sites/default/files/supply_chain_failures_2013_FINAL_web.pdf

4. http://www.ers.usda.gov/topics/in-the-news/us-drought-2012-farm-and-food-impacts.aspx

5. http://www.emdat.be/final-result-request

6. Business Continuity Institute and Zurich, Supply Chain Resilience: BCI Survey Report 2009, http://www.bcifiles.com/BCISupplyChainResilienceSurvey2009MainReport2.pdf

7. Business Continuity Institute and Zurich, Supply Chain Resilience: BCI Survey Report 2010, http://www.bcipartnership.com/BCISupplyChainResilienceSurvey2010EXECUTIVESUMMARY.pdf

8. Business Continuity Institute and Zurich, Supply Chain Resilience: BCI Survey Report 2011, http://www.zurichna.com/internet/zna/SiteCollectionDocuments/en/corporatebusiness/riskengineering/Supply_Chain_Resilience_2011.pdf

9. Business Continuity Institute and Zurich, Supply Chain Resilience 2012, http://www.zurich.com/internet/main/sitecollectiondocuments/reports/supply-chain-resilience2012.pdf

10. Business Continuity Institute and Zurich, Supply Chain Resilience 2013, http://www.zurich.com/internet/main/sitecollectiondocuments/reports/supply-chain-resilience-2013-en.pdf

11. http://www.wired.com/wiredscience/2012/12/mississippi-low-water-cd/

12. Julie Cart, "Drought Has Mississippi River Barge Traffic All Choked Up," *Los Angeles Times*, September 1, 2012.

13. Darryl Fears, "Drought Threatens to Halt Critical Barge Traffic on Mississippi," *Washington Post*, January 6, 2013, http://www.washingtonpost.com/national/health-science/drought-threatens-to-halt-critical-barge-traffic-on-mississippidrought-threatens-to-halt-critical-barge-traffic-on-mississippi drought-threatens-to-halt-critical-barge-traffic-on-mississippi/2013/01/06/92498b88-5694-11e2-bf3e-76c0a789346f_story.html

14. http://www.bloomberg.com/news/2012-04-13/auto-supplier-warns-of-resin-shortage-disrupting-output.html

15. http://bulk-distributor.com/wp-content/uploads/2012/04/Bulk-Distributor-February-Low-Res.pdf

16. http://money.cnn.com/2007/08/01/news/companies/fisherpricerecall/index.htm?cnn=yes

17. http://www.faa.gov/news/press_releases/news_story.cfm?newsId=14233

18. http://www.forbes.com/sites/afontevecchia/2013/05/21/boeing-bleeding-cash-as-787-dreamliners-cost-200m-but-sell-for-116m-but-productivity-is-improving/

19. John Rogers, "LA Mayor Says Both Sides in West Coast Port Strike Have Agreed to Mediation," *CommercialAppeal.com News*, December 4, 2012

20. Ibid.

21. Greenpeace,. "Greenpeace Protests at Nestle Shareholder Meeting," 2010, http://www.youtube.com/watch?v=s8kwVU5pujg

22. The 2002 port lockout of the US Pacific Coast ports, which necessitated a presidential back-to-work order, also took place during the high season.

23. http://en.wikipedia.org/wiki/Voluntary_export_restraints

24. Clayton Christensen, *The Innovator's Dilemma* (Harper Business [reprint edition], October 2011).

25. Nassim Taleb, *Antifragile: Things That Gain from Disorder* (New York: Random House, 2014).

26. http://www.bbc.com/news/business-18508071

27. http://www.businessweek.com/articles/2013-01-17/inside-pfizers-fight-against-counterfeit-drugs

28. http://news.microsoft.com/download/presskits/antipiracy/docs/IDC030513.pdf

29. P. Chaudhry and A. Zimmerman, *Protecting Your Intellectual Property Rights*, 7; Management for Professionals, DOI 10.1007/978-1-4614-5568-4_2,(New York: Springer Science+Business Media, 2013).

30. http://www.businessweek.com/1998/47/b3605129.htm

31. Charles Arthur, "Google Faces Complaints to European Regulators over 'Predatory Pricing,'" *Guardian*, April 9, 2013.

32. http://www.washingtonpost.com/wp-dyn/content/article/2009/09/20/AR2009092001299.html

33. International Monetary Fund, "The Asian Crisis: Causes and Cures," http://www.imf.org/external/pubs/ft/fandd/1998/06/imfstaff.htm

34. http://www.pbs.org/wgbh/pages/frontline/shows/crash/etc/cron.html

35. http://www.cdc.gov/sars/about/index.html

36. http://www.cnn.com/2003/WORLD/asiapcf/east/04/25/sars/

37. http://www.cdc.gov/coronavirus/mers/

38. http://www.nytimes.com/interactive/2014/07/31/world/africa/ebola-virus-outbreak-qa.html?_r=0

39. http://www.who.int/influenza/human_animal_interface/en/

40. Jane Perlez, "As Dispute over Island Escalates, Japan and China Send Fighter Jets to the Scene," *New York Times*, January 18, 2013.

41. Demetri Sevatopulo, Michael Peel, and Jeremy Grant, "Vietnamese Mobs Ransack Foreign Factories in Anti-China Violence," *Financial Times*, May 15, 2014.

42. http://www.bbc.com/news/world-europe-13637130

43. http://earthquake.usgs.gov/earthquakes/eqarchives/year/eqstats.php

44. The figure appears in multiple places. See, for example, Bilal Ayyub and Massoud Amin, "Infrastructure Risk Analysis and Management," in *Handbook of Energy Efficiency and Renewable Energy*, ed..D. Yogi Goswami and Frank Kreith (CRC Press, 2007).

45. http://en.wikipedia.org/wiki/Chelyabinsk_meteor

46. http://www.gpo.gov/fdsys/pkg/CHRG-113hhrg80552/pdf/CHRG-113hhrg80552.pdf

47. David Marples, "The Decade of Despair," *Bulletin of the Atomic Scientists* 52 (3 (May–June 1996)): 20–31.

48. Ingrid Eckerman. *The Bhopal Saga—Causes and Consequences of the World's Largest Industrial Disaster* (Hyderabad, India: Universities Press, 2005).

49. Campbell Robertson and Clifford Kraus, "Gulf Spill Is the Largest of Its Kind, Scientists Say," *New York Times*, August 2, 2010.

50. Nassim Taleb, *The Black Swan: The Impact of the Highly Improbable* (New York: Random House, 2007).

51. http://www.aoml.noaa.gov/hrd/tcfaq/E11.html

52. http://stateimpact.npr.org/texas/2012/08/28/hurricane-isaac-shuts-down-oil-production-in-the-gulf/

53. Carolyn Kellogg, "Donald Rumsfeld Talks about His Upcoming Memoir," *Los Angeles Times,* January 24, 2011, http://latimesblogs.latimes.com/jacketcopy/2011/01/donald-rumsfeld-talks-about-his-upcoming-memoir.html

54. John Zinkin, *Challenges in Implementing Corporate Governance: Whose Business is it Anyway* (New York: Wiley, 2011), p. 137.

55. Gartner Case Study http://www.cisco.com/web/strategy/docs/manufacturing/Cisco_Case_Study_AMR_10-0917.pdf

56. University of Michigan Case 1-428–881, July 17, 2012, http://globalens.com/DocFiles/PDF/cases/inspection/GL1428881I.pdf

57. Gartner Case Study, http://www.cisco.com/web/strategy/docs/manufacturing/Cisco_Case_Study_AMR_10-0917.pdf

58. http://www.supplychainmovement.com/wp-content/uploads/Supply-Chain-Movement-Quarterly-No3-2011.pdf p. 12.

59. NAND flash is used in main memory, memory cards, USB flash drives, solid-state drives, and similar products, for general storage and transfer of data. The acronym NAND derives from "Not And," and refers to the choice of the logic gates that store the data. A NAND gate produces an output that is false only if all the incoming elements are true.

60. Don Clark and Juro Osawa, "Power Blip Jolts Supply of Gadget Chips," *Wall Street Journal,* December 10, 2010.

61. iSupply, Spansion cited in http://online.wsj.com/article/SB10001424052748703766704576009071694055878.html

62. Clark and Osawa, "Power Blip Jolts Supply of Gadget Chips."

63. John Farmer, "United 93: The Real Picture," *Washington Post*, April 30, 2006, http://www.washingtonpost.com/wp-dyn/content/article/2006/04/29/AR2006042900129.html

64. http://www.industryweek.com/blog/how-mattel-fiasco-really-happened

65. Louise Story, "Lead Paint Prompts Mattel to Recall 967,000 Toys," *New York Times*, August 2, 2007, http://www.nytimes.com/2007/08/02/business/02toy
.html?_r=1

66. Joel Wisner, "The Chinese-Made Toy Recall at Mattel, Inc.," University of Nevada Faculty Websites, http://faculty.unlv.edu/wisnerj/mba720_files/Mattel_case2.pdf

67. http://money.cnn.com/2009/06/05/news/companies/cpsc/

68. http://money.cnn.com/2007/10/12/markets/spotlight_mat/

69. http://www.msnbc.msn.com/id/20254745/ns/business-consumer_news/t/mattel-issues-new-massive-china-toy-recall/

70. See a discussion of such approaches in Yossi Sheffi, *The Resilient Enterprise: Overcoming Vulnerability for Competitive Advantage* (Cambridge, MA: MIT Press, 2005).

71. https://www.youtube.com/watch?v=sX8luPQZ2I0&feature=related

72. http://www.tnooz.com/article/inside-social-media-at-delta-air-lines-a-behind-the-scenes-look/

73. https://www.youtube.com/watch?v=5YGc4zOqozo&feature=kp

74. https://www.youtube.com/watch?v=P45E0uGVyeg

Chapter 3

1. Interview with Rob Thom, manager, GM global vehicle engineering operations, August 2012.

2. Interview with Ron Mills, director, GM components holding, August 2012.

3. Interview with Rob Thom, August 2012.

4. Interview with Bill Hurles, executive director of global supply chain at GM, August 2012.

5. Interview with Rob Thom, August 2012.

6. Interview with Ron Mills, August 2012.

7. Interview with Daniel Ackerson, CNBC, April 19, 2011, http://www.cnbc.com/id/42500044/CNBC_TRANSCRIPT_FIRST_ON_CNBC_GENERAL_MOTORS_CHAIRMAN_CEO_DANIEL_AKERSON_SPEAKS_WITH_CNBC_S_PHIL_LEBEAU_TODAY_ON_THE_CALL

8. http://www.autonews.com/article/20110425/OEM02/304259930

9. http://www.nytimes.com/2011/05/13/business/global/13auto.html?pagewanted=all

10. Interview with Ackerson, April 19, 2011.

11. Interview with Bill Hurles, August 2012.

12. Interview with Bob Glubzinski, manager of North American scheduling and order fulfillment at GM, August 2012.

13. Interview with Dr. Marc Robinson, assistant director and economist, Enterprise Risk Management at GM, August 2012.

14. Interview with Bob Glubzinski, August 2012.

15. Interview with Bill Hurles, August 2012.

16. Interview with Rob Thom, August 2012.

17. The disruption of production occurs before the disruption of sales, which occurs before the disruption of deliveries to customers. For purposes of calculating VaR, a company will need to measure the timing of disruption and recovery events in some consistent way.

18. https://www.semiconportal.com/en/archive/news/main-news/110602-renesas-naka-200mm.html

19. "Renesas Moves TargetDate for Full Supply Restoration," *EE Times-Asia*, June 14, 2011 http://www.eetasia.com/ART_8800644802_480200_NT_938fdf93.HTM

20. Under *fair allocation*, the company satisfies the same partial fraction of demand for each product or customer.

21. If $p > (1\text{-}TTI/TTR)$, the initial inventories plus partial supply will suffice to cover the entire duration of the *TTR*.

22. Of course different products may have different finished goods inventories and varying rates of demand, which may fluctuate throughout the year, making the VaR calculation a little more nuanced. In addition, a company could also ration its DOS over the duration of the disruption. (In that case, the DOS increases the effective partial supply by DOS divided by *CIT*, in which case the *CIT* will be longer but the VaR will be the same.).

23. http://news.techworld.com/personal-tech/3320401/thailand-floods-hard-drive-shortage-makes-small-pc-makers-hike-prices/

24. http://www.docstoc.com/docs/88638192/Japan-Earthquake---Related-Industry-News-Update-Compiled-by

25. Peter Borrows, "After Floods, a Sea of Disk Drive Shortages," *Bloomberg-Businessweek*, November 17, 2011, http://www.businessweek.com/magazine/after-the-floods-a-sea-of-disk-drive-shortages-11172011.html

26. This can be a fraction of customers' actual orders unless the company thinks customers are trying to game the allocation system. If customers are intentionally over-ordering to get more than their fair share, the company might limit orders to the pre-disruption forecasts or levels of demand.

27. The mathematics of such calculations, including a case study, are reported in: Jennifer Yip, "Evaluating Upstream Supply Chain Disruptions with Partial Availability," master thesis, Center for Transportation and Logistics, MIT, May 2015.

28. Don Clark, "Seagate Preps for Drive Shortages Amid Flooding," *Wall Street Journal*, January 31, 2012.

29. Mark Hachman, "Want a Seagate Drive? Then Pay Up," *PC Magazine*, February 2, 2012.

30. Ibid.

31. Ibid.

32. http://evertiq.com/news/21036

33. http://www.backupworks.com/hdd-market-share-western-digital-seagate.aspx

34. Lawrence Ausubel and Peter Cramton, *Demand Reduction and Inefficiency in Multi-Unit Auctions*, University of Maryland Working Paper, 1998.

35. http://money.cnn.com/2013/02/10/news/makers-mark-bourbon/

36. Ibid.

Chapter 4

1. http://en.wikipedia.org/wiki/Atlantic_hurricane_season

2. Cath Malseed, director of coffee supply P&G, presentation at MIT CTL's conference, "At the Crossroads of Supply Chain and Strategy: Simulating Disruption to Business Recovery," held on April 11, 2006, in Cambridge, MA.

3. http://en.wikipedia.org/wiki/Timeline_of_Hurricane_Katrina

4. Doug MacCash and James O'Byrne, "Levee Breach Floods Lakeview, Mid-City, Carrollton, Gentilly, City Park," *Times Picayune*, August 30, 2005, http://www.nola.com/katrina/index.ssf/2005/08/levee_breach_floods_lakeview_mid-city_carrollton_gentilly_city_park.html

5. Kim Ann Zimmermann, "Hurricane Katrina: Facts, Damage & Aftermath" August 20, 2012 http://www.livescience.com/22522-hurricane-katrina-facts.html

6. Malseed, Cath. MIT CTL's conference, "At the Crossroads of Supply Chain and Strategy," April 11, 2006. Most of the details in this chapter about P&G's preparations and recovery efforts are based on the MIT presentation and subsequent discussions with Cath Malseed.

7. http://usatoday30.usatoday.com/news/washington/2005-09-20-bush-gulf_x.htm

8. http://news.bbc.co.uk/2/hi/uk_news/england/leicestershire/4398514.stm

9. "Primark Risk Strategy Reduces Impact of Fire," *Finance Week*, November 9, 2005, p. 2.

10. Will Hadfield, "Blaze-Hit Primark Back on Track as Continuity Plan Saves the Day," *Computer Weekly*, November 8, 2005.

11. "Primark Risk Strategy Reduces Impact of Fire," p. 2.

12. Hadfield, "Blaze-Hit Primark Back on Track as Continuity Plan Saves the Day."

13. "Primark Rushes to Replace Stock after Massive Blaze." Europe Intelligence Wire, November 3, 2005.

14. http://www.brisc2013.com/blog/Weakest%20Supply%20Chain%20 Link%20Apr11.pdf

15. Hadfield, "Blaze-Hit Primark Back on Track as Continuity Plan Saves the Day."

16. Peter Borrows, "After Floods, a Sea of Disk Drive Shortages," *Bloomberg-Businessweek,* November 17, 2011, http://www.businessweek.com/magazine/after-the-floods-a-sea-of-disk-drive-shortages-11172011.html

17. Ploy Ten Kate, "Thailand Surreal Industrial Park: Crocodiles but No Chips," Reuters, November 24, 2011, http://www.reuters.com/article/2011/11/24/uk-thailand-floods-hana-idUSLNE7AN02C20111124

18. Fabrinet Updates Thailand Flood Situation, http://evertiq.com/news/21005

19. http://www.cbsnews.com/8301-201_162-57542015/superstorm-sandy-more-than-7-million-without-power/

20. Thomas Gryta, "AT&T, T-Mobile, Team Up as Damaged Networks Still Strained," *Wall Street Journal*, October 31, 2012.

21. http://www.hrw.org/news/2011/01/28/egypt-demonstrators-defy-riot-police-censorship

22. Interview with Jim Holko, July 31, 2012.

23. Interview with Rick Birch, global director, operational excellence at Delphi, August 2012.

24. Interview with Joe McBeth, vice president of global supply chain at Jabil, September 2012.

25. http://www.cnn.com/2014/03/19/world/asia/malaysia-airlines-plane-ground-witnesses/

26. http://www.theaustralian.com.au/news/latest-news/mh370-search-highlights-indian-ocean-trash/story-fn3dxiwe-1226884181607?nk=b59546d46230b8bd9f2ba4efaead80c8

27. http://www.themalaysianinsider.com/malaysia/article/as-leads-pan-out-search-for-mh370-stretches-from-sumatra-to-hong-kong

28. http://www.theguardian.com/world/2014/mar/15/flight-mh370-malaysia-hunt-speculation

29. Ibid.

30. http://www.theguardian.com/world/2014/mar/14/malaysia-flight-mh370-hunt-sees-suspicion-and-cooperation-china-us

31. http://archive.org/details/CNNW_20140315_183000_CNN_Newsroom?q=%22all+right+good+night%22#start/176/end/236

32. http://www.cnn.com/2014/03/31/world/asia/malaysia-airlines-plane/

33. http://www.abc.net.au/news/2014-04-03/malaysia-airlines-mh370-missing-director-general-abdul-rahman/5365992

34. http://www.themalaysianinsider.com/malaysia/article/malaysian-authorities-slammed-for-contradicting-statements-in-search-for-mh

35. http://www.theguardian.com/world/2014/mar/13/malaysian-officials-deny-flight-mh370-missing-plane-flew-hours

36. http://www.theguardian.com/world/2014/mar/15/flight-mh370-malaysia-hunt-speculation

37. http://www.theguardian.com/world/2014/mar/14/malaysia-flight-mh370-hunt-sees-suspicion-and-cooperation-china-us

38. http://www.theguardian.com/world/2014/mar/13/malaysian-officials-deny-flight-mh370-missing-plane-flew-hours

39. http://www.cnn.com/2014/03/31/world/asia/malaysia-airlines-plane/

40. http://www.reuters.com/article/2014/10/17/us-health-ebola-usa-message-analysis-idUSKCN0I62DU20141017

41. http://www.usatoday.com/story/news/nation/2014/10/27/ebola-christie-cuomo-quinn-pentagon/18022791/

42. http://www.wsj.com/articles/airasia-chief-tony-fernandes-takes-lead-on-crash-response-1419989212

43. A. Strickler, "Stormy Weather: Waiting til They're Blue; JetBlue Passengers Stranded on Planes for Hours amid Icy Snarl at JFK Gates." *New York Newsday*, February 15, 2007, and New Word City, *How JetBlue Got Its Wings Back*, Financial Times Press, 2010.

44. http://www.awpagesociety.com/wp-content/uploads/2011/09/08JetBlue_CaseStudy.pdf

45. Jeff Bailey, "JetBlue's CEO Is 'Mortified' after Flyers Are Stranded," *New York Times*, February 19, 2007, http://www.nytimes.com/2007/02/19/business/19jetblue.html

46. Bailey, "JetBlue's CEO Is 'Mortified' after Flyers Are Stranded."

47. http://www.autonews.com/article/20110425/OEM02/304259930/chasing-chips:-gms-ace-in-the-hole

48. http://www.reuters.com/article/2011/03/18/us-japan-quake-gm-idUSTRE72H7RH20110318

49. http://www.youtube.com/watch?v=5uggXdzRZ3s

50. http://www.just-auto.com/news/gm-working-through-quake-supply-issues-ceo_id110331.aspx

51. This section is based on Malseed, "At the Crossroads of Supply Chain & Strategy."

52. http://www.npr.org/blogs/thesalt/2013/02/11/171732213/less-potent-makers-mark-not-going-down-smooth-in-kentucky

53. http://www.forbes.com/sites/larryolmsted/2013/02/14/whiskey-or-water-marketing-nightmare-as-bourbon-fans-incensed-over-choice/

54. Ibid.

55. http://nypost.com/2013/02/17/cheers-makers-mark-not-cutting-alcohol-in-whiskey-after-all/

56. Ibid.

57. http://www.forbes.com/sites/avidan/2013/05/06/makers-marks-plain-dumb-move-proved-to-be-pure-marketing-genius/

58. http://business.time.com/2013/05/03/proof-positive-makers-mark-blunder-results-in-surprise-profit/

59. http://www.autonews.com/apps/pbcs.dll/article?AID=/20111011/OEM10/111019989/1424

60. Marc Reisch, "Explosion at German Chemical Plant Kills Two," *Chemical and Engineering News*, April 2, 2012, http://cen.acs.org/articles/90/web/2012/04/Explosion-German-Chemical-Plant-Kills.html

61. http://www.plastics-car.com/lightvehiclereport

62. http://plastics.dupont.com/plastics/pdflit/americas/markets/nylon_under_hood.pdf

63. http://www.daicel-evonik.com/english/products/manufacture/C12,C8/index.html

64. http://www.bloomberg.com/news/2012-04-13/auto-supplier-warns-of-resin-shortage-disrupting-output.html

65. https://www.aiag.org/staticcontent/about/index.cfm

66. Melissa Burden, "Auto Group Looks for Ways to Work around Resin Shortage," *Detroit News*, April 19, 2012.

67. http://www.aiag.org/staticcontent/press/releases/GENERAL/AIAG%20Post%20Summit%20UPDATE%20-%20FINAL4-18.pdf

68. Burden, "Auto Group Looks for Ways to Work around Resin Shortage."

69. Jeff Bennett," Nylon-12 Haunts Car Makers," *Wall Street Journal*, April 17, 2012.

70. http://www.crainsdetroit.com/article/20120417/STAFFBLOG12/120419913/auto-industry-tries-to-head-off-resin-shortage-but-what-can-it-do

71. http://www.businessweek.com/news/2012-04-19/dupont-sees-boost-to-polymers-from-automakers-seeking-resins

72. Criag Trudell, "Automakers to Speed Part-Validation Process," *Bloomberg-Businessweek*, April 24, 2012.

73. http://www.plasticsnews.com/headlines2.html?id=25223

74. Stefan Baumgarten, "Evonik Gets Permit to Restart Germany CDT Plant after Explosion," 04 December 2012, *ISCIS News* http://www.icis.com/resources/news/2012/12/04/9621085/evonik-gets-permit-to-restart-germany-cdt-plant-after-explosion/

75. http://energy.gov/sites/prod/files/Derecho%202012_%20Review_0.pdf

76. http://www.outagecentral.com/mutual-assistance-group/mid-atlantic-mutual-assistance-group

77. http://www.theexchange.org/

78. http://www.publicpower.org/Media/magazine/ArticleDetail.cfm?Item Number=34001

79. Ibid.

80. http://energy.gov/sites/prod/files/Derecho%202012_%20Review_0.pdf

81. http://www.oe.netl.doe.gov/docs/Northeast%20Storm%20Comparison_FINAL_041513c.pdf

82. http://water.epa.gov/infrastructure/watersecurity/mutualaid/index.cfm

83. Interview with Tim Harden, president of supply chain and fleet operations at AT&T, July 29, 2014.

84. Thomas Gryta, "AT&T, T-Mobile Team Up as Damaged Networks Still Strained," *Wall Street Journal*, October 31, 2012, http://online.wsj.com/articles/SB10001424052970204846304578091442059702404

85. Malseed, MIT CTL's conference, "At the Crossroads of Supply Chain and Strategy," April 11, 2006.

86. http://en.wikipedia.org/wiki/2008_Sichuan_earthquake

87. Interview with Rob Thom, August 3. 2012.

88. Interview with Ron Mills, August 3, 2012.

89. http://www.scrlc.com/articles/Supply_Chain_Risk_Management_A_Compilation_of_Best_Practices_final%5B1%5D.pdf

90. http://tech.fortune.cnn.com/tag/automakers/

Chapter 5

1. S&P Case-Shiller 20-City Home Price Index, http://research.stlouisfed.org.

2. Barclays Capital reprinted in http://soberlook.com/2012/06/in-spite-of-large-corrections-housing.html

3. http://www.jchs.harvard.edu/sites/jchs.harvard.edu/files/son2008.pdf

4. http://www.cbo.gov/sites/default/files/cbofiles/ftpdocs/120xx/doc12032/12-23-fanniefreddie.pdf

5. http://www.nber.org/papers/w15362

6. http://research.stlouisfed.org/fred2/graph/?id=EXPGS

7. http://research.stlouisfed.org/fred2/graph/?id=IMPGS

8. http://www.federalreserve.gov/boarddocs/hh/2005/february/testimony.htm

9. http://research.stlouisfed.org/fred2/graph/?id=SPCS20RSA

10. http://www.federalreserve.gov/boarddocs/snloansurvey/201208/chartdata.htm

11. Ibid.

12. http://siteresources.worldbank.org/INTRANETTRADE/Resources/TradeFinancech06.pdf

13. http://www.nber.org/cycles/dec2008.html

14. http://www.cnbc.com/id/101573765

15. https://en.wikipedia.org/wiki/Lehman_Brothers

16. http://en.wikipedia.org/wiki/American_International_Group

17. http://blogs.wsj.com/deals/2008/09/16/the-aig-crisis-by-the-numbers/ and http://www.federalreserve.gov/newsevents/press/other/20080916a.htm

18. https://en.wikipedia.org/wiki/American_International_Group

19. http://www.bls.gov/spotlight/2012/recession/pdf/recession_bls_spotlight.pdf

20. http://i2.cdn.turner.com/money/2011/04/25/news/economy/new_home_sales/chart_new_home_sales2.top.jpg

21. http://www.calculatedriskblog.com/2011/12/us-light-vehicle-sales-at-136-million.html

22. http://research.stlouisfed.org/fred2/series/DGORDER

23. Hau L. Lee, V. Padmanabhan, and Seungjin Whang, "The Bullwhip Effect in Supply Chains," *Sloan Management Review* 38, no. 3 (Spring 1997): 93–102, http://sloanreview.mit.edu/article/the-bullwhip-effect-in-supply-chains/

24. Ibid.

25. Janice Hammond, Barilla SpA (a). Harvard Business School Case no. 9-694-046, 1994.

26. Li Chen and Hau Lee, "Bullwhip Effect Measurement and Its Implications, http://citeseerx.ist.psu.edu/viewdoc/download?doi=10.1.1.163.3773&rep=rep1&type=pdf

27. A. G. de Kok, F. B. S. L. P. Janssen, J. B. M. Doremalen, E. van Wachem, M. van Clerkx, and W. Peeters, "Philips Electronics Synchronizes Its Supply Chain to End the Bullwhip Effect," *Interfaces* 35, no. 1 (2005): 37–48, http://www.tue.nl/en/publication/ep/p/d/ep-uid/194396/

28. http://research.stlouisfed.org/fred2/graph/?id=IMPGS and Jan Fransoo, Robert Peels, and Maximiliano Udenio, "Supply Chain Dynamics Have Major Impact on Course of Credit crisi"s—Essay11-SupplyChainCreditCrisis.pdf.

29. Altomonte, Carlo and di Mauro, Filippo and Ottaviano, Gianmarco Ireo Paolo and Rungi, Armando and Vicard, Vincent, Global Value Chains during the Great Trade Collapse: A Bullwhip Effect? (December 16, 2011). ECB Working Paper No. 1412. Available at SSRN: http://ssrn.com/abstract=1973497

30. Robert Peels, Maximiliano Udenio, Jan C. Fransoo, Marcel Wolfs, and Tom Hendrikx, "Responding to the Lehman Wave: Sales Forecasting and Supply Management during the Credit Crisis," December 5, 2009, http://www.flostock.nl/fileadmin/user_upload/PDF_upload/2009_December_BETA_Working_Papers_University_of_Technology_Eindhoven.pdf

31. Ibid.

32. Altomonte, Carlo and di Mauro, Filippo and Ottaviano, Gianmarco Ireo Paolo and Rungi, Armando and Vicard, Vincent, Global Value Chains during the

Great Trade Collapse: A Bullwhip Effect? (December 16, 2011). ECB Working Paper No. 1412. Available at SSRN: http://ssrn.com/abstract=1973497

33. http://www.nber.org/papers/w15556.pdf

34. http://siteresources.worldbank.org/INTRANETTRADE/Resources/TradeFinancech06.pdf].

35. TED is an acronym formed from T-Bill and ED. The TED spread is the difference between the T-Bill rate (interest paid on short-term US Government debt) and ED rate (the ticker symbol for the Eurodollar futures contract as represented by short-term interbank lending rates).

36. http://www.princeton.edu/~markus/research/papers/liquidity_credit_crunch.pdf

37. http://www.imf.org/external/pubs/ft/wp/2011/wp1116.pdf

38. Society for Worldwide Interbank Financial Telecommunication, http://www.swift.com/index.page?lang=en

39. http://www.jpmorgan.com/tss/General/A_Counterintuitive_Development_Supply_Chain_Finance_in_the_New_Economic_/1275699773419

40. http://www.imf.org/external/pubs/ft/wp/2011/wp1116.pdf

41. http://www.newyorkfed.org/research/economists/amiti/Trade%20Finance.pdf

42. http://www.bls.gov/mls/mlsreport1025.pdf

43. http://www.bea.gov/industry/gdpbyind_data.htm

44. http://www.booz.com/media/file/The_New_Consumer_Frugality.pdf

45. http://www.time.com/time/business/article/0,8599,1885133,00.html

46. http://www.nbcnews.com/id/31171643/ns/business-food_inc/wid/7468326/

47. http://money.cnn.com/2009/02/17/news/companies/starbucks_instant/?postversion=2009021716

48. Panel discussion with a representative from Shaw's Supermarkets, at MIT CTL's conference, "Crossroads: Managing Supply Chains during Turbulent Times," March 26, 2009, http://ctl-test1.mit.edu/sites/default/files/library/public/CTL-Crossroads-2009-SynthesisReport.pdf

49. KPMG, ConsumerCurrents Issue #10, April 2011, http://www.kpmg.com/CN/en/IssuesAndInsights/ArticlesPublications/Newsletters/ConsumerCurrents/Documents/Consumer-Currents-O-1104-10.pdf

50. MIT CTL's conference, "Crossroads," March 26, 2009.

51. Ibid.

52. http://supply-chain.org/f/1-Hoole-Ready%20for%20Recovery.pdf

53. http://www.reuters.com/article/2008/11/11/us-techcompanies-analysis-idUSTRE4AA8EJ20081111

54. S. John Tilak, "Circuit City Bankruptcy a Blip for Tech Firms," *Reuters*, Nov 11, 2008 http://www.reuters.com/article/2008/11/11/us-techcompanies-analysis-idUSTRE4AA8EJ20081111

55. MIT CTL's conference, "Crossroads," March 26, 2009.

56. http://www.grantthornton.com/staticfiles/GTCom/CIP/Consumer%20and%20industrial%20products%20publications/Supply%20Chain%20Solutions/GrantThornton_SupplyChainSolutionsPart1.pdf

57. MIT CTL's conference, "Crossroads," March 26, 2009.

58. http://faculty.poly.edu/~brao/The%20FDX%20Group_files/image007.jpg

59. http://centreforaviation.com/analysis/airlines-and-airports-feeling-impact-of-global-economic-weakness-with-continued-freight-pressures-ev-63705

60. MIT CTL's conference, "Crossroads," March 26, 2009.

61. http://www.lr.org/Images/CS%20Focus5_tcm155-175189.pdf

62. Maersk, "Slow Steaming Here to Stay." Maersk Press Release, 01 September, 2010 http://www.maersk.com/en/the-maersk-group/press-room/press-release-archive/2010/9/slow-steaming-here-to-stay

63. BASF, "About Us: Verbund," https://www.basf.com/en/company/about-us/strategy-and-organization/verbund.html

64. http://www.nytimes.com/2009/08/02/magazine/02FOB-onlanguage-t.html

65. http://online.wsj.com/article/SB100014240527487038943045750471601 51066820.html

66. "Companies Concerned About Retention," @Work, posted on 06/28/2011, accessed 03/19/2015, https://challengeratwork.wordpress.com/tag/perks/

67. http://online.wsj.com/article/SB100014240527487038943045750471601 51066820.html

68. http://www.industryweek.com/global-economy/staying-true-toyota-way-during-recession

69. http://www.guardian.co.uk/education/2009/oct/22/tefl-germany

70. http://www.reuters.com/article/2009/02/10/us-singapore-recession-acronyms-idUSTRE5190X520090210

71. http://bits.blogs.nytimes.com/2009/10/30/innovation-spending-looks-recession-resistant/

72. http://commons.wikimedia.org/wiki/File:IPhone_sales_per_quarter_simple.svg

73. http://www.informationweek.com/mobility/business/t-mobile-usa-and-htc-have-sold-1-million/229206890

74. MIT CTL's conference, "Crossroads," March 26, 2009.

75. Flextronics Annual Report, 2009, http://investors.flextronics.com/annuals.cfm

76. Roland Berger Strategy Consultants, "Restructuring for Automotive Suppliers," Business Breakfast, Budapest, Hungary, March 31, 2010.

77. http://www.handelsblatt.com/unternehmen/industrie/dramatischer-umsatzeinbruch-autozulieferer-edscha-geht-in-die-insolvenz/3102330.html

78. http://www.bbc.co.uk/news/business-17769466

79. Roland Berger Strategy Consultants, "Restructuring for Automotive Suppliers," Business Breakfast, Budapest, Hungary, March 31, 2010.

80. http://www.bcifiles.com/BCISupplyChainResilienceSurvey2009MainReport2.pdf

81. http://www.bcifiles.com/BCISupplyChainResilienceSurvey2009MainReport2.pdf

82. 2011 APICS, the Association for Operations Management survey.

83. C. Blome and T. Schönherr, "Supply Risk Management in Financial Crises: A Multiple Case-Study Approach," *International Journal of Production Economics* 134, no. 1 (2011): 43–57.

84. Ibid.

85. http://www.ft.com/intl/cms/s/0/ec98b5e4-17c5-11de-8c9d-0000779fd2ac.html

86. http://www.grantthornton.es/publicaciones/AHGT.ES%20supply%20chain%20solutions.pdf

87. http://supply-chain.org/f/1-Hoole-Ready%20for%20Recovery.pdf

88. MIT CTL's symposium, "Advancing Supply Chain Risk Management: Emerging Challenges and Strategies," October 10, 2012.

89. Interview with Jackie Sturm, July 31, 2012.

90. http://phx.corporate-ir.net/External.File?item=UGFyZW50SUQ9OTc0NDh8Q2hpbGRJRD0tMXxUeXBlPTM=&t=1

91. http://www.grantthornton.es/publicaciones/AHGT.ES%20supply%20chain%20solutions.pdf

92. http://www.grantthornton.com/staticfiles/GTCom/CIP/Consumer%20and%20industrial%20products%20publications/Supply%20Chain%20Solutions/CIP% 20-%20WT%20Distribution%20part2.PDF

93. http://research.stlouisfed.org/fred2/graph/?id=UNRATE

94. http://www.bls.gov/spotlight/2012/recession/pdf/recession_bls_spotlight.pdf

95. http://graphics.eiu.com/upload/eb/Oracle_Supply_Chain_WEB.pdf

96. http://graphics.eiu.com/upload/eb/Oracle_Supply_Chain_WEB.pdf

97. http://graphics.eiu.com/upload/eb/Oracle_Supply_Chain_WEB.pdf

98. http://graphics.eiu.com/upload/eb/Oracle_Supply_Chain_WEB.pdf

99. http://www.plasticsnews.com/article/20130415/NEWS/130419948/risk-averse-suppliers-become-bottlenecks-pinch-automakers

100. http://www.plasticsnews.com/article/20130415/NEWS/130419948/risk-averse-suppliers-become-bottlenecks-pinch-automakers

101. Heimo Losbichler and Farzad Mahmoodi, "Why Working Capital Should Matter to You," *Supply Chain Management Review*, November 13, 2012, http://www.scmr.com/article/why_working_capital_should_matter_to_you

102. http://www.grantthornton.com/staticfiles/GTCom/CIP/Consumer%20and%20industrial%20products%20publications/Supply%20Chain%20Solutions/CIP%20-%20WT%20Distribution%20part2.PDF

103. http://www.churchdwight.com/PDF/AnnualReports/2009-CDH-Annual-Report.pdf

104. http://www.grantthornton.es/publicaciones/AHGT.ES%20supply%20chain%20solutions.pdf

105. http://www.grantthornton.com/staticfiles/GTCom/CIP/Consumer%20and%20industrial%20products%20publications/Supply%20Chain%20Solutions/GrantThornton_SupplyChainSolutionsPart1.pdf

106. Church & Dwight benchmarked its inventory performance against its peers and found that it ranked #1, even though the company did not explicitly try to reach the top slot.

107. http://www.calculatedriskblog.com/2011/12/us-light-vehicle-sales-at-136-million.html

108. http://business.time.com/2011/09/19/the-worse-the-economy-the-better-business-is-at-auto-repair-shops/

109. http://www.fpsc.com/DB/TreasuryPulse/PDF/Winter10_article2.pdf

110. MIT CTL's conference, "The Changing Dynamics of Supply Chain and Finance," October 21, 2009.

111. Although this looks like routine financing of account receivables, it's different in several ways, including: (i) it's being arranged by the customer, not the supplier—AAP paid the upfront costs to set up the program; (ii) the interest rate is based on AAP's credit rating; and (iii) it's a three-way relationship: the supplier sends goods to AAP, AAP sends a notice to the bank, and the bank sends money to the supplier when the supplier asks for it.

Chapter 6

1. Lenos Trigeorgis, *Real Options* (Cambridge, MA: MIT Press, 1995).

2. Interested readers can get an introduction to the subject in many books. See, for example, Richard De Neufville and Stefan Scholtes, *Flexibility in Engineering Design*, Engineering Systems Series (Cambridge, MA: MIT Press, 2011).

3. Catherine Bolgar, "Virtuality: Competing Supply/Demand Trends Pose Complications for Companies," *Supply Chain Risk Insights*, October 4, 2010, http://www.zurichna.com/internet/zna/SiteCollectionDocuments/en/Products/riskengineering/SCRI_Virtuality.pdf

4. http://9to5mac.com/2013/05/19/inside-atts-83gbhour-mobile-cell-tower-or-why-your-iphone-no-longer-drops-out-at-huge-events/

5. http://www.theinquirer.net/inquirer/feature/2231811/at-t-talks-about-its-disaster-recovery-strategy-during-hurricane-sandy

6. http://www.gottabemobile.com/2012/01/31/att-brings-9-cows-to-indianapolis-for-super-bowl-46-video/

7. http://www.supplychainmovement.com/wp-content/uploads/Supply-Chain-Movement-Quarterly-No3-2011.pdf; "Do or Die," p. 13.

8. Author's note: Once I learned about this, I started having dreams involving huge mountains of milk chocolate...

9. http://www.ism.ws/files/RichterAwards/CiscoSubmissionSupportDoc2012.pdf

10. http://www.supplychainmovement.com/wp-content/uploads/Supply-Chain-Movement-Quarterly-No3-2011.pdf

11. Panos Kouvelis, Lingxiu Dong, Onur Boyabatli, and Rong Li, *Handbook of Integrated Risk Management in Global Supply Chains,* citing Martine Van Campenhout. Private correspondence on "Mechelen's Position on Handling the Consequences of the Jackson Tornado," October 22, 2004.

12. William C. Jordan and Stephen C. Graves, "Principles on the Benefits of Manufacturing Process Flexibility." *Management Science* 41, no. 4 (April 1995): 577–594.

13. http://corporate.walmart.com/our-story/our-business/logistics

14. http://www.drpeppersnapplegroup.com/files/Beverage_Industry-DrPepper_125th_CoverStory_Victorville_Plant_Opening.pdf

15. Christopher Tang and Brian Tomlin, "The Power of Flexibility for Mitigating Supply Chain Risks," *International Journal of Production Economics* 116 (2008): 12–27.

16. Susan Rietze, "Case Studies of Postponement in the Supply Chain," master's thesis, MIT Department of Civil and Environmental Engineering, 2006.

17. Ibid.

18. http://www.embedded.com/print/4314610

19. Venu Nagali et al., "Procurement Risk Management (PRM) at Hewlett-Packard Company," *Interfaces* 38, no. 1 (2008): 51–60.

20. http://www.pwc.com/mx/es/forms/archivo/PwC-PRTM_SupplyChain_092811_r_v3.pdf

21. Susan Ratcliffe, *Oxford Essential Quotations*, Oxford University Press, 2014.

22. Nghi Luu, "The Cisco Method" presentation at Advancing Supply Chain Risk Management: Emerging Challenges and Strategies, MIT Center for Transportation and Logistics Conference, Cambridge, MA, October 10, 2012.

23. http://scrmblog.com/review/practitioner-views-on-supply-chain-risk-management

24. http://www.continuityinsights.com/sites/continuityinsights.com/files/legacyfiles/Microsoft%20PowerPoint%20-%20A3%20Raso.pdf

25. http://www.continuityinsights.com/sites/continuityinsights.com/files/legacyfiles/Microsoft%20PowerPoint%20-%20A3%20Raso.pdf

26. http://www.continuityinsights.com/sites/continuityinsights.com/files/legacyfiles/Microsoft%20PowerPoint%20-%20A3%20Raso.pdf

27. http://www.medtronic.com/wcm/groups/mdtcom_sg/@mdt/@corp/documents/documents/019-g034.pdf

28. http://www.continuitycentral.com/news06887.html

29. http://www.continuityinsights.com/sites/continuityinsights.com/files/legacyfiles/Microsoft%20PowerPoint%20-%20A3%20Raso.pdf

30. http://businessfinancemag.com/risk-management/when-erm-meets-sox

31. http://en.wikipedia.org/wiki/Top-down_risk_assessment

32. http://www.coso.org/Publications/ERM/COSO_ERM_ExecutiveSummary.pdf

33. http://www.iso.org/iso/home/standards/iso31000.htm

34. Andrew Grove, *Only the Paranoid Survive* (New York: Crown Business, 2010).

35. Lars Leemhorst and Roberto Crippa, "Do or Die: Manage or Ignore Supply Chain Risks," *Supply Chain Movement Quarterly,* no. 3 Q4 2011, pp. 10–17.

36. http://www.usresilienceproject.org/pdfs/USRP_Priorities_Final_020112.pdf

37. Luu, "The Cisco Method."

38. http://www.continuityinsights.com/sites/continuityinsights.com/files/legacyfiles/Microsoft%20PowerPoint%20-%20A3%20Raso.pdf

39. Kevin Harrington and John O'Connor, "How Cisco Succeeds," *Supply Chain Management Review*, July/August 2009, http://www.imperiallogistics.co.za/documents/06.HowCiscoSucceeds_.pdf

40. http://www.zurich.com/internet/main/sitecollectiondocuments/reports/supply-chain-resilience2012.pdf

41. http://www.sedexglobal.com/wp-content/uploads/2011/06/Sedex-Transparency-Briefing-Nov-2013.pdf

42. http://www.cbs12.com/news/top-stories/stories/vid_8457.shtml

43. David Rath, "Private-Sector Organizations Earn a Seat in Emergency Operations Center," *Emergency Management*, May 17, 2010, http://www.emergencymgmt.com/disaster/Private-Sector-Organizations-Emergency-Operations-Center.html

44. Mark Cooper, "Industry Perspective: The Importance of Public-Private Partnerships," *Emergency Management*, April 30, 2012, http://www.emergencymgmt.com/disaster/Industry-Perspective-Importance-Public-Private-Partnerships.html

45. Rath, "Private-Sector Organizations Earn a Seat in Emergency Operations Center."

46. Margaret Steen, "Business EOCs Improve Public-Private Partnerships," *Emergency Management*, May 21, 2012.

47. https://s3-us-gov-west-1.amazonaws.com/dam-production/uploads/20130726-1852-25045-2704/fema_factsheet_nbeoc_final_508.pdf

48. Rath, "Private-Sector Organizations Earn a Seat in Emergency Operations Center."

49. https://s3-us-gov-west-1.amazonaws.com/dam-production/uploads/20130726-1852-25045-2704/fema_factsheet_nbeoc_final_508.pdf

50. Dan Milkovic and Roberta Witty, *Case Study: Cisco Addresses Supply Chain Risk Management*, Gartner Industry Research no. G00206060, September 17, 2010, http://www.cisco.com/web/strategy/docs/manufacturing/Cisco_Case_Study_AMR_10-0917.pdf

51. http://www.ism.ws/files/RichterAwards/CiscoSubmissionSupportDoc2012.pdf

52. Luu, "The Cisco Method."

53. http://www.sec.gov/answers/form8k.htm

54. http://investor.shareholder.com/seagate/secfiling.cfm?filingid=1104659-11-55849&cik=1137789

55. http://www.sec.gov/answers/form8k.htm

56. http://www.sec.gov/News/Speech/Detail/Speech/1370539878806#.VIHCV2NHCbQ

57. The US Supreme Court has stated that a fact is not material merely because a shareholder might find it important. A fact is material if "there is a substantial likelihood that a reasonable shareholder would consider it important in deciding how to vote." See *TSC Industries, Inc. et al. v. Northway, Inc. 426 US 438 (1976)*.

58. http://www.continuityinsights.com/sites/continuityinsights.com/files/legacyfiles/Microsoft%20PowerPoint%20-%20A3%20Raso.pdf

59. Luu, "The Cisco Method."

60. Interview with Jim Holko, July 31, 2012.

61. http://www.usresilienceproject.org/pdfs/USRP_Priorities_Final_020112.pdf

62. Adam Smith, "The Cost of Europe Volcanic-Ash Travel Crisis," *Time*, April 20, 2010, http://www.time.com/time/business/article/0,8599,1983169,00.html

63. http://www.propertycasualty360.com/2012/11/26/pocket-size-risk-tools-10-apps-for-risk-managers

64. http://www.quantivate.com/app.php

65. http://www.esi911.com/esi/index.php/products-mainmenu-68

66. Gerald Baron, "Online Team Communications Gets Easier," *Emergency Management*, April 26, 2012, http://www.emergencymgmt.com/emergency-blogs/crisis-comm/Online-team-collaboration-gets-042612.html

67. http://www.continuityinsights.com/sites/continuityinsights.com/files/legacyfiles/Microsoft%20PowerPoint%20-%20A3%20Raso.pdf

68. Leemhorst and Crippa, "Do or Die."

69. http://www.google.com/search?q=solar+powered+Wifi+repeater

70. Ravi Anupindi, *Supply Chain Risk Management at Cisco: Response to H1N1*, case 1-428-881, March 7, 2011.

71. Ibid.

72. Ibid.

73. Luu, "The Cisco Method."

74. Michael Barbaro and Justin Gillis, "Wal-Mart at Forefront of Hurricane Relief," *Washington Post*, September 6, 2005.

75. Ibid.

76. Debra van Opstal, "Transform. The Resilient Economy: Integrating Competitiveness and Security," Council on Competitiveness, July 2007. http://www.nyu
.edu/intercep/research/pubs/annotated-business-case_20-aug-2007.pdf

77. Barbaro and Gillis, "Wal-Mart at Forefront of Hurricane Relief."

Chapter 7

1. BCI Supply Chain Resilience 2011. http://www.zurichna.com/internet/zna/sitecollectiondocuments/en/corporatebusiness/riskengineering/supply_chain_resilience_2011.pdf. Unfortunately, later surveys did not probe this issue.

2. Boston Scientific presentation at MIT CTL, "Crossroads," March 26, 2009.

3. Zurich, "Avoiding the Pitfalls of Supply Chain Disruptions," Insights, Supply Chain Risks: Issue 2011 http://www.zurich.com/internet/main/SiteCollectionDocuments/products-and-services/SCI_Risk_Insight_WSJ_articles.pdf

4. Kevin Harrington and John O'Connor, "How Cisco Succeeds," *Supply Chain Management Review*, July/August 2009, http://www.imperiallogistics.co.za/documents/06.HowCiscoSucceeds_.pdf

5. http://www.resilinc.com

6. http://www.razient.com/

7. http://sourcemap.com/

8. Boston Scientific Presentation "Boston Scientific Corporation (BSC) Supplier Risk Management Program" in Northeast Supply Chain Conference, October 1, 2007, http://www.nescon.org/docs/2007/3A-Weinstein-Millson--Kalfopoulos.pdf

9. http://www.greenpeace.org/kitkat

10. Jeremiah Owyang, "Greenpeace Vs. Brands: Social Media Attacks To Continue," *Forbes*, July 19, 2010, http://www.forbes.com/2010/07/19/greenpeace-bp-nestle-twitter-facebook-forbes-cmo-network-jeremiah-owyang.html

11. The Economist, "The Other Oil Spill," June 24, 2010, http://www.economist.com/node/16423833

12. http://forestethics.org/tar-sands

13. http://www.forbes.com/sites/amywestervelt/2011/08/17/the-big-pr-lesson-companies-still-need-to-learn-about-facebook/

14. C. Blome and T. Schönherr, "Supply Risk Management in Financial Crises—A Multiple Case-Study Approach, *International Journal of Production Economics* 134, no. 1: 43–57.

15. Zurich, "Avoiding the Pitfalls of Supply Chain Disruptions," *Insights, Supply Chain Risks:* Issue 2011, http://www.zurich.com/internet/main/SiteCollectionDocuments/products-and-services/SCI_Risk_Insight_WSJ_articles.pdf

16. Kevin Harrington and John O'Connor, "How Cisco Succeeds," *Supply Chain Management Review*, July/August 2009, http://www.imperiallogistics.co.za/documents/06.HowCiscoSucceeds_.pdf

17. Zurich, "Avoiding the Pitfalls of Supply Chain Disruptions," *Insights, Supply Chain Risks:* Issue 2011, http://www.zurich.com/internet/main/SiteCollectionDocuments/products-and-services/SCI_Risk_Insight_WSJ_articles.pdf

18. Mike Kalfopoulos, presentation at MIT CTL, "Crossroads," March 26, 2009.

19. http://www.zurichna.com/internet/zna/SiteCollectionDocuments/en/corporatebusiness/Supply%20Chain/10-0894_FINAL_W%20Supply%20Chain%20Guide.pdf

20. http://www.annualreport2012.philips.com/annual_report_2012/en/sustainability_statements/supplier_indicators.aspx

21. http://www.supplybusiness.com/debates/executive-debate-supply-base-consolidation-how-far-is-too-far/

22. Zurich, "Avoiding the Pitfalls of Supply Chain Disruptions," *Insights, Supply Chain Risks*: Issue 2011 http://www.zurich.com/internet/main/SiteCollectionDocuments/products-and-services/SCI_Risk_Insight_WSJ_articles.pdf

23. http://graphics.eiu.com/upload/eb/Oracle_Supply_Chain_WEB.pdf

24. Economist Intelligence Unit, *Resilient Supply Chains in a Time of Uncertainty*. 2010, http://www.m2mevolution.com/conference/east-13/presentations/oracle_supply_chain_web.pdf

25. http://online.wsj.com/article/SB10001424127887323415304578369403991284398.html

26. http://graphics.eiu.com/upload/eb/Oracle_Supply_Chain_WEB.pdf

27. The Economist Intelligence Unit, *Resilient Supply Chains in a Time of Uncertainty.*

28. Ibid.

29. Ibid.

30. http://www.autonews.com/apps/pbcs.dll/article?AID=/20110419/BLOG06/110419849/1503&template=printart

31. http://press.ihs.com/sites/ihs.newshq.businesswire.com/files/2011-09-06_HDD_Market_Share_0.jpg

32. http://thoughtleadership.aonbenfield.com/Documents/20120314_impact_forecasting_thailand_flood_event_recap.pdf

33. http://www.digitimes.com/news/a20111117PD210.html

34. http://news.techworld.com/personal-tech/3320401/thailand-floods-hard-drive-shortage-makes-small-pc-makers-hike-prices/

35. http://www.digitimes.com/news/a20111127PD201.html

36. See the full story in Sheffi, *The Resilient Enterprise*.

37. http://www.mwpvl.com/html/walmart.html

38. http://www.us.am.joneslanglasalle.com/Lists/ExpertiseInAction/Attachments/108/SupplyChain_%20eBulletin_final.pdf

39. http://www.bbc.co.uk/news/business-12891710

40. Interview with Tim Griffin, General Manager of Flextronics's Milipas Operations, July 31, 2012.

41. Interview with Mike Lypka, Director, Powertrain/GMCH Supply Chain at GM, August 3, 2012.

42. http://www.plasticsnews.com/article/20120418/NEWS/304189961/nylon-12-shortage-creates-opportunities-for-material-substitution

43. http://www.ism.ws/files/RichterAwards/CiscoSubmissionSupportDoc2012.pdf

44. James Healy, "6 Chrysler Recalls: Airbag Lights, Brakes, Fuel Tubes," *USA Today*, April 9, 2013, http://www.usatoday.com/story/money/cars/2013/04/09/chrysler-300-dodge-charger-challenger-recall-airbag/2067947/

45. http://us.mobile.reuters.com/article/Deals/idUSTRE73K08C20110421?irpc=932

46. http://www.supplybusiness.com/debates/executive-debate-supply-base-consolidation-how-far-is-too-far/

47. http://www.unido.org/fileadmin/import/29959_CSR.pdf

48. Interview with Patrick McGivern, senior vice president of global supply chain at Verifone, July 30, 2012.

49. Colum Murphy, Joseph White and Jake Maxwell Watts, "GM Doesn't Plan to Change Supply-Chain Safety Process," *Wall Street Journal*, August 5, 2014.

50. https://supplier.intel.com/static/bc/considerations.htm

51. Tony Sundermeier, "Simulating Disruption to Business Recovery," presentation at MIT CTL, "At the Crossroads of Supply Chain and Strategy: Simulating Disruption to Business Recovery," April 11, 2006.

52. https://supplier.intel.com/static/bc/

53. Kevin Harrington and John O'Connor, "How Cisco Succeeds," *Supply Chain Management Review*, July/August 2009, http://www.imperiallogistics.co.za/documents/06.HowCiscoSucceeds_.pdf

54. BCI 2009 Survey, http://www.bcifiles.com/BCISupplyChainResilienceSurvey2009MainReport2.pdf

55. BCI 2011 Survey, http://www.zurichna.com/internet/zna/sitecollectiondocuments/en/corporatebusiness/riskengineering/supply_chain_resilience_2011.pdf

56. Dan Miklovic and Roberta Witty, *Case Study: Cisco Addresses Supply Chain Risk Management*. Gartner Industry Research, September 17, 2010.

57. BCI 2011 Survey, http://www.zurichna.com/internet/zna/sitecollectiondocuments/en/corporatebusiness/riskengineering/supply_chain_resilience_2011.pdf

58. http://globalens.com/DocFiles/PDF/cases/inspection/GL1428881I.pdf

59. Rebecca Ellinor, "BA Joins Fight for Suppliers," *Supply Management*, February 14, 2008, http://www.supplymanagement.com/news/2008/ba-joins-fight-for-suppliers/

60. http://www.supplybusiness.com/debates/executive-debate-supply-base-consolidation-how-far-is-too-far/

61. Rebecca Ellinor, "BA Joins Fight for Suppliers," *Supply Management*, February 14, 2008, http://www.supplymanagement.com/news/2008/ba-joins-fight-for-suppliers/

62. Jerome Chandler, "Thrust Alignment," *Air Transport World*, March 31, 2008, http://atwonline.com/operations/thrust-alignment

63. http://www.supplybusiness.com/debates/executive-debate-supply-base-consolidation-how-far-is-too-far/

64. https://www.ism.ws/files/Pubs/Proceedings/BBBew.pdf

65. http://www.supplymanagement.com/news/2014/strong-supplier-relationships-leads-to-higher-profitability

66. http://www.cnn.com/2013/02/09/world/europe/uk-horsemeat-probe/index.html

67. Greg Weston, "Canada Dismisses U.S. Concern Over Fake Chinese Military Parts" CBS News, Jun 11, 2012 http://www.cbc.ca/news/politics/canada-dismisses-u-s-concern-over-fake-chinese-military-parts-1.1157278

68. http://manufacturing-geek.com/electronics/2012/11/coming-revolution-preventing-counterfeit-electronics/

69. http://www.cbsnews.com/8301-202_162-57569474/

70. http://www.bbc.co.uk/news/world-europe-21501568

71. Stephen Castle, "Iglo and Birds Eye Pull Meat After Finding Horse Meat," *New York Times*, February 22, 2013.

72. http://www.bbc.co.uk/news/world-21453370

73. Anna Molin and John Stoll, "Ikea's Iconic Meatball Drawn Into Horse-Meat Scandal," *Wall Street Journal*, February 25, 2013.

74. http://www.bbc.co.uk/news/world-europe-21501568

75. http://www.theguardian.com/world/2013/feb/08/how-horsemeat-scandal-unfolded-timeline

76. http://www.theguardian.com/uk/2013/mar/01/horsemeat-taco-bell-with draws-beef-uk

77. Nicola Clark and Stephen Castle, "Anger Flares in Europe as Scandal Over Meat Widens," *New York Times*, February 11, 2013.

78. http://www.independent.co.uk/news/uk/home-news/horsemeat-found-in -british-supermarkets-may-be-donkey-8489030.html

79. http://www.bbc.co.uk/news/world-europe-21501568

80. Neil Buckley, "Romania Hits Back over Horsemeat Scandal," *The Financial Times*, Feb 11, 2013, http://www.ft.com/intl/cms/s/0/6b4c75ce-7465-11e2-b323 -00144feabdc0.html#axzz3I9kPtOI0

81. Ibid.

82. http://www.couriermail.com.au/news/breaking-news/german-horsemeat -scandal-traced-to-poland/story-e6freoo6-1226584628884

83. James Meikle and Simon Naville, "Horsemeat Scandal: Welsh Firm Recalls Burgers after Tests Show Illicit Meat," *Guardian*, February 21, 2013.

84. Jens Hansegard, "A Horse Is a Horse—But Not in IKEA Meatballs, *Wall Street Journal*, December 26, 2013, http://online.wsj.com/news/articles/SB10001 424052702304854804579236373135317120

85. http://www.gpo.gov/fdsys/pkg/CRPT-112srpt167/pdf/CRPT-112srpt167 .pdf

86. http://www.gpo.gov/fdsys/pkg/CRPT-112srpt167/pdf/CRPT-112srpt167 .pdf

87. http://www.cbc.ca/news/politics/fake-parts-in-hercules-aircraft-called-a -genuine-risk-1.1345862

88. http://www.gpo.gov/fdsys/pkg/CHRG-112shrg72702/html/CHRG -112shrg72702.htm

89. http://www.gpo.gov/fdsys/pkg/CRPT-112srpt167/pdf/CRPT-112srpt167 .pdf

90. http://www.gpo.gov/fdsys/pkg/CHRG-112shrg72702/pdf/CHRG -112shrg72702.pdf

91. http://www.gpo.gov/fdsys/pkg/CRPT-112srpt167/pdf/CRPT-112srpt167 .pdf

92. http://www.gpo.gov/fdsys/pkg/CHRG-112shrg72702/pdf/CHRG -112shrg72702.pdf

93. http://www.gpo.gov/fdsys/pkg/CHRG-112shrg72702/pdf/CHRG -112shrg72702.pdf

94. "Senate Armed Services Committee Releases Report on Counterfeit Electronic Parts," May 21, 2012 http://www.armed-services.senate.gov/press-releases/senate-armed-services-committee-releases-report-on-counterfeit-electronic-parts

95. "Senate Armed Services Committee Releases Report on Counterfeit Electronic Parts," May 21, 2012 http://www.armed-services.senate.gov/

press-releases/senate-armed-services-committee-releases-report-on-counterfeit-electronic-parts

96. Caroline Winter, "How the Pentagon Is Using DNA to Combat Counterfeiters," *BloombergBusinessweek*, August 14, 2013, http://www.businessweek.com/articles/2013-08-14/how-the-pentagon-is-using-dna-to-combat-counterfeiters#r=shared

97. Greg Weston, "Canada dismisses U.S. concern over fake Chinese military parts" CBS News, Jun 11, 2012 http://www.cbc.ca/news/politics/canada-dismisses-u-s-concern-over-fake-chinese-military-parts-1.1157278

98. Winter, "How the Pentagon Is Using DNA to Combat Counterfeiters."

99. http://www.cbc.ca/m/touch/news/story/1.1157278

100. http://www.highbeam.com/doc/1G1-146197861.html

101. IHS Press Release, "One of Every Two Counterfeit Parts is Obsolete—But Managing Obsolescence Is Not Enough," June 11, 2012, http://press.ihs.com/press
-release/design-supply-chain/one-every-two-counterfeit-parts-obsolete-managing-obsolescence-no

102. James Carbone, "Most Counterfeit Parts Involve Obsolete Semiconductors and Other EOL Components," *The Source*, August 2012, http://www.eciaonline.org/documents/August2012.pdf

103. "Most Counterfeit Parts Involve Obsolete Semiconductors and ECIA," http://www.docstoc.com/docs/131368522/Most-Counterfeit-Parts-Involve-obsolete
-Semiconductors-and-ECIA

104. "One of Every Two Counterfeit Parts is Obsolete," *Integrated Circuit Electronics*, June 12, 2012

105. http://www.electronicsweekly.com/news/business/counterfeits-driven-by-obsolete-parts-says-ihs-2012-06/

106. http://eur-lex.europa.eu/LexUriServ/LexUriServ.do?uri=OJ:L:2003:037:0019:0023:EN:PDF

107. http://www.slideshare.net/rorykingihs/security-economics-technology-and-the-sustainability-paradox (slide #7).

108. IHS Press Release, "One of Every Two Counterfeit Parts is Obsolete—But Managing Obsolescence Is Not Enough," June 11, 2012, http://press.ihs.com/press-release/design-supply-chain/one-every-two-counterfeit-parts-obsolete—-managing
-obsolescence-no

109. Ibid.

110. Ibid

111. Carbone, "Most Counterfeit parts Involve Obsolete Semiconductors and Other EOL Components."

112. http://www.electronicsnews.com.au/features/countering-counterfeits

113. http://www.adnas.com/signature-dna-marking-authentication-for-anticounterfeiting-diversion-security

114. Caroline Winter, "How the Pentagon Is Using DNA to Combat Counterfeiters, *BloombergBusinessweek*, August 14, 2013, http://www.businessweek.com/articles/2013-08-14/how-the-pentagon-is-using-dna-to-combat-counter feiters#r=shared

115. Ibid.

116. http://www.who.int/impact/events/IMPACT-ACTechnologiesv3LIS.pdf

117. http://www.bbc.co.uk/news/world-europe-21501568

118. http://www.examiner.com/article/birds-eye-and-taco-bell-now-involved-horse-meat-scandal

119. http://www.e-certa.com/assets/counterfeit-symposium-paper.pdf.

120. http://www.gscreview.com/feb10_john_interview.php

121. http://www.gscreview.com/feb10_john_interview.php

Chapter 8

1. http://www.craneaccidents.com/2008/05/report/three-injured-two-critically-in-black-thunder-crane-accident/

2. http://trib.com/special_breaking_news/three-injured-two-critically-in-black-thunder-crane-accident/article_09ba2344-f94f-5e66-822b-8cc1cd9a6f8a.html

3. http://skywarn.org/about/

4. http://www.aoml.noaa.gov/hrd/tcfaq/E11.html

5. http://www.goes.noaa.gov/

6. http://www.nwas.org/committees/rs/radar.html

7. http://www.noaa.gov/features/02_monitoring/weather_stations.html

8. http://skywarn.org/about/].

9. UPS Logistics - http://thenewlogistics.ups.com/customers/ontime-delivery/

10. A. Pawlowski, "UPS, Fedex Meteorologists get Your Packages to You on Time," *USA Today*, December 20, 2012, http://www.today.com/money/ups-fedex-meteorologists-get-your-packages-you-time-1C7695990

11. UPS Logistics - http://thenewlogistics.ups.com/customers/ontime-delivery/

12. http://www.esi911.com/esi/index.php/products-mainmenu-68/resources-mainmenu-105/doc_download/52-walgreens-gains-real-time-awareness-of-more-than-8-000-stores

13. http://www.esi911.com/esi/index.php/products-mainmenu-68/resources-mainmenu-105/doc_download/52-walgreens-gains-real-time-awareness-of-more-than-8-000-stores

14. http://www.sec.gov/about/laws/wallstreetreform-cpa.pdf

15. http://www.flextronics.com/supplier/supplierquality/Files/Conflict%20 Minerals%20Supplier%20Training.pdf

16. http://www.whitehouse.gov/the-press-office/proclamation-address-market -disruption-imports-certain-passenger-vehicle-and-light-

17. http://www.businessinsider.com/china-announces-another-massive-cut-in -rare-earth-exports-2011-12

18. "The Hidden Persuaders," *Economist*, October 12, 2013, http://www. economist
.com/node/21587381

19. http://cei.org/sites/default/files/Wayne%20Crews%20-%2010,000%20 Commandments%202013.pdf

20. http://www.poole.ncsu.edu/erm/index.php/articles/entry/regulatory-risk -cost/

21. Nghi Luu, presentation at MIT CTL, "Advancing Supply Chain Risk Management: Emerging Challenges and Strategies," October 10, 2012, in Cambridge, MA.

22. Ibid.

23. www.nc4.us

24. http://www.anvilgroup.com

25. http://www.ijet.com

26. https://www.osac.gov/Pages/Home.aspx

27. www.cargonet.com/⊠,

28. https://www.osac.gov/Pages/Home.aspx

29. http://www.nc4.us/RiskCenterStats.php

30. http://www.nc4.us/FI_Archived.php

31. http://www.nc4.us/riskcenter_security.php

32. http://www.cisco.com/web/strategy/docs/manufacturing/Cisco_Case_Study _AMR_10-0917.pdf

33. http://www.supplychainriskinsights.com/archive/scri-protection

34. Luu, presentation at MIT CTL, "Advancing Supply Chain Risk Management," on October 10, 2012.

35. http://www.nj.com/news/index.ssf/2012/10/gov_christie_blasts_ac_mayor_f .html

36. http://hw-lab.com/cougar-point-sandy-bridge-chipset-lineups.html

37. http://www.anandtech.com/show/4142/intel-discovers-bug-in-6series -chipset-begins-recall

38. http://www.anandtech.com/show/4142/intel-discovers-bug-in-6series -chipset-begins-recall

39. http://www.wired.com/2011/02/intels-chipset-fail/

40. http://www.notebookcheck.net/Intel-s-defective-Sandy-Bridge-Chipsets-Status-Report.45596.0.html

41. Verne Kopytoff, "Intel, Finding a Chip Flaw, Expect to Lose $1 Billion," *New York Times*, January 1, 2011.

42. http://seekingalpha.com/article/264363-intels-ceo-discusses-q1-2011-results-earnings-call-transcript?source=cc

43. http://www.utrechtlawreview.org/index.php/ulr/article/viewFile/URN%3ANBN%3ANL%3AUI%3A10-1-101040/21

44. http://www.fwi.co.uk/articles/12/11/2004/21719/dioxin-in-milk-scare-shuts-farms.htm

45. http://archive.newsweaver.com/fsai/newsweaver.ie/fsai/e_article00034042864e4.html?x=b11,0,w

46. http://ec.europa.eu/transparency/regcomitology/index.cfm?do=Search.getPDF&2ZAqunybzgEqS2dzX8g/PeCXCTkEMvjCaXWhWTT3prm5SVAw47eF02NzJJLXFBE77kGvLzo2Pu5uyjPyPE0HGhn1Yyu8a5hceFqN5ixnqYI=

47. http://ec.europa.eu/food/food/foodlaw/traceability/factsheet_trace_2007_en.pdf

48. http://archive.newsweaver.com/fsai/newsweaver.ie/fsai/e_article00034042864e4.html?x=b11,0,w

49. http://www.cdc.gov/foodsafety/facts.html#tracking

50. Cory Young, and Arhlene Flowers, "Fight Viral with Viral: A Case Study of Domino's Pizza's Crisis Communication Strategies." *Case Studies in Strategic Communication, 1*, article 6. 2012, Available online: http://cssc.uscannenberg.org/cases/v1/v1art6

51. GM Board Report, http://s3.documentcloud.org/documents/1183506/valukas-report-from-gm-redacted.txt

52. NHTSA Review http://energycommerce.house.gov/sites/republicans.energycommerce.house.gov/files/Hearings/OI/20140915GMFootnotes/NHTSAreportfinal.pdf

53. GM Board Report, http://s3.documentcloud.org/documents/1183506/valukas-report-from-gm-redacted.txt

54. NHTSA Review http://energycommerce.house.gov/sites/republicans.energycommerce.house.gov/files/Hearings/OI/20140915GMFootnotes/NHTSAreportfinal.pdf

55. http://www.npr.org/2014/03/31/297158876/timeline-a-history-of-gms-ignition-switch-defect

56. NHTSA Review http://energycommerce.house.gov/sites/republicans.energycommerce.house.gov/files/Hearings/OI/20140915GMFootnotes/NHTSAreportfinal.pdf

57. http://www.thecarconnection.com/news/1090367_2005-2007-chevrolet-cobalt-2007-pontiac-g5-recalled-for-faulty-ignition-switch

58. http://time.com/2819690/gm-recall-deaths-ignition-switch/

59. GM Board Report, http://s3.documentcloud.org/documents/1183506/valukas-report-from-gm-redacted.txt

60. http://www.ibtimes.com/ignition-switch-recall-only-1-5-cars-key-rotation-problem-are-covered-gm-compensation-fund-1694984

61. http://fortune.com/2014/09/25/chrysler-recalls-350000-cars-due-to-faulty-ignition-switch/

62. http://www.theverge.com/2014/6/30/5858108/gm-announces-it-will-recall-another-7-6-million-cars

63. http://www.businessweek.com/news/2014-04-06/gm-investors-unshaken-as-recall-cuts-3-billion-in-market-value

64. http://www.conflictfreesmelter.org/ConflictMineralsReportingTemplateDashboard.htm

65. http://www.flextronics.com/supplier/supplierquality/Files/Conflict%20Minerals%20Supplier%20Training.pdf

66. https://www.wewear.org/assets/1/7/ConflictMineralsGuideline_v2_May2013.pdf

67. http://ec.europa.eu/environment/forests/pdf/EUTR_Leaflet_EN.pdf

68. http://www.fda.gov/Food/GuidanceRegulation/FSMA/ucm270851.htm

69. US Government Publishing Office, "Public Law 113 - 54 - Drug Quality and Security Act" http://www.gpo.gov/fdsys/pkg/PLAW-113publ54/content-detail.html

70. http://www.resilinc.com/index.aspx

71. http://www.razient.com/

72. http://www.metricstream.com/solutions/supply_chain_risk_management.htm

73. Yossi Sheffi, Bindiya Vakil and Tim Griffin, "New Software Tools to Manage Risk and Disruptions: Part II" *Supply Chain Management Review*, March 29, 2012, http://www.scmr.com/article/new_software_tools_to_manage_risk_and_disruptions1/

74. http://www.cdcsoftware.com/en/Solutions/CDC-Event-Management-Framework-EMF/Solutions/Supply-Chain-Event-Management

75. http://www.manh.com/solutions/supply-chain-event-management

76. http://www.pwc.be/en/pharma/pdf/supply-chain-risk-assessment-PwC-09.pdf

77. http://www.jltgroup.com/Supply-Chain-Risk-Management/

78. http://usa.marsh.com/ProductsServices/MarshRiskConsulting.aspx

79. https://www.linkedin.com/company/capitol-risk-concepts-ltd.

80. http://www.lmi.org/Services/Logistics-%281%29/Planning/Supply-Chain-Risk-Mitigation.aspx

81. Mike Kalfopoulos, Senior Manager, Global Sourcing at Boston Scientific, presentation at MIT CTL, "Crossroads," March 26, 2009.

82. http://www.turnaround.org/Publications/Articles.aspx?objectID=6850

83. MIT CTL, "Crossroads," March 26, 2009.

84. Naturally, if the supplier is a public company, they cannot release meaningful financial data before its time. This works better with private companies, which many suppliers are, even though the early data may be subject to revisions.

85. http://www.nexis.co.uk/pdf/LexisNexis_Early_Warning_Investigation.pdf

86. http://www.turnaround.org/Publications/Articles.aspx?objectID=6850

87. MIT CTL, "Advancing Supply Chain Risk Management," October 10, 2012.

88. http://www.supplychainmovement.com/wp-content/uploads/Supply-Chain-Movement-Quarterly-No3-2011.pdf

89. MIT CTL, "Advancing Supply Chain Risk Management," October 10, 2012.

90. MIT CTL, "Crossroads," March 26, 2009.

91. http://report.basf.com/2012/en/managementsanalysis/responsibilityalongthevaluechain/supplychainmanagement/print.html

92. en.wikipedia.org/wiki/Melamine.

93. http://www.ncbi.nlm.nih.gov/pubmed/17823396

94. http://www.cbsnews.com/8301-504763_162-57466913-10391704/u.n-panel-sets-limits-for-chemical-melamine-in-infant-milk-following-2008-china-scandal/

95. http://www.law.uh.edu/healthlaw/perspectives/2008/(SB)%20heparin.pdf

96. Jacob Goldstein, "Heparin Likely Cut with Cheap Counterfeit Ingredient," *Wall Street Journal Health Blog*, March 19, 2008, http://blogs.wsj.com/health/2008/03/19/heparin-likely-cut-with-cheap-counterfeit-ingredient/?mod

97. Walt Bogdanich, "F.D.A. Tracked Poisoned Drugs but Trail Went Cold in China," *New York Times*, June 17, 2007, http://www.nytimes.com/2007/06/17/health/17poison.html?pagewanted=all&_r=0

98. http://www.verisk.com/

99. http://www.supplychainbrain.com/content/general-scm/sc-security-risk-mgmt/single-article-page/article/using-data-to-mitigate-risk-and-build-supply-chain-resiliency-1

100. http://www.cisco.com/web/strategy/docs/manufacturing/Cisco_Case_Study_AMR_10-0917.pdf

101. http://www.spc.noaa.gov/products/outlook/archive/2012/day2otlk_20120413_0600.html

102. http://www.srh.noaa.gov/oun/?n=events-20120413-norman

103. http://enterprisesolutions.accuweather.com/assets/documents/AccuWeather_Success_Better_Radar__Better_Tornado_Tracking.pdf

104. http://enterprisesolutions.accuweather.com/assets/documents/AccuWeather_Success_BNSF_Receives_41_Minutes_Advance_Tornado.pdf

105. http://www.senseaware.com/what-is-senseaware/

106. http://www.mckinsey.com/insights/high_tech_telecoms_internet/the_internet_of_things

107. http://www.schneider.com/groups/public/@marketing-public/documents/document/prd006124.htm

108. http://fleet.omnitracs.com/rs/omnitracsllc1/images/LCL1135_11-13_TT210_Brochure.pdf

109. Sheffi, *The Resilient Enterprise.*

110. https://www.abiresearch.com/press/45-million-windows-phone-and-20-million-blackberry

111. http://mobiledeviceinsight.com/2011/12/sensors-in-smartphones/]

112. http://www.consumerreports.org/cro/news/2011/08/irene-disaster-recovery-there-are-smartphone-apps-for-that/index.htm

113. http://www.capgemini-consulting.com/sites/default/files/resource/pdf/Global_Supply_Chain_Control_Towers.pdf

114. http://www.amberroad.com/pdf/June-2013-JOC-Control-Towers.pdf

115. http://www.dinalog.nl/en/themes/4c__cross_chain_control_center/

116. Greg Johnsen, "Your Global Supply Chain Control Tower Has A Memory," Supply Chain Digest, February 25, 2010, http://www.scdigest.com/assets/Experts/Guest_10-02-25.php and Richard Strollo, "The Rise of Global Controls Towers, Logistics Insight Asia, June 1, 2014, http://www.logasiamag.com/article/the-rise
-of-global-control-towers/3987

117. http://info.e2open.com/rs/e2open/images/WP_E2open_ControlTower.pdf

118. http://www.rfidjournal.net/masterPresentations/rfid_live2012/np/casto_apr4_220_enhancVis_Trac.pdf

119. William Tate and Mark Abkwitz, "Emerging Technologies Applicable to Hazardous Materials Transportation Safety and Security" *Hazardous Materials Cooperative Research Program Report* #4, Washington, DC: TRB, 2011. http://onlinepubs.trb.org/onlinepubs/hmcrp/hmcrp_rpt_004.pdf

120. MIT CTL, "Advancing Supply Chain Risk Management," October 10, 2012.

121. http://newsfeed.time.com/2013/03/25/more-people-have-cell-phones-than-toilets-u-n-study-shows/

122. http://www.bloomberg.com/news/2012-08-31/twitter-beats-u-s-geological-survey-to-philippines-quake-news.html

123. http://www.slideshare.net/USArmySocialMedia/army-social-media-handbook-2011

124. http://connectedcops.net/2013/07/18/social-media-is-the-new-face-of-disaster-response/

125. http://seeclickfix.com

126. http://wis.ewi.tudelft.nl/twitcident/

127. http://www.newscientist.com/blogs/onepercent/2012/04/making-twitter-make-sense-for.html

128. http://www.digitaltrends.com/social-media/how-on-earth-can-twitter-fight-fires-save-you-from-earthquakes-or-find-help-during-hurricanes/

129. http://mashable.com/2010/12/08/dell-social-listening-center/

130. http://socialaxis.wordpress.com/2012/05/15/how-dell-reinvented-itself-thanks-to-social-media/

131. http://www.cmo.com/articles/2011/2/23/listen-up-dell-lends-its-ear-to-social-media.html

132. http://www.idfblog.com/facts-figures/rocket-attacks-toward-israel/

133. http://www.haaretz.com/business/1.549524

134. http://static1.businessinsider.com/image/4fe4dec26bb3f7267800000a-480/iron-dome.jpg

135. http://en.wikipedia.org/wiki/Reverse_911

136. http://www.missionmode.com/solutions/emergency_notification/technical.htm

137. http://emcomus.org/index1.html

138. http://earthquake.usgs.gov/earthquakes/ted/

139. USGS, Earthquake Notification Service, https://sslearthquake.usgs.gov/ens/

140. http://en.wikipedia.org/wiki/Earthquake_Early_Warning_(Japan)

141. http://en.wikipedia.org/wiki/P-wave

142. Jane Lee, "How do Earthquake Early Warning Systems Work?" *National Geographic*, September 27, 2013, http://news.nationalgeographic.com/news/2013/09/130927-earthquake-early-warning-system-earth-science/

143. http://www.jma.go.jp/jma/en/Activities/eew2.html

144. http://www.scientificamerican.com/article.cfm?id=tsunami-seconds-before-the-big-one&page=3

145. http://en.wikipedia.org/wiki/Tsunami_warning_system

146. Thomas Choi and Tom Linton, "Don't Let Your Supply Chain Control Your Business," *Harvard Business Review*, December 2011, http://hbr.org/2011/12/dont-let-your-supply-chain-control-your-business/ar/

Chapter 9

1. Business Continuity Institute, "Supply Chain Resilience, BCI Survey Report" 2009, 2010, 2011, 2012.

2. Council on Competitiveness, "The Resilient Economy: Integrating Competitiveness and Security," 2007 www.tisp.org/index.cfm?pk=download&id=11018&pid=10261

3. http://spectrum.ieee.org/telecom/security/the-real-story-of-stuxnet

4. Robert McMillan, Siemens: "Stuxnet Worm Hit Industrial Systems," *Computerworld*, September 14, 2010, http://www.computerworld.com/s/article/9185419/Siemens_Stuxnet_worm_hit_industrial_systems?taxonomyId=142&pageNumber=1

5. Joseph Gross, "A Declaration of Cyber-War," *Vanity Fair*, April 2011, http://www.vanityfair.com/culture/features/2011/04/stuxnet-201104

6. http://blogs.wsj.com/cio/2012/11/08/stuxnet-infected-chevrons-it-network/

7. http://www.symantec.com/content/en/us/enterprise/media/security_response/whitepapers/w32_stuxnet_dossier.pdf

8. Robert O'Harrow, "Tridium's Niagara Framework: Marvel of Connectivity Illustrates New Cyber Risks," *Washington Post,* July 11, 2012.

9. Ibid.

10. Ibid.

11. http://www.informationweek.com/security/attacks/zombie-hackers-exploited-emergency-alert/240148682

12. Andrew Bagrin, "What Will 2015 Bring for Cybersecurity?" Wired Innovation Insights, December 30, 2014 http://insights.wired.com/profiles/blogs/what-will-2015-bring-for-cyber-security#ixzz3U5auW8lU

13. http://www.usatoday.com/story/tech/personal/2013/11/12/iphone-hack-while-charging/3505753/

14. http://www.wired.com/2014/07/usb-security/

15. Antone Gonsalves "Georgia Tech Warns of Emerging Threats in Cloud, Mobile," CSO, Nov 8, 2013 http://www.csoonline.com/article/2134150/network-security/georgia-tech-warns-of-emerging-threats-in-cloud--mobile.html

16. http://investors.target.com/phoenix.zhtml?c=65828&p=irol-newsArticle&ID=1903678&highlight=

17. http://op.bna.com/der.nsf/id/sbay-9hktrf/$File/Rockefeller%20report%20on%20Target%20breach.pdf

18. http://krebsonsecurity.com/tag/fazio-mechanical-services/

19. http://www.reuters.com/article/2014/02/05/us-target-breach-vendor-idUSBREA1425O20140205

20. http://faziomechanical.com/Target-Breach-Statement.pdf

21. http://www.reuters.com/article/2014/02/05/us-target-breach-vendor-idUSBREA1425O20140205

22. http://krebsonsecurity.com/2014/02/target-hackers-broke-in-via-hvac-company/

23. http://krebsonsecurity.com/2014/01/new-clues-in-the-target-breach/

24. http://www.seculert.com/blog/2014/01/pos-malware-targeted-target.html

25. Monica Langley, "Inside Target: CEO Gregg Steinhafel Struggles to Contain Giant Cybertheft," *Wall Street Journal*, February 18, 2014.

26. http://krebsonsecurity.com/2013/12/cards-stolen-in-target-breach-flood-underground-markets/

27. Langley, "Inside Target."

28. http://investors.target.com/phoenix.zhtml?c=65828&p=irol-newsArticle&ID=1903678&highlight=

29. Ibid.

30. http://news.yahoo.com/data-breach-costs-toll-target-profit-123047290--finance.html

31. http://www.cbanet.org/News%20and%20Media/Press%20Releases%202014/02182014_pressrelease.aspx

32. Langley, "Inside Target."

33. http://www.supermoney.com/2013/12/target-faces-potential-3-6-billion-liability-credit-card-breach/#.UriH-2RDtdE

34. http://www.safenet-inc.com/news/2014/breach-level-index-q2-375-million-data-records-lost-stolen-2014/

35. Ellen Nakashima, "DHS Contractor Suffers Major Computer Breach, officials say," *Washington Post*, August 6, 2014.

36. Nicole Perlroth, "Hackers Lurking in Vents and Soda Machines," *New York Times*, April 7, 2014.

37. Ibid.

38. Tim Worstall, "Analyzing Friday's Google Outage," *Forbes*, August 8, 2013, http://www.forbes.com/sites/timworstall/2013/08/19/analysing-fridays-google-outage/

39. https://engineering.gosquared.com/googles-downtime-40-drop-in-traffic

40. http://www.google.com/intl/en/about/products/

41. http://www.slashgear.com/expired-ssl-certificate-causes-microsoft-azure-outages-23270828/

42. http://www.theregister.co.uk/2013/10/30/windows_azure_global_fail/

43. http://www.informationweek.com/news/cloud-computing/infrastructure/240002170?google_editors_picks=true

44. Cisco Annual Security Report, 2013, https://www.cisco.com/web/offer/gist_ty2_asset/Cisco_2013_ASR.pdf

45. Georgia Tech Information Security Center, Emerging Cyber Threats Reports, 2014, http://www.gtsecuritysummit.com/2014Report.pdf

46. http://blogs.cisco.com/security/byod-many-call-it-bring-your-own-malware-byom/

47. http://www.mobilepaymentstoday.com/article/219713/Mobile-malware-to-have-doubled-in-2013-says-McAfee

48. http://www.trendmicro.com/cloud-content/us/pdfs/business/reports/rpt_implementing_byod_plans.pdf

49. http://www.scmagazine.com/android-malware-spreads-via-mail-tracking-sms-spam/article/364236/

50. http://www.trendmicro.com/cloud-content/us/pdfs/business/reports/rpt_implementing_byod_plans.pdf

51. https://www.securelist.com/en/analysis/204792326/Mobile_Malware_Evolution_2013

52. Jeff Drew, "Managing Cybersecurity Risks," *Journal of Accountancy* July 31, 2012 http://www.journalofaccountancy.com/Issues/2012/Aug/20125900.htm

53. https://www.securelist.com/en/analysis/204792326/Mobile_Malware_Evolution_2013

54. http://www.networkworld.com/news/2012/112912-cisco-csirt-264643.html?page=1

55. http://www.computerworld.com/s/article/9241352/Researchers_reveal_methods_behind_car_hack_at_Defcon][http://illmatics.com/car_hacking.pdf

56. http://www.ibtimes.com/car-hacking-white-paper-released-darpa-funded-researchers-shows-how-hack-ford-escape-toyota-prius

57. http://www.digitaltrends.com/range-reviews/dacor-discovery-iq-wall-oven-review/

58. http://www.digitaltrends.com/home/wemo-crock-pot-adds-smart-features-slow-cooker/

59. http://www.cnet.com/products/samsung-4-5-cu-ft-front-load-washer-w-vrt-plus-white/

60. http://www.globaltoynews.com/2013/12/for-cyber-monday-a-connected-toys-round-up-a-guide-to-whats-available-and-whats-coming-.html

61. http://www.kb.cert.org/vuls/id/656302

62. http://en.wikipedia.org/wiki/Heartbleed

63. http://www.zdnet.com/belkin-patches-vulnerabilities-in-wemo-devices-7000026499/

64. http://www.truckinginfo.com/channel/fleet-management/article/story/2014/02/pushing-the-telematics-boundaries.aspx

65. Abel Sanchez, "Cyber Security," presentation at MIT CTL's roundtable, "Supply Chain Visualization Analytics," June 27, 2013, in Cambridge, MA.

66. Cisco Annual Security Report, 2013, https://www.cisco.com/web/offer/gist_ty2
_asset/Cisco_2013_ASR.pdf

67. http://www.pcworld.com/article/2036177/one-in-five-data-breaches-are-the-result-of-cyberespionage-verizon-says.html

68. http://www.pcworld.com/article/2036177/one-in-five-data-breaches-are-the-result-of-cyberespionage-verizon-says.html

69. Michael Fitzgerald, "Organized Cybercrime Revealed," CSO, September 28, 2009 http://www.csoonline.com/article/2124411/malware-cybercrime/organized-cybercrime-revealed.html

70. http://en.wikipedia.org/wiki/Melissa_(computer_worm)

71. http://en.wikipedia.org/wiki/ILOVEYOU

72. http://en.wikipedia.org/wiki/Bagle_(computer_worm)]

73. Tom Simonite, "Welcome to the Maleware-Industrial Complex, *MIT Technology Review*, February 13, 2013

74. Michael Fitzgerald, "Organized Cybercrime Revealed," CSO, September 28, 2009 http://www.csoonline.com/article/2124411/malware-cybercrime/organized-cybercrime-revealed.html

75. https://scm.symantec.com/resources/b-symantec_report_on_attack_kits_and_malicious_websites_21169171_WP.en-us.pdf

76. http://news.cnet.com/8301-1009_3-10105963-83.html

77. Joseph Gross, "A Declaration of Cyber-War," *Vanity Fair*, April 2011, http://www.vanityfair.com/culture/features/2011/04/stuxnet-201104

78. Michael Fitzgerald, "Organized Cybercrime Revealed," *CSO Magazine*, September. 28, 2009. Accessed 03/19/2015. http://www.csoonline.com/article/2124411/malware-cybercrime/organized-cybercrime-revealed.html

79. http://www.bbc.co.uk/news/world-asia-china-21272613

80. http://en.wikipedia.org/wiki/Operation_Aurora

81. http://articles.washingtonpost.com/2010-01-14/news/36876544_1_cyber-intrusion-that-google-attributes-computer-attacks-china

82. http://www.informationweek.com/security/attacks/google-aurora-hack-was-chinese-counteres/240155268

83. Kim Zetter, "Google Hack Attack was Ultra Sophisticated, New Details Show," Wired Magazine, January 14, 2010, http://www.wired.com/threatlevel/2010/01/operation-aurora/

84. Ariana Eunjung and Ellen Nakashima, "Google China Cyberattack Part of Vast Espionage Campaign, Expert Say," *Washington Post*, January 14, 2010.

85. Kim Zetter, Google Hack Attack Was Ultra Sophisticated, New Details Show," *Wired*, January 14, 2010, http://www.wired.com/threatlevel/2010/01/operation-aurora/

86. http://intelreport.mandiant.com/Mandiant_APT1_Report.pdf

87. Ibid.

88. http://www.net-security.org/malware_news.php?id=2422

89. David Goldman, "Wake up, America! China Is Attacking," *CNN Money*, February 19, 2013, http://money.cnn.com/2013/02/19/technology/security/china-hacking-war/index.html

90. http://www.reuters.com/article/2012/06/17/us-media-tech-summit-cyber-strikeback-idUSBRE85G07S20120617

91. http://www.pcworld.com/article/2036177/one-in-five-data-breaches-are-the-result-of-cyberespionage-verizon-says.html

92. Ibid.

93. David Goldman, "Wake up, America! China is Attacking," *CNN Money*, February 19, 2013, http://money.cnn.com/2013/02/19/technology/security/china-hacking-war/index.html

94. http://www.bbc.co.uk/news/world-asia-china-21272613

95. http://www.securelist.com/en/blog/208193767/

96. Nicole Perlroth, "In Cyberattacks on Saudi Firm, U.S. Sees Iran Firing Back, *New York Times*, October 23, 2012

97. http://www.reuters.com/article/2013/08/29/us-syria-crisis-cyberspace-analysis-idUSBRE97S04Z20130829

98. David Sanger and Steven Erlanger, "Suspicion Falls on Russia as 'Snake' Cyberattacks Target Ukraine's Government," *New York Times*, March 8, 2014.

99. http://www.reuters.com/article/2013/02/24/us-cybersecurity-battle-idUSBRE91N03520130224

100. http://intelreport.mandiant.com/Mandiant_APT1_Report.pdf

101. http://www.theatlantic.com/technology/archive/2010/11/the-stuxnet-worm-more-than-30-people-built-it/66156/

102. http://www.economist.com/blogs/analects/2013/02/chinese-cyber-attacks

103. David Sanger, David Barboza, and Nicole Perlroth, "Chinese Army Unit is Seen as Tied to Hacking Against U.S.," *New York Times*, February 18, 2013.

104. http://www.economist.com/blogs/analects/2013/02/chinese-cyber-attacks

105. Ibid.

106. Nicole Perlroth and David Sanger, "Cyberattacks Seem Meant to Destroy, Not Just Disrupt," *New York Times*, March 28, 2013.

107. Joseph Gross, "A Declaration of Cyber-War," *Vanity Fair*, April 2011, http://www.vanityfair.com/culture/features/2011/04/stuxnet-201104

108. Nicole Perlroth and David Sanger, "Cyberattacks Seem Meant to Destroy, Not Just Disrupt," *New York Times*, March 28, 2013.

109. http://www.cnet.com/8301-1009_3-57501066-83/saudi-oil-firm-says-30000-computers-hit-by-virus/

110. Perlroth and Sanger, "Cyberattacks Seem Meant to Destroy, Not Just Disrupt."

111. Geoff Dyer, "Panetta warns US of 'Cyber Pearl Harbor,'" *Financial Times*, October 12, 2012.

112. Elizabeth Bumiller and Thom Shanker, "Panetta Warns of a Dire Threat of Cyberattacks on the U.S.," *New York Times*, October 11th, 2012.

113. http://secunia.com/vulnerability-review/vulnerability_update_all.html

114. Eric Hutchins, Michael Cloppert, and Rohan Amin, "Intelligence-Driven Computer Network Defense Informed by Analysis of Adversary Campaigns and

Intrusion Kill Chains," Lockheed Martin Corporation, ttp://www.lockheedmartin.com/content/dam/lockheed/data/corporate/documents/LM-White-Paper-Intel-Driven-Defense.pdf

115. Kelly Higgins, "How Lockheed Martin's 'Kill Chain' Stopped SecurID Attack," *InformationWeek*, February 12, 2013. http://www.darkreading.com/attacks-breaches/how-lockheed-martins-kill-chain-stopped-securid-attack/d/d-id/1139125?

116. Hutchins, Cloppert, and Amin, "Intelligence-Driven Computer Network Defense Informed by Analysis of Adversary Campaigns and Intrusion Kill Chains."

117. http://www.appliednsm.com/making-mandiant-apt1-report-actionable/

118. http://gigaom.com/2013/05/15/google-io-statshot-900-million-android-devices-activated/

119. http://www.theverge.com/2013/6/10/4415258/apple-announces-600-million-ios-devices-sold

120. https://www.securelist.com/en/analysis/204792326/Mobile_Malware_Evolution_2013

121. http://www.sophos.com/en-us/security-news-trends/security-trends/malware-goes-mobile/why-ios-is-safer-than-android.aspx

122. http://www.forbes.com/sites/timworstall/2013/06/27/googles-android-malware-problem-its-the-os-fragmentation-that-makes-it-so-bad/

123. http://www.csoonline.com/article/2134117/mobile-security/the-department-of-homeland-security-and-its-obsolete-android-os-problem.html

124. http://techcrunch.com/2014/03/23/mixpanel-ios-7-adoption-at-90-while-android-kit-kat-remains-at-under-10/

125. http://searchconsumerization.techtarget.com/feature/Mobile-device-security-policies-Asserting-control-over-mobile-devices

126. http://searchconsumerization.techtarget.com/tip/Remote-wipe-101-Policy-and-how-tos-for-protecting-mobile-data

127. http://technet.microsoft.com/en-us/library/dn283963.aspx

128. Geoffrey Fowler, "You Won't Believe How Adorable This Kitty Is! Click For More!," *Wall Street Journal*, March 26, 2013.

129. Ibid.

130. Supply Chain Leadership Council, Emerging Threats in the Supply Chain, 2013, http://www.scrlc.com/articles/Emerging_Risks_2013_feb_v10.pdf

131. Deloitte, "Aftershock: Adjusting to the New World of Risk Management" *Forbes*, June 2012, http://www.forbes.com/forbesinsights/risk_management_2012/index.html#sthash.41mnuy6L.zcBPrTfu.dpuf

132. Supply Chain Leadership Council, *Emerging Threats in the Supply Chain, 2013*, http://www.scrlc.com/articles/Emerging_Risks_2013_feb_v10.pdf

133. Joel Schectman, "Netflix Amazon Outage Shows Any Company Can Fail," *Wall Street Journal*, December 27, 2012, http://blogs.wsj.com/cio/2012/12/27/netflix-amazon-outage-shows-any-company-can-fail/

134. Forrester Research analyst Rachel Dines, cited in http://blogs.wsj.com/cio/2012/12/27/netflix-amazon-outage-shows-any-company-can-fail

135. Dan Raywood, "ENISA Organizes European Stress Test against DDoS Attacks," *SC Magazine*, October 5, 2012, http://www.scmagazineuk.com/enisa-organises-european-stress-test-against-ddos-attacks/article/262382/

136. http://en.wikipedia.org/wiki/White_hat_(computer_security)

137. Raywood, "ENISA Organizes European Stress Test against DDoS Attacks."

138. https://www.cs.purdue.edu/homes/fahmy/papers/catch.pdf

139. http://www.procurementleaders.com/news-archive/news-archive/european-banks-and-companies-warned-of-cyber-attacks-

140. http://www.reuters.com/article/2012/06/17/us-media-tech-summit-cyber-strikeback-idUSBRE85G07S20120617

141. http://venturebeat.com/2013/03/19/investors-clamber-to-back-fraud-fighting-startup-sift-science/

142. Kelly Higgins, "How Lockheed Martin's 'Kill Chain' Stopped SecurID Attack," *InformationWeek*, February 12, 2013, http://www.darkreading.com/attacks-breaches/how-lockheed-martins-kill-chain-stopped-securid-attack/d/d-id/1139125?

143. http://mobile.reuters.com/article/idUSBRE91N03520130224?irpc=932

144. Bruce Schneier, "The Story Behind the Stuxnet Virus," *Forbes*, October 7, 2010, http://www.forbes.com/2010/10/06/iran-nuclear-computer-technology-security
-stuxnet-worm.html

145. https://threatpost.com/microsoft-closes-door-stuxnet-december-patch-121410

146. http://www.esecurityplanet.com/windows-security/did-microsoft-improve-security-in-2012.html

147. http://technet.microsoft.com/en-us/security/dn436305

148. http://www.esecurityplanet.com/windows-security/did-microsoft-improve-security-in-2012.html

149. https://community.qualys.com/blogs/laws-of-vulnerabilities/2013/12/05/december-2013-patch-tuesday-preview

150. http://www.gfi.com/blog/security-patching-trends-for-major-software-vendors/

151. http://news.softpedia.com/newsTag/botched+update

152. http://nakedsecurity.sophos.com/2013/04/12/patch-tuesday-fatal-system-error/

153. http://www.computerworld.com/s/article/9153638/Windows_7_stability_update_makes_PCs_unstable_users_report

154. http://www-03.ibm.com/press/us/en/pressrelease/37257.wss

155. Nicole Perlroth, "Hackers Lurking in Vents and Soda Machines," *New York Times*, April 7, 2014 http://www.nytimes.com/2014/04/08/technology/the-spy-in-the-soda-machine.html?_r=0

156. http://www.theiia.org/bookstore/downloads/freetoall/5036.dl_GRC%20Cyber%20Security%20Research%20Report.pdf

Chapter 10

1. http://research.stlouisfed.org/fred2/graph/?id=GASDESW

2. Catherine Bolgar, "Getting a handle on those quickly shifting corporate risks," *Supply Chain Risk Insights*, October 18, 2010 http://www.supplychainriskinsights.com/archive/scri-future

3. World Economic Forum report, *Global Risks 2012*, World Economic Forum, January 2012.

4. Charles Shehadi III and Michael Witalec, *How to Utilize hedging and a Fuel Surcharge Program to Stabilize the Cost of Fuel, Master of Engineering in Logistics Thesis*, MIT Center for Transportation and Logistics, May 2010.

5. MIT CTL's roundtable, "Exploring the Impact of Energy Volatility on the Global Supply Chain," held on October 22, 2008, in Cambridge, MA.

6. Dave Blanchard, Portrait of Best-In-Class Risk Management, *IndustryWeek*, January 9, 2009. http://www.industryweek.com/planning-amp-forecasting/portrait-best-class-risk-management

7. Y. Cynthia Lin and Lea Prince, "Gasoline Price Volatility and the Elasticity of Demand for Gasoline," *Journal of Energy Economics* 38: 111–117, 2013.

8. James D. Hamilton, "Causes and Consequences of the Oil Shock of 2007–08" Brookings Papers on Economic Activity, Spring 2009, http://www.brookings.edu/~/media/Projects/BPEA/Spring%202009/2009a_bpea_hamilton.PDF

9. This observation is based on 1949–2007 US data. The phenomenon of declining income elasticity of oil consumption as countries become more developed has been observed in other developed countries. For discussion see James Hamilton, "Understanding Crude Oil Prices," *Energy Journal* 30, no.2 (2009): 179–206.

10. Micheline Maynard, "Southwest Has First Loss in 17 Years," *New York Times*, October 16, 2008, http://www.nytimes.com/2008/10/17/business/17air.html

11. Rick Blasgen, presentation at MIT CTL's conference "Achieving the Energy-Efficient Supply Chain," held on April 30, 2007, in Cambridge, MA.

12. Interview with Annette Prochaska, manager of vehicle scheduling at GM, August 2012.

13. MIT CTL's roundtable, "Exploring the Impact of Energy Volatility on the Global Supply Chain," October 22, 2008.

14. Ibid.

15. Ibid.

16. Jill Dunn, "Study: Fuel Efficiency Efforts Pay Off for Carriers," September 8, 2014, *Commercial Carrier Journal*, http://www.ccjdigital.com/study-fuel-efficiency-efforts-pay-off-for-carriers/

17. http://nacfe.org/wp-content/uploads/2014/06/June-26-TE-Workshop-Master-Little-Rock-061614.pdf

18. By the end of 2014 the largest container ship in the world was the Globe operated by China Shipping Container Lines. It has capacity for carrying 19,100 TEUs. In 2015 the Swiss vessel MSC Oscar took the title with capacity for 19,224 TEUs.

19. http://www.greencarcongress.com/2011/02/maersk-20110221.html

20. http://www.boeing.com/commercial/aeromagazine/articles/qtr_4_07/AERO_Q407_article2.pdf

21. Mike Ramsey, "Will Cheap Gas Hurt Sales of Ford's New Pickup?" *Wall Street Journal*, October 21, 2014, http://online.wsj.com/articles/will-cheap-gas-hurt-sales-of-fords-new-pickup-1413921646. See also Alex Taylor III, "Ford's Epic Gamble: The Inside Story," *Fortune*, July 24, 2014, http://fortune.com/2014/07/24/f-150-fords-epic-gamble/

22. http://abcnews.go.com/US/wireStory/gas-prices-gallon-texas-oklahoma-27395888

23. http://time.com/money/3614039/suv-sales-increase-luxury/

24. Ramsey, "Will Cheap Gas Hurt Sales of Ford's New Pickup?"

25. http://www.morningstar.com/invest/articles/1169113-update-these-u-s-oil-producers-have-the-most-lose.html

26. http://www.industryweek.com/planning-amp-forecasting/majority-companies-have-suffered-supply-chain-disruptions

27. http://science.time.com/2013/12/20/rare-earths-are-too-rare/

28. http://blogs.ei.columbia.edu/2012/09/19/rare-earth-metals-will-we-have-enough/

29. Marc Humphries, "Rare Earth Elements: The Global Supply Chain," Congressional Research Services, June 8, 2012, http://www.fas.org/sgp/crs/natsec/R41347.pdf

30. Ibid.

31. Randolph Kirchain, presentation at the MIT CTL's conference, "Crossroads 2012: "Supply Chains in Transition," held on June 28, 2012, in Cambridge, MA.

32. Ibid.

33. Humphries, "Rare Earth Elements."

34. Randolph Kirchain, presentation at the MIT CTL's conference, "Crossroads 2010: Building Supply Chains that Deliver Sustainability," held on March 25, 2010, in Cambridge, MA.

35. http://www.farmdocdaily.illinois.edu/2012/07/update_on_the_shutdown_price_o.html

36. Simon Romero, "Big Tires in Short Supply," *New York Times*, April 20, 2006.

37. http://www.kitcometals.com/charts/copper_historical.html

38. Soroya Permalasari, David Stringer and Liezel Hill, "Gold Miners Lose $169 Billion as Price Slump Adds EFT Pain," *Bloomberg*, April 18, 2013, http://www.bloomberg.com/news/2013-04-17/gold-miners-lose-169-billion-as-price-slump-compounds-etf-pain.html

39. Josh OKane, "Gold Producers Need to Stop Piling on Debt, S&P Warns," *Globe and Mail*, December 18, 2012, and Ernst and Young, *A New World, A New Strategy, Global Steel 2013 Report,* http://www.ey.com/Publication/vwLUAssets/Global-Steel-Report-2013/$FILE/Global-Steel-Report-2013_ER0046.pdf

40. http://www.forbes.com/sites/larrybell/2012/04/15/chinas-rare-earth-metals-monopoly-neednt-put-an-electronics-stranglehold-on-america/

41. Eric Martin and Jennifer Freedman, "Obama Says China Rare-Earth Case is Warning for WTO Violators," *Bloomberg*, March 13, 2012, http://www.bloomberg.com/news/2012-03-13/eu-joins-u-s-japan-in-challenging-china-s-rare-earth-export-restrictions.html.

42. http://www3.weforum.org/docs/WEF_SCT_RRN_NewModelsAddressingSupplyChainTransportRisk_IndustryAgenda_2012.pdf

43. http://www.kitcometals.com/charts/copper_historical.html

44. http://blogs.ei.columbia.edu/2012/09/19/rare-earth-metals-will-we-have-enough

45. Ernst and Young, "Resource Nationalism Remains Number One Risk for Miners" http://www.ey.com/RU/en/Newsroom/News-releases/PressRelease---2012-07-10

46. http://www.bbc.co.uk/news/business-17441170

47. http://www.cnbc.com/id/46714747

48. Wayne Morrison and Rachel Tang, "China's Rare Earth Industry and Export Regime: Economic and Trade Implications for the United States," *Congressional Research Service Report*, April 30, 2012.

49. http://www.nbcnews.com/id/9146363/ns/business-local_business/t/pump-prices-jump-across-us-after-katrina/

50. Grant Thornton Report, *Creating a Reliable, Profitable Supply Chain: Navigating Exchange Rate, Working Capital and Business Uncertainties,* http://www.grantthornton.es/publicaciones/AHGT.ES%20supply%20chain%20solutions.pdf]

50. BASF 2011 Annual Report, report.basf.com/2011/.

52. http://www3.weforum.org/docs/WEF_SCT_RRN_NewModelsAddressingSupplyChainTransportRisk_IndustryAgenda_2012.pdf

53. http://www.ag.senate.gov/download/schloss-testimony

54. http://report.basf.com/2013/en/servicepages/downloads/files/BASF_Report_2013.pdf

55. http://www.cfo.com/article.cfm/14504913

56. Maynard, "Southwest Has First Loss in 17 Years."

57. Jack Nicas, "Delta Expect Lower Fuel Prices to Boost Profits in 2015," *Wall Street Journal*, December 11, 2014.

58. http://www.chron.com/business/steffy/article/Hedging-turned-out-to-be-a-bad-idea-for-oil-1566272.php

59. http://www.uschamber.com/sites/default/files/international/agenda/files/G20-B20%20Bridge%20Report.pdf

60. Nicole Hing, "Small Importers, Travel Firms, Take to Hedging," *Wall Street Journal*, December 5, 2012, http://online.wsj.com/article/SB10001424127887324784404578144911472475622.html

61. Maynard, "Southwest Has First Loss in 17 Years."

62. http://www.grantthornton.com/staticfiles/GTCom/CIP/Consumer%20and%20industrial%20products%20publications/Supply%20Chain%20Solutions/GrantThornton_SupplyChainSolutionsPart1.pdf

63. http://www.hybridcars.com/ghosn-localization-key-to-nissans-success/

64. MIT CTL, "Exploring the Impact of Energy Volatility on the Global Supply Chain," October 22, 2008.

65. http://www.bcg.com/media/PressReleaseDetails.aspx?id=tcm:12-104216

66. Susan Carey, "Delta Flies New Route to Profits: Older Jets," *Wall Street Journal*, November 15, 2012.

67. Jad Mouawad, "Delta Buys refinery to Get Control of Fuel Costs" *New York Times*, April 30, 2012.

68. http://www.forbes.com/sites/steveschaefer/2012/04/30/delta-pulls-the-trigger-on-purchase-of-philly-refinery-from-phillips-66/

69. http://www.ey.com/Publication/vwLUAssets/Global-Steel-Report-2013/$FILE/Global-Steel-Report-2013_ER0046.pdf

70. Jerry DiColo, "Delta Air Says Trainer Refinery Lost $22 Million in First Quarter," *Wall Street Journal*, August 23, 2013.

71. http://www.ey.com/Publication/vwLUAssets/Global-Steel-Report-2013/$FILE/Global-Steel-Report-2013_ER0046.pdf

72. http://www.platinum.matthey.com/media/820682/07_palladium.pdf

73. http://www.stillwaterpalladium.com/production.html

74. http://www.people.hofstra.edu/geotrans/eng/ch8en/conc8en/fuel_consumption_containerships.html

75. http://ports.com/sea-route/port-of-shanghai,china/port-of-rotterdam,netherlands/

76. http://www.bairdmaritime.com/index.php?option=com_content&view=article&id=13224

77. http://www.bridgestonetrucktires.com/us_eng/real/magazines/ra_special-edit_4/ra_special4_fuel-speed.asp

78. http://205.186.149.248/wp/wp-content/uploads/Slow-Steaming-Research-Study-by-Centrx-BDP-International-and-SJU.pdf

79. http://www.inboundlogistics.com/cms/article/is-slow-steaming-good-for-the-supply-chain/

80. http://www.scientificamerican.com/article/rare-earths-elemental-needs-of-the-clean-energy-economy/

81. http://serc.carleton.edu/integrate/teaching_materials/mineral_resources/student_materials/unit2cobaltexample.html

82. http://www1.eere.energy.gov/cleancities/waste_management.html

83. Rebecca Smith, "Will Truckers Ditch Diesel?" *Wall Street Journal*, May 23, 2012.

84. Ibid.

85. http://www.eia.gov/dnav/ng/hist/rngwhhdm.htm

86. http://research.stlouisfed.org/fred2/graph/?id=GASDESW

87. Smith, "Will Truckers Ditch Diesel?"

88. http://www.platinum.matthey.com/media/820682/07_palladium.pdf

89. http://www.pwc.com/mx/es/forms/archivo/PwC-PRTM_SupplyChain_092811_r_v3.pdf

90. E. Alonso, F. Field and R. Kirchain, "Platinum Availability for Future Automotive Technologies," *Environmental Science & Technology* 46, no. 23 (2012): 12986–12993.

91. Ibid.

92. http://www.johnsoncontrols.com/content/us/en/products/power_solutions/global_battery_recycling.html

93. http://www.dell.com/learn/us/en/uscorp1/corp-comm/us-goodwill-reconnect

94. http://www.recycling-guide.org.uk/materials/computers.html

95. http://www.theguardian.com/environment/2011/dec/29/japan-leads-field-plastic-recycling?newsfeed=true

96. http://www.environmentalleader.com/2014/02/05/epas-toxic-substances-rules-discourage-recycling/

97. http://usatoday30.usatoday.com/money/industries/manufacturing/2004-02-20-steel_x.htm

98. http://energy.gov/sites/prod/files/DOE_CMS2011_FINAL_Full.pdf

99. http://minerals.usgs.gov/minerals/pubs/mcs/2013/mcs2013.pdf

100. http://www.eia.gov/petroleum/gasdiesel/

101. Randolph Kirchain, presentation at MIT CTL, "Crossroads 2012: "Supply Chains in Transition," June 28, 2012.

102. http://seekingalpha.com/article/424331-ford-motors-management-host-ford-university-conference-call-transcript?source=cc

103. http://www.nasdaq.com/markets/copper.aspx?timeframe=5y

104. http://ir.tyson.com/files/doc_financials/2013/TSN-2013-Annual-Report-on-Form-10-K.PDF

105. https://www.google.com/url?q=http://www.wsj.com/articles/commodities-go-from-hoard-to-floored-heard-on-the-street-1418583983

106. http://www.ag.senate.gov/download/schloss-testimony

107. Charles Mulford and Eugene E. Comiskey, "The Non-designation of Derivatives as Hedges for Accounting Purposes," Georgia Tech Financial Analysis Lab, Georgia Institute of Technology, September 2008, http://scheller.gatech.edu/centers-initiatives/financial-analysis-lab/files/2008/ga_tech_cf_hedges_2008.pdf

108. https://www.wellsfargo.com/downloads/pdf/com/focus/fx_survey/FX_Survey_Summary_2011.pdf

Chapter 11

1. http://www.reocities.com/Athens/Acropolis/5232/edmonton.htm

2. http://www.insurancejournal.com/news/international/2011/10/11/219349.htm

3. http://business.time.com/2010/03/01/warren-buffetts-boring-brilliant-wisdom/

4. See, for example, http://www.brandchannel.com/papers_review.asp?sp_id=357

5. http://www.rankingthebrands.com/PDF/2012%20RepTrak%20100-Global_Report,%20Reputation%20Institute.pdf

6. http://www.bloomberg.com/news/2010-06-06/foxconn-to-double-china-factory-worker-salaries-by-october-after-suicides.html

7. Reed Albergotti and Elizabeth Rappaport, "US Not Seeking Goldman Charges," *Wall Street Journal*, August 9, 2012.

8. http://www.bbc.co.uk/news/world-asia-22476774

9. http://www.guardian.co.uk/commentisfree/2013/may/12/savar-bangladesh-international-minimum-wage

10. http://abcnews.go.com/Blotter/fire-kills-112-workers-making-clothes-us-brands/story?id=17807229

11. http://www.bbc.co.uk/news/world-asia-22474601

12. http://www.nytimes.com/2013/05/02/business/some-retailers-rethink-their-role-in-bangladesh.html?_r=0

13. http://online.wsj.com/article/SB10001424127887323401904578159512118148362.html?google_editors_picks=true

14. http://www.nytimes.com/2013/05/02/business/some-retailers-rethink-their-role-in-bangladesh.html?pagewanted=all

15. http://www.nytimes.com/2013/05/02/business/some-retailers-rethink-their-role-in-bangladesh.html?_r=0

16. http://www.nytimes.com/2013/05/14/world/asia/bangladeshs-cabinet-approves-changes-to-labor-laws.html?pagewanted=all&_r=0

17. http://www.autonews.com/article/20140803/GLOBAL02/140809957/gm-looks-for-alternative-supplies-in-china-after-deadly-factory-blast

18. Colum Murphy, Joseph White and Jake Maxwell Watts, "GM Doesn't Plan to Change Supply-Chain Safety Process," *Wall Street Journal*, August 5, 2014.

19. Ibid.

20. http://asq.org/qualitynews/qnt/execute/displaySetup?newsID=18877

21. http://www.dicastal.com/en/index_mnewlook_t12_i16.html

22. http://media.gm.com/media/us/en/gm/news.detail.html/content/Pages/news/us/en/2011/Mar/0311_soy.html

23. http://english.caixin.com/2014-08-26/100721484.html

24. http://www.bjreview.com.cn/nation/txt/2014-08/11/content_633994.htm

25. www.gscreview.com/feb10_john_interview.php

26. Steven Greenhouse, "Some Retailers Rethink Their Role in Bangladesh," *New York Times*, May 1, 2013.

27. Ibid.

28. Nazli Kibria, *Becoming a Garments Worker: The Mobilization of Women into the Garments Factories of Bangladesh*, Occasional Paper 9, March 1998, UN Research Institute for Social Development, http://www.unrisd.org/unrisd/website/document.nsf/0/523115d41019b9d980256b67005b6ef8/$FILE/opb9.pdf

29. See http://www.enoughproject.org/

30. http://www.enoughproject.org/publications/can-you-hear-congo-now-cell-phones-conflict-minerals-and-worst-sexual-violence-world

31. Interview with Gary Niekerk, director of global citizenship at Intel, July 23, 2012.

32. Ibid.

33. Ibid.

34. Ibid.

35. Ibid.

36. http://www.eiccoalition.org/about/members/

37. http://www.intel.com/content/dam/doc/policy/policy-conflict-minerals.pdf

38. http://thinkprogress.org/security/2014/01/07/3126271/intel-announces-launch-conflict-free-microprocessors/

39. Jim Low, "Dodd-Frank and the Conflict Minerals Rule," *KPMG Directors and Boards,* 4th Quarter, 2012, pp.44–45.

40. http://www.csr360gpn.org/magazine/feature/ms-ethical-model-factories/

41. http://betterwork.org/global

42. Steven Greenhouse, "Some Retailers Rethink Their Role in Bangladesh," *New York Times*, May 1, 2013.

43. http://www.sedex.org.uk

44. http://www.fairtrade.net

45. http://www.fairtrade.net/products.html

46. Jens Hainmueller, Michael J. Hiscox, and Sandra Sequeira, *Consumer Demand for the Fair Trade Label: Evidence from a Field Experiment* (April 1, 2011). MIT Political Science Department Research Paper no. 2011-9B. Available at SSRN, http://ssrn.com/abstract=1801942 or http://dx.doi.org/10.2139/ssrn.1801942

47. http://www.coca-colacompany.com/our-company/hours-of-work-improvement-guide

48. Tom Mitchell and Jonathan Birchall, "Wal-Mart Orders Chinese Suppliers to Lift Standards," *Financial Times*, October 23, 2008.

49. http://articles.businessinsider.com/2011-03-24/strategy/30081749. 1_routes-engineers-map-ups#ixzz1gGl5niKg.

50. Mark Buckley, VP Environmental Affairs at Staples, "Implementing Sustainability at the Corporate Level," presentation at MIT "Crossroads 2010," March 25, 2010.

51. http://www.brightfleet.com/blog/2012/interview-with-mike-payette-at-staples-about-speed-limiters-fuel-economy-and-safety/

52. William Newman, "The Race to Greener Bottles Could Be Long," *New York Times*, December 15, 2011.

53. MIT CTL, "Crossroads 2010," March 25, 2010.

54. http://www.staples.com/sbd/cre/marketing/easy-on-the-planet/our-goals-and-initiatives.html

55. "In Hot Water," *Economist*, October 6, 2005, http://www.economist.com/node/4492835

56. http://www.ens-newswire.com/ens/jun2007/2007-06-05-07.asp

57. http://www3.weforum.org/docs/GAC12/IssueBrief/IB_WaterSecurity.pdf

58. http://www.ens-newswire.com/ens/jun2007/2007-06-05-07.asp

59. MIT CTL, "Crossroads 2012," June 28, 2012.

60. Alexa Olesen, "Coca Cola Begins Water Conservation Bid," *Washington Post*, June 4, 2007, http://www.washingtonpost.com/wp-dyn/content/article/2007/06/05/AR2007060500265_pf.html

61. http://www.coca-colacompany.com/sustainabilityreport/world/water-stewardship.html

62. Alexa Olesen, "Coca Cola Begins Water Conservation Bid," *Washington Post*, June 4, 2007, http://www.washingtonpost.com/wp-dyn/content/article/2007/06/05/AR2007060500265_pf.html

63. http://www.unilever.com/mediacentre/pressreleases/2002/safety.aspx

64. MIT CTL, "Crossroads 2010," March 25, 2010.

65. http://www.pwc.com/us/en/supply-chain-management/assets/pwc-sci-112008.pdf

66. Interface Flor, RePrise Collection Brochure, 2007. Interface products.

67. Carpet Recovery, "Carpet Cycle, InterFace Flor Named CARE Recyclers of the Year," 2007, http://www.carpetrecovery.org/070509_CARE_Conference.php

68. YouTube, "I AM Mission Zero," 2007, http://www.youtube.com/watch?v=chPD3g4dMJI

69. Prof. Randy Kirchain, presentation at MIT CTL "Crossroads 2010," March 25, 2010.

70. http://www.environmentalleader.com/2014/10/17/zero-interest-loans-to-develop-recycling-infrastructure-available/

71. P&G, presentation at MIT CTL "Crossroads 2010," March 25, 2010.

72. http://www.guardian.co.uk/sustainable-business/best-practice-exchange/marks-and-spencer-change-better

73. "Plan A: Doing the Right Thing," http://global.marksandspencer.com/hk/en/about-ms/

74. MIT CTL, "Crossroads 2010," March 25, 2010.

75. http://www.pwc.com/us/en/supply-chain-management/assets/pwc-sci-112008.pdf

76. http://www.imdb.com/title/tt0390521/

77. http://www.dailymail.co.uk/news/article-2529302/McDonalds-shuts-website-telling-staff-not-eat-food.html

78. *The Economist*, "Coulrophobia," May 19, 2012, http://www.economist.com/node/18713690

79. http://www.stopcorporateabuse.org/news/national-campaign-against-mcdonalds-mascot-kicks-cedar-mill

80. http://www.cspinet.org/new/201204041.html and http://newsandinsight.thomsonreuters.com/Legal/News/2012/04_-_April/Judge_tosses_Happy_Meal_lawsuit_against_McDonald_s/

81. http://fitbie.msn.com/eat-right/mcdonald-s-announces-healthier-happy-meal

82. Lisa Baertlein, "Anti-obesity Proposal Fails Again at McDonald's," *Chicago Tribune*, May 24, 2012, http://articles.chicagotribune.com/2012-05-24/lifestyle/sns-rt-us-mcdonalds-obesitybre84n1ci-20120524_1_childhood-obesity-happy-meals-chief-executive-jim-skinner

83. Stephanie Strom, "McDonald's Menu to Post Calorie Count," *New York Times*, September 12, 2012.

84. http://www.usatoday.com/story/money/business/2014/01/06/mcdonalds-nutrition-fast-food-mcdonalds-menu/4339395/

85. Allison Aubrey, "Bowing to Pressure, McDonald's Makes Happy Meals More Healthful," NPR, July 26, 2011 http://www.npr.org/blogs/health/2011/07/26/138702964/bowing-to-pressure-mcdonalds-makes-happy-meals-more-healthful

86. http://www.yaleruddcenter.org/newsletter/issue.aspx?id=36

87. Stephanie Strom, "McDonald's Trims Its Happy Meal," *New York Times*, July 26, 2011.

88. D M Klurfeld, J Foreyt, T J Angelopoulos and J M Rippe, "Lack of Evidence for High Fructose Corn Syrup as the Cause of the Obesity Epidemic" *International Journal of Obesity* (2013) 37, 771–773; doi:10.1038/ijo.2012.157; published online 18 September 2012, http://www.nature.com/ijo/journal/v37/n6/full/ijo2012157a.html and Tara Parker-Pope "Still Spooked by High-Fructose Corn Syrup," *New York Times*, October 30, 2008 http://well.blogs.nytimes.com/2008/10/30/still-spooked-by-high-fructose-corn-syrup/?_r=0

89. http://www.nytimes.com/2012/05/31/nyregion/bloomberg-plans-a-ban-on-large-sugared-drinks.html?pagewanted=all&_r=0

90. http://www.npr.org/blogs/thesalt/2012/01/12/145112865/could-a-soda-tax-prevent-26-000-deaths-per-year

91. http://en.wikipedia.org/wiki/Golden_rice

92. http://www2.ca.uky.edu/entomology/entfacts/ef130.asp

93. http://en.wikipedia.org/wiki/Roundup_Ready_soybean

94. http://www.scientificamerican.com/article/corn-genetically-modified-to-tolerate-drought/

95. Ibid.

96. Godfray, C., J. Beddington, I. Crute, et al., *Food Security: The Challenge of Feeding 9 Billion People* 327 (2010): 812–818.

97. "China Pushes Genetically Modified Food," *Wall Street Journal*, http://blogs.wsj.com/chinarealtime/2013/10/23/china-pushes-genetically-modified-food-draft/?KEYWORDS=gmo

98. Mark Lynas, "Time to call out the anti-GMO conspiracy theory." Retrieved from: http://www.marklynas.org/2013/04/time-to-call-out-the-anti-gmo-conspiracy-theory/

99. http://www.medicalnewstoday.com/articles/260022.php

100. http://www.fda.gov/Food/GuidanceRegulation/GuidanceDocumentsRegulatoryInformation/Allergens/ucm106187.htm

101. http://www.bbc.co.uk/news/technology-15671823

102. Srini S..Srinivasan, Brian D. Till, (2002) "Evaluation of Search, Experience and Credence Attributes: Role of Brand Name and Product Trial," *Journal of Product & Brand Management* 11 (7): 417–431.

103. Darby, M. and Karni, E. (1973). "Free Competition and the Optimal Amount of Fraud," *Journal of Law and Economics* 16, no. 1 (1973): 67–88.

104. http://www.greenpeace.org/international/en/news/features/Clickers-and-Stickers-Make-HM-Detox/

105. http://www.oxfam.org/sites/www.oxfam.org/files/rr-unilever-supply-chain-labor-rights-vietnam-310113-en.pdf

106. http://www.insead.edu/facultyresearch/centres/isic/ecsr/research/documents/UnderstandingtheImpactsofBusinessonPoverty.pdf

107. MIT CTL, "Crossroads 2010," March 25, 2010.

108. Ariel Schwartz, "Walmart Plans to Cut 20 Million Metric Tons of Greenhouse Gas Emissions from Supply Chain," *Fast Company*, February 25, 2010, http://www.fastcompany.com/1563121/walmart-plans-cut-20-million-metric-tons-greenhouse-gas-emissions-supply-chain

109. http://www.ab-inbev.com/go/social_responsibility/environment/water_use.cfm

110. http://www.coca-colacompany.com/setting-a-new-goal-for-water-efficiency

111. http://www.ghgprotocol.org

112. http://www.ghgprotocol.org/about-ghgp

113. http://sustainability.baxter.com/environment-health-safety/environmental-performance/ghg-emissions-across-value-chain.html

114. Lynn Beavis, "M&S: Doing the Right Thing Leads to Change—for the Better" *Guardian*, May 30, 2012, http://www.guardian.co.uk/sustainable-business/best-practice-exchange/marks-and-spencer-change-better

115. MIT CTL's, conference "Crossroads 2011: Disruptive Innovations That Will Shape the Future of Supply Chains," held on June 16, 2011, in Cambridge, MA.

116. http://www.conservation.org/partners/Pages/starbucks.aspx

117. http://www.conservation.org/campaigns/starbucks/Pages/default.aspx

118. Interview with Kelly Goodejohn, director of ethical sourcing, Starbucks, May 2014.

119. Jonathan Johnson, professor of management at the Sam M. Walton College of Business, University of Arkansas, presentation at MIT CTL's symposium "Future Freight Flows," held on March 11–12, 2010, in Cambridge, MA.

120. Georgina Grenon, director of operations PSO at Booz Allen Hamilton, presentation at MIT CTL "Achieving the Energy-Efficient Supply Chain," April 30, 2007.

121. Alexandra Alter, "Yet Another 'Footprint' to Worry About: Water," *Wall Street Journal*, February 17, 2009.

122. Tesco (2007. Prepared remarks, T. Leahy, http://www.tesco.com/climatechange/speech.asp

123. Charles Boyle, "Aon, Zurich Launch Innovative $100 Million Reputational Risk Coverage," *Insurance Journal*, October 11, 2011, http://www.insurancejournal.com/news/international/2011/10/11/219349.htm

124. MIT CTL, "Advancing Supply Chain Risk Management," October 10, 2012.

125. Ibid.

126. Klout is a score calculated on Klout.com, measuring a person's influence (how their social media writings influence people's responses and actions).

127. MIT CTL, "Advancing Supply Chain Risk Management," October 10, 2012.

128. http://www.theguardian.com/environment/2014/mar/03/tim-cook-climate-change-sceptics-ditch-apple-shares

129. http://www.guardian.co.uk/sustainable-business/best-practice-exchange/marks-and-spencer-change-better

130. Theodore F. Piepenbrock, *Toward a Theory of the Evolution of Business Ecosystems: Enterprise Architectures, Competitive Dynamics,Ffirm Performance, and Industrial Co-evolution,* MIT dissertation, 2009.

131. http://www.accenture.com/SiteCollectionDocuments/PDF/Driving_Value_from_Integrated_Sustainability_High_Performance_Lessons_from_the_Leaders.pdf (Of course, this could only be a correlation and it is possible that only the more profitable companies have the luxury to invest in stakeholders' concerns.)

132. Kevin Wrenn, vice president of PC business and operations at Fujitsu Computer Systems Corp., presentation at MIT CTL "Achieving the Energy-Efficient Supply Chain," April 30, 2007.

133. http://repository.law.umich.edu/cgi/viewcontent.cgi?article=1158&context=law_econ_current

Chapter 12

1. http://www.marketingcharts.com/direct/landline-phone-penetration-dwindles-as-cell-only-households-grow-22577/cdc-us-household-phone-status-h12008-h22011-jul2012png/

2. http://www.gallup.com/poll/156833/one-five-adults-smoke-tied-time-low.aspx

3. http://news.bbc.co.uk/2/hi/8074663.stm

4. http://www.sportingnews.com/mlb/story/2011-04-15/declining-attendance-could-signal-deeper-problems-for-baseball

5. http://atruegolfer.com/2012/12/the-decline-of-golf/

6. http://assets.aarp.org/rgcenter/general/approaching-65.pdf

7. Joseph Coughlin, presentation at MIT CTL, "Future of Freight Flows," March 11–12, 2010.

8. OECD statistics, http://www.oecd.org/els/health-systems/47884543.pdf

9. Joseph Coughlin, presentation at MIT CTL, "Future of Freight Flows," March 11–12, 2010.

10. "Demography, China's Achilles Heel," *Economist*, April 21, 2012.

11. http://www.telegraph.co.uk/women/sex/divorce/9705967/Silver-separation-the-surge-in-older-divorce.html

12. http://www.dailymail.co.uk/femail/article-1285392/The-40-year-itch-Divorce-falling-age-group-60s--ARE-couples-splitting-lifetime-together.html

13. Coughlin, presentation at MIT CTL, "Future of Freight Flows," March 11–12, 2010.

14. MetLife Mature Market Institute, David DeLong & Associates, and Zogby International, *Living Longer, Working Longer: The Changing Landscape of the Aging Workforce–A MetLife Study*, April 2006. https://www.whymetlife.com/downloads/MetLife_LivingLongerWorkingLongerStudy.pdf

15. http://www.ncdc.noaa.gov/sotc/global/2013/13

16. http://en.wikipedia.org/wiki/List_of_scientists_opposing_the_mainstream_scientific_assessment_of_global_warming

17. http://ipcc-wg2.gov/SREX/images/uploads/SREX-SPMbrochure_FINAL.pdf

18. Ross McKitrick, "IPCC Models Getting Mushy," *Financial Post*, September 16, 2013.

19. Bruna Waterfield, "EU Policy on Climate Change Is Right Even if Science Was Wrong, Says Commissioner," *Telegraph*, September 16, 2013.

20. George Shultz in a speech at MIT, September 30, 2014.

21. http://www.epa.gov/climatechange/basics/

22. http://www.esrl.noaa.gov/news/2013/CO2400.html

23. Ernst Moniz presentation at MIT CTL, "Achieving the Energy-Efficient Supply Chain," April 30, 2007.

24. http://www.ipcc.ch/pdf/assessment-report/ar4/syr/ar4_syr.pdf

25. http://www.thelocal.de/national/20111122-39035.html

26. http://www.hellenicshippingnews.com/News.aspx?ElementId=553a8ae3-1663-4fe7-beac-0d9f4cfd26ed

27. http://www.thelocal.de/national/20111122-39035.html

28. http://www.rita.dot.gov/bts/sites/rita.dot.gov.bts/files/publications/freight_in_america/html/table_01.html

29. Alan McKinnon, *European Freight Transport Statistics: Limitations, misinterpretations and Aspirations*, Logistics Research Center, Heriot-Watt University, Edinburgh, UK. Report prepared for the 15 ACEA Scientific Conference Advisory Group Meeting, Brussels, September 8, 2010. See figure 1 on p. 6.

30. http://www.basf.com/group/corporate/us/en/function/conversions:/publishdownload/content/sustainability/economy/basf-shares/images/Programme_Response_Investor_CDP_2012.pdf

31. http://www.csmonitor.com/World/Americas/2011/0506/Food-inflation-land-grabs-spur-Latin-America-to-restrict-foreign-ownership

32. http://www.thejakartaglobe.com/archive/aging-farmers-threaten-indonesian-food-security/446190/

33. S. F. Balica, N. G. Wright, and F. van der Meulen, "A Flood Vulnerability Index for Coastal Cities and Its Use in Assessing Climate Change Impacts," *Journal of International Society for the Prevention and Mitigation of Natural Hazards* 64 (2012): 73–105, http://link.springer.com/content/pdf/10.1007%2Fs11069-012-0234-1.pdf, section 5.1.

34. Ibid. See section 5.1, figure 8, p.96.

35. http://www.worldshipping.org/about-the-industry/global-trade/top-50-world-container-ports

36. Balica, Wright, and van der Meulen, "A Flood Vulnerability Index for Coastal Cities and Its Use in Assessing Climate Change Impacts." See section 4.2, p. 90.

37. http://www.nationmultimedia.com/national/Severe-drought-looms-nationwide-30188892.html

38. http://www.hiso.or.th/hiso/picture/reportHealth/ThaiHealth2011/eng2011_15.pdf

39. http://thoughtleadership.aonbenfield.com/ThoughtLeadership/Documents/20120314_impact_forecasting_thailand_flood_event_recap.pdf

40. http://geology.com/articles/northwest-passage.shtml

41. http://www.epa.gov/climatechange/ghgemissions/sources/transportation.html

42. http://www.guardian.co.uk/environment/damian-carrington-blog/2011/aug/25/food-price-arab-middle-east-protests

43. Maria Godoy, "Can Riots Be Predicted? Experts Watch Food Prices," Oct. 02, 2012, http://www.npr.org/blogs/thesalt/2012/09/20/161501075/high-food-prices-forcast-more-global-riots-ahead-researchers-say

44. David Tenenbaum, "Food vs. Fuel: Diversion of Crops Could Cause More Hunger," *Environmental Health Perspectives*. 2008 June; 116(6): A254–A257.

45. Adam Thomson, Tortilla Riots' Give Foretaste of Food Challenge, *Financial Times*, October 12h, 2012.

46. http://news.bbc.co.uk/2/hi/6319093.stm

47. http://www.cnn.com/WORLD/9802/12/indonesia/

48. Leon C. Megginson, "Lessons from Europe for American Business," *Southwestern Social Science Quarterly* 44 (1).

49. Sheffi, *The Resilient Enterprise*.

50. http://tech.fortune.cnn.com/2011/01/13/iphone-sales-in-the-pre-verizon-era/

51. http://www.gartner.com/it/page.jsp?id=612207

52. http://www.canalys.com/newsroom/smart-mobile-device-shipments-hit-118-million-2007-53-2006

53. Jack Gold, "Will Anyone Answer When Apple iPhone Home?" *Computerworld*, January 10, 2007. http://www.computerworld.com/s/article/9007753/Will_anyone_answer_when_Apple_iPhones_home_

54. http://blogs-images.forbes.com/canaccordgenuity/files/2012/02/Smartphone-unit-sales-and-market-share-estimates-by-OEM-millions.png

55. http://www.statista.com/statistics/12861/market-share-of-nokia-smartphones-since-2007/

56. Nick Wingfield, "Microsoft Gets Nokia Units, and Leader," *New York Times*, September 3, 2013.

57. http://bgr.com/2011/12/13/apple-and-google-dominate-smartphone-space-while-other-vendors-scramble/

58. Anton Troianovski and Sven Grundberg, "Nokia's Bad Call on Smartphones," *Wall Street Journal*, July 18, 2012.

59. Mathew Lynn, "Apple iPhone Will Fail in a Late, Defensive Move," *Bloomberg*, January 15, 2007, http://www.bloomberg.com/apps/news?pid=newsarchive&sid=aRelVKWbMAv0

60. Clayton Christensen, *The Innovator's Dilemma* (Boston: Harvard Business School Press, 1997).

61. http://technologizer.com/2010/02/01/iphone-skeptics/

62. http://www.hung-truong.com/blog/2007/01/09/4-reasons-why-the-apple-iphone-will-fail/

63. Rory Prior, ThinkMac Blog, "Will the iPhone Fail?" *Macworld*, January 12, 2007, as cited in http://www.macworld.co.uk/ipad-iphone/news/?newsid=28556&pn=5

644. Christensen, *The Innovator's Dilemma.*

65. http://www.bloomberg.com/news/2013-02-05/dell-s-drop-mirrors-descent-of-pc-industry-in-mobile-world-tech.html

66. Christensen, *The Innovator's Dilemma.*

67. http://www.forbes.com/sites/stevedenning/2011/11/18/clayton-christensen-how-pursuit-of-profits-kills-innovation-and-the-us-economy/

68. http://www.businessweek.com/news/2014-03-10/sbarro-files-second-bankruptcy-as-mall-traffic-dwindles-1

69. https://www.fidelity.com/viewpoints/investing-ideas/mall-shopping

70. http://www.utsandiego.com/news/2014/Feb/03/hot-dog-on-stick-bankruptcy-carlsbad/

71. "Welcome to the 'Sharing Economy.'" *New York Times* (2013), http://www.nytimes.com/2013/07/21/opinion/sunday/friedman-welcome-to-the-sharing-economy.html?pagewanted=all&_r=0

72. http://techcrunch.com/2013/12/19/airbnb-10m/

73. http://techcrunch.com/2014/04/18/airbnb-has-closed-its-500m-round-of-funding-at-a-10b-valuation-led-by-tpg/

74. http://www.hospitalitynet.org/news/4060119.html

75. http://venturebeat.com/2013/10/01/relayrides-changes-direction-to-focus-on-airport-and-long-term-car-rentals/

76. http://www.pmgbenchmarking.com/public/product/scorecard/PIB/metrics.aspx

77. http://www.15inno.com/2010/01/22/innovationmetrics/

78. The quote is also known as Amara's law. See http://www.pcmag.com/encyclopedia/term/37701/amara-s-law

79. A rigorous process of developing scenarios is described in: Shardul Phadnis, Chris Caplice, Mahender Singh, and Yossi Sheffi, "Axiomatic Foundation and a Structured Process for Developing Firm-Specific Intuitive Logics Scenarios," *Technological Forecasting & Social Change* 88 (July 2014): 122–139.

80. NCHRP Report 750, http://onlinepubs.trb.org/onlinepubs/nchrp/nchrp_rpt_750v1.pdf

81. Ibid.

82. http://www.forumforthefuture.org/sites/default/files/project/downloads/consumer-futures-2020-full-document.pdf

83. NCHRP Report 750, http://onlinepubs.trb.org/onlinepubs/nchrp/nchrp_rpt_750v1.pdf

84. Shardul Phadnis, Chris Caplice, Mahender Singh, and Yossi Sheffi, "Effect of Scenario Planning on Field Experts' Judgment of Long Range Investment Decisions," *Strategic Management Journal*, June 2014.

85. Ibid.

86. Presentation at MIT CTL's conference "Crossroads 2013: Supply Chain as Future Enabler," held on June 26, 2013, in Cambridge, MA.

87. http://www.economist.com/news/special-report/21569570-growing-number-american-companies-are-moving-their-manufacturing-back-united

88. http://www.bloomberg.com/news/2013-01-28/latin-america-commits-to-open-trade-after-year-of-protectionism.html

89. http://www.washingtonpost.com/blogs/worldviews/wp/2014/05/09/china-may-build-an-undersea-train-to-america/

90. http://bigstory.ap.org/article/vigilantes-reject-disarming-mexico-standoff

91. Kate Galbraith, "Strong Rules on Fracking in Wyoming Seen as Model," *New York Times*, November 22, 2013.

92. http://www.forbes.com/2010/08/17/business-obama-finance-companies-opinions-contributors-brook-watkins.html

Chapter 13

1. http://www.mckinsey.com/features/leading_in_the_21st_century/ellen_kullman

2. http://www.mckinsey.com/features/leading_in_the_21st_century/ellen_kullman

3. iSupply, Spansion cited in http://online.wsj.com/article/SB10001424052748703766704576009071694055878.html

4. Barry Lynn, "Built to Break: The International System of Bottlenecks in the New Era of Monopoly," *Challenge* 55, no. 2 (March/April 2012): 87–107.

5. http://www.intel.com/content/dam/www/public/us/en/documents/packaging-databooks/packaging-chapter-14-databook.pdf

6. http://www.docstoc.com/docs/88638192/Japan-Earthquake---Related-Industry-News-Update-Compiled-by

7. "Japan Earthquake Aftermath—Related Industry News Update," compiled by Advanced MP Technology, http://www.docstoc.com/docs/88638192/Japan-Earthquake-Related-Industry-News-Update-Compiled-by

8. Mark LaPedus. "Quake to Cause Prices Hikes, Shortages," 3/15/2011 http://www.eetimes.com/document.asp?doc_id=1258944

9. "Japan Earthquake Aftermath—Related Industry News Update.

10. www.researchinchina.com/news/NewsInfo.aspx?Id=18292

11. http://www.paintsquare.com/news/?fuseaction=view&id=5329&nl_versionid=859

12. Mariko Sanchanta, "Chemical Reaction: iPod Is Short Key Material," *Wall Street Journal*, March 29, 2011.

13. http://www.advisorperspectives.com/commentaries/gmo_112612.php

14. Interview with Jackie Sturm, July 31, 2012.

15. Stephen Wagner and Christoph Bode, "An Empirical Investigation into Supply Chain Vulnerability," *Journal of Purchasing & Supply Management* 12, no. 6 (2006): 301–312.

16. http://www.reuters.com/article/2013/04/11/us-toyota-recall-idUSBRE93A04D20130411

17. http://www.blumenthal.senate.gov/newsroom/press/release/blumenthal-markey-call-on-department-of-justice-to-open-criminal-investigation-of-takata

18. http://www.cdc.gov/salmonella/bredeney-09-12/index.html

19. http://concord-ca.patch.com/groups/politics-and-elections/p/peanut-butter-recall-expands-as-salmonella-outbreak-worsens

20. http://www.cdc.gov/salmonella/bredeney-09-12/index.html

21. "Peanut Industry: Recall Price Tag $1 billion," Associated Press, March. 11, 2009, http://www.msnbc.msn.com/id/29634279/

22. http://en.wikipedia.org/wiki/Air_travel_disruption_after_the_2010 _Eyjafjallajökull_eruption

23. http://pubs.usgs.gov/ds/545/DS545.pdf

24. http://blog.van.fedex.com/blog/business-unusual-flight-planning-and -iceland-volcano-eruption

25. http://in.reuters.com/article/2010/04/20/idINIndia-47840520100420

26. Richard Wray and Graeme Wearden, "Flight Ban Could Leave the UK Short of Fruit and Veg," *Guardian*, April 16, 2010, http://www.guardian.co.uk/ business/2010/apr/16/flight-ban-shortages-uk-supermarkets

27. Bernice Lee and Felix Preston, with Gemma Green, "Preparing for High Impact, Low Probability Events: Lessons from Eyjafjallajokull," *Chatham House Report*, January 2012, http://www.chathamhouse.org/sites/default/files/public/ Research/Energy,%20Environment%20and%20Development/r0112 _highimpact.pdf

28. Lee and Preston, "Preparing for High Impact, Low Probability Events."

29. Jeffrey Gettleman, "With Flights Grounded, Kenya's Produce Wilts," *New York Times*, April 19, 2010 http://www.nytimes.com/2010/04/20/world/ africa/20kenya.html?_r=0

30. Lee and Preston, "Preparing for High Impact, Low Probability Events," and Airmic Technical, "Supply Chain Failures" http://www.airmic.com/sites/default/ files/supply_chain_failures_2013_FINAL_web.pdf.

31. https://www.cia.gov/library/publications/the-world-factbook/geos/ke.html

32. Gettleman, J. "With Flights Grounded, Kenya's Produce Wilts." *New York Times*, April 19, 2010 http://www.nytimes.com/2010/04/20/world/ africa/20kenya.html?_r=0

33. http://www.worldtradewt100.com/blogs/14-wt100-blog/post/iceland-s -volcano-does-a-number-on-global-supply-chains

34. http://news.bbc.co.uk/2/hi/8631676.stm

35. Wray and Wearden, "Flight Ban Could Leave the UK Short of Fruit and Veg,"http://www.guardian.co.uk/business/2010/apr/16/flight-ban-shortages-uk -supermarkets

36. http://money.cnn.com/2010/04/19/news/companies/airlines_volcano/

37. James Pomfret, "Ash Cloud Disrupts Asia's Links to Global Supply Chain," April 20, 2010, http://in.mobile.reuters.com/article/worldNews/ idINIndia-47839520100420

38. Gettleman, "With Flights Grounded, Kenya's Produce Wilts."

39. http://virtualofficefaq.wordpress.com/2010/04/19/update-mail-and-courier -delays-due-to-eyjafjallajokull-ash/

40. www.science20.com/planetbye/volcanic_eruptions_science_and_risk _management-79456

41. Wray and Wearden, "Flight Ban Could Leave the UK Short of Fruit and Veg,"

42. www.science20.com/planetbye/volcanic_eruptions_science_and_risk_management-79456

43. http://news.bbc.co.uk/2/hi/8631676.stm

44. Ibid.

45. http://www.thestate.com/2010/04/20/1251405/volcano-disrupts-bmw-supply-chain.html

46. http://news.bbc.co.uk/2/hi/8631676.stm

47. http://www.toponline.org/books/kits/welcome%20to%20germany/WTGpdf/Handout%204.pdf

48. http://www.handyshippingguide.com/shipping-news/more-misery-for-rhine-shippers-as-drought-continues_626

49. http://www.hellenicshippingnews.com/News.aspx?ElementId=1c36a1ec-edf3-4a27-a8c5-d107b0a268c2

50. http://www.csmonitor.com/World/Latest-News-Wires/2011/0113/Acid-tanker-capsizes-on-Rhine-in-Germany

51. Mathew Day, "War Bombs Cause Chaos on the Rhine," *Telegraph*, November 23, 2011.

52. http://www.nytimes.com/2012/05/08/us/chicago-train-congestion-slows-whole-country.html?pagewanted=all

53. John Rogers, "LA Mayor Says Both Sides in West Coast Port Strike Have Agreed To Mediation," *CommercialAppeal.com News*, December 4, 2012

54. Ibid.

55. "NRF Renews Call for Obama to Intervene in Port Strike," December 3, 2012, http://www.reuters.com/article/2012/12/03/idUS191936+03-Dec-2012+BW20121203

56. Lori Ann LaRocco, "Strike by East Coast Port Workers Could Devastate US Supply Chains," *Alaska Dispatch News*, December 21, 2012, http://www.adn.com/article/strike-east-coast-port-workers-could-devastate-us-supply-chains

57. http://labusinessjournal.com/news/2012/dec/05/ports-reopen-following-tentative-labor-deal/

58. Lori Ann LaRocco, "'Container Cliff': East Coast Faces 'Devastating' Port Strike," December 21, 2012, http://www.cnbc.com/id/100332472

59. See, for example, Sheffi, *The Resilient Enterprise*.

60. http://www.bloomberg.com/news/2011-12-08/floods-tsunami-may-dent-black-box-of-supply-chain-insurance.html

61. Ibid.

62. http://www.canadianunderwriter.ca/news/supply-chain-and-business-interruption-losses-due-to-earthquake-in-japan-may-end-up-on-the-low-end/1000617448/?&er=NA

63. European Food Safety Authority, "E. coli: Rapid Response in a Crisis," http://www.efsa.europa.eu/en/press/news/120711.htm

64. Joshua Chaffin, "Source of E. coli Eludes Experts," *Financial Times*, May 31st, 2011.

65. "New Epidemiological Data Corroborate Eexisting Recommendation on Consumption by BfR." Bundesinstitut für Risikobewertung.

66. http://www.bbc.co.uk/news/world-europe-13605910

67. http://www.thejournal.ie/spanish-cucumbers-not-responsible-for-e-coli-outbreak-146922-Jun2011/

68. http://www.theguardian.com/uk/2011/may/31/e-coli-deaths-16-germany-sweden

69. http://www.bbc.co.uk/news/world-europe-13605910

70. http://metro.co.uk/2011/06/01/1500-now-hit-by-e-coli-bug-as-spain-sues-for-damages-30231/

71. http://www.thejournal.ie/spanish-cucumbers-not-responsible-for-e-coli-outbreak-146922-Jun2011/

72. http://english.cntv.cn/program/newsupdate/20110601/103130.shtml

73. http://english.cntv.cn/program/newsupdate/20110601/103130.shtml

74. Peter Walker, Abby D'Arcy Hughes, and Adam Gabbatt, "E. coli Outbreak 'Trail' Leads to German Bean Sprouts, Authorities Say," *Guardian*, June 6, 2011.

75. "German Farmer Denies E. coli Link to Farm's Bean Sprouts," *Telegraph*, June 6, 2011, http://www.telegraph.co.uk/health/healthnews/8558899/German-farmer-denies-E.coli-link-to-farms-bean-sprouts.html

76. http://www.bfr.bund.de/cm/349/ehec-outbreak-2011-updated-analysis-as-a-basis-for-recommended-measures.pdf

77. Quentin Hardy, "Intel Sees Opportunity in Storage Drives," *New York Times*, December 12, 2011.

78. http://www.digitimes.com/news/a20111127PD201.html

79. Eric Smally, "Thai Flood Sink Intel Chip Orders," *Wired*, December 12, 2011.

80. http://www.bloomberg.com/news/2011-12-12/intel-reduces-forecast-for-fourth-quarter-sales-on-hard-disk-drive-supply.html

81. Charles Arthur, "Intel Cuts Revenue Forecast as Thai Floods Hit PC Sales," *Guardian*, December 12, 2011.

82. Interview with Jackie Sturm, July 31, 2012.

83. http://www.zurich.com/internet/main/SiteCollectionDocuments/products-and-services/SCI_Risk_Insight_WSJ_articles.pdf

84. http://www.dailykos.com/story/2008/12/01/668305/-Side-Product-of-the-Economic-Meltdown-160-Important-Research-Chemical-in-Short-Supply

85. http://www.dupont.com/products-and-services/plastics-polymers-resins/thermoplastics/press-releases/teams-help-pa12-shortage.html

86. http://www.plasticsnews.com/article/20120426/NEWS/304269984/evonik-offers-nylon-12-alternatives-while-plant-is-repaired

87. http://pipeline.corante.com/archives/2009/01/22/the_great_acetonitrile_shortage.php

88. http://www.broughtonlaboratories.co.uk/downloads_bl/acetonitrileshortage.pdf

89. Ibid.

90. http://cen.acs.org/articles/87/i42/Acetonitrile.html

91. Mark Szakoyi, "Iceland's Volcano Disruption Put Vistakon in Response Mode," *Jacksonville Business Journal*, October 29, 2010, http://www.bizjournals.com/jacksonville/print-edition/2010/10/29/icelands-volcano-eruption-put.html?page=all

92. Mark Pearson and Bill Read, "A Volcano's Fallout: Strategies for Disruption," *BloombergBusinessweek*, June 15, 2010, http://www.businessweek.com/stories/2010-06-15/a-volcanos-fallout-strategies-for-disruptionbusinessweek-business-news-stock-market-and-financial-advice

93. http://www.thestate.com/2010/04/20/1251405/volcano-disrupts-bmw-supply-chain.html

94. http://erm.ncsu.edu/az/erm/i/chan/library/AICPA_ERM_Research_Study_20142.pdf

95. http://www.coso.org/documents/coso_erm_executivesummary.pdf

96. http://www.iso.org/iso/home/standards/iso31000.htm

97. http://www.iso.org/iso/home/standards.htm

98. http://www.pwc.com/us/en/corporate-governance/annual-corporate-directors-survey/assets/annual-corporate-directors-survey-full-report-pwc.pdf

99. http://erm.ncsu.edu/az/erm/i/chan/library/AICPA_ERM_Research_Study_20142.pdf

100. See, for example, the discussion by the World Economic Forum in http://www.weforum.org/issues/supply-chain-risk

101. Nassim Taleb, *Antifragile: Things that Gain from Disorder* (New York: Random House, 2012).

102. http://researchnews.osu.edu/archive/restfail.htm

103. http://www.businessinsider.com/new-york-restaurants-fail-rate-2011-8

104. Peter March, "Industry Left High and Dry," *Financial Times*, April 12, 2011.

105. Andy Hooper, "Iceland Volcano: And You Thought the Last Disruption was Bad…," *Telegraph*, April 10, 2012.

106. http://en.wikipedia.org/wiki/Types_of_volcanic_eruptions

107. http://www.reuters.com/article/2011/03/16/us-japan-quake-california-idUSTRE72F5KG20110316

108. http://news.discovery.com/earth/megaquake-schedule-pacific-northwest.htm

109. http://www.dw.de/tokyo-prepares-for-long-overdue-big-one/a-16524572

110. http://www.theguardian.com/science/2010/sep/16/british-science-festival-2010-british-science-festival

111. Amy Chozick, "Toyota Sticks By 'Just in Time' Strategy After Quake," *Wall Street Journal*, July 24, 2007.

112. Timothy J. Pettit, "Supply Chain Resilience: Development of a Conceptual Framework, an Assessment Tool and an Implementation Process." PHD dissertation, Ohio State University, 2008, www.dtic.mil/cgi-bin/GetTRDoc?AD=ADA488407

113. Barry Lynn, "Built to Break: The International System of Bottlenecks in the New Era of Monopoly," *Challenge*, 55, no. 2 (March/April 2012): 87–107.

114. Juro Osawa, "Chip Maker Runs at Half Speed," *Wall Street Journal*, March 26, 2011.

115. http://www.gpo.gov/fdsys/pkg/CHRG-110shrg50418/html/CHRG-110shrg50418.htm

116. http://www.gpo.gov/fdsys/pkg/CHRG-110shrg50418/html/CHRG-110shrg50418.htm

117. http://asq.org/qualitynews/qnt/execute/displaySetup?newsID=13192

118. Bryce Hoffman, "Inside Ford's Fight to Avoid Disaster," *Wall Street Journal*, March 8, 2012.

119. http://www.theferrarigroup.com/supply-chain-matters/2012/03/09/

120. http://asq.org/qualitynews/qnt/execute/displaySetup?newsID=13192

121. Richard Milne, "Early warnings in the supply chain," *Financial Times*, March 24, 2009, http://www.ft.com/intl/cms/s/0/cfaf418e-1813-11de-8c9d-0000779fd2ac.html?siteedition=intl#axzz2u4SRMn6w

122. http://ec.europa.eu/environment/waste/rohs_eee/events_rohs1_en.htm

123. http://www.earth.columbia.edu/news/2005/story03-29-05.html

124. Peter March, "Industry Left High and Dry," *Financial Times*, April 12, 2011.

125. http://www.emsnow.com/npps/story.cfm?pg=story&id=45416

126. Lisa Eadicicco, "Korean conflict could nuke your next phone, experts say," *Laptop Magazine*, April 16, 2013, http://www.foxnews.com/tech/2013/04/16/korean-conflict-could-nuke-your-next-phone/

127. Sheffi, *Logistics Clusters*.

128. http://www.siemens.com/innovation/apps/pof_microsite/_pof-spring-2012/_html_en/global-logistics-chains.html

129. Allianz, *Managing Disruptions*, http://www.agcs.allianz.com/assets/PDFs/white%20papers/AGCS%20Managing%20disruptions%20Nov2012.pdf

130. Ibid.

131. David Turner, "Credit Crunch Failure Explained to Queen," *Financial Times*, July 26 2009.

132. "The Tragedy of the Commons," *Science* 162, no. 3859 (1968): 1243–1248.

133. William Forster Lloyd, *Two Lectures on the Checks to Population*, 1833.

134. Anton Troianovski and Sarah Portlock, "Outage Exposes Carriers' Backup Plans," *Wall Street Journal*, November 2, 2012.

135. Peter March, "Industry Left High and Dry," *Financial Times*, April 12, 2011.

136. Interview with Tom Linton, chief procurement and supply chain officer at Flextronics, July 2012.

137. MIT CTL's conference, "Global Ocean Transportation Initiative," held on November 29, 2012, in Cambridge, MA.

138. Micheline Maynard, "Southwest Has First Loss in 17 Years."

139. www.science20.com/planetbye/volcanic_eruptions_science_and_risk_management-79456

Chapter 14

1. See also, for example, Myron Gordon and Jeffrey Rosenthal, "Capitalism's Growth Imperative," *Cambridge Journal of Economics* 27 (1):25–48.

2. S&P Global Credit Portal, http://www.standardandpoors.com/servlet/BlobServer?blobheadername3=MDT-Type&blobcol=urldata&blobtable=MungoBlobs&blobheadervalue2=inline%3B+filename%3DCorporates_ERM_FAQ_06_24_10.pdf&blobheadername2=Content-Disposition&blobheadervalue1=application%2Fpdf&blobkey=id&blobheadername1=content-type&blobwhere=1243731092522&blobheadervalue3=UTF-8

3. Mateo Tonello, *Emerging Governance Practices In Enterprise Risk Management*, Research Report R-1398-07-WG, The Conference Board, 2007 and http://www.bcifiles.com/Engaging%26Sustaining.pdf and http://hal.archives-ouvertes.fr/docs/00/85/74/35/PDF/Gates_Nicolas_Walker_MAQ_2012.pdf and Stephen Gates and Ellen Hexter, *From Risk Management to Risk Strategy*, The Conference Board Research Report, R-1363–05-R, 2005, p. 32. Data is based on a survey of management executives from 271 companies based in North America and Europe.

4. http://www.ralphkeyes.com/quote-verifier/

5. Scott Price, *A Bright Light on the Darkest of Days: The U.S. Coast Guard's Response to Hurricane Katrina*, US Coast Guard, http://www.uscg.mil/history/katrina/docs/DarkestDay.pdf

6. Ibid.

7. Ibid.

8. Ibid.

9. http://www.uscg.mil/history/katrina/katrinaindex.asp

10. http://www.cnn.com/2006/POLITICS/04/14/fema.ig/

11. http://www.fema.gov/news-release/2004/07/23/hurricane-pam-exercise-concludes

12. GAO Report, *COAST GUARD: Observations on the Preparation, Response, and Recovery Missions Related to Hurricane Katrina*, GAO-06-903, June 2006, http://www.gao.gov/new.items/d06903.pdf

13. Ibid.

14. http://www.economist.com/node/4086117

15. GAO Report, COAST GUARD.

16. Price, *A Bright Light on the Darkest of Days.*

17. Ibid.

18. Sheffi, *The Resilient Enterprise*

19. Price, *A Bright Light on the Darkest of Days.*

20. http://www.greenpeace.org/usa/en/campaigns/toxics/justice-for-bhopal/

21. Lee Wilkins, *Shared Vulnerability: The Mass Media and American Perceptions of the Bhopal Disaster* (Westport, CT: Greenwood Press, 1987).

22. http://finance.yahoo.com/echarts?s=bp+interactive

23. Chris Bryant. "BASF to Focus Investments Outside Europe," *Financial Times*, February 25, 2014, http://www.ft.com/intl/cms/s/0/c0c9b448-9e2c-11e3-95fe
-00144feab7de.html?siteedition=intl#axzz3JMRe1BBN

24. BASF 2013 Report, http://www.basf.com/group/corporate/en/function/conversions:/publish/content/about-basf/facts-reports/reports/2013/BASF_Report_2013.pdf

25. http://www.coso.org/documents/coso_erm_executivesummary.pdf

26. http://rzv113.rz.tu-bs.de/Bieleschweig/pdfB4/Bieleschweig4_Folien_Kuhn.pdf

27. Trevor Kletz, *An Engineer's View of Human Error*. IChemE, 2009 p1.

28. http://www.academia.edu/4194035/Sources_of_Industrial_Accidents?login=sheffi@mit.edu&email_was_taken=true

29. BASF 2013 Report.

30. http://view.fdu.edu/files/brkpreswallwarrenbasfdec10.pdf]

31. BASF 2012 Report, https://www.basf.com/group/corporate/us/en/function/conversions:/publishdownload/content/about-basf/facts-reports/reports/2012/BASF_Report_2012.pdf

32. http://www.cefic.org/Documents/Annual%20reports/ICCA-Responsible-Care-annual-report-2002-2012.pdf

33. http://www.basf.com/group/corporate/en/function/conversions:/publish/content/about-basf/facts-reports/reports/2013/BASF_Report_2013.pdf

34. http://www.businessinsider.com/these-are-the-20-most-valuable-brands-in-the-world-2013-9?op=1

35. Disney, International Labor Standards, http://thewaltdisneycompany.com/sites/default/files/ILSProgramManualFINAL4_10_12.pdf

36. FM Global, "A Conversation with Susan Shaw," http://www.fmglobal.com/assets/pdf/p09094a_0309.pdf

37. http://www.grifols.com/en/web/singapore/view-news/-/new/grifols-los-angeles-site-is-awarded-highly-protected-risk-hpr-status

38. FM Global, "A Conversation with Susan Shaw."

39. http://www.wsj.com/articles/malaysia-air-mystery-fails-to-spur-changes-1420000398

40. http://www.ism.ws/files/RichterAwards/CiscoSubmissionSupportDoc2012.pdf

41. http://www.scientificamerican.com/article.cfm?id=tsunami-seconds-before-the-big-one&page=3

42. Christopher Bode, Stephan Wagner, Kenneth Petersen, and Lisa Ellram, "Understanding Responses to Supply Chain Disruptions: Insights from Information Processing and Resource Dependent Perspectives," *Academy of Science Journal* 54 (5) (2011): 833–856.

43. Ford,*Code of Conduct Handbook* http://corporate.ford.com/doc/sr13-corporate-conduct-standards-2007.pdf

44. Ibid.

45. http://report.basf.com/2012/en/managementsanalysis/responsibilityalongthevaluechain/responsiblecare.html

46. Ibid.

47. Kevin Harrington and John O'Connor, "How Cisco Succeeds," *Supply Chain Management Review*, July/August 2009, pp. 10–17.

48. Dave Turbide, "Insurance for Your Business: The Value of Risk Prevention – Even if You Never Need It," *APICS Magazine*, January/February 2013, p. 21.

49. http://www.propertycasualty360.com/2010/04/26/volcano-claims-success-unlikely-for-business-interruption-aviation

50. http://www.intc.com/intel-annual-report/2012/other-information/risk-factors/

51. http://www.shlegal.com/Asp/uploadedFiles/File/Newsletters/2010_newsletters/10_10/Briefing_note_October_2010_Business_interruption_cover.pdf

52. http://www.cnn.com/2004/US/12/06/chicago.fire/ and http://www.chicagotribune.com/news/local/chi-0412220352dec22,0,144514.story

53. http://training.fema.gov/EMIWeb/edu/docs/busind/BCCM%20-%20Session%2015%20-%20Handout%20II%20-%20The%20LaSalle%20Bank%20Fire.pdf and http://www.bcifiles.com/Continuity_Magazinejan2008.pdf

54. Constance Hays, "What Walmart Knows About Customer Habits," *New York Times*, November 14, 2004.

55. http://www.imperiallogistics.co.za/documents/Global-Supply-Chain-Trends-2010-2012.pdf p.7.

56. Ibid.

57. Ibid.

58. Interview with Frank Jones, vice president and general manager, customer fulfillment, planning, and logistics at Intel, July 31, 2012.

59. http://supplychain.dhl.com/Resilience-360 (required free registration).

60. Ibid.

61. MIT, March 26, 2009.

62. http://www.bcifiles.com/Engaging%26Sustaining.pdf

63. www.nescon.org/docs/2007/3A-Weinstein-Millson--Kalfopoulos.pdf

64. Interview with Hiro Fukutomi, http://www.pharmaboardroom.com/article/interview-with-hiro-fukutomi-managing-director-takeda-uk

65. http://www.pwc.com/en_US/us/risk-performance/assets/pwc-risk-performance-2009.pdf

66. PricewaterhouseCoopers, *Management Information and Performance: CFOs Face New Demands for High-Quality Data That Drives Decisions* (June 2007).

67. Tom Aabo, John Fraser, and Betty Simkins, "The Rise and Evolution of the Chief Risk Officer," *Journal of Applied Corporate Finance*, Summer 2005.

68. PWC, *Risk Performance,* http://www.pwc.com/en_US/us/risk-performance/assets/pwc-risk-performance-2009.pdf

69. http://www.standardandpoors.com/servlet/BlobServer?blobheadername3=MDT-Type&blobcol=urldata&blobtable=MungoBlobs&blobheadervalue2=inline%3B+filename%3DSafety_8_23_11.pdf&blobheadername2=Content-Disposition&blobheadervalue1=application%2Fpdf&blobkey=id&blobheadername1=content-type&blobwhere=1243952370388&blobheadervalue3=UTF-8

70. PWC, *Risk Performance.*

71. http://www.ferma.eu/app/uploads/2012/11/ferma-survey-part-1-the-maturity-of-risk-management-in-europe.pdf

72. Stephen Gates and Ellen Hexter, "From Risk Management to Risk Strategy," *The Conference Board Research Report,* R-1363-05-R, 2005, p. 32.

73. http://www.bcifiles.com/Engaging%26Sustaining.pdf

74. http://wrap.warwick.ac.uk/36084/

75. http://www.standardandpoors.com/servlet/BlobServer?blobheadername3=MDT-Type&blobcol=urldata&blobtable=MungoBlobs&blobheadervalue2=inline%3B+filename%3DSafety_8_23_11.pdf&blobheadername2=Content-Disposition&blobheadervalue1=application%2Fpdf&blobkey=id&blobheadername1=content-type&blobwhere=1243952370388&blobheadervalue3=UTF-8

76. Brian Hindo, “Rewiring Westinghouse,” *BloombergBusinessweek* Magazine, May 7, 2008, http://www.businessweek.com/stories/2008-05-07/rewiring-westinghouse

77. Jeanne Liedtka, Robert Rosen, and Robert Wiltbank, “The Catalyst: How You Can Become an Extraordinary Growth Leader” (New York: Racom Communications, 2011).

78. Brian Hindo, “Rewiring Westinghouse,” *BloombergBusinessweek Magazine*, May 7, 2008, http://www.businessweek.com/stories/2008-05-07/rewiring-westinghouse

79. http://triblive.com/business/headlines/3685293-74/westinghouse-nuclear-reactors#axzz34wPpJkL7

80. http://www.automationregion.com/library/081111_westinghouse1.pdf

81. Liedtka, Rosen, and Wiltbank, *The Catalyst.*

82. Andrew S. Grove, *Only the Paranoid Survive.* Crown Publishing Group, May 5, 2010.

83. David Rogers, “Rising Global Middle Classes Pose Huge Resource Threat,” *Global Construction Review*, May 8, 2014, http://www.globalconreview.com/trends/rising-global-middle-classes8-pose-huge100/

84. http://wwf.panda.org/?204732%2FRising-consumption-increased-resource-use-by-a-growing--population-puts-unbearable-pressure-on-our-Planet--WWF-2012--Living-Planet-Report

TABLE OF THANKS

Armada	Paul Newbourne	Senior Vice President, Operations
Audi AG	Hermann Krog	Executive Director of Logistics
AT&T	Tim Harden	President, Supply Chain and Fleet Operations for AT&T Services, Inc.
BASF SE	Andreas Backhaus	Senior Vice President—Global Supply Chain and Process Innovation
	Stefan Bartens	Vice President, Logistics Procurement
	Robert Blackburn	President, Supply Chain Operations and Information Services
	Dirk Hopmann	Vice President, Supply Chain Strategy
	Thomas Nitzlader	Vice President, Service Center Distribution Logistics
	Andreas Rausch	Vice President, Global Strategic Supply Chain Management and Governance
	Steve Stair	Vice President, Supply Chain Service, North American Operations
BNSF Railway	David L. Freeman	Vice President Transportation
	Kristen Rabe	General Director, Internal Communications
Boston Scientific	Mike Kalfopoulos	Senior Manager, Global Sourcing
C.H. Robinson	Steve Weiby	Vice President, Transportation
Chrysler	Kimberly Baxter	Head of Component Supply Risk Mitigation
	Mary Gauthier	Head of Sustainability Communications
	Bill Hall	Head of Sustainability
	Scott Marcantonio	Head of Inbound Logistics

Chrysler	Amy Scott	Senior Manager, Global Sourcing
Cintas	Dave Wheeler	Senior Vice President, Global Supply Chain
Cisco	Karen Ashley	Vice President, Supply Chain
	Tom Bandoni	Senior Manager, Treasury, Risk Management
	Edna Conway	Senior Director, Advanced Compliance and Social Responsibility, Customer Value Chain Management
	Kristi Kilpatrick	Senior Public Relations Advisor, Supply Chain Operations
	Nghi Luu	Senior Manager, Supply Chain Risk Management
	Kathleen Shaver	Director, Sustainability and Risk
Coca-Cola	Carletta Ooton	Vice President, Global Technical Operations
Damco Int'l	Aaron Baker	Senior Director, Supply Chain
Delphi	Rick Birch	Global Director, Operational Excellence
Disney	John Lund	Senior Vice President, Integrated Supply Chain Management
Dow AgroSciences	Dave Winstone	Global Supply Chain Expertise Leader
US Dept. of Homeland Security	Keith Holtermann	Director of FEMA's National Exercise Division
	Justin Legary	Supervisory IT Specialist at FEMA
	Jalal Mapar	Director, Resilient Systems Division at FEMA
	Doug Maughan	Director, Cyber Security Division, DHS Science and Technology Directorate
Disney	John Lund	Senior Vice President, Integrated Supply Chain Management
ETH Zurich	Didier Sornette	Professor and Chair of Entrepreneurial Risks
Expediters Int'l	Steve Grimmer	Senior Vice President, Account Management
Flextronics	Tim Griffin	General Manager, Milpitas Operations
	Tom Linton	Chief Procurement and Supply Chain Officer
	David Marks	Chief Strategy Officer
General Motors	Fred Brown	Director, Assembly and Stamping Plants
	Bob Glubzinski	Manager of North America Scheduling and Order Fulfillment
	Bill Hurles	Executive Director, Global Supply Chain

	Matt Joshua	Executive Director, Electrical Systems, Batteries/Hybrids, New Technology
	Christine Krathwohl	Executive Director, Global Logistics
	Mike Lypka	Director, Powertrain Plants Global Supply Chain
	Ron Mills	Director, GM Components Holding
	Randy Pappal	Executive Director, Global Body/Exteriors
	Annette Prochaska	Manager, Vehicle Scheduling
	Marc Robinson	Assistant Director & Economist, Enterprise Risk Management
	Anne Schneider	Director, North America Fulfillment and Risk Management
	Rob Thom	Manager, Global Vehicle Engineering Operations
	Katherine Worthen	Executive Director, Global Purchasing and Supply Chain—Chassis Systems
Hershey	Terence O'Day	Senior Vice President, Chief Supply Chain Officer
Intel	Malcolm Harkins	Chief Information Security Officer
	Tim Hendry	Vice President, Technology and Manufacturing Group, Director of Fab Materials
	Jim Holko	Program Manager, Corporate Emergency Management
	Frank Jones	Vice President and General Manager, Customer Fulfillment, Planning and Logistics
	Steve Lund	Director of Security
	Jim Kellso	Senior Supply Chain Master
	Gary Niekerk	Director, Global Citizenship
	Rotem Rayhany	Chief of Security, Kiryat Gat Fab
	Tony Romero	General Manager, Customer Fulfillment Planning and Logistics
	Jeff Selvala	Director, Assembly Test Global Materials
	Wendy Spratt	Consumer Products Logistics Group
	Jacklyn Sturm	Vice President, Technology and Manufacturing; General Manager, Global Sourcing and Procurement
	Dovev Viess	FMS Manager, Israel and Russia

International Association of Insurance Supervisors	Daniel Hofmann	Economic Counsellor
Jabil	Joe McBeth	Vice President, Global Supply Chain
Johnson Controls	Jelle Van Der Haak	Senior Manager Materials and Logistics, Logistics Purchasing, Product Business Unit Foam, Automotive Experience
	Michael Harsh	Executive Director, Supply Chain
	Robert C. Melcher	Director of Supply Chain Management, Product Group Metals and Mechanisms, Automotive Experience
	Armando X. Murillo	Director of Supply Chain Management, Product Group Metals and Mechanisms, Automotive Experience
	Derrick Redding	Automotive Systems, CBU Finance
Juniper Networks	Joe Carson	Global Operations Executive
	Steve Darendinger	Vice President, Worldwide Procurement
	Dmitri Kamensky	Regional Vice President, Eastern Europe
Patagonia	Cara Chacon	Director of Social &and Environmental Responsibility
Procter & Gamble	Cath Malseed	Director of Coffee Supply
	Stefano Zenezini	Vice President, Product Supply, Beauty Care
Railex	Adrian Neuhauser	President
Resilinc	Bindiya Vakil	CEO and Founder
Ryder Systems	Gary Allen	Vice President of Engineering
Siemens	Barbara Kux	Head of Supply Chain Management and Member of the Managing Board
Starbucks	Troy Alstead	Chief Operating Officer
	Cliff Burrows	Group President, U.S., Americas and Teavana
	John Culver	Group President, Starbucks Coffee China and Asia Pacific, Channel Development and Emerging Brands
	Kelly Goodejohn	Director of Ethical Sourcing
	Steven Lovejoy	Senior Vice President, Global Supply Chain
	Deverl Maserang	Executive Vice President, Global Supply Chain
	Craig Russell	Executive Vice President, Global Coffee

Tel Aviv University	Kobi Peleg	Professor, Head of the Program for Emergency Management
	Gili Shenhar	Director of the Academic Program for Emergency Management
UPS	Charlie Covert	Vice President, Global Customer Solutions
Verifone	Patrick McGivern	Senior Vice President of Global Supply Chain
Verizon	Mariano Legaz	Vice President, Sourcing
	Viju Menon	Senior Vice President, Supply Chain Services
	Bill Roesch	Manager, Supply Chain Services
Walmart	David Blackorby	Senior Vice President, Global Security Operations
	Mark Cooper	Senior Director of Global Emergency Management
	Elizabeth Fretheim	Director, Business Strategy and Sustainability—Logistics
	Tracy Rosser	Senior Vice President, Transportation
	Ken Senser	Senior Vice President, Global Security, Aviation and Travel
	Chris Sultemeier	Executive Vice President, Logistics
	Andrea Thomas	Senior Vice President, Sustainability
Washington State DOT	Barbara Ivanov	Director, Freight Strategy and Policy
Zurich Insurance	Linda Conrad	Director of Strategic Business Risk

Index